The post-modern and the post-industrial

This book offers an historical and critical guide to the concepts of the post-modern and the post-industrial. It brings admirable clarity and thoroughness to a discussion of the many different uses made of the term post-modern across a number of different disciplines (literature, architecture, art history, philosophy, anthropology and geography, to name but a few). It also analyses the concept of the post-industrial society to which the concept of the post-modern has often been related. Dr Rose discusses the work of many major theorists in the area, from Hassan, Lyotard, Jameson and Foster to the architectural historian Charles Jencks, and also looks at analyses and uses of the concepts of the post-modern and post-industrial by Frampton, Portoghesi, Peter Fuller and some feminist critics.

This book provides a clear and much-needed guide to a highly controversial discussion.

The post-modern and
the post-industrial

A critical analysis

Margaret A. Rose

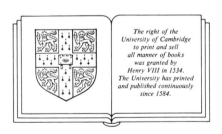

The right of the
University of Cambridge
to print and sell
all manner of books
was granted by
Henry VIII in 1534.
The University has printed
and published continuously
since 1584.

Cambridge University Press

Cambridge
New York   Port Chester
Melbourne   Sydney

Published by the Press Syndicate of the University of Cambridge
The Pitt Building, Trumpington Street, Cambridge CB2 1RP
40 West 20th Street, New York, NY 10011–4211, USA
10 Stamford Road, Oakleigh, Melbourne 3166, Australia

First published 1991

Printed in Great Britain
at the University Press, Cambridge

British Library cataloguing in publication data

Rose, Margaret A.
The post-modern and the post-industrial: a critical
analysis.
1. Culture.   Postmodernism
I. Title
306

Library of Congress cataloguing in publication data

Rose, Margaret A.
The post-modern and the post-industrial: a critical analysis /
Margaret A. Rose.
    p.   cm.
Includes bibliographical references and index.
ISBN 0 521 40131 3 (hardback), – ISBN 0 521 40952 7 (paperback)
1. Postmodernism.   I. Title
B831.2.R67   1991
909.82–dc20   90-39993 CIP

ISBN 0 521 40131 3 hardback
ISBN 0 521 40952 7 paperback

w v

Contents

List of illustrations   *page* ix

Preface   xi

Introduction   1

1   Defining the post-modern   3

2   Defining the post-industrial   21

3   Deconstructionist theories   40

4   Double-coded theories   101

5   Alternative theories   150

6   Conclusion and summary   169

Notes   180

Bibliography   286

Index   298

Illustrations

page

1 Chase's 'Heisenberg Department of Physics', *Chance:
New Directions for Statistics and Computing*, vol. 2, no. 2
(courtesy of Springer-Verlag, Heidelberg)   54

2 John Portman, Bonaventure Hotel, Los Angeles, 1976
model (courtesy of Clyde May Photography, Inc.)   77

3 Renzo Piano and Richard Rogers, Pompidou Centre,
1971–7 (courtesy of Charles Jencks)   81

4 'Banking Hall', Hongkong Shanghai Bank, Norman
Foster and Foster Associates, 1982–6 (courtesy of Foster
Associates and Ian Lambot)   82

5 The blowing-up of the Pruitt-Igoe housing estate
(Minoru Yamasaki and Associates)   108

6 'High Rise', Osbert Lancaster, *A Cartoon History of
Architecture* (courtesy of John Murray (Publishers) Ltd)   109

7 Paolo Portoghesi, *Casa Baldi*, 1959–61 (Paolo Portoghesi)   114

8 Sculpture Court, New Wuerttemberg State Gallery,
Stuttgart, 1977–84, James Stirling, Michael Wilford and
Associates (courtesy of R. Bryant/Arcaid)   117

9 Carlo Maria Mariani, *The Hand Submits to the Intellect
(La Mano ubbidisce all'inteletto)*, 1983 (courtesy of the
artist.   120

10 Saul Steinberg, drawing from *The New World*   121

11 Carlo Maria Mariani, *The constellation of Leo*, 1980–1
(courtesy of the artist)   126

12 Raphael, *School of Athens* (courtesy of the Vatican
Muscums)   127

13 View of part of the exterior of the New Wuerttemberg
State Gallery, Stuttgart, 1977–85, James Stirling and
Michael Wilford and Associates (courtesy of R.
Bryant/Arcaid)   128
14 Peter Eisenman, Biocenter for the University of
Frankfurt, 1987, Site Model A (courtesy of Eisenman
Robertson Architects, New York)   132
15 Julian Schnabel, *Winter*, 1982 (courtesy of the Saatchi
Collection, London)   136
16 Peter Blake, *'The Meeting'* or *'Have a Nice Day, Mr
Hockney'*, 1981–3 (courtesy of the Tate Gallery, London) 138
17 Gustave Courbet, *'Bonjour, Monsieur Courbet'*, 1854
(courtesy of Musée Fabre, Montpellier)   139
18 'Crouching Aphrodite' (Archaeological Museum of
Rhodes)   140
19 Philip Taaffe, *Chi-Chi Meets the Death of Painting*, 1985
(courtesy of the Massimo Audiello Gallery, New York)   142

Preface

Now, as this century comes into its last decade and closer to its conclusion, it is interesting to look back on the variety of different theories which have been developed from its earliest decades onwards to describe a culture or its arts as 'post-modern' and a society as 'post-industrial'. As the following history and analysis of those theories and their terms will show, a significant use of the term post-industrial may be found at least as early as the year 1914, and one of the term post-modernism by 1934.[1] What is also interesting about these terms and their uses as the new century approaches is that that history will illustrate how the use of them has arisen not only from a variety of different and sometimes conflicting criticisms of the modern cultures or modern industrial societies of the twentieth century, but from a variety of different ideals and programmes for both the present and the future.[2]

Because many of the theories using the terms post-modern or post-industrial have been developed in different decades and on the basis of a variety of understandings of the terms modern, modernism, modernisation, modernity, industrial and post,[3] there is, however, now a real need for those theories to be clearly and critically delineated and analysed if we are to be able to assess the usefulness – or potential dangers – of their various examples for either the present decade or future century.

As one of the prime purposes of this book will be to bring some clarity into the discussion of terms used in the twentieth century to describe a culture as post-modern and its society as post-industrial, so that such assessments can be made, it will first of all give an historical and analytical overview of the most influential or significant uses of the terms in question and then a critical analysis of the presuppositions and arguments used with them in recent theories and applications.

With regard to the specific contents of the book, a brief introduction is first of all given into the more general issues involved in the definition of the terms in question. This then is followed by a chapter on the history and problems of defining the word post-modern and related terms such as post-modernism, post-modernisation and post-modernity, while the next chapter introduces the concept of the post-industrial society to which the concept of the post-modern has so often been attached in recent years, and which is in itself an important topic for the understanding of current developments in the description and analysis of contemporary society and technology.

From this point the book moves on to give an account of what will be termed the major 'deconstructionist' theories of post-modernism, and of their views on the post-industrial society,[4] and deals here specifically with the work of Ihab Hassan, Jean Baudrillard, Jean-François Lyotard, Fredric Jameson, Juergen Habermas and Hal Foster amongst others.[5]

In chapter 4 of the text the view of post-modernism as a 'double-coding' of modernism with other codes put forward by the architectural critic and historian Charles Jencks is discussed together with his critique of what will be described here as 'deconstructionist post-modernism', as a body of theory describing phenomena which are 'Late-Modern' rather than 'Post-Modern'. Here the development of Jencks's definitions of post-modernism is also traced from his earliest work on the subject of post-modern architecture up to his more recent discussions of 'Post-Modern Classicism' and post-modernism in the visual arts, as well as to his comments on some of the newer but for him still 'late-modern' 'deconstructionist' theories of architecture.[6]

As mentioned in chapter 3, in the comparison of Fredric Jameson's reading of John Portman's Bonaventure Hotel as 'postmodern' with Jencks's description of it as 'Late-Modern', Jencks has used the category of the late-modern in several of his works on contemporary architecture to describe buildings which have carried aspects of the Modern Movement into the 1960s and beyond and, in many cases, exaggerated them. In 1980 Jencks also published a table of differences between the 'Modern', the 'Late-Modern' and the Post-Modern[7] in which the 'Late-Modern' and the 'Post-Modern' are shown as running concurrently from the 1960s onwards. Following this, Jencks suggested that the subjects described by such as Lyotard, Hassan, Jameson and Foster should also be regarded as late-modern rather than as post-modern,[8] and even though those writers had themselves appropriated the term post-modern rather than the other for their descriptions of contemporary society and culture. As most of the latter theorists have borrowed at least some ideas from deconstructionist theory for their theories of the post-modern, I suggest with my choice of terms in this text that one way out of this problem – where they claim they are post-modernist and Jencks suggests they are late-modernist, and where a category of late-modernist post-modernists would be a nonsense to both sides – is to describe them as deconstructionist post-modernists, while also noting the objections of Jencks to their appropriation of the term post-modern, and, as will be pointed out again in the beginning of chapter 3, the very general way in which the adjective deconstructionist is being used to cover a variety of different 'deconstructionist' as well as 'post-modernist' ideas in this new term.

From these topics the fifth chapter of the book moves on to consider a variety of other discussions of the post-modern and the post-industrial, including those of Paolo Portoghesi, Kenneth Frampton, John Fekete, Peter Fuller and some feminist critics, before a final, sixth, chapter concludes the book with a summary of the history of the uses of the terms given in the preceding pages of the text, and final commentary on their values.

While this study will concentrate its analysis largely on the most influential theories of the post-modern and the post-industrial from which have been derived other recent theories and applications of the term to the arts, architecture, film, philosophy and the social sciences which are now too numerous to discuss in detail in any serious overview of the subject as a whole, cross-referencing to a variety of different recent uses of the concepts of the post-modern and the post-industrial is also made throughout the book, in both text and notes, and an Index provided at its end by means of which its readers may make their own connections where necessary, and trace the major theories from which other applications have been made.[9]

Because there are still many writers throughout the world who are interested in developing the concepts of the post-modern and the post-industrial further, it is also hoped that the approach used in this book, to provide a critical analysis of the basic parts of the major theories of those concepts from which more recent ones have developed, and are developing still, will mean that readers may continue to find the following study useful for the analysis of works published after its own completion, as well as for the development of any of their own uses of the concepts in question.[10] As emphasised elsewhere in the text which follows, only the increased use of clarity in the formulation and development of concepts of the post-modern and the post-industrial will, moreover, ensure that they will continue to be of interest and of use for the present or future towards which they are orientated.[11]

INTRODUCTION

To begin at the beginning, the term post-modern[1] is a word which has so far been used by a variety of thinkers on the basis of several different understandings of both the concept of the modern and the meaning of the prefix post (as, for instance, a 'break with' or a 'continuation of' the modern). Not only has the term 'post-modern' been used with reference to a variety of different concepts of the modern epoch (the dating of which has been stretched to cover periods from the Renaissance to contemporary times, despite the fact that the word 'modern' is derived from one for 'now' or 'today'[1]), but it has also been used on the basis of a variety of understandings of the meaning of modernism in the arts or architecture, modernisation (the economic and technological developments of the last century of industrialist and capital-based expansion which have been seen to be characteristic of 'modern' societies[2]) and modernity, which has been defined as the sum total of 'modernism', the 'modern' and 'modernisation'.

As will be seen in the following chapters, the term post-modern has further been used as a synonym for post-modernism by some writers without reference to the fact that it may also be used to refer to a reaction to the modern epoch or modernisation, while others have used it to refer to all three of these phenomena at once, and yet others to designate just one or another of the latter two terms. In addition to these uses others again have utilised the more specific terms such as post-modernism in a general way to cover more than one aesthetic, political or philosophic reaction to that which they have defined as modern.

1

While the more general uses of the concept of the post-modern may also present a very general view of the modern, many of the more specifically defined concepts of post-modernism will be seen to have been built up on the basis of an antagonism to, or reform of, a modernism which has been understood in some particular way as, for instance, functionalism in architecture or abstraction in art, just as most specific uses of the concepts of post-modernisation and post-modernity will be seen to have been based on a particular concept of modernisation or modernity. As our pages on the post-industrial will show, many contemporary uses of this concept have also been based on some specific concept of industrial society, and authors will be seen to have differed in both their attitudes to how the post-industrial should be distinguished from the industrial, and in their attitudes to concepts such as that of post-modernism.

As suggested earlier, it will not just be our definition or understanding of the latter part of our term (of the modern, modernism, modernisation, modernity, or the industrial) which will be crucial to our understanding of the post-modern and its concomitants, but also our definition of the prefix post, as a 'break from' or as a 'continuation of' its modern component, or as an amalgamation, or dialectic, of break and continuation.[3] Although it has not been possible to analyse all statements about the post-modern, or the post-industrial here, it is hoped, as stated earlier, that enough analysis of the major theories and their presuppositions will have been given to enable the reader to make his or her own analysis of any other theory or application of theory not specifically treated in the following pages of text or notes, and to trace them back where necessary to those other theories and their protagonists.[4]

1

DEFINING THE POST-MODERN

Dick Hebdige opens the section on post-modernism in his *Hiding in the Light: On Images and Things* of 1988 with the statement that 'The success of the term postmodernism ... has generated its own problems', and that

> It becomes more and more difficult as the 1980s wear on to specify exactly what it is that 'postmodernism' is supposed to refer to as the term gets stretched in all directions across different debates, different disciplinary and discursive boundaries, as different factions seek to make it their own, using it to designate a plethora of incommensurable objects, tendencies, emergencies.[1]

Despite this and other similar complaints,[2] there is, however, no necessary reason why some of the 'factional' or other differences behind the variety of definitions of post-modernism and the post-modern in general which we now have may not be defined as such, and the different meanings which have been given the term be categorised more succinctly. One major source for the idea that post-modernism is a movement in which 'anything goes' is, in fact, to be found in an attack by the French theorist Lyotard on a rival concept of post-modernism, which, in addition, cannot be said to describe its target accurately.[3]

Many (although certainly not all) recent discussions of post-modernism have also followed Lyotard's writings on the subject in some regard. Hebdige himself, for example, goes on after summarising a variety of uses of the term 'postmodernism' to use it, without specifically saying so, in the Lyotardian sense of a critique of meta-narratives,[4] when he claims that his following overview of the term will entail his 'going against the spirit of

3

postmodernism', understood as being 'founded in the renunciation of claims to mastery and dominant specularity'.[5]

While the 'renunciation of claims to mastery' evokes Lyotard's
deconstruction of the 'meta-narratives' of modernity,[6] the positing of a 'dominant specularity' as yet another target of the post-
modernist also recalls the terminology of works such as Guy
Debord's *Society of the Spectacle* of 1967, and the use of it by
Jean Baudrillard in his contribution to Hal Foster's *Postmodern
Culture*[7] or his 'The Orders of Simulacra' of 1975. In this latter
text Baudrillard had not only spoken of the 'burlesque spectacle'
of the political class,[8] but had also divided history into three
dominant 'orders of appearance' since the Renaissance: of
Counterfeit for the period from the Renaissance to the industrial
revolution; *Production* for the industrial era; and *Simulation* for
the current phase, in which reality is said to be continuously
overtaken by its images and to be ruled by indeterminacy.[9] While
Baudrillard had been speaking here, as elsewhere, largely of the
modern world, rather than of something termed the post-
modern (or 'postmodern'), one theorist of post-modernism
writing prior to both Hebdige and Lyotard, Ihab Hassan, will
be seen to have taken the post-modern age to be an age of
'indeterminacy',[10] while others, such as Fredric Jameson, will be
seen to have echoed Baudrillard in viewing the present age as a
'neo-capitalist cybernetic order' which aims at total control.[11]

Hebdige's commentary on post-modernism also continues in a
Baudrillardian vein when he claims that 'postmodernity is
modernity without the hopes and dreams which made
modernity bearable'[12] and adds that 'it is a hydra-headed,
decentred condition in which we get dragged along from pillar to
post across a succession of reflecting surfaces, drawn by the call
of the wild signifier'.[13] Further to this we shall see later that
Hebdige's description of post-modernism as 'bricolage, pastiche,
allegory, and the hyperspace of the new architecture'[14] echoes a
'Baudrillardian' characterisation of post-modernism by Fredric
Jameson which has projected characteristics onto post-modernism[15] which others, such as Charles Jencks, have preferred to
describe as 'Late-Modern' rather than as 'Post-Modern'.[16]

Problems arising from the theories referred to above will be
returned to in following chapters. Although it gives a somewhat

broader account of the concept of the post-modern than Hebdige's survey, and those like it,[17] the *Oxford English Dictionary*'s (*OED*) *Supplement* of 1982 was of necessity also too restricted in its coverage of the use of the term to give all the details required for an accurate history of it or of the sometimes related term 'post-modernism'.[18]

The *OED Supplement*'s entry begins:

post-mo.dern, *a*. Also **post-Modern**. [POST-B. 1b.] Subsequent to, or later than, what is 'modern'; *spec.* in the arts, esp. *Archit.*, applied to a movement in reaction against that designated 'modern' (cf. MODERN a. 2h.)[19] Hence **post-mo.dernism, post-mo.dernist**, *a*. and *sb*.

Despite the generally scientific appearance of the above entry, it contains a number of problems which the reader aware of the possible variety of definitions of the post-modern may already have been able to discern. Firstly, the word 'post-modern' is not always thought to be subsequent to or later than the 'modern', but may both be contemporary with it, or, as in the writings of Lyotard, 'prior' to the modern. Secondly, although one other theorist of post-modernism, Charles Jencks, has questioned the sense of Lyotard's claims, he himself has not seen the post-modern in architecture as simply a reaction against the 'modern', but has described it as a 'double-coding' of the modern style with some other style or 'code'.[20]

Further to the above, the *OED Supplement*'s cross-reference to its '2h' definition of the 'modern' in its characterisation of the 'post-modern' as, 'with reference to the arts and architecture', a 'movement in reaction against that designated "modern" ', creates some problems not only on account of its conflation of the terms 'modern' and 'modernism' in its application of the former to the arts, where the two terms might not always be able to describe the same phenomena, but also because its 2h definition of the modern has described the 'modern' in terms of its 'departure from or . . . repudiation of accepted or traditional styles and values'.[21] Hence we have a definition of the post-modern which not only describes it negatively as a reaction against the modern, but which also relates it to a description of the modern which secs it too in negative terms as a reaction against other traditions. Although the latter may be true for some modernisms, it is not the only aspect of the modern, or of modernism, which has been addressed by post-modernists who have reacted specifically to modernist alternatives to other traditions as well as to modernist rejections of the past.

Other problems abound in giving a history of today's usage of the term post-modern. The *OED Supplement*'s reference to Joseph Hudnut's use of the term post-modern in relation to architecture (which the dictionary's entry goes on to date as being from 1949 and as the earliest use of the term 'post-modern', whereas it is in fact used by Hudnut from at least 1945 on, and by others prior to that[22]) is, for example, to a concept of 'post-modern' architecture as mass-produced prefabricated building which would today be rejected by many post-modernist architects as describing an 'ultra-modern' rather than a 'post-modern' form of architecture.[23] Further to this, the quotation given by the dictionary entry from Hudnut gives little idea of the application of the term to the prefabricated house in his article: 'He shall be a modern owner, a post-modern owner, if such a thing is conceivable. Free from all sentimentality or fantasy or caprice.'[24]

Hudnut had published these words in an article of 1945 entitled 'the post-modern house' as well as in a 1949 collection of essays entitled *Architecture and the Spirit of Man*.[25] The passage from which they are taken reads in full:

I shall not imagine for my future house a romantic owner, nor shall I defend my client's preferences as those foibles and aberrations usually referred to as 'human nature'. No, he shall be a modern owner, a post-modern owner, if such a thing is conceivable. Free from all sentimentality or fantasy or caprice, his vision, his tastes, his habits of thought shall be those most necessary to a collective–industrial scheme of life; the world shall, if it pleases him, appear as a system of casual sequences transformed each day by the cumulative miracles of science. Even so he will claim for himself some inner experiences, free from outward control, unprofaned by the collective conscience. That opportunity, when the universe is socialized, mechanized and standardized, will yet be discoverable in the home. Though his house is the most precise product of modern processes there will be entrenched within it this ancient loyalty invulnerable against the siege of our machines. It will be the architect's task, as it is today, to comprehend that loyalty – to comprehend it more firmly than anyone else – and, undefeated by all the armaments of industry, to bring it out in its true and beautiful character.[26]

I have quoted this passage at length because there are several points made in it which are of interest for understanding Hudnut's concept of the post-modern. Firstly, the concept of the post-modern is clearly used to describe what could also be denoted in Hudnut's own terms a modern or ultra-modern owner. Secondly, Hudnut had spoken in the opening of his 1945 article on the 'post-modern house' of the 'prefabricated' hut or house as the house of the future,[27] and had also suggested in his 1949 text that his vision had been produced by 'thinking about those factory-built houses, pure products of technological research and manufacture, which are promised us as soon as a few remaining details of finance and distribution are worked out'.[28] As Hudnut envisaged these houses in 1949 they were to be 'pressed by giant machines out of plastics or chromium steel, pouring out of assembly lines by the tens of thousands, delivered anywhere in response to a telephone call, and upon delivery made ready for occupancy by the simple process of tightening a screw'.[29] After flying over a parking lot beside a baseball stadium, Hudnut had also been inspired to see the thousands of automobiles parked there in herringbone patterns as a foreshadowing of those future suburbs in which 'every family will have each its standardized mass-produced and movable shell, indistinguishable from those of its thousand neighbours except by a choice of paint and the (relative) ambitions of their owners to be housed in the latest model'.[30]

In addition to this, Hudnut's post-modern owner's house is described in his conclusion as the epitome of the results of 'the cumulative miracles of science', which might even be termed the forces of 'modernisation', given that Hudnut had also spoken in his article of the coming of a 'collective–industrial scheme of life' which now appears to have looked back to the relations of modern industrial society rather than forward to any new 'post-industrial' scheme of things similar to those spoken of by Jencks in his writings on the post-modern in architecture.[31] For this reason too Hudnut's vision could be said to be 'ultra' rather than 'post'-modern. Only when Hudnut goes on to speak of the architect as providing an antidote to the machine, by providing the way of bringing out the 'true and beautiful character' of the post-modern house, might we in fact find something which looks forward to at least some of the post-modern architectural theory of the 1970s.

Charles Jencks has even written of Hudnut in his *What is Post-Modernism?* of 1986 that he had 'introduced the term "Post-Modernism" into the "architectural subconscious" ', and, in being at Harvard with Walter Gropius, 'may have wished to give this pioneer of the Modern Movement a few sleepless nights'.[32] Although Jencks does not refer specifically to the passage, Hudnut's 1945 article had also contained the statement that while the author would not advise a return to 'that harlequinade of Colonial, Regency, French Provincial, Tudor and Small Italian Villa which adds such dreary variety to our suburban landscapes', he sometimes thought 'that the eclectic soul of these suburbs is, by intuition if not by understanding, nearer the heart of architecture than those rigid minds which understand nothing but the economics of shelter and the arid technicalities of construction'.[33] In that the Modern Movement had not yet achieved all it should achieve for Hudnut, who also wrote that 'we have not yet learned to give them [i.e. the modern techniques and motives] any persuasive meanings',[34] he may well have placed the concept of the post-modern into the 'architectural subconscious', as suggested by Jencks.[35] At the same time it has also to be noted that Hudnut was writing in the 1940s largely within the debates of his time, and that, while critical of the distortion of modernism into pure functionalism, still saw many of the ideals of the Modern Movement as being basically sound.[36] Added to this it must again be recalled that Hudnut has used the term post-modern itself not to describe a better alternative to the modern, but to describe an ultra-functionalist version of the modern house. If Hudnut is to be understood to have sought to give his Modernist colleagues 'a scare' with his vision of the 'post-modern house' of the coming years it was therefore with what might now be seen as a dystopian vision of what their modernism could degenerate into, rather than with a utopian insight into any of the post-modern alternatives recommended by post-modernist architects of today.

Although Arnold J. Toynbee had used the term post-modern in several volumes of his *A Study of History* of 1939 and 1954, and it had also been used in the 1946 D. C. Somervell abridgement of the early volumes of 1939 written prior to Hudnut's articles, it is only to his *Historian's Approach to Religion* of 1956 to which the *OED* entry next makes reference, and again without giving an explanation of the specific meaning of the term there.[37] In addition to using the term post-modern in his 1956 text to describe the changes experienced by Western civilization since the end of the nineteenth century, Toynbee had used it in volume V of his *A Study of History* of 1939 to describe the age inaugurated by the war of 1914–18.[38] Only after the end of the Second World War had Toynbee gone on to apply it, as indicated by D. C. Somervell's abridgement of the first six volumes of that work of 1946,[39] to the period of Western civilization from 1875 on.[40] While this is the period to which the term 'post-Modern' is attached by Toynbee in the post-World War Two volumes of his *A Study of History* of 1954,[41] it should be noted that when that period is mentioned in volume I of 1934, at the place related to that in which the term 'Post-Modern' appears in Somervell's abridgement of 1946, the term 'Post-Modern' is not used.[42]

Further to being used in the post-war volumes of Toynbee's *A Study of History* to describe the period from the end of the nineteenth century, the term post-modern (now written 'post-Modern') had been used by Toynbee in those volumes to describe the rise of an industrial urban working class, and after the term 'Modern' had been used by him to describe the 'middle classes' of Western civilization. Toynbee wrote, for example, in volume VIII of his *A Study of History*:

The most significant of the conclusions that suggest themselves is that the word 'modern' in the term 'Modern Western Civilization', can, without inaccuracy, be given a more precise and concrete connotation by being translated 'middle class'. Western communities became 'modern' in the accepted Modern Western meaning of the word, just as soon as they had succeeded in producing a bourgeoisie that was both numerous enough and competent enough to become the predominant element in Society. We think of the new chapter of Western history that opened at the turn of the fifteenth and sixteenth centuries as being 'modern' *par excellence* because, for the next four centuries and more, until the opening of a 'post-Modern Age' at the turn of the nineteenth and twentieth centuries, the middle class was in the saddle in the larger and more prominent part of the Western World as a whole.

Toynbee added:

This definition of the Modern Western culture as being a phase of Western cultural development that is distinguished by the ascendancy of the middle class throws light on the conditions under which, before the advent in the West of a post-Modern Age marked by the rise of an industrial urban working class, any alien recipients of this Modern Western culture would be likely to be successful in making it their own. During the currency of the Modern Age of Western history the ability of aliens to become Westerners would be proportionate to their capacity for entering into the middle-class Western way of life.[43]

As later notes will show, to Toynbee the 'post-Modern Age' was also to be marked not only by the rise of a new industrial urban working class in the West, but by both the rise of other nations and their proletariats and the rise of a variety of 'post-Christian' religious cults as well as sciences.

While Charles Jencks has written in his *Post-Modernism: The New Classicism in Art and Architecture* of 1987 that the term post-modern had also acquired an element of Spenglerian doom in Toynbee's *A Study of History* in being used there to refer to 'the end of Western dominance, Christian culture and individualism',[44] it should also be noted that Toynbee had used the term in post-Second World War (1954) volumes of his *History* which he himself saw as optimistic rather than pessimistic. Toynbee wrote, for instance, in the opening of the chapter on 'Law and Freedom in History' of volume IX of his *A Study of History* that when he was planning his study in the summer of 1927 he had seen that he would have to 'grapple with the problem of the respective roles of Law and Freedom in human history before he could attempt to win a Pisgah sight of the prospects of the Western Civilization'. It was, however, only in June 1950 when, after a seven-years-long interruption extending over the years 1939 to 1946, he at last reached this point in the writing of the book, that he found himself working in a new atmosphere that was 'decidedly more congenial to his theme'.

Toynbee's discussion of the 'post-Modern' age is also carried out largely in this post-war work, where he dates the post-modern period from the end of the nineteenth century.[45] Further to this, these post-war volumes by Toynbee had also criticised those who had taken the end of their own period to be the end of history as such.[46] This criticism was directed, moreover, against both the 'complacent' view that a period was as good as could be (Toynbee quotes Sellar and Yeatman's ironic *1066 and All That* of 1930: 'History is now at an end; this History is therefore final'[47]) and the 'antithetical' view that things were so bad that nothing new could arise.

While Toynbee counters the first view by pointing out that a 'post-Modern Age' was to follow the 'Modern' which would bring 'new tragedies as well as new developments', he counters the second by pointing out that the pessimistic view of the end of history is as 'subjective' and 'egocentric' as the former.[48] Both views, the complacent view that no further improvement is needed in history, and the pessimistic view that history itself is in some way 'at an end', look no further than the view-point of the viewer for Toynbee, and are described by him as 'rationalizations of feelings that are irrationally subjective'.[49] Following this discussion, Toynbee adds that in 'studying the breakdowns of civilizations, we found that the cause was, in every case, some failure of self-determination, and that, when human beings thus lost control over their own destinies, this social disaster usually turned out to have been the consequence of a moral aberration'.[50]

Although the question of Spengler's pessimism is complex, the conclusion of his *Decline of the West* that 'a task that historic necessity has set *will* be accomplished with the individual or against him' may also be said to present a much more pessimistic view of the possibility of individual intervention in the direction of history than that suggested by Toynbee.[51]

Further examples of the use of the term 'post-modern' given by the *OED* include C. Wright Mills's use of it in his *The Sociological Imagination* of 1959 to describe a new 'Fourth Epoch' after the 'Modern Age';[52] Leslie Fiedler's 1965 reference to post-modernist literature (again the quotation given by the dictionary is not very explanatory, being Fiedler's sentence: 'I am not now interested in analyzing . . . the diction and imagery which have passed from Science Fiction into post-Modernist literature');[53] Frank Kermode's 1966 remarks that Pop Fiction demonstrates 'a growing sense of the irrelevance of the past', and that 'post-Modernists are catching on';[54] Nikolaus Pevsner's reference in *The Listener* of 29 December 1966, to a 'new style', a 'successor' to his 'International Modern' of the nineteen-thirties which he 'was tempted to call . . . a post-modern style';[55] a reference in the *New York Review of Books* of 28 April 1977 to 'the post-modernist demand for the abolition of art and its assimilation to "reality" ';[56] two somewhat different remarks in the *Journal of the Royal Society of Arts* of November 1979 to 'Post-Modern architects [who] use motifs . . . in questionable taste', and to 'Post-Modernists who have substituted the body metaphor for the machine metaphor'; a reference in *Time* of January 1979 to Philip Johnson as 'the nearest Post-Modernism has to a senior partner'; and another, finally, to *The Times Higher Education Supplement* of 7 March 1980 in which 'Postmodernism, structuralism, and neo-dada' are all said to represent 'a reaction against modernism'.

Several of these uses of the term post-modernism will be discussed at greater length, or referred to again in either text or notes, presently. Other early uses of the term not listed by the *OED* have included several given by Michael Koehler in his article entitled ' "Postmodernismus": Ein begriffsgeschichtlicher Ueberblick', which was completed in November 1976 and published in 1977.[57] Here Koehler drew attention to the use made of the term and its variants by the professor Federico de Onis in 1934, the anthologist Dudley Fitts in 1942 (although the use ascribed to Fitts is attributed by Fitts himself to his assistant H. R. Hays), Arnold J. Toynbee (whose usage of the term post-modern Koehler dates only from 1947), Charles Olson (in the years between 1950 and 1958), Irving Howe (1959), Harry Levin (1960), Leslie Fiedler (1965) and John Perreault,[58] as well as Amitai Etzioni in his *The Active Society* of 1968,[59] Ihab Hassan in his *The Dismemberment of Orpheus* and 'POSTmodernISM' essay of 1971,[60] and Ralph Cohen in his autumn 1971 edition of *New Literary History* in which Hassan's 'POSTmodernISM' essay was published.[61]

Details of Koehler's own assessment of these varying definitions will be given presently. First of all it has, however, to be noted that Koehler has not only given one of the most extensive surveys of the term 'postmodernism' (as it is written in the brief abstract in English which precedes his essay), but has also referred us to one of its earliest uses in his documentation of the 1934 use made of it by de Onis.[62]

Koehler writes of de Onis's *Antologica de la poesia española e hispanoamericano* (Madrid 1934) that its Introduction had dated Modernism from the years 1896 to 1905 and had added two other phases to it, of 'postmodernismo' (of 1905 to 1914) and 'ultramodernismo' (of 1914 to 1932). While the first had been defined as a reaction to the 'excesses' of modernism (de Onis describes it as a 'reining in' of modernist excesses which sometimes resulted in more prosaic or ironic works), the second had been seen as an attempt to extend the 'Modernist search for poetic innovation and freedom'.[63]

Further to de Onis's use of the term 'postmodernismo' to describe works of Spanish and Latin-American verse which could be said to be reacting to the excesses of modernism, the anthologist and poet Dudley Fitts's *Anthology of Contemporary Latin-American Poetry* of 1942 had also used the term 'post-modernism' in its 'Note' on the Mexican poet Enrique Gonzalez Martinez:

He more than any other single force, is responsible for the revolt against the decorative rhetoric of the school of Ruben Dario. From his work – stripped, hard, clear – the new poets derive much of their strength. It is not exaggeration to say that his sonnet on the Swan, used as a general epigraph for this anthology, is the manifesto of post-Modernism – one of the significant landmarks in world literature.[64]

While, according to Fitts's Preface, the Notes to his anthology had been written by H. R. Hays,[65] it is also clear from the Preface that Fitts had agreed with them.[66] As indicated in the Note just cited, Fitts's anthology had also used Martinez's sonnet as a 'general epigraph':

THEN TWIST THE NECK OF THIS DELUSIVE SWAN

Then twist the neck of this delusive swan,
white stress upon the fountain's overflow,
that merely drifts in grace and cannot know
the reed's green soul and the mute cry of stone.

Avoid all form, all speech, that does not go
shifting its beat in secret unison
with life . . . Love life to adoration!
Let life accept the homage you bestow.

See how the sapient owl, winging the gap
from high Olympus, even from Pallas' lap,
closes upon this tree its noiseless flight . . .

Here is no swan's grace. But an unquiet stare
interprets through the penetrable air
the inscrutable volume of the silent night.[67]

In addition to using Martinez's poem as the epigraph for his anthology, Fitts had spoken in his Preface of how the anthology was an introductory survey of Latin-American poetry since the death, in 1916, of Ruben Dario, and of how the reaction to the Dario tradition since then was prefigured in Enrique Gonzalez Martinez's sonnet.[68] Although this might be taken to extend the dates of the 'postmodernismo' spoken of by de Onis as taking place only between 1905 and 1914, Fitts continued to speak of the movement prefigured by Martinez's sonnet in terms comparable to those used by de Onis to describe 'postmodernismo':

The new verse is tougher, more intellectualized: its symbol is the 'sapient owl', as opposed to the graceful but vague and somewhat decadent Swan so beloved by Dario and his precursors among the French symbolists. Native themes and native rhythms – whether Indian, Afro-Antillean or Gaucho – have energized it, transforming it into something that is peculiarly American and wholly of our own time. It has never lost the profound tones of its European ancestry, but it speaks to us with a voice that is authentically its own. Poetry, after long absence, has returned to the people.

Here the modernism of which Fitts speaks is not the modernism to which Joseph Hudnut will refer in his articles on the 'post-modern' house of the 1940s but the decorative Symbolism of the end of the nineteenth century.[69] Despite this, both Hudnut's 'post-modernism' and the 'postmodernism' spoken of by de Onis and Fitts/Hays may be said to share the common element of a lack of sentimentality and decorativeness because the post-modernism of which de Onis and Fitts/Hays have spoken was conceived of as a *reaction to* a late nineteenth-century decorative modernism, while Hudnut's post-modern house may be understood as an *extension of* the abstract and decoration-free ('less is more') modernism of the International Style and its offshoots.[70] Here we may again note that the term post-modernism will always need to be read alongside the author's understanding of both modernism and the prefix 'post'.

Michael Koehler concludes his survey of the term 'post-modernism' with the statement that it not only shows that there is still no agreement over that which may be counted as 'post-modern', but that one of the reasons for this is the double meaning of the concept of the 'modern' period. This, Koehler writes, can be used as a synonym for 'die Neuzeit' (literally, 'the new age', although it is usually translated as 'the modern period' or 'modern times'), which for Koehler refers to the time since the European Renaissance, from around 1500,[71] or it can be used to designate the most recent historical period from around 1900 and is then concurrent with the cultural concept of modernism. As has just been seen from our comparison of the uses of the term post-modernism by de Onis and Hudnut, this 'cultural concept of modernism' can itself be divided into several different periods and movements – from, for instance, Symbolism to Abstractionism, Expressionism, Surrealism or any other such modern '-ism' selected by the theorist. Further to this, several other meanings of the term modern could be added to those given by Koehler, such as, for instance, those given it in the phrase describing 'the battle of the ancients and the moderns' from the late seventeenth century on.[72]

Koehler himself continues to argue from his set of alternatives that while Toynbee and Olson may be said to have used the word 'modern' in the first sense given by him (to refer, that is, to a modern period dating from around 1500),[73] they have produced confusion by using the word post-modern to cover a period in which modernism was also born and developed.[74] Koehler adds that this use of the term post-modern is therefore comparable with all those theories which contest the view that the most recent art has broken with the paradigm of modernism. Whether this is either an accurate or a helpful view of Arnold Toynbee's position may, however, be questioned, especially as although Toynbee had used the term 'post-Modern' to refer to a new 'post-Middle class' age, he had continued to see the middle class as the force behind the production of 'Modern' art of both archaic and futurist kinds and to criticise both those types of art.[75] While it is clear that the question of whether a new 'post-Modernist' art might still arise from the 'post-Modern Age' and its proletariats was one left unanswered by Toynbee, it is also clear that he believed that there was much in existing modernist art which needed to be changed.[76]

One other point which needs to be made here, and which Koehler himself suggests in a footnote,[77] is also that a comparison of Toynbee's views on the 'post-Modern' with more recent views on post-modernism and its relationship to modernism is problematic in that the 'post-modernist' art spoken of in the last two decades was not only unknown to Toynbee, but is inclusive of a great many reactions to, and extensions of, a variety of modernisms.

From the subject described above, Koehler goes on to speak of those theories which have equated the modern with modernism[78] and to detail those by, for example, Irving Howe and Harry Levin which date the end of the modern period from the end of World War Two. According to Koehler the years of the 1950s then see a reaction to the extremes of modernist Formalism and a return to Realism which is not so evident in the more 'avant-garde' 1960s, which, Koehler suggests (in an echo of de Onís's terminology), might rather be seen as 'ultra-modern' if the 1950s are to be described as post-modern.

One other hypothesis – which Koehler sees as having been put by Leslie Fiedler and Ihab Hassan – views, by contrast, the 1960s as representative of a 'postmodern sensibility'. (In fact, Hassan will be seen to have taken his 'postmodernism' back much further than this.)[79] According to this view, continues Koehler, the 1950s are seen as being only an early phase of 'postmodernity'.[80]

For Koehler this approach also revolts against the canonisation of a classical modernism which suppresses the 'aesthetic praxis' of 'alternative' modern 'traditions' such as Dadaism and Surrealism. Koehler adds, however, that 'insofar as the "post" in "postmodern" does not just imply a temporal relation, but also designates a break with the preceding style', this approach leads to an 'internal contradiction', for here 'the postmodernism in question breaks only with the conventions of the (so-called) classical Modern, but not with its "alternative" tradition'. Although it could be argued (as others have since Koehler) that the term post-modern need not necessarily designate a total break with the modern (or 'post-modernism' with 'modernism') in the first place,[81] Koehler goes on to conclude from the above that the 1960s should be seen as 'late modern' rather than as 'postmodern'.[82]

The argument over whether a movement is 'late' or 'post'-modern is also one around which several post-modernist debates have circled since Koehler wrote his article. As we shall see, they include the contributions made by Charles Jencks that the 'Post-Modern' in both art and architecture involves a 'double-coding' of the 'Modern' with other 'codes' where the 'Late-Modern' does not, and that theories of the post-modern which do not see it as aiming to double-code the modern with another code, but at simply 'deconstructing' the modern, should themselves only be seen as being 'late modern'.[83]

Koehler's last alternative, and preferred, view of the post-modern is that of a 'model' which would cover the last two decades from the point of view of two 'sometimes intersecting developments'. During the 1950s, Koehler claims, a 'traditional-ism' born of the 'modern classics' was dominant, but at the same time a 'Neo-Avantgardism' developed from the premisses of Dadaism and Surrealism which finally 'wore itself out' in the 1960s.[84] In the second half of that period a new sensibility was evident which was, however, no longer in harmony with either of the modernisms previously mentioned. Koehler adds that this 'tentative postmodernism' only begins to take form in the 1970s, but is still not easy to define. For Koehler the 'postmodern' thus begins only after 1970, and the period from 1945 to 1970 must therefore be called 'late modern'.

Despite the above vagueness over the nature of the 'post-modern', as well as some lack of clarity in Koehler's text over the boundaries between the words 'postmodern', 'postmodernity' and 'postmodernism',[85] and some minor errors,[86] it must still be seen as one of the earliest systematic attempts to give a history of the term post-modernism, although it may also now seem ironic, given the growth of post-modernist architecture in recent years and the use of the term post-modern in theoretical writings on the subject of architecture from at least 1945 on, that the one field omitted from its survey was that of architecture.[87]

Amongst the other early uses of the term post-modernism not listed by either the *OED Supplement* of 1982 or by Koehler in his 1977 essay[88] is, moreover, one by the Australian art historian Bernard Smith which may well be one of the first twentieth-century applications of the term to the visual arts.[89] Smith (who had been reading Toynbee's *A Study of History* through the war years[90]) had used the word 'post-Modernist' in the Conclusion of his *Place, Taste and Tradition* of 1945 (the text of which was completed in February 1944) with reference to the emergence of a new social and political realism in the Australian work of the artists Noel Counihan, Josl Bergner and Victor O'Connor. This 'new' form of Realism (in which elements from Expressionism and other twentieth-century styles mixed with the realistic depiction of the subject-matter of poverty and labour) represented for Smith a move away from modernist abstract art, as well as a reaction to what he saw to be the 'l'art pour l'art' mentality of many of the modernists of the twentieth century,[91] and was described by him as having arisen in the 'post-Modernist world' of the 1940s.[92]

In addition to the above, the 'post-Modernist' Realism of Counihan, Bergner and O'Connor was also described by Smith as having arisen in the place of the prophecies for a 'Post-Byzantine' form of modernism which would see the latter reduced further to the cold geometric forms favoured by Abstractionists. Here Smith was speaking in particular of a prophecy by Clive Bell and Pitirim Sorokin that modernism would develop into a 'sort of Post-Byzantinism that would catch the "spirit" of machinery in a vague symbolic fashion, in abstract geometric forms'.[93]

Further to referring us to the theories of Bell and Sorokin, Smith's use of the term 'Post-Byzantine' again recalls the work of Arnold J. Toynbee in that the latter had both described the contemporary world as a 'machine age' in the pre-World War Two volumes of his *A Study of History* and used the word 'Byzantine' in his fifth volume of 1939 to describe the 'archaism' of movements such as that of the 'Pre-Raphaelites' and 'Neo-Gothicists'.[94] Following Toynbee's use of the term 'Byzantine' to describe those forms of modernism which he thought to be 'archaic', Smith had used the term 'Post-Byzantine' to designate the reaction of modernist abstractionists against the 'Byzantine'. While de Onis's and Fitts/Hays's post-modernisms could be said to share some characteristics with that which Smith has termed 'Post-Byzantine' art, of, for instance, a reaction against earlier modernist Symbolist art, Smith's chosen category of 'post-Modernist' art is understood as standing in contrast to the cold abstractions of the 'Post-Byzantine'. Put in summary this could read:

Toynbee (1939): Post-World War One = *Post-Modern Age*; *Modern Art* = either Byzantine Archaism (Neo-Gothic or Pre-Raphaelite) or Futurism;

De Onis (1934) and Fitts/Hays (1942): 'postmodernismo' poetry = a reaction to earlier Modernist decorativeness;

Hudnut (1945): the *'post-modern* house' = (1) extension of Modern Movement functionalism and lack of decorativeness, and (2) in need of architect's sensibility;

Smith (1945): modern *'Post-Byzantine' Art* = a reaction to decorativeness and a move towards greater abstraction; *'Post-Modernist'* Art (of the 1940s) = a reaction against Modernist abstraction.[95]

Here the Modernism to which de Onis and Fitts/Hays's 'post-modernismo' was an alternative may be aligned (though not equated) with the Byzantine Archaism condemned by Toynbee[96] and their 'postmodernist' alternatives compared with the 'post-Byzantinism' to which Smith's 'post-Modernism' was seen by him to have acted as an alternative.[97] Although the Realism described by Smith as 'post-Modernist' in 1944 might now be described as a modern form of nineteenth-century social realism, and, hence, as also carrying on a tradition of modernism which existed prior to abstract modernism,[98] the use made by Smith of the term 'post-Modernism' in 1944/5 to describe a reaction to abstract modernism has also been echoed, despite Smith's own more recent condemnation of contemporary post-modernism,[99] in some contemporary uses of the term post-modernism and its concomitants in the fields of both art and architecture to denote a turning-away from the modernist obsession with abstraction.[100]

This is true, for example, of Achille Bonito Oliva's concept of the 'transavantgarde', as well as of some other contemporary concepts of post-modernist art.[101] Further to this, Michael Koehler's history of the term 'postmodern' refers to the American art critic John Perreault as having used the term in the mid-1960s for art works which 'did not seem to fit within the rules of modernism in art' or which revived 'art styles "wiped out" by modernism', or 'Anti-Object Art' or 'what have you'.[102] As with some later concepts of 'post-modernism', such accounts of post-modernist art have also thought it legitimate for that art to go back to movements prior to modernism as well as to go beyond them.[103] Whether the work of Counihan, Bergner or O'Connor could be said to be 'post-modernist' in any of the contemporary senses given the word by those discussed in the following chapters could, however, be questioned on the basis of the absence of other basic criteria listed for today's 'post-modernisms' or 'trans-avantgardes', such as the ironic awareness that all the modernist styles of the past are now historic and archaic rather than truly of the present, and that any opposition to modernist abstraction should also be aware of the naiveté of many 'pre-abstractionist' concepts of representation or Realism.[104]

Many of the early uses of the terms post-modern and post-modernism discussed in this section have also become outdated now because that which was for them post-modern has come to be seen in more recent years as a part of a now historical modern period. Whether current uses of the term will prove to have a better foot-hold in history remains to be seen, but they do at least seem at this point of time to have a wider distribution than that enjoyed by those of the 1930s and 1940s in their time.

One of the other factors distinguishing more recent theories of post-modernism from the earlier theories discussed in this chapter will also be found in the relating of the concept of the post-modern to concepts of post-industrial society which have been formulated in the last two or three decades of this century to describe certain changes in technology, scientific knowledge and the nature of work. Although the concept of the post-industrial society has not been explicitly used in the early definitions of the post-modern discussed in this chapter, the explanation of it which follows will be found to be relevant to the understanding of the more recent theories of the post-modern which are to be discussed in chapters 3, 4 and 5.

2

DEFINING THE POST-INDUSTRIAL

As will be seen from the following chapters, many of the more recent uses of the term post-modernism have included, or been defined alongside, a concept of contemporary society as a post-industrial society. Although this term has frequently been used in recent works to refer to a computerised, 'information', or 'knowledge' society, a history of its usage will show it to have been utilised to cover a variety of different concepts of 'information' or 'knowledge', and to have contained a variety of presuppositions about the nature of the relationship of the post-industrial to industrial society.

While there is no entry on the post-industrial in the *Oxford English Dictionary* comparable to its entry on the 'post-modern', there have been several brief discussions of the history of the term in recent studies of it, including Daniel Bell's important *The Coming of Post-Industrial Society* of 1973.[1]

Amongst the earlier uses of the idea of the post-industrial listed by Bell are those by Arthur J. Penty in his *Old Worlds for New: a Study of the Post-Industrial State* of 1917, David Riesman in 1958,[2] Herman Kahn and Anthony J. Wiener in 1967, Zbigniew Brzezinski in 1970 and Kenneth Keniston and Paul Goodman in 1971. In addition to listing these names, Bell also adds a brief reference to the work of what he calls 'a number of European neo-Marxist theoreticians', including Radovan Richta, Serge Mallet, André Gorz, Alain Touraine and Roger Garaudy.[3]

Arthur J. Penty, whom Bell describes as a follower of William Morris and John Ruskin as well as a Guild Socialist, was an architect and publicist who had worked with Alfred R. Orage on the weekly periodical *The New Age* in the early 1900s.[4] One other contributor to that journal, Ananda K. Coomaraswamy, had co-edited a volume of essays with Penty in 1914 entitled *Essays in Post-Industrialism: A Symposium of Prophecy concerning the Future of Society*.[5] While Coomaraswamy's contribution had been entitled 'The Religious Foundation of Art and Life', Penty's was on the unsuitability of industrial products for architecture and the impossibility of forming any new architecture from them.[6] This was also a subject to which Penty was to return in his 1922 book entitled *Post-Industrialism*, where he wrote:

There is no branch of art that in one way or another is not threatened with extinction at the hands of mechanical production, and nothing appears to take its place. The problem of architecture, it may be said, is too complex to be capable of any simple generalization. But it may be said that it is attacked on all sides by a combination of influences against which the architect is apt to struggle in vain, most of which are directly or indirectly the consequence of unregulated machine production. For a long time the only serious difficulty which the competent architect had to face was the difficulty of getting decent bricks and tiles to build with. But of late years he has got buried under a perfect avalanche of artificial materials, asbestos tiles, concrete blocks, standardized window frames, doors and other abominations which cut at the base of any possible architectural treatment. Only on the more expensive work, which is rapidly declining in quality, can he escape from the necessity of using such things. To believe that any new style of architecture can arise out of such conditions is to take refuge in a faith that has no relation to reality. No one in architecture really believes it, though there are some who try.[7]

Later, in a book entitled *The Elements of Domestic Design* of 1930, Penty named 'the clear cut, massive simplicity of Norman work' as his own ideal architecture.[8] Although he was a critic of the modern machine aesthetic in architecture,[9] Penty did not automatically fall back on the more decorated styles of the past for an alternative, and wrote critically of the way in which 'the idea of architecture becomes increasingly identified with its trimmings, and as time elapses it becomes so over-moulded that the essential form is obscured'. To Penty, Gothic architecture had also 'degenerated into confectionery, into a phantasmagoria of glass and stone', and it was only with the Renaissance that 'the sense of space which is so essential to architecture' was recovered. For him it was, moreover, essentially 'the primitive' in architecture which represented the best way 'to be equipped for dealing with the modern', and was even 'the modern' 'in the best sense'.[10]

Penty had also praised the Arts and Crafts movement in both his early and later works for their revival of craft,[11] but criticised it in his 1922 text for directing most of its energies towards decoration rather than to the solution of what he saw to be the broader problems created by industrialism,[12] such as the control of work by the machine and the continuing dominance of the 'artificial' sub-divisions of labour which he saw to be typical of industrialism.

Penty's co-editor of 1914, Ananda K. Coomaraswamy, had both spoken in his earlier works of the lack of industrial divisions of labour in the arts and crafts of pre-industrial India and its villages[13] and provided Penty with some details of the Indian guilds[14] as well as with the word 'post-industrial'.[15] Penty's Preface to his *Post-Industrialism* of 1922 acknowledges Coomaraswamy as the author of the term used in his title and gives the following explanation of the meaning given it in Penty's text:

A word about the title of the book. From one point of view, Post Industrialism connotes Medievalism, from another it could be defined as 'inverted Marxism'. But in any case it means the state of society that will follow the break-up of Industrialism, and might therefore be used to cover the speculations of all who recognize Industrialism is doomed. The need of some such term sufficiently inclusive to cover the ideas of those who, while sympathizing with the ideals of the Socialists, yet differed with them in their attitude towards Industrialism has long been felt, and the term Post-Industrialism, which I owe to Dr A.K. Coomaraswamy, seems to me well suited to supply this want.[16]

Penty's use of the term post-industrial here is, despite his acknowledgement to Coomaraswamy, also specific to Penty in his use of it to counter the criticisms of some Marxists that the true target of socialism was not industrialism but capitalism.[17] To Penty Marx had sometimes been too optimistic about the benefits of new machinery, even though he had pointed to some of its deleterious effects.[18] Armed with this interpretation of Marx, Penty was able to argue that the immediate target of socialism (and, in particular, of Guild Socialism) must be the regulation of machinery by its users, and the abolition of the divisions of labour typical of industrialism by means of which the tasks formerly undertaken by the craftsman had been split between a variety of men and machines.[19]

Although Penty has been criticised in more recent years as offering a reactionary and unrealistic vision of the new post-industrial society as one in which the industrialism of the past will be 'broken-up',[20] his specification of the central issues of both industrialism and post-industrialism as the regulation of machines and the sub-division of labour between both persons and machines has been one which has continued to feature in most recent theories of the post-industrial society.[21] While few of these theorists since Penty have used the term post-industrial to demand the abolition of industrial practices,[22] almost all have directed their attention to the new divisions of labour and new machinery (or technology) which have been added to those of industrial society by that which they have termed the new 'post-industrial society'. Even if these more recent theories of the post-industrial society have used the prefix 'post' to designate a development of industrialism rather than a break from it, as suggested by Penty's use of the term, most have therefore also happened to continue Penty's emphasis on the centrality of industrial issues such as the sub-division of labour and the role of machinery to both industrial and post-industrial theory.

Similarities between Penty's use of the term post-industrial and those of more recent theorists have, however, been less frequently looked at than the differences between them. Although Penty's 1917 text had spoken (like his 1922 work) of the relations of society, the 'growth of large organizations, the division of labour, and the application of machinery' in industrialism,[23] Daniel Bell, for instance, has related Penty's use of the term post-industrial in his 1917 text only to Penty's denunciation of the 'Leisure State' as 'collectivist' and 'servile' and to his call for a return to the decentralised, small workshop artisan society in which work could be 'ennobled'.[24] Bell's description of Penty's ideas had even been followed by an exclamation mark:

Ironically, I have recently discovered that the phrase occurs in the title of a book by Arthur J. Penty, *Old Worlds for New: A Study of the Post-*

Industrial State (London 1917). Penty, a well-known Guild Socialist of the time and a follower of William Morris and John Ruskin, denounced the 'Leisure State' as collectivist and associated with the Servile State, and called for a return to the decentralized, small workshop artisan society, ennobling work, which he called the 'post-industrial state'!

While the latter state also presupposed the reform of the industrial divisions of labour for Penty, such descriptions of his theory do not appear to have made clear the central importance of the question of those divisions of labour to Penty's 'post-industrial' theory, and, hence, its similarity to, as well as difference from, more recent post-industrial theory.[25]

Penty's criticisms of the 'Leisure State' in his 1917 text had, however, also offered Bell a contrast to the use of the term 'post-industrial' by David Riesman.[26] While Penty had argued that the Leisure State would entail the slavery of some to others, and that even with the replacement of slaves by machines, the pursuit of pleasure would inevitably lead to selfishness so that a post-industrial ennoblement of work would have to counter that alternative,[27] Riesman had spoken of the post-industrial society itself as a 'leisure society'.[28] Although this view of post-industrial society also suggests an affluent society, it had, however, not gone as far as to equate the post-industrial society with a 'post-scarcity' society.

Bell not only criticises this last concept as unrealistic,[29] but also goes on to question the use of the term 'the technetronic society' by Zbigniew Brzezinski in his *Between Two Ages: America's Role in the Technetronic Era* of 1970 to refer to society as dominated by the new technologies and electronics of the post-war years. Despite the relevance of this term to many contemporary uses of the concept of the post-industrial,[30] it is criticised by Bell for 'shifting the focus of change from theoretical knowledge to the practical applications of technology', and for a certain 'technological determinism'.[31]

In addition to the works which Bell mentions as having characterised the post-industrial society as one dominated by technology, other more popular works of the 1970s, such as Alvin Toffler's *Future Shock* of 1970, had painted a picture of future society as dominated by both new technologies and their effects.[32] Even earlier than Toffler, the writings of Marshall McLuhan on the growth of electronic communications systems had also suggested the world to be entering a new technological age, and one in which the electronic media would create a new 'global village'.[33]

Interestingly, it is also McLuhan's view of modern society as characterised by new technological and electronic developments which has been taken up by theorists such as Jean Baudrillard who have since been appropriated to the canon of 'postmodernist' theorists.[34] Baudrillard's 'The Orders of Simulacra' calls, for example, on McLuhan for confirmation of Baudrillard's belief in the ubiquity of the media in contemporary society,[35] while his earlier article 'Requiem for the Media' had summarised McLuhan in the following manner: 'The media make – indeed they are – the revolution, independently of their content, by virtue of their technological structure alone. After the phonetic alphabet and the printed book comes the radio and the cinema. After radio, television. We live, here and now, in the age of instantaneous, global communication'.[36] The 'Baudrillardian' vision of contemporary society as one dominated by electronic media which has since been taken over by so many recent theorists of 'postmodernism' may also be seen to owe much to McLuhan. Although Baudrillard is critical of some aspects of McLuhan's theories in the text from which the above passage is taken, the summary which he gives in it of McLuhan's ideas also expresses thoughts which Baudrillard himself will take over and repeat in other of his works.

In addition to mentioning ideas from McLuhan at several points in his 'The Orders of Simulacra',[37] Baudrillard's contribution to Hal Foster's 1983 volume on 'Postmodern Culture',[38] 'The Ecstasy of Communication', contains passages such as the following:

Something has changed, and the Faustian, Promethean (perhaps Oedipal) period of production and consumption gives way to the 'proteinic' era of networks, to the narcissistic and protean era of connections, contact, contiguity, feedback and generalized interface that goes with the universe of communication. With the television image – the television being the ultimate and perfect object for this new era – our own body and the whole surrounding universe become a control screen.[39]

McLuhan is not named in the above passage, or in the article from which it is taken, but his theories are specifically mentioned by Baudrillard in an article published in a volume on 'Post-industrial Culture',[40] in which he also claims that 'we live in a world of proliferating information and shrinking sense'. In contrast to McLuhan's belief in the possibility of controlling the electronic media,[41] Baudrillard here presents a much more cynical picture of the individual as controlled by the latter. Baudrillard also shows himself to be aware of this difference from McLuhan when he writes in his essay, 'Design and Environment', of the twentieth century's 'cybernetic idealism, blind faith in radiating information' and 'mystique of information services and the media': 'This optimism can seem to be in good faith, it can take on the benign air of the designer who plans, for his small part, to contribute to increased information by his creativity, or the prophetic air of McLuhan, who exalts the "already present" global communication'.[42]

Previously, Baudrillard had criticised McLuhan in his 'Requiem for the Media' for being both 'empirical' and 'mystical'.[43] Here as there, however, Baudrillard will both criticise McLuhan for his optimism, and take over McLuhan's description of the modern world as one characterised by a growing utilisation of electronic media. Like McLuhan's, the 'Baudrillardian' view of contemporary society as one dominated by electronic media and other 'cybernetic orders' is one which may, moreover, be said to describe late modernity and its forces of modernisation rather than anything which is 'post-modern' in the sense of having broken from the latter.[44]

Despite this, Baudrillard's characterisations of contemporary society as dominated by the electronic media have been taken up by several cultural theorists to describe a new post-modern age.[45] One of these writers, Dick Hebdige, has also spoken of 'post-modernisation', in a combination of terms from industrial and post-industrial theory, as 'automation, micro-technologies, decline of manual labour and traditional work forms, consumerism, multinational media conglomerates, and deregulation of the airwaves'.[46] Although Hebdige has run several different concepts together here, and from post-modern as well as industrial and post-industrial theory, most of them may also be described as aspects of modernisation rather than of post-modernisation understood as a break from the forces of modernisation.[47]

This is so because, while automation may clearly be said to be a product of what is normally understood as modernisation, micro-technologies, the rise of multinational media conglomerates, and the 'deregulation of the airwaves' may also be understood as the products of processes of technology and their divisions of labour developed from those initiated under modernisation. Most important of all, however, the latter, 'modern', forms of production, do not simply cease with the advent of the newer information-industries. If we are to speak of contemporary societies as 'post-modernisation' societies in this way, then we shall at least have to make it clear that the prefix 'post' in this term will almost always designate a continuation of modernisation rather than a break from it, and either because modernisation and earlier forms of production will continue to support the economies of the world together with newer forms, and/or because some of those newer forms may be able to be seen as continuations of the other rather than as breaks.

Prior to Baudrillard's use of McLuhan in his essays of the 1970s the French sociologist Alain Touraine had also spoken of the post-industrial society as 'programmed' by its technologies and dominated by 'technocratic power', although without the total pessimism about the possibility for change which is evident in so many of Baudrillard's texts.[48] Touraine's 1969 text, *The Post-Industrial Society, Tomorrow's Social History: Classes, Conflicts and Culture in the Programmed Society* began: 'A new type of society is now being formed. These new societies can be labeled post-industrial to stress how different they are from the industrial societies that preceded them, although – in both capitalist and socialist nations – they retain some characteristics of these earlier societies'. Touraine continued: 'They may also be called technocratic because of the power that dominates them. Or one can call them programmed societies to define them according to the nature of their production methods and economic organization'.[49]

Although Touraine adds that the last of these definers seems to be the most useful, 'because it most accurately indicates the nature of these societies' inner workings and economic activity',[50] he goes on in his chapter entitled 'The Programmed Society' to repeat his claims about the power held by technocrats and to suggest that it must be rebelled against.[51] Touraine adds in his following chapter, 'Old and New Social Classes': 'A new kind of society is being born. If we want to define it by its technology, by its "production forces", let's call it the programmed society. If we choose to name it from the nature of its ruling class, we'll call it technocratic society.'[52]

Further to this, Touraine writes of the 'technocrats' that they support a 'self-devouring technical development, which transforms itself into the non-rational accumulation of power',[53] and that the technocratic society will also control and inhibit new forms of building as well as social interaction.[54] Although Touraine is not totally pessimistic about the possibilities for change,[55] his vision of post-industrial society as a society dominated by bureaucrats and technology is, as we shall soon see, a long way from both the optimistic vision of industrial society presented by Saint-Simon at the beginning of the nineteenth century and the vision of the post-industrial society as presented by Daniel Bell in his *The Coming of Post-Industrial Society* of 1973.

Bell's *The Coming of Post-Industrial Society* is not only critical of the 'technological determinism' of some other theories of the post-industrial society, but also sets out to propose that the 'axial principle' of the post-industrial society will not be technology but theoretical scientific knowledge.[56] While even Arthur Penty may be said to have been aware of the importance of science in the twentieth century when he had written with reference to the attention paid to scientists, that they were 'the high priests of the modern world, and when they speak they are listened to',[57] his depiction of the post-industrial society of the future had had no specific place for such men. Indeed, while one of the characteristics of the post-industrial society as described by Daniel Bell will be an increase in the divisions of mental labour, and information-sector work, Penty had also specifically argued against the increased specialisation of the professions.[58]

In the Preface to his *The Coming of Post-Industrial Society*[59] Bell had first described his thesis as being that in the 'next thirty to fifty years' we will see the emergence of 'the post-industrial society', and that while this will be 'primarily a change in the social structure'[60] (with varying consequences in different countries), it will not be understood by him in any deterministic manner as 'a "substructure" initiating changes in a "superstructure" '.[61] In contrast to this view (and to those theories of technological determinism discussed previously in this chapter) Bell goes on to refer to the 'new and decisive role of theoretical knowledge in determining social innovation and the direction of change'.[62]

Unlike some other theories of the post-modern and the post-industrial, the post-industrial developments forecast by Bell in his 1973 book are also to make up but 'one important dimension of a society'.[63] As such statements show, the post-industrial society discussed by Bell in 1973 is not one which will displace completely the industrial society of previous decades,[64] but it is to represent changes which may be described as significant enough to warrant the new title of 'post-industrial'.[65]

Bell, according to the Preface to his 1973 text,[66] had originally formulated its concept of the post-industrial society in an unpublished paper presented at a forum on technology and social change in Boston in 1962. As Bell goes on to explain in the Introduction to his book, this paper was entitled 'The Post-Industrial Society: a Speculative View of the United States in 1958 and Beyond', and it was in it that he had turned his attention to the role played by intellectual technology and science in social change.[67] Further to this, Bell's Introduction had explained that he had earlier used the term 'post-industrial society' in a series of lectures in Salzburg in 1959[68] to denote a society 'which had passed from a goods-producing stage to a service society', and that he had also been using the term 'post-industrial' there in contrast to Ralf Dahrendorf's 'post-capitalist' because Bell was dealing with 'sector changes in the economy' while Dahrendorf was discussing 'authority relations in the factory'.[69]

While Bell will concentrate his concept of the post-industrial society on 'changes *in the social structure*' and the 'way in which the economy is being transformed and the occupational system reworked' with 'new relations between science and technology' in his 1973 text, he will also be concerned with the widening gap between the economy, the polity and culture in both his *The Coming of Post-Industrial Society* and in his later *The Cultural Contradictions of Capitalism* of 1976. There, as will be seen presently, post-modern culture will, moreover, be seen as an extension of modern narcissistic culture, and as an extension of the gap between society and its values.

Hence it is also important to note that the theoretical knowledge which Bell understands to be organising and changing post-industrial society will not be the discourses of 'postmodern culture' (or, at least, of post-modern culture as understood by Bell) so much as the 'theoretical discourses of science' which he sees as affecting the basic structures of modern society. In contrast to the French philosopher Jean-François Lyotard, whose writings on the post-modern society will be discussed in the following chapter, Bell also makes a division between the 'technical intelligentsia who are committed to functional rationality and technocratic modes of operation' and the 'literary intellectuals who have become increasingly apocalyptic, hedonistic and nihilistic'.[70]

Further to this, Bell may also be seen to be using the concept of science in a very different sense from that used by Lyotard[71] in using it in the sense of Robert Merton's 1942 rules for science, of universalism, communalism, disinterestedness and organised scepticism.[72] In contrast to the Mertonian view of science propounded by Bell in his depiction of the post-industrial society that science will be carried out without self-interest, Lyotard has written in his 1979 study of the 'postmodern condition' that 'What happened at the end of the eighteenth century, with the first industrial revolution, is that the reciprocal of [the] equation was discovered: no technology without wealth, but no wealth without technology',[73] and that the present 'commercialization' of research has also meant that 'scientists, technicians, and instruments are purchased not to find truth, but to augment power'.[74]

Lyotard's work will be returned to presently. Because Bell is aware that his concept of the post-industrial society is, to use his own words, 'a large generalization',[75] he also breaks it down into five main components:

1. Economic sector: the change from a goods-producing to a service economy;
2. Occupational distribution: the pre-eminence of the professional and technical class;
3. Axial principle: the centrality of theoretical knowledge as

the source of innovation and of policy formulation for the
society;
4.   Future orientation: the control of technology and technological assessment;
5.   Decision-making: the creation of a new 'intellectual
technology'.[76]

A closer look at all of these components will suggest, however,
not only that they too are generalizations, but also that they
may, according to some interpretations of their terms, just as
well describe some aspects and philosophies of the industrial
societies of the last century. Thus the change from a 'goods-
producing' to a 'service' economy may be questioned if certain
categories of nineteenth-century workers are also included in the
service industries other than those which Bell goes on to specify
as the service industries typical of post-industrial society – of the
health, education, research and government industries[77] – or if,
conversely, the service workers of the post-industrial society are
interpreted as 'goods-producing' workers of some kind.[78]

Further to this, Bell's three other components of the post-
industrial society – of the centrality of knowledge to innovation
and policy formation, control of technology and decision-making
– are all factors which, together with his list of reasons for the
significance of the post-industrial,[79] are not only to be found in
some form in the nineteenth-century industrial societies of the
West, but are also foreshadowed in the writings of one of the
major pioneers of modern industrial social theory mentioned by
Bell in his works on the post-industrial society, the Count
Claude-Henri de Saint-Simon (1760–1825).

Not only may Saint-Simon be said to have introduced the idea
of an intellectual avant-garde into modern social theory, but he
had also used this and other concepts to argue that a leading role
should be taken by scientists and engineers in restructuring the
labour relationships of feudal society for the new 'industrial'
society of the nineteenth century.[80] Here Saint-Simon's 'avant-
garde' of 'producers' or 'industrialists' is also comparable in at
least some senses to the knowledge elites spoken of by Daniel
Bell as characteristic of the post-industrial society.[81] This is so
because of the way in which Saint-Simon's avant-garde was to

guide society both politically and by way of the application of science to the increase of economic productivity, but also because Saint-Simon had explicitly included theoretical scientists as well as technologists and engineers in it.

Saint-Simon wrote, for example, in the fourth fragment of his *On the Social Organization*:

> The high administration of society encompasses the invention, examination and execution of projects which are useful to the mass of mankind.
>
> High administration, therefore, involves three abilities; that of the artists, that of the scientists and that of the industrialists, and the combination of all three fulfils all the necessary conditions satisfying the moral and physical needs of society.[82]

Saint-Simon's 'avant-garde' (a term he took from military terminology as early as 1802[83]) was also to live up to its name in looking to the future of society rather than to its past. Earlier, in the first fragment of his *On the Social Organization*, he had written with regard to the period preceding the abolition of slavery: 'Hitherto men have walked backwards on the path of civilization, turning their backs on the future; they have usually had their gaze fixed on the past and they have glanced only very seldom and cursorily at the future. Now that slavery has been destroyed, it is upon the future that men should mainly concentrate'.[84] In contrast to those 'deconstructionist' post-modernists who have found themselves fascinated by Walter Benjamin's image of the angel of history as having his face 'turned toward the past' while being propelled backwards into the future by the 'storm' of progress,[85] Saint-Simon's image of his avant-garde places their gaze firmly on the future, and their feet firmly on the material path to it.[86]

As Ken'ichi Tominaga has argued in his contribution to the winter 1971 edition of *Survey*'s symposium on 'Post-Industrial Society',[87] similarities in the thoughts of Saint-Simon on industrial society[88] with those of Bell on post-industrial society also suggest that Bell's post-industrial society must be understood as an extension of industrial society rather than as an entirely different new stage.[89] This is true, Tominaga writes, not only of the various characteristics which post-industrial society has 'inherited' from industrial society, such as 'differentiated

systems of the division of labour' and 'achievement orientation',[90] but also of the role played by science and technology in
the post-industrial society. Tominaga continues: 'Throughout
the entire process of industrialization and including its present
post-industrial stage, the development of science and technology has consistently played the part of prime mover. The
increasing preponderance of the knowledge society in post-
industrial society is merely the end result of this process.'[91]

While Daniel Bell's contribution to the symposium had
acknowledged Saint-Simon as having 'popularized' the word
industrialism – to 'designate the emergent society, wherein
wealth would be created by production and machinery rather
than be seized through plunder and war'[92] – it had also dismissed Saint-Simon and his followers for having turned scientists
into the priests of society in a 'cultish fashion'.[93] Later, in his *The
Coming of Post-Industrial Society* of 1973, Bell does agree with
Tominaga that the post-industrial society is 'a continuation of
trends unfolding out of industrial society',[94] but again appears to
underplay the importance of scientists in Saint-Simon's
industrial society. Bell also argues:[95]

Both Saint-Simon and Marx ... were obsessed with the crucial role of
engineers (in the one case) and science (in the other) in transforming
society, though neither of them had, or could have, any sense of the
change in the fundamental relation of science to economic and technological development, the fact, for instance, that most of the major
industries of the nineteenth and early twentieth centuries – steel,
telegraph, telephone, electricity, auto, aviation – were developed largely
by talented tinkerers who worked independently of the fundamental
work in science; while the first modern industry is chemistry, since one
has to have a theoretical *a priori* knowledge of the properties of the
macromolecules one is manipulating in order to create new products.[96]

Bell adds at a later point: 'If the dominant figures of the past
hundred years have been the entrepreneur, the businessman,
and the industrial executive, the "new men" are the scientists,
the mathematicians, the economists, and the engineers of the
new intellectual technology.'[97]

Several points could be made about Bell's claims here. Firstly,
it can be noted that his implication that Marx could have no idea
that 'technological development' would be controlled by scien-

tists rather than by 'tinkerers' may be said to have overlooked the fact, amongst others, that Marx had certainly read Charles Babbage's *On the Economy of Machinery and Manufactures* of 1832 not only once but at least twice,[98] and could have learned from that work that Babbage (1792–1871), who was the Lucasian Professor of Mathematics at Cambridge from 1828 to 1839 as well as a Fellow of the Royal Society from 1816 on, had published it in tandem with the development of his 'Calculating' or 'Difference' Machine.[99] This machine was, moreover, not only developed by a Swedish engineer named Georg Scheutz and exhibited in Marx's time in London, in 1854,[100] but was also the forerunner of Babbage's more complex 'Analytical Machine', which has since been described as the prototype of the modern computer.[101] Despite the fact that Babbage was never to see the production of this latter 'computer' in his lifetime, his work on it, and mathematical expertise, clearly show that not all nineteenth-century inventors were 'tinkerers'.

Secondly, in addition to developing a prototype of the machine which has done so much to encourage theorists to speak of contemporary society as a 'post-industrial' society, Babbage had not only suggested in his 1832 text that the future would see an increase in the education of the sons of manufacturers in science,[102] but had argued, following the French engineer de Prony, that the divisions of manual labour spoken of by Adam Smith as leading to the increase of national wealth should be extended to mental labour, through, for example, the distribution of mathematical tasks amongst several persons.[103] Further to this, Babbage suggested both that new developments in chemistry could aid manufacturers and that at least two of the most significant discoveries in chemistry – of iodine and brome (the term then used for bromine) – had been made by manufacturers themselves.[104]

Without referring to the figure of Babbage, and to his attempts to bring the theoretical and practical sciences closer together in the early and mid-nineteenth century,[105] Bell had also written in his *The Coming of Post-Industrial Society* of 1973 that the post-industrial society has not only been characterised by the joining of science, technology and economics in recent years (symbolised for Bell by the phrase 'research and development'), but that the science-based, computer, electronics, optics and polymers industries of the post-industrial society are unlike industries which arose in the nineteenth century in being 'primarily dependent on theoretical work prior to production',[106] and that the computer would not exist without the work in solid-state physics initiated forty years ago by Felix Bloch.[107] Although Bell might be right about Bloch, there would seem to be no reason given in his text as to why Babbage's work might not also be accorded a similar status, if not even a greater one given Babbage's added contribution to recent 'post-industrial theory' through his extension of the discussion of the advantages of the divisions of manual labour spoken of by Adam Smith to the realms of both science and technology.[108]

The case of Babbage, and of his relationship to the post-industrial principles defined by Bell, may also lead us to question the usefulness of Bell's axial principle – of the growth of theoretical knowledge – for the rise of what he has termed the 'post-industrial society', or question how different that society is from industrial society if looked at from the view-point of that principle alone. Rather than distinguish the post-industrial from the industrial from the point of view of such abstract and loosely interpretable principles, it may, for instance, still be better to look more closely at the way in which any apparently new developments in technology and divisions of labour have marked a development of, or departure from, those of industrial society, although here again we must be prepared to discuss and deal with problems of categorisation, and/or insufficient appropriate data on earlier industrial communities more thoroughly than in the past.[109]

Not only have we seen that the axial principle of Bell's society may be taken back to nineteenth-century thinkers, including Babbage and Saint-Simon, but Bell's interest in it may also be seen to follow in at least a broad sense from the sociological tradition begun by Saint-Simon and theorised by his secretary Auguste Comte of seeing the growth of something termed 'modern science' as being of importance to the future of human society.[110] Where Bell does appear to move onto a different and less optimistic path from that taken by earlier utopian social theorists such as Saint-Simon or Comte, is, however, in the concluding 'Coda' to his 1973 work on the break-down of values in the modern world, and in the book which followed that work in 1976, his *The Cultural Contradictions of Capitalism*.

It is here too, moreover, that Bell describes both 'modernism' and 'post-modernism' as having been incapable so far of providing the values needed for contemporary society. While some elements of the 'Protestant ethic' may still be said to be at work in some areas of production in society, the 'culture of capitalism' (which includes both modernism and post-modernism for Bell) has in his view been based on a contradictory movement towards 'pleasure and play'.[111]

Although Juergen Habermas has claimed that Bell has blamed modernist culture for the dissolution of the Protestant ethic,[112] Bell himself has stated in both his 1973 and 1976 texts that the Protestant ethic has been undermined not by modernism but 'by capitalism itself'.[113] *Contra* Habermas's misreadings of Bell in his 1980 lecture[114] and elsewhere,[115] Bell's 1973 and 1976 works clearly show him to have put the 'blame' for the problems of modernity onto aspects of capitalist modernisation such as its introduction of 'instant credit' rather than onto cultural modernism, and to have seen the reduction of the latter to a subjective hedonism to be a product of the destruction by the former of the ethical elements in the 'Protestant ethic'.[116]

Bell writes, for example, in his 1973 work, of the destruction of the 'integrated whole in which culture, character, structure and economy were infused by a single value system' in nineteenth-century bourgeois (and capitalist) society: 'Ironically, all this was undermined by capitalism itself. Through mass production and mass consumption, it destroyed the Protestant ethic by zealously promoting a hedonistic way of life'. Later, in his 1976 text, Bell reiterates this argument: 'The Protestant ethic had served to limit sumptuary (though not capital) accumulation. When the Protestant ethic was sundered [by capitalism's invention of "instant credit"] from bourgeois society, only the hedonism remained, and the capitalist system lost its transcendental ethic.'[117] And he continues: 'The real problem of *modernity* is the problem of belief [or] a spiritual crisis, ... a situation which brings us back to nihilism.'[118]

For Bell the 'deconstructionist', 'structuralist' and 'neo-

Freudian' theories of 'postmodernism' are also as symptomatic of this crisis as is 'modernist hedonism'. Bell makes a specific reference to what he sees to be the 'de-constructionist' nature of post-modernism in describing the ideas of Michel Foucault: 'Foucault sees man as a short-lived historical incarnation, "a trace on the sand" to be washed away by the waves. The "ruined and pest-ridden cities of man called 'soul' and 'being' will be deconstructed".' Bell continues: 'It is no longer the decline of the West, but the end of all civilization. Much of this is modish, a play of words pushing a thought to an absurd logicality. Like the angry playfulness of Dada or surrealism, it will probably be remembered, if at all, as a footnote to cultural history.'[119]

Just prior to these passages Bell had named Foucault together with Norman O. Brown, William S. Burroughs, Jean Genet and 'porno-pop culture' as representative of the 1960s post-modernist extension of modernism,[120] and this and other statements by Bell on post-modernism are repeated in his 1977 essay 'Beyond Modernism, Beyond Self',[121] where it is also suggested that Bell's conception of post-modernism as hedonistic and antipathetic to the Protestant ethic may have been following the description, given of post-modern culture by Leslie Fiedler in his 1965 essay 'The New Mutants'.[122]

In addition to naming writers such as William S. Burroughs and Norman O. Brown as representatives of a new 'post-Modernist' literature,[123] Fiedler had written of those involved in the new post-modernist cults that they were replacing the Protestant ethic of modern America and were 'mystics' but not 'Christians'.[124] In addition to describing both modern and post-modern culture as antipathetic to the Protestant ethic Bell had also written in his 1976 text that present-day art was both 'post-modern' and 'post-Christian'.[125]

Earlier, Bell had also referred to both Brown and Foucault in the Coda to his *The Coming of Post-Industrial Society*[126] and had then gone on to relate a later depiction in that text[127] of the 'anti-institutional' and 'antinomian' character of contemporary culture to post-modernism in his 1977 essay 'Beyond Modernism, Beyond Self'.[128] Bell had written first in his *The Coming of Post-Industrial Society*:

Contemporary culture, with the victory of modernism, has become anti-institutional and antinomian. Few writers 'defend' society or institutions against the 'imperial self' ... The older artistic imagination, however wild or perverse, was constrained by the shaping disciplines of art. The new sensibility tears down all genres and denies that there is any distinction between art and life.[129]

In his 1977 essay Bell then wrote of post-modernism that it was a 'culmination of modernist intentions', the substitution of the 'instinctual' for the 'aesthetic justification of life', the 'tearing down' of boundaries and the 'onslaught on the values and motivational patterns of "ordinary" behaviour'.[130] Prior to this, in his *The Cultural Contradictions of Capitalism*, Bell had also written:

The effort to find excitement and meaning in literature and art as a substitute for religion led to modernism as a cultural mode. Yet modernism is exhausted and the various kinds of post-modernism (in the psychedelic effort to expand consciousness without boundaries) are simply the decomposition of the self in an effort to erase individual ego.[131]

Although Bell views post-modernism here as elsewhere in a largely negative manner as an attempt at the further 'deconstruction' of earlier values,[132] it must be remembered that he was then not only using a concept of post-modernism born of the late 1960s, and descriptive of those years, but was also writing prior to the growth of those more recent post-modernisms which have challenged the 'deconstructionist' and late modernist theories of which he was writing in the 1970s.[133] While the following chapter will look in greater detail at the 'deconstructionist postmodernisms' of the 1970s, chapters 4 and 5 will discuss some of the other post-modernisms which were not yet known to Bell in the early and mid-1970s.

3

DECONSTRUCTIONIST THEORIES

Introduction

What's the difference between the Mafia and a deconstructionist?
A deconstructionist makes you an offer you can't understand.[1]

As the above lines suggest, deconstructionist theory has often been seen to have avoided giving clear definitions, and even of itself. Christopher Norris has written of this latter problem in his *The Deconstructive Turn*[2] that 'to treat it [Deconstruction] as amenable to handy definition is to foster a misleadingly reductive account of that activity and hence to render one's text redundant as it originates'. Having said this, Norris then goes on to admit that 'on the other hand such purist attitudes can all too easily become an excuse for mere conceptual laziness and muddled thinking'.[3]

Norris continues his search for a definition of Deconstruction with a timely limitation of its drive for universal questioning: 'Deconstructionist rigour – if we are to use that term – belongs to a discourse which can only question all standard, regulative notions of logical consistency.' One problem for deconstructionist theory here, however, is how to determine how these 'standard' notions are to be identified or categorised as such without practising the 'hierarchical' analysis which its theorists have so often condemned. Despite the existence of this problem, many of the 'deconstructionist' post-modernists whose work will be discussed in this chapter will be seen to have directed their attention towards the 'deconstruction' of selected modernist canons (selected – and sometimes also constructed – by these 'deconstructionist post-modernists' themselves), whilst also replacing them with new ones containing their ideal post-modernist alternatives.[4]

As an introduction to what will generally be termed 'deconstructionist post-modernism' in this chapter (for reasons previously outlined in the Preface), rather than to 'Deconstruction' as such, the following paragraphs will be concerned first of all with providing some definition of the adjective used for this particular type of post-modernism by both its supporters and critics, before the various different forms which 'deconstructionist post-modernism' has taken in the last two decades are described in greater detail.[5]

With regard to the word 'Deconstruction' and its use as an adjective in the term 'deconstructionist post-modernism', Jacques Derrida, for instance, has written in his *The Truth in Painting* of 1978 in a manner which, despite his own reluctances to use the term post-modernism, presages Lyotard's direction of post-modernism towards the deconstruction of the 'metanarratives' of modernity in his *The Postmodern Condition* of 1979, that it (Deconstruction) 'attacks not only the internal edifice, both semantic and formal, of philosophemes, but also . . . its extrinsic conditions of practice: the historical forms of its pedagogy, the social, economic or political structures of this pedagogical institution'.[6]

Other characteristics of Deconstruction listed by Norris which may be found to be relevant to the deconstructionist post-modernism of such as Lyotard include its questioning of 'exclusive or privileged orders of valorization'[7] and of the 'authorial point of view'.[8] In addition to listing these characteristics, Norris's *The Deconstructive Turn* presents Deconstruction as a move which both 'overturns' assumptions of 'classical philosophy', such as the claim (as Norris puts it) that philosophy has 'access to truths which literature can only obscure and pervert by its dissimulating play with language and fiction', and shows both philosophy and scientific thought to be 'bound up with linguistic structures which crucially influence and complicate' their 'logical workings'.[9] Norris continues: 'Deconstruction is first and last a textual activity, a putting-into-question of the root metaphysical prejudice which posits self-identical concepts outside and above the disseminating play of language.'[10]

To summarise this brief introduction to the concept of deconstructionist post-modernism, we may say that that term will refer here largely to theories of post-modernism which have used concepts from or related to deconstructionist theory to either construct their idea of post-modernism as breaking from earlier modern or modernist canons, as in the work of both Hassan and Lyotard, or to criticise other kinds of post-modernism and their 'canons', as in the cases, for example, of both Lyotard and Jameson and their criticisms of post-modernist architecture and its theories.[11] In each of these instances ideas or techniques similar to those of Deconstruction may be seen to have been used to criticise the establishment of what is described as either a 'modern' or 'post-modern' canon. While the choice of such canons may also serve to distinguish these deconstructionist post-modernisms from other forms of deconstructionist theory or analysis, as well as from each other, the 'indeterminacy' of their alternatives to those canons, and emphasis on the importance of continual critique, will further identify their links with deconstructionist theory.

Ihab Hassan

When Ihab Hassan suggests that the concept, and we may add 'deconstructionist' concept, of post-modernism had begun its international travels in the 1970s from American papers such as his own to the ears and eyes of such as Jean-François Lyotard,[12] we might also note that it had thereby brought back to France many of its previously formulated deconstructionist ideas in new form.

While Lyotard's use of the terms 'postmodern' and 'post-modernism' can be said to post-date Hassan's, deconstructionist concepts found in Hassan's work on post-modernism, such as that of the need to break free from the canons of modernism, or of the 'indeterminacy' of truth, may be found in the works of French theorists from Derrida through to others such as Baudrillard and to Lyotard himself which pre-date Hassan's work on post-modernism.[13] If Hassan's use of the term 'postmodern' also owes something to the use made of it by such as Arnold J. Toynbee, as Koehler has suggested,[14] the sources of many of its more specific and deconstructionist characteristics may, hence, be found in other more contemporary works of philosophic and literary theory.

Despite the origin of some of its underlying concepts in the work of other theorists, Hassan's 'postmodernism', as he writes it, is generally dated from 1971 and the publication of both his book *The Dismemberment of Orpheus: Toward a Postmodern Literature* and his article 'POSTmodernISM: A Paracritical Bibliography'.[15] Charles Jencks, for example, has written of this latter work that it had both 'christened' post-modernism and 'provided a pedigree for it'.[16] Having said this, Jencks, however, had also criticised what he saw to be the 'anarchic' biases of the concept as formulated by Hassan, and preferred to it his own 'double-coded' concept of post-modernism.[17]

While Jencks's early writings on post-modernism were concerned largely with the architecture of recent years, Hassan's concept of post-modernism had originally been directed at the area of the literary arts and their criticism.[18] After asking 'when will the Modern Period end?',[19] Hassan's 1971 essay had gone on to claim that a change had already occurred in Modernism that could be called 'Postmodernism' which could be found in a contrast between Edmund Wilson's *Axel's Castle: a Study in the Imaginative Literature of 1870–1930* of 1931 (Contents: Symbolism, Yeats, Valéry, Eliot, Proust, Joyce, Stein), as the 'classic text of Modernism', and, forty years later, Hassan's own alternative view, *The Dismemberment of Orpheus: Toward a Postmodern Literature* of 1971 (Contents: Sade, Pataphysics to Surrealism, Hemingway, Kafka, Existentialism to Aliterature, Genet and Beckett). Following his listing of these latter names, Hassan adds that Gertrude Stein should also have appeared in the latter canon as she had contributed to both 'Modernism' and 'Postmodernism', but that 'without a doubt' the 'crucial text' is *Finnegan's Wake*.

Having also asked, 'If we can arbitrarily state literary Modernism includes certain works between Jarry's *Ubu Roi* (1896) and Joyce's *Finnegan's Wake* (1939), where will we arbitrarily say that Postmodernism begins?',[20] Hassan had continued with ironic awareness of the difficulty of giving a 'deconstructionist' canon for post-modernism: 'A year earlier than the *Wake*? With

Sartre's *La Nausée* (1938) or Beckett's *Murphy* (1938)?' Hassan concluded:

> In any case Postmodernism includes works by writers as different as Barth, arthelme, ecker, eckett, ense, lanchot, orges, recht, urroughs, utor.
>
> *Query.* But is not *Ubu Roi* itself as Postmodern as it is Modern?[21]

Hassan's 'Postmodernism' here begins not just where Wilson's modernism ends, in the 1930s, but several decades prior to this, in the 1890s. Ironically, Hassan's choice of 'indeterminacy' as a characteristic of post-modernism will itself make any definite characterisation by him of post-modernism, and division of it from the canons of modernism it is to help question, difficult. Not only will Hassan's post-modernism be further defined by way of characteristics such as irony and parody which may also be said to have been characteristic of modernism,[22] but modernism will be seen to continue to exist alongside post-modernism and to entail certain elements – of, for example, urbanism, technologism, dehumanisation, primitivism, eroticism, antinomianism, experimentalism – which Hassan will see 'carried forward toward Postmodernism'.[23]

Despite the similarities between his concepts of modernism and post-modernism, Hassan goes on to set up a series of 'contrasts' between the two which may be summarised in the follow-

MODERNISM	POSTMODERNISM
Urbanism	The City and also the Global Village, ... leading either to more or less destruction, anarchy.
Technologism	Runaway technology, New art forms, Boundless dispersal by media, The computer as substitute consciousness or as an extension of consciousness?
Dehumanization	Antielitism, antiauthoritarianism. Diffusion of the ego. Participation. Art becomes communal, optional, anarchic. At the same time, Irony becomes radical, self-consuming play, entropy of meaning. Also comedy of the absurd, black humour, insane parody and slapstick, Camp. Negation.

	Abstraction taken to the limit and coming back as New Concreteness: the found object, the signed Brillo box or soup can, the nonfiction novel as history.

The range is from Concept Art (abstract) to Environmental Art (concrete).

Primitivism   Away from the mythic, toward the existential.

Eroticism   Beyond censorship.

Antinomianism   Counter Cultures.

Beyond alienation from the whole culture, acceptance of discreteness and discontinuity.

Evolution of radical empiricism in art as in politics or morality.

Counter Western 'ways' or metaphysics.

Experimentalism   Open, discontinuous, improvisational, indeterminate, or aleatory structures, together with simultaneism, fantasy, play, humour, happening, parody, increasing self-reflexiveness, intermedia, the fusion of forms, the confusion of realms.

An end to traditional aesthetic focused on the 'beauty' or 'uniqueness' of the art work?

Against interpretation (Sontag).[24]

Here it may also be noted that Hassan's list of characteristics for post-modernism contains characteristics previously described as 'post-modernist' by critics such as Leslie Fiedler.[25] These characteristics also include, however, elements of the literary work such as parody, which some others have seen to be typical of modernist writing, and which could and should, moreover, simply be described as devices used for several different purposes by different authors of different periods.[26] Further to this, Hassan's first sets of characteristics for the postmodern city and its technology recall the ideas of Marshall McLuhan on the way in which increased communications technology will create a 'global village' which other theorists, including Baudrillard,[27] have used to describe modernity.

As with some other definitions of post-modernism, Hassan's may, however, be understood as having used the prefix 'post' not to designate a 'break' from modernism so much as a continuation of it. While this may also suggest that its 'deconstruction' of the canons of modernism may in fact have the function of taking them over rather than of criticising them, it may also help to explain why Jencks for one has found Hassan's theories to be 'late modern' rather than a new 'post-modern' alternative to, or reform of, the modern. Here we might also note that, while the prefix 'post' in the term post-modernism will generally be understood as designating either a break from, or a continuation of, modernism,[28] the degree to which it will describe a change to the modernism to which it is attached will depend on the particular use made of it by the theorist.[29]

While many of the characteristics which Hassan describes as 'postmodern' may equally describe the modern, or modernism,[30] some of them have also been echoed by other theorists and practitioners of post-modernism, and from within different theorisations of the meaning of the modern and post-modern to Hassan's. Hence the dual-coded architecture of post-modernism has been described by Charles Jencks as both an essentially 'urban' form and as one built by the inhabitants of the 'world village' with the aid of its communications networks, while he and others have also discussed the 'environmental art' of Ian Hamilton Finlay in works on post-modernism.[31] Here it should again be noted, however, that Jencks's definer for the post-modern of 'double-coding' will also mean that aspects of the modern or of modernism will need to be 'double-coded' with other codes to help constitute the 'post-modern' in his view. Further to this, other theorists aside from Jencks, such as, for instance, Achille Bonito Oliva, might also not agree with Hassan's claim that the range of post-modernist art could include abstract modernist forms of 'Concept Art'. As noted in chapter 1, Bonito Oliva has represented the view-point that post-modernist art offers a turning away from modernist abstraction.[32] While this position might appear to have been covered by Hassan's claim that 'Abstraction will be taken to the limit and come back as New Concreteness', this 'Concreteness' has been illustrated by Hassan with examples taken from both early and late modernist Pop Art, from Marcel Duchamp to Andy Warhol.[33]

Although Jencks has also written that the idea of 'participation' is one characteristic listed by Hassan which might be relevant to post-modern architecture, but not that of anarchy,[34] Hassan's concept of participation had also been given a 'deconstructionist turn' in his 1971 list by its proximity to the dictum that 'Art becomes communal, optional, anarchic'.[35] Similarly, the irony which Jencks will see to be characteristic of post-modern art and architecture because of its ability to increase the number of 'codes' used by the modernist architect is also described there by Hassan as 'becoming radical, self-consuming play' and 'entropy of meaning', while parody is described as being 'insane'.[36] In contrast to the 'Negation' with which Hassan ends this list, the irony which Jencks describes as a definer of post-modernism is presented by him as a device for 'double-coding' the modern with another code[37] which assists in the expansion of meaning rather than in 'negation'.[38]

Hassan's vagueness about both the nature and chronology of post-modernism in his article of 1971 was followed, however, not only by the discussion and rewriting of his ideas by others, but also by his own further exploration of the subject in articles such as his 'The Question of Postmodernism' of 1980. Here Hassan gave a more extensive history of the early use of the term, from Federico de Onis and Arnold J. Toynbee,[39] and discussed other relevant uses of it such as Fiedler's 1969 argument that post-modernism had 'crossed the gap' between high and pop culture.[40]

With regard to Fiedler, Hassan also writes that Fiedler had 'had it in mind to challenge the elitism of the high modernist tradition in the name of pop', but that he, Hassan, had 'wanted to explore that impulse of self-unmaking which is part of the literary tradition of silence'. None the less, despite having suggested a contrast between himself and Fiedler, Hassan continues: 'Pop and silence, or mass culture and deconstruction – or, as I shall later argue, immanence and indeterminacy – may all be aspects of postmodern culture.'[41]

It is also from this point that Hassan goes on to list the nine 'conceptual problems' which constitute post-modernism for him at this moment of time. Put in summary these are:

1. 'The word postmodernism . . . evokes what it wishes to surpass or suppress, modernism itself. The term thus contains its enemy within . . . Moreover, it denotes temporal linearity and connotes belatedness, even decadence.' Hassan also asks here what better name could be given the Postmodern Age: could it,

for example, best be called the Atomic, Space, Television, Semiotic, or Deconstructive Age, or should it be called 'the Age of Indetermanence'?[42]

2.   'No clear consensus about its meaning exists among scholars.' (Hassan adds here that some mean by post-modernism what others would call avant-gardism, while others still would call the same phenomenon simply modernism.)

3.   'The concept (like others) is also open to change.'

4.   'Modernism and postmodernism are not separated by an Iron Curtain or Chinese Wall, for history is a palimpsest, and culture is permeable to time past, time present, and time future.'

5.   'This means that a period must be perceived in terms of *both* continuity *and* discontinuity . . . postmodernism . . . demands a double view.' 'Sameness and difference, unity and rupture, filiation and revolt, all must be honored if we are to *attend* to history, *apprehend* (perceive, understand) change.' (Here Jencks's description of post-modernism as a 'double-coding' – used by him from 1978, and echoing Robert Venturi's advocacy of 'both–and' rather than 'either–or' statements in architecture[43] – could also be said to be accommodated to at least some extent, although the more 'anarchic' elements of Hassan's 'both–ands' – of, for instance, 'rupture' and 'revolt' – will not be reflected in the majority of examples of the post-modern chosen by Jencks.)

6.   'But a "period" is generally not a period at all: it is rather both a diachronic and synchronic construct . . . we have created in our mind a model of postmodernism, a particular typology of culture and imagination, and have proceeded to "rediscover" the affinities of various authors and various moments with that model.' Hassan continues: 'We have, that is, reinvented our ancestors . . . Consequently, "older" authors can be postmodern – Beckett, Borges, Nabokov, Gombrowicz – while "younger" authors need not be – Styron, Updike, Gardner.' (One problem for post-modernist studies here, however, is the problem of who may select whom to be 'postmodern', and why. Because many of Hassan's other definers remain indeterminate, it is also difficult to tell from them who else might or might not be classified as a 'post-modernist'.)

7. 'A definition of the subject also requires a dialectical vision, for defining traits are often antithetical . . . and also plural: to elect a single trait as an absolute criterion of postmodern grace is to make of all other writers preterites.' Hassan adds: 'Thus we cannot simply rest – as I have sometimes done – on the assumption that postmodernism is antiformal, anarchic, or decreative: for though it is indeed all these, and despite its will to unmaking, it also contains the need to discover a "unitary sensibility" (Sontag), to "cross the border and close the gap" (Fiedler), and to obtain, as I have suggested, an immanence of discourse, a neo-gnostic im-mediacy of mind.'[44]

8. 'The concept of postmodernism assumes a theory of innovation or cultural change. Which one? Viconian? Marxist? Freudian? Derridean? Semiotic? Paradigmatic? Eclectic? Or should postmodernism be left undefined, unconceptualized, at least for the moment?' (Hassan gives no answer but leaves the question open.)

9. 'Is postmodernism only a literary tendency, or is it also a cultural phenomenon, perhaps even a mutation in Western humanism? If so, how are the various aspects of this phenomenon – psychological, philosophical, economic, political – joined or disjoined? In short can we understand postmodernism in literature without some attempt to perceive the lineaments of a postmodern society, a Toynbeean postmodernity, so to speak, of which the tendency I have been discussing is but a single elitist strain?'[45]

Hassan, though aware of the limits of dichotomies,[46] moves on to give a set of what appear to be contrasting characteristics for 'Modernism' and 'Postmodernism':

Modernism	Postmodernism
Romanticism/Symbolism	Pataphysics/Dadaism
Form (conjunctive, closed)	Antiform (disjunctive, open)
Purpose	Play
Design	Chance
Hierarchy	Anarchy
Mastery/Logos	Exhaustion/Silence
Art Object/Finished Work	Process/Performance/Happening
Distance	Participation

Creation/Totalization	Decreation/Deconstruction
Synthesis	Antithesis
Presence	Absence
Centering	Dispersal
Genre/Boundary	Text/Intertext
Paradigm	Syntagm
Hypotaxis	Parataxis
Metaphor	Metonymy
Selection	Combination
Root/Depth	Rhizome/Surface
Interpretation/Reading	Against Interpretation/Misreading
Signified	Signifier
Lisible (Readerly)	*Scriptible* (Writerly)
Narrative	Antinarrative
God the Father	The Holy Ghost
Symptom	Desire
Genital/Phallic	Polymorphous/Androgynous
Paranoia	Schizophrenia
Origin/Cause	Difference –Differance/Trace
Metaphysics	Irony
Determinacy	Indeterminacy
Transcendence	Immanence

As Hassan himself notes, these characteristics are drawn from a great variety of fields and authors. Despite this, and the fact that many of the characteristics previously associated with anarchy or indeterminacy have now been separated from the latter,[47] the view of post-modernism given here is still one which Jencks for one will read as 'late modern' rather than as post-modern, and because, as with other 'late-modernisms', it extends the language and categories of modernism rather than adding some new, or even older, meanings.[48]

Here it might also be said that although Hassan's table has chosen to split certain dichotomies into contrasting lists for 'Modernism' and 'Postmodernism', many of those dichotomies are ones which are to be found in modernist works themselves – such as, to name but one, the 'dichotomy' of 'Narrative/Antinarrative' which is to be found in many modernist parodies, and from earlier classic parodistic works such as *Don Quixote* and *Tristram Shandy* onwards. Further to this, many other of the apparent oppositions such as 'Metaphor/Metonymy' and

'Metaphysics/Irony' are not strictly dichotomies at all but groupings of rhetorical devices and philosophic attitudes, the parts of
which are to be found together or separately in both modern and
pre-modern works. In addition to splitting a variety of different
dichotomies and groupings without making their original
modernist relationships or origins clear, Hassan's list for post-
modernism also has enough elements in it which can be clearly
associated with modernism and late-modernism, such as 'Dadaism', 'Performance', 'Happening' and even 'Deconstruction'
itself, to suggest that it may be seen by others quite apart from
Jencks to have canonised aspects of the modern rather than the
'post' modern in its list for the latter. While the issue of the
possibility, or desirability, of periodising certain styles or movements is of course fraught with many problems, it can at least be
said with regard to the categorisation of the modern and the
post-modern that there are some more objective methods of categorisation available (by, for example, period or style) than the
simply arbitrary division of dichotomies and groupings found in
works which are, according to some existing categories of period
or style, not just modernist but even pre-modernist.

Perhaps the biggest problem with Hassan's depiction of the
post-modern as 'indeterminate' (in both his 1971 and 1980
articles), is that this too, together with the other characteristics
listed by Hassan, does not appear to add anything very new to
the trends which others have characterised as typical of
modernity or modernism in the past. Given that Hassan's 1971
article had described post-modernism as going back to the 1930s
(and even 1890s), one may also wonder about the extent to
which the principles guiding his choice in that chronology had
themselves been derived from the literary and theoretical works
of the period which others have been used to calling 'modern'.[49]
(Here it might also be noted that Hassan does not follow de Onis
or Fitts/Hays in describing the more abstract works of modernism as representing the birth of 'postmodernism', but rather
takes up the characteristics of de Onis's 'ultra-modernism' and
its extension of the 'modernist' 'search for poetic innovation and
freedom'.) Hassan's continued use of the term 'indeterminacy'
to characterise post-modernism may bear witness to his lack of
desire to define the 'postmodern' too precisely, but does not

itself offer anything which could not also be found in late modernist theory, or in some other theories which have not redefined themselves as 'postmodern'.

Hassan's conclusion to his 1980 essay had also presented 'Five Paratactical Propositions about the Culture of Postmodernism', which again demonstrate a turn which is both 'indeterminate' and 'deconstructive':[50]

1.   Postmodernism depends on the violent transhumanization of the earth, wherein terror and totalitarianism, fractions and wholes, poverty and power summon each other. The end may be cataclysm and/or the beginning of genuine planetization, a new era for the One and the Many . . .

2.   Postmodernism derives from the technological extension of consciousness, a kind of twentieth century gnosis . . . The result is a paradoxical view of consciousness as information and history as happening.

3.   Postmodernism, at the same time, reveals itself in the dispersal of the human – that is, of language – in the immanence of discourse and mind . . .

4.   Postmodernism, as a mode of literary change, could be distinguished from the older avant-gardes (Cubism, Futurism, Dadaism, Surrealism etc.) as well as from modernism. Neither Olympian and detached like the latter nor Bohemian and fractious like the former, postmodernism suggests a different kind of accommodation between art and society . . .[51]

5.   Postmodernism veers toward open, playful, optative, disjunctive, displaced, or indeterminate forms, a discourse of fragments, an ideology of fracture, a will to unmaking, an invocation of silences – veers toward all these and yet implies their very opposites, their antithetical realities. It is as if *Waiting for Godot* found an echo, if not an answer, in *Superman*.[52]

Again the overriding theme is indeterminacy, and although Hassan has added 'Constructionism' to his list of definers of post-modernism in one of his more recent essays of 1986,[53] this term is not only defined there as referring to the 'construction of its reality', but is also joined by other definers such as 'Indeterminacy', 'Fragmentation', 'Decanonization', 'Self-less-ness', 'Depth-less-ness', 'The Unpresentable', 'Unrepresent-

able', 'Irony', 'Hybridization', 'Carnivalization', 'Performance'
and 'Immanence'. Again many of Hassan's definers also go back
to those of Deconstruction and late modernism, while Bakhtin's
concept of 'Carnivalization' is derived, as Hassan himself is
aware, from texts ranging from Rabelais to the early twentieth
century.[54] Indeed, Hassan himself admits[55] that the definers
given in his 1986 essay do not serve to distinguish post-modernism from modernism, and concludes with the again somewhat
'indeterminate' point that his preceding paragraphs argue the
twin conclusions that '(a) critical pluralism is deeply implicated
in the cultural field of postmodernism' and '(b) a limited critical
pluralism is in some measure a reaction against the radical
relativism, the ironic indetermanences, of the postmodern condition', and is 'an attempt to contain them'. Despite this latter
suggestion that the indeterminacy of post-modernism may be in
need of some reduction or control, if only by its own forces,
Hassan appears to continue his own indeterminacy when he
writes that 'Clearly, the imagination of postmodern criticism is a
disestablished imagination. Yet clearly, too, it is an intellectual
imagination of enormous vibrancy and scope.'[56]

Perhaps Daniel Bell might comment here that such passages
suggest that we have not moved very much further along the
path to understanding what the post-modern is from when
Amitai Etzioni had written in the opening of his *The Active
Society* of 1968 that that post-modern period would see *either* an
increase *or* a decrease in the control of the technologies developed in the modern period and of their effects.[57] Despite, and
also because of, the lack of certainty about the nature of post-
modernism which may be noted in Hassan's writings on post-
modernism, they will, however, also be seen to have been taken
up, in one way or another, in many of the other descriptions of
the post-modern discussed in the following pages of this
chapter.[58]

Jean-François Lyotard

As Ihab Hassan has suggested in his *The Postmodern Turn* of
1987, the term 'postmodernism' as used by himself and others in
America in the early 1970s had also entered the work of the

1   Chase's 'Heisenberg Department of Physics', from *Chance: New Directions for Statistics and Computing*, as illustrated in the *Times Higher Education Supplement*, 16 February 1990, p. 25

French theorist Jean-François Lyotard by the end of that decade.[59] Lyotard's Introduction to his *The Postmodern Condition* of 1979 itself begins by claiming that he has decided to use the word 'postmodern' to describe 'the condition of knowledge in the most highly developed societies',[60] and that the word was in 'current use on the American continent among sociologists and critics'.[61] While Lyotard also goes on to claim here that the term 'designates the state of our culture following the transformations which, since the end of the nineteenth century have altered the game rules for science, literature and the arts', his next definition of the 'postmodern', as 'incredulity toward metanarratives' gives us yet another, more specific, description of the term, and one which will serve to distinguish his usage of it from that of both 'the sociologists' and Hassan while also retaining, and expanding, 'deconstructionist' elements in the latter.[62]

Just as it has been seen previously with reference to definitions of the post-modern that the basis for the specific meaning given the term post-modern in them can be found in part at least in their author's definition of the modern, so it will be seen in following passages that Lyotard's definition of the 'postmodern' must also be read against the background of his particular understanding and characterisation of the modern.

Lyotard had written, for instance, between his two definitions of the 'postmodern' given above that he will be using the term 'modern' to 'designate any science that legitimates itself with reference to a metadiscourse ... making an explicit appeal to some grand narrative, such as the dialectics of Spirit, the hermeneutics of meaning, the emancipation of the rational or working subject, or the creation of wealth', or, as he continues, 'the rule of consensus between the sender and addressee of a statement'. Here Lyotard is including amongst the meta-narratives of modernity such philosophies as those of Hegel, the hermeneuticists, Marxism, capitalism and Habermas, the last of which Lyotard will also return to attack with even greater vigour in his 'Answering the Question: What is Postmodernism?' of 1982[63] because of Habermas's post-1979 attempt to defend 'the project of modernity' in his Adorno Prize lecture of 1980 against the 'postmodernism' of the 'neo-conservatives'.[64] The question of what that attack actually says, and in what Habermas's defence of the 'project of modernity' consists, will also be answered after we have first made clear what Lyotard had meant by the word 'postmodern' in his 1979 text.

Lyotard's *The Postmodern Condition* begins: 'Our working

hypothesis is that the status of knowledge is altered as societies enter what is known as the postindustrial age and cultures enter what is known as the postmodern age.'[65] This development is also dated by Lyotard from the end of the 1950s, 'or the completion of reconstruction in Europe', although he adds (as Bell had done with reference to the 'post-industrial society') that 'the pace is faster or slower depending on the country' and their 'different sectors'.[66]

While Lyotard's use of the term 'post-industrial' in the above passage may also appear to refer to the term used by Daniel Bell in his *The Coming of Post-Industrial Society*, differences from Bell's terminology arise when Lyotard goes on to say that the main feature upon which he will be concentrating will be that of scientific knowledge understood as discourse. Now while Bell had defined the post-industrial society as a society in which theoretical knowledge or science should be regarded as the 'axial principle', he had not spoken of it merely as discourse, and, as seen previously in chapter 2, had also clearly distinguished it from any discourse shared with the literati or critics of 'post-modern' culture. In contrast to Bell's use of the concept of 'scientific knowledge', Lyotard's reduction of scientific knowledge to 'a kind of discourse' will also allow him to treat it in a 'deconstructionist' manner like other forms of literary or philosophical discourse (as described by Norris in the passages quoted from him in the Introduction to this chapter), and as something which stands or falls depending upon its relationship to other discourses or 'metanarratives' of 'totality'.[67]

Mixed together with Lyotard's 'deconstructionist' reduction of science to a form of discourse is, moreover, a treatment of the discourse as something which can be commodified and alienated from its producer, which is closer to Marx's description of the production and alienation of the goods of *industrial* society under capitalism than to Bell's depiction of the role of theoretical knowledge in what he has termed the *post-industrial* society.[68]

Here, despite his criticism of modernist meta-narratives inclusive of Marxism, we also see Lyotard's argument being coloured by both the Marxist 'metanarrative' of the reduction of labour to the production of exchange value rather than use value,[69] and by the related concepts of alienation[70] and reification.[71]

Lyotard continues his extrapolations from Marx's theory of the circulation of capital:

> It is not hard to visualize learning circulating along the same lines as money, instead of for its 'educational' value or political . . . importance; the pertinent distinction would no longer be between knowledge and ignorance, but rather, as is the case with money, between 'payment knowledge' and 'investment knowledge'.[72]

As with the Marxist distinction between use and exchange value, we may find that Lyotard's distinction is much too black and white here. It is, however, necessary for his further arguments that the knowledge society may also be an exploitative and alienating one if built on 'modern' capitalist lines with one elite class of decision-makers having access to its knowledge and distribution, and that the 'postmodern culture' may hence also come to stand in an adversary place to it for such reasons.[73]

One of the ways in which 'the postmodern' is to counter the institutions which may seek to appropriate power to themselves and their 'metanarratives' for Lyotard is, moreover, not by way of the 'communicative action' which Habermas has seen as the way to producing consensus,[74] but by way of an 'atomization of the social into flexible networks of language games',[75] and by the critique of games which, like those aimed at producing 'greater performance', may attempt to appropriate power unto themselves.[76] Later Lyotard will also claim that 'postmodern science' concerns itself, by contrast, with such things as 'undecidables, the limits of precise control, conflicts characterized by incomplete information, *"fracta"*, catastrophes, and pragmatic paradoxes' and suggests 'a model of legitimation that has nothing to do with maximized performance, but has as its basis difference understood as paralogy'.[77]

Not only has the gap between Lyotard's concept of 'postmodern science' and Bell's of 'post-industrial science' widened even further here, but the fact that the maximisation of language games and their 'quest for paralogy'[78] now appears to him to be the goal of that science leads Lyotard to conclude[79] that the computerisation of society (which was so germane to other descriptions of the post-industrial society) can only help if it be redirected from 'performativity' to the 'opening up' of all memory and data banks to the public. Mixing what might be termed, following his own guidelines, the 'metanarratives' of utopian socialism with anarchism, Lyotard continues: 'Language games would then be games of perfect information at any given moment.'

One very serious problem with this statement is, moreover, its apparent optimism that the information freed in this way would not either itself be false, or be misused by those 'freeing' it. Here all of Lyotard's previous statements on the dangers of the modernist 'metanarrative' of progress, and of others like it, seem forgotten. The question of whose progress or freedom would ultimately be achieved by the act described by Lyotard also remains unasked, as do the related questions of the intended and unintended consequences of that act, given all the possible types of agents involved in such actions, and the continued existence of other structural social and cultural forces, drives for power and restraints. Even Ihab Hassan, whose work on the term post-modern has, as noted previously, been described by himself as having travelled with that of others from America to Lyotard, has recently suggested that 'Lyotard is on treacherous ground . . . when he claims that "recognition of the heteromorphous nature of language games" leads to "a renunciation of terror, which assumes that they are isomorphic and tries to make them so".' Hassan continues: 'terror is rarely "renounced" by rational perceptions of any kind', and adds, 'Let us also recall that these "language games" commit genocide, despoil the earth, vaporize cities.'[80]

To those who have long found deconstructionist language games, in which the agency of the individual as well as the possibility of determining truth are undermined, to be themselves at least partly responsible for a diminution of the idea of the moral responsibility of the subject, in speech or action, it will, however, also be the stress on both the 'diffusion of the ego' and the indeterminacy of truth in deconstructionist 'postmodernist' theory from Hassan to Lyotard and beyond which will be seen to have increased rather than decreased the likelihood of irrational or 'terroristic' actions committed without regard for other individuals or their social contexts. To say that 'rational perceptions of any kind' 'rarely renounce terror' may also appear to such critics of deconstruction to be yet another expression of those post-structuralist critiques of modern rationality which have often been based on a generalised caricature of it, and which may themselves be said to have contributed to the weakening of the effective rational critique of terror because of their attacks on both concepts of rational discourse and the concept of the subject as an agent strong enough or 'centred' enough to participate in effective rational action.

In order to bring the beginning of this section together with its conclusion, we may briefly summarise Lyotard's description of the postmodern condition in his 1979 text in the following manner:

1. It suggests that the 'postmodern' represents a scepticism towards what are termed the 'metanarratives' of the modern period.
2. It claims that some of the discourses of the 'postindustrial' society are still influenced by narratives such as 'performativity'.
3. It suggests that the solution to such problems will be the opening up of all data banks.

Apart from the criticisms which have just been made of this last point, other charges which can be placed against Lyotard here include the criticism that he has not only reduced the elements of the post-industrial society to discourses or data in a 'late-modernist' 'post-structuralist' manner, but that his criticisms of the remaining capitalist elements in post-industrial society are themselves derived from 'modernist metanarratives' condemned by him in earlier pages.

The charge made here against Lyotard that he has in fact remained within the boundaries of the modern 'metanarratives' he would deconstruct, may also be added to the criticisms made of him by the architectural historian of post-modernism and critic Charles Jencks, that he has remained a modernist in aesthetic matters. While Jencks specifically targets Lyotard's claim in his 1982 article 'Answering the Question: What is Postmodernism?' that the post-modern work 'is undoubtedly a part of the modern', and that 'a work can become modern only if it is first postmodern',[81] Lyotard had also used that text to refer critically to post-modernist architecture as having thrown out what he has called the experimental elements of modernism: 'I have read that under the name of postmodernism, architects are getting rid of the Bauhaus project, throwing out the baby of experimentation with the bathwater of functionalism.'[82] Although Lyotard might well have taken these words from the very same Adorno Prize lecture by Habermas which he will also attack in this text, he had prefaced both them and his remarks on Habermas with the statement that 'This is a period of slackening' and a period in which 'From every direction we are being urged to put an end to experimentation in the arts and elsewhere.'

Later Lyotard also associates the post-modernism of Jencks with both capitalism and what he describes as its philosophy of 'anything goes':[83]

When power is that of capital and not that of a party, the 'transavant-gardist' or 'postmodern' (in Jencks's sense) solution proves to be better adapted than the antimodern solution. Eclecticism is the degree zero of contemporary general culture: one listens to reggae, watches a Western, eats McDonald's food for lunch and local cuisine for dinner, wears Paris perfume in Tokyo and 'retro' clothes in Hong Kong; knowledge is a matter for TV games. It is easy to find a public for eclectic works. By becoming kitsch, art panders to the confusion which reigns in the 'tastes' of the patrons. Artists, gallery owners, critics and public wallow together in the 'anything goes', and the epoch is one of slackening. But this realism of the 'anything goes' is in fact that of money; in the absence of aesthetic criteria, it remains possible and useful to assess the value of works of art according to the profits they yield. Such realism accommodates all tendencies, just as capital accommodates all 'needs', providing that the tendencies and needs have purchasing power. As for taste, there is no need to be delicate when one speculates or entertains oneself.[84]

Jencks's theories, and their lack of similarity to such caricatures, will be dealt with in detail in chapter 4. Although appearing to follow Habermas's condemnation of post-modernist architecture in his Adorno Prize lecture of 1980 referred to previously,[85] Lyotard's 1982 text had also attacked that same Habermas for criticising post-modernists for trying to get rid of the uncompleted 'project of modernity':[86] 'I have read a thinker of repute who defends modernity against those he calls the neo-conservatives. Under the banner of postmodernism, the latter would like, he believes, to get rid of the uncompleted project of [the modern[87]], that of the Enlightenment.' Lyotard continues:

Even the last advocates of the *Aufklaerung*, such as Popper or Adorno, were only able, according to him, to defend the project in a few particular spheres of life – that of politics for the author of *The Open Society*, and that of art for the author of the *Aesthetische Theorie*. Juergen Habermas (everyone had recognized him) thinks that if modernity has failed, it is in allowing the totality of life to be splintered into independent specialties which are left to the narrow competence of experts.[88]

As noted earlier, Habermas had in fact been referring to Daniel Bell and others in speaking of 'neoconservatives' in his 1980 talk, and via a misreading of Bell which sees him as having put the blame for the 'uncompleted project of modernity' onto cultural modernism.[89] Lyotard's reading of Habermas does not correct this error, however, and even creates a new misreading of Habermas when he proceeds to claim that that thinker 'requires from the arts and the experiences they provide . . . to bridge the gap between cognitive, ethical and political discourses, thus opening the way to a unity of experience'.[90] While this claim is not a misreading in the same sense as Habermas's is of Bell, it is an oversimplification of Habermas's theories (Habermas speaks, for instance, of consensus being produced from intersubjective communicative action, rather than of a 'unity of experience'), and a simplification which (ironically, in view of Lyotard's defence of the same) also gives a much greater 'avant-garde' role to the aesthetic sphere than Habermas himself has suggested.[91]

On the basis of his misreading of Habermas, Lyotard also proceeds to ask what sort of a 'unity' Habermas has in mind. Avoiding what Habermas himself has said on the issue of consensus, Lyotard inquires:

Is the aim of modernity the constitution of sociocultural unity within which all the elements of daily life and of thought would take their places as in an organic whole? Or does the passage that has to be charted between heterogeneous language games – those of cognition, of ethics, of politics – belong to a different order from that? And if so, would it be capable of affecting a real synthesis between them?[92]

To Lyotard both positions (as he has described them) present as their goal an ideal unity or totality which must be challenged:

The first hypothesis, of a Hegelian inspiration, does not challenge the notion of a dialectically totalizing *experience*, the second is closer to the spirit of Kant's *Critique of Judgement*, but must be submitted, like the *Critique* to that severe reexamination which postmodernity imposes on the thought of the Enlightenment, on the idea of a unitary end of history and of a subject.[93]

In contrast to the Habermas which he has constructed in these passages as a searcher for such false unities, Lyotard goes on to suggest that the 'postmodern' is characterised by a new (post-Kantian) concept of the sublime, by virtue of which 'the post-modern' would be that which not only 'puts forward the unpresentable in presentation itself', but also 'denies itself the solace of good forms, the consensus of a taste which would make it possible to share collectively the nostalgia for the unattainable' and 'searches for new presentations, not in order to enjoy them but in order to impart a stronger sense of the unpresentable'. Lyotard concludes his 1982 text by adding: 'The answer is: Let us wage a war on totality; let us be witnesses to the unpresentable; let us activate the differences and save the honor of the name.'[94]

Earlier Lyotard had also written that the difference between the modern aesthetic and the 'postmodern' is that 'modern aesthetics is an aesthetic of the sublime, though a nostalgic one' which 'allows the presentable to be put forward only as the missing contents; but the form because of its recognizable consistency, continues to offer to the reader or viewer matter for solace and pleasure'.[95] He continued: 'Yet these sentiments do not constitute the real sublime sentiment, which is in an intrinsic combination of pleasure and pain: the pleasure that reason should exceed all presentation, the pain that imagination or sensibility should not be equal to the concept.'

Unfortunately Lyotard gives, however, no specific examples of either the modernist or 'postmodernist' 'sublimes' of which he is speaking here. It could be that the work of the modern artist Mark Rothko might well fit in with Lyotard's description of the modernist sublime, although others might argue that it could equally well fit in with his criteria for the 'postmodern sublime'.

Carlo Maria Mariani is, for example, one artist who has been dubbed a 'post-modernist' who has both admired Rothko and spoken of his work as having 'its dimension of the sublime'.[96] If one of Lyotard's more recent texts[97] has also taken up some of the questions of representation and nostalgia in the visual arts touched upon in his 1982 text, it would, however, appear to be largely with reference to artists who have been described in recent years as 'new modernist deconstructionists'.[98]

Lyotard's presentation of his concept of the post-modern sublime in his 1982 text may be summarised in the following way:

1. It is not 'nostalgic' for the unpresentable.
2. It does not offer only solace or pleasure in presenting the unpresentable.
3. It combines pleasure and pain: the pleasure that reason should exceed all presentation, the pain that imagination or sensibility should not be equal to the concept.
4. It puts forward the 'unpresentable' in presentation without seeking the solace of good forms or a consensus of taste which would enable the nostalgia for the unattainable to be shared collectively.
5. It seeks for new presentations to impart a stronger sense of the unpresentable.
6. It does not seek to supply reality but to invent allusions to the conceivable which cannot be presented.
7. Work and texts have the character of an *event* because artist and writer 'work without rules in order to formulate the rules of what will have been done'. Lyotard writes further on this that there can be no 'preestablished rules' for this task, and it cannot be judged 'according to a determining judgement'. 'Those rules and categories', Lyotard continues in 'post-structuralist' manner, 'are what the work of art itself is looking for.'[99]

While Lyotard has previously been seen to have defended experimental elements of modernism which others have described as avant-garde, the apparent elimination of the agency of the artist in passages such as the last also suggest that his belief in these elements cannot be completely equated with earlier modernist beliefs in the avant-garde role of the individual artist.[100]

Although most, if not all, modern avant-garde actions could also be said to have had unintentional as well as intentional effects, Lyotard's reduction of the agency of the artist to what appears to be largely the former, unintentional, type of effect, must also mean that any avant-garde or 'experimental' action will have to wait to see what effects are produced by it before being able to define itself in any more specific way.[101]

Robert Hughes's account of the demise of the in more ways than one 'late' modernist performance artist Rudolf Schwarzkogler – as having involved 'successive acts of self-amputation which finally did Schwarzkogler in'[102] – may well come to mind here as an example of an avant-garde action whose consequences had got out of hand. While this might also be considered an innovatory 'experimental' action on the basis of at least some of the criteria suggested in Lyotard's text, it had served Hughes, however, as a graphic example of the 'death of the avant-garde'.[103]

Some other problems in Lyotard's text may also be raised at this point. For example, not only does point 7 appear to question the rule-like character of Lyotard's other points, but it also raises the question of how a 'war on totality' may be waged with any certainty that the correct 'targets' will be defeated. One may also be reminded of this problem when we see it put to the side in Lyotard's later texts where the forces of modernisation, rather than the post-modern questioning of its meta-narratives referred to in Lyotard's earlier works, are named as having achieved the 'destruction of the project of modernity' by themselves.[104]

This later position of Lyotard's would also seem to be more pessimistic about the possibility of changing the problems of modernity, including the forces of modernisation, via the post-modern, than his earlier theoretical works on post-modernism. A consistent development in Lyotard's thought towards this position is, however, not easy to find as, for one thing, not all of his works address the issue explicitly or in the same terms. Although his 1982 text might be seen as having moved closer towards his later, more pessimistic, position in its reduction of the agency of the artist and writer, Lyotard's April 1984 manifesto for his exhibition *Les Immatériaux* of 1985, for example, had suggested that while the modern age might be seen as an age in which the human subject saw itself as mastering matter, the post-modern was that which questioned this mastery and redefined it as a question of the interaction of man and matter, rather than of control.[105] By contrast to such statements, Lyotard's 1984 claim in his 'Apostille aux récits' of February 1984, that the project of modernity is not just incomplete, but 'dead', and destroyed by the 'capitalist techno-science' which had appeared to be keeping it alive, appear to suggest that matter, rather than either man or interaction, is now again in charge.[106] Here it might also be suggested that Lyotard's more pessimistic 1984 view of post-modernity as modernisation run wild has even brought his position closer to that held by Baudrillard in the early 1980s,[107] and to the 'post-Baudrillardian' interpretations of post-modernism and its conditions given in the mid-1980s by such as Fredric Jameson.[108]

Fredric Jameson

Jameson's Foreword to the 1984 English translation of Lyotard's *The Postmodern Condition* had not only referred to how Lyotard's voice had been 'more combative' in other works,[109] but had also suggested that 'postmodernism as it is generally understood involves a radical break, both with a dominant culture and aesthetic, and with a rather different moment of socioeconomic organization against which its structural novelties and innovations are measured'.[110] In addition to defining the general understanding of post-modernism here as involving a radical break with a dominant aesthetic (a position rejected by Jencks as well as others when referring to their concepts of post-modernism), Jameson had gone on to say of Lyotard's 'Answering the Question: What is Postmodernism?' of 1982 that it had also given an adversary, critical voice to post-modernism by assimilating it to something similar to the experimental avant-garde element of high modernism.[111] Although the avant-garde nature of Lyotard's post-modernism has been seen to be more problematic than this in the preceding pages of this chapter, Jameson's comments on Lyotard make it clear that these are at least some of the adversary or critical aspects of Lyotard's post-modernism which Jameson believes should be stressed.

Given the above, it may also be not too surprising to find that Jencks will criticise Jameson for defending elements which Jencks has understood to be late-modernist rather than post-modernist. In addition to this, differences between Jameson and Jencks also become obvious when Jameson chooses to follow both Lyotard and Habermas in criticising post-modernist architecture as a rejection of the modernist tradition, and to extend Lyotard's suggestion that the architecture of post-modernism is an expression of modern capitalism.

As seen previously, Lyotard had not only accused post-modernist architecture of having thrown out the experimental moments from modernism in its rejection of the Bauhaus,[112] but had also attacked it in his 1982 text for having become a part of the culture of capital.[113] Although Jameson had written in his Foreword to Lyotard's *The Postmodern Condition* that post-modernist architecture can be a 'rich and creative moment, of the greatest aesthetic play and delight', counter to what he calls the 'terrorist stance of the older modernism',[114] he also goes on there to agree with Habermas that it is an insufficiently 'ethical' answer to the problems of modernity,[115] and to extend Lyotard's characterisation of it as a part of the culture of capitalism in other essays of the mid-1980s.

Jameson writes, for instance, in his *New Left Review* article of 1984, 'Postmodernism, or the Cultural Logic of Capitalism', with reference to post-modern architecture as well as to some other art forms such as Pop Art which he has described as 'postmodernist':

The postmodernisms have in fact been fascinated precisely by this whole 'degraded' landscape of schlock and kitsch, of TV series and Readers' Digest culture, of advertising and motels, of the late show and the grade-B Hollywood film, of so-called paraliterature with its airport paperback categories of the gothic and the romance, the popular biography, the murder mystery and science-fiction or fantasy novel: materials they no longer simply 'quote', as a Joyce or a Mahler might have done, but incorporate into their very substance.[116]

To Jameson the society named 'post-industrial' by Daniel Bell, is, moreover, in no way 'postmodern' in the sense of being opposed to the 'metanarratives' of capitalism, but is, in the words of the Marxist economist Ernest Mandel, a 'Late Capitalist' society of an even 'purer' stage of capitalism than those preceding it.[117] Although Daniel Bell would not necessarily dispute the fact that the post-industrial society as he has described it may be supported by capitalism in some way or another, he has, as has been seen in the previous chapter, not only criticised the late 'post-ethical' capitalism of modern and post-modern culture but has also made other significant distinctions between the post-industrial and the industrial which Jameson's Mandelian terminology does not address.[118]

Despite Jameson's suggestion that he will not view the post-industrial society from a technologically deterministic viewpoint,[119] but from that of its capitalist elements,[120] he also goes on to speak of late-capitalism in terms of a 'new decentred global network' reminiscent of Baudrillard's 'McLuhanite' description of contemporary communications technology,[121] and to write of the 'incapacity of our minds, at least at present, to map the great global multinational and decentred communicational network in which we find ourselves caught as individual subjects'. In reintroducing the language of technological determinism, this argument also problematically suggests, however, that we are in fact not yet capable of fully understanding the real nature of that which Jameson has previously claimed we should describe as 'late-capitalist'.[122]

Jameson's 1984 equation of the post-modern with the culture of capital and of post-industrial society with late capitalism had also been preceded by the following description of the post-modern and the post-industrial in his contribution to Hal Foster's volume on post-modern culture of 1983:

It ['postmodernism'] is not just another word for the description of a particular style. It is also, at least in my use, a periodizing concept whose function is to correlate the emergence of new formal features in culture with the emergence of a new type of social life and a new economic order – what is euphemistically called modernization, postindustrial or consumer society, the society of the media or the spectacle, or multinational capitalism.[123]

In addition to combining, and confusing, concepts of the post-modern, the post-industrial, modernisation and capitalism here, Jameson's description of post-modernism in his contribution to Foster's *Postmodern Culture* as a part of the 'media society', the 'society of the spectacle', the 'bureaucratic society of controlled consumption', and what he calls 'postindustrial or consumer society' also associates it with elements to which Lyotard's post-modernism was to be an antidote or critique.[124] Jameson expatiates further on his equation of the post-modern, the post-industrial and capital in a passage of his 'Postmodernism, or the Cultural Logic of Late Capitalism', recently criticised by Ihab Hassan as 'pressed down by the yoke of ideology':[125] 'This whole global, yet American, postmodern culture is the internal and superstructural expression of a whole new wave of American military and economic domination throughout the world: in this sense, as throughout class history, the underside of culture is blood, torture, death and horror.'[126] Not only is metaphor used here to equate post-modernism with terror (where in his Fore-word to Lyotard's 1979 text Jameson had reserved that latter term for modernism), but a hidden metonymy is also utilised to reduce the 'postmodern' to those elements which are said to produce the latter.

Similarly, Jameson's critiques of post-modernist architecture also reduce it to but a few of the many characteristics which architectural historians such as Charles Jencks have outlined for it, such as, most notably, *pastiche*.[127] In his *New Left Review* article 'Postmodernism, or The Cultural Logic of Late Capitalism' of 1984 Jameson writes of the pastiche which he sees to be generally characteristic of post-modernist architecture:[128]

parody finds itself without a vocation; it has lived, and that strange new thing pastiche slowly comes to take its place. Pastiche is, like parody, the imitation of a peculiar mask, speech in a dead language: but it is a neutral practice of such mimicry, without any of parody's ulterior motives, amputated of the satiric impulse, devoid of laughter and any conviction that alongside the abnormal tongue you have momentarily borrowed, some healthy linguistic normality still exists. Pastiche is thus blank parody, a statue with blind eyeballs: it is to parody what that other interesting and historically original modern thing, the practice of a kind of blank irony, is to what Wayne Booth calls the 'stable ironies' of the 18th century.[129]

One of the reasons given by Jameson for the 'rise' of this apparently new form of parody had been, moreover, the 'normlessness' of 'the advanced capitalist countries'.[130]

Earlier Jameson's contribution to Foster's volume on post-modern culture had also characterised pastiche not just as an expression of consumer culture, but as a normless or 'blank' form of the parody that was to be found in modernism:

> Pastiche is, like parody, the imitation of a peculiar or unique style, the wearing of a stylistic mask, speech in a dead language: but it is a neutral practice of such mimicry, without parody's ulterior motive, without the satirical impulse, without laughter, without that still latent feeling that there exists something *normal* compared to which what is being imitated is rather comic. Pastiche is blank parody, parody that has lost its sense of humor: pastiche is to parody what that curious thing, the modern practice of a kind of blank irony is to what Wayne Booth calls the stable and comic ironies of, say, the 18th century.[131]

What is interesting about Jameson's characterisations of 'post-modern' pastiche in both of these works is not, however, their derivation from the theory of post-modernist architecture,[132] so much as their echo of the depiction of the contemporary capitalist world by Baudrillard as one in which 'a kind of non-intentional parody hovers over everything' in a space in which art is said to be 'everywhere' and 'dead'. This is so, Baudrillard had added, not only 'because its critical transcendence is gone', but 'because reality itself, entirely impregnated by an aesthetic which is inseparable from its own structure, has been confused with its own image'.[133]

Baudrillard's use of the terms 'hyperreality' and 'hyperspace' in this essay to characterise aspects of this same condition will be returned to presently in the discussion of Jameson's use of the term 'hyperspace' to describe what he understands to be the 'postmodernism' of the Bonaventure Hotel in Los Angeles in his 1984 essay 'Postmodernism, or The Cultural Logic of Late Capitalism'. One other use of the term 'parody' by Baudrillard which may be of relevance to understanding the tenor of Jameson's use of the term 'blank parody' in his descriptions of 'postmodern' pastiche is, moreover, to be found in his essay 'Gesture and Signature: Semiurgy in Contemporary Art',[134] in which modern art is described as being both critical in appearance and yet in collusion with the contemporary world: 'It plays with it, and is included in the game. It can parody this world, illustrate it, simulate it, alter it; it never disturbs the order, which is also its own.'

Although Baudrillard is speaking of modern art here, it is also of modern art of which he is speaking in his 'The Orders of Simulacra' when describing the condition in which art is everywhere and dead, and a 'non-intentional' parody all-present over everything. While Jameson has made a distinction between the critical forms of modernism and the 'blindness' of post-modernism in his essays on the latter, it is none the less the characteristics of Baudrillard's depictions of modernism which are echoed by him in his description of the post-modern.[135] To put this in other words, what Jameson appears to have done in his characterisations of post-modern parody as 'blank' or 'blind' parody or 'pastiche' is to have taken Baudrillard's characterisations of modern art and of its use of parody and to have applied them to what he (Jameson) has termed the 'postmodern', so that once again the problems of modernity, and of its capitalist elements, are projected onto the post-modern.

Further to the characterisations of modern parody already quoted, Baudrillard had also written of the contemporary world in his 'The Precession of Simulacra' that 'simulation is master and nostalgia, the phantasmal parodic rehabilitation of all lost referentials, alone remains'.[136] Here too a connection with Jameson's characterisation of post-modern pastiche may be made, in that Jameson has not only criticised post-modernist pastiche for indulging in a nostalgia for the past in his 'Postmodernism, or the Cultural Logic of Late Capitalism' of 1984,[137] but has also gone on to write in a 'Baudrillardian' manner that 'we are [now] condemned to seek history by way of our own pop images and simulacra of that history, which itself remains forever out of reach'.[138] To Jameson the nostalgia which he claims to be shown by post-modernist pastiche is also no better than that shown by modernism to Lyotard[139] – and offers no other alternative to the other.

One of the reasons for the 'blindness' of post-modernism for Jameson is, moreover, the 'death of the old individualist subject'. Jameson had written of this in his contribution to Foster's volume,[140] and had added:

Hence, once again, pastiche; in a world in which stylistic innovation is no longer possible, all that is left is to imitate dead styles, to speak through the masks and with the voices of the styles in the imaginary museum. But this means that contemporary or postmodernist art is going to be about art itself in a new kind of way; even more, it means that one of its essential messages will involve the necessary failure of art and the aesthetic, the failure of the new, the 'imprisonment' in the past.[141]

It may well be that this position could also be described as the logical conclusion of the reduction of the agency of the artist spoken of by Lyotard in his text of 1982. One of the problems with the literature on 'postmodernism' which follows that text is, however, that where Lyotard had appeared to wish still to preserve some critical role for the truly 'postmodernist' work in it, the works of Jameson, and of those who have followed him, have tended to depict a diminution of the subject as a part of the decadence of the post-modern condition as a whole. Here no alternative post-modern avant-garde is present to counter what are seen to be the failings of post-modernist architecture and its ilk, and the latter are contrasted with a lost modernist tradition of criticism.

While the idea of the 'death of the subject' may also be traced back to what may be described as 'late modernist' post-structuralism, and, as suggested earlier, to the modernist theories of alienation and reification taken up by the former, Jameson has not explicitly noted this, or that it may link his post-modernism with late modernist theory, but has simply, and confusingly, claimed in his 1984 essay on 'Postmodernism, or the Cultural Logic of Late Capitalism' that the 'alienation of the subject' spoken of in modernism has been replaced by a 'fragmentation of the subject' in the 'postmodern', which recalls the 'fashionable' theme of 'the end of the autonomous bourgeois monad or ego or individual'.[142]

It is, as stated previously, also from this claim about the death of the old individualist subject as something characteristic of post-modernism, that Jameson proceeds to describe the pastiche of post-modernism as a form of 'blind parody'. What is again to be noted here about Jameson's definitions and their application to the pastiche of post-modernist architecture is, however, that it is not post-modernist architecture, or, more precisely, its theorists or practitioners, who have ascribed to the theory of the 'death of the subject', but the late-modernist post-structuralist and 'deconstructionist' post-modernists from whom Jameson has developed some of his theories.[143]

Further to this it should also be pointed out that the term 'pastiche', which Jameson has used to make a distinction between modernist parody and post-modernism, is a term which has been used throughout modernism, and sometimes as a synonym of 'parody', and has also been used in English from at least the early eighteenth century.[144] Although several writers have followed Jameson in describing pastiche as peculiarly post-modern, and as a 'blind form of parody', it is, like parody and irony, essentially a device, and one which has been used in several periods for several different purposes. Here it may also be noted that Jameson's misinterpretation of Jencks as an 'anti-modernist'[145] is also accompanied by a lack of acknowledgement of the fact that the post-modernist architecture praised by Jencks has also used some techniques of modernism, if for different purposes and in different ways from in the past.[146]

Some of these points will be returned to presently with specific reference to Jencks's discussion of pastiche. For the moment it may be said in summary of the above that what we have with Jameson's projection of a Baudrillardian concept of modern parody onto the use of pastiche in post-modern architecture is essentially the creation of a category error in which at least two different meanings and their sources (let us call them A: Jameson's concept of normless pastiche, and B: the pastiche used in post-modern architecture) have been confused and meaning A ('normlessness') projected onto source B (the use of pastiche in post-modern architecture) as if the two different sources and meanings did not exist.[147]

Recently Ihab Hassan has also written on Jameson's characterisation of post-modern culture as one in which 'only the imitation of dead styles is left' that this is not only a 'partial presentation' of the post-modern, but one which 'bends post-modernism to older, in some ways reactionary, presuppositions'. Hassan continues: 'the judgement *both* defines and critiques innovation in modernist, even Edwardian terms, applicable to a society very different in its modes of self-representation, its immanent procedures'.[148]

Hassan adds that the dissatisfactions that Jameson and others vent about post-modernism are real, but that such dissatisfactions 'call for imaginative assessments', and for 'truly radical reflections on our interpretative frames', and because, Hassan concludes, in an echo of Toynbee's ninth volume of his *A Study of History*, the world may be no more or less baneful 'than our perception of its bane'.[149]

Although Jameson has acknowledged that 'architectural post-modernism is itself no unified or monolithic period style', 'but spans a whole gamut of allusions to styles of the past, such that within it can be distinguished a baroque postmodernism (say, Michael Graves) a rococo postmodernism (Charles Moore or Venturi), a classical and neoclassical postmodernism (Rossi and De Porzemparc respectively), and perhaps even a Mannerist and a Romantic variety, not to speak of a high modernist postmodernism itself'[150] he has also not clearly differentiated between the various different uses of pastiche by post-modernist architects – as, for example, an expression of nostalgia, or as a way to achieving the complexity and contradiction spoken of by, for instance, both Venturi and Jencks.[151]

Jencks himself, moreover, has made a distinction between weak eclecticism and the 'stronger more radical variety' to be developed by post-modernism in the revised and enlarged editions of his *The Language of Post-Modern Architecture* of 1977 and elsewhere which has not been adequately acknowledged by Jameson and those following him: 'In contrast to . . . weak eclecticism, it seems . . . that Post-Modernism has at least the potential to develop a stronger more radical variety.'[152] As Jencks goes on to argue here, it is, moreover, the process of *selection* (which Jencks also sees as the original meaning of *eclectic*) which can give strength to the new 'radical eclecticism' of the post-modern.

Jencks's concept of the post-modern in these and other passages hence also contains an affirmation of the ability of the architect to make choices about the values to be expressed in the post-modern work which bears little relationship to the post-structuralist belief in the 'death of the subject' spoken of by Jameson as lying behind what he has described as the 'normlessness' of post-modernist pastiche. The post-modern architect as presented by Jencks, is, by contrast, one who is able to return value to architecture while also opening up the paths to the 'intersubjective' evaluation of those values.[153] Variety rather than conformism can thus also be the result of post-modernist building for Jencks, and a variety which affirms rather than negates the values of both architect and user.[154]

Jencks also specifically relates this last issue to that of 'Radical Eclecticism' in the 1978 and later editions of his 1977 text:

> Radical Eclecticism ... starts design from the tastes and languages prevailing in any one place and overcodes architecture (with many redundant clues) so that it can be understood and enjoyed by different taste cultures – both the inhabitants and the elite. Although it starts from these codes it doesn't necessarily use them to send the expected messages, or ones which simply confirm the existing values. In this sense it is both contextual and dialectical, attempting to set up a discourse between different and often opposed taste cultures.[155]

This aspect of Jencks's theory of the post-modern, and of its underlying belief in the need for post-modern architecture to 'double-code' modernism with a variety of other 'codes' is, however, not dealt with in any depth by Jameson, who, as stated previously, not only sees a 'normless' form of pastiche as a major definer of architectural post-modernism, but also fails to discuss Jencks's concept of post-modernism as a 'double-coding' of modernism with other codes. This latter omission further appears to lead Jameson not only to describe Jencks as an 'anti-modernist' in his article on post-modernism of 1984 entitled 'The Politics of Theory: Ideological Positions in the Postmodernism Debate',[156] but to categorise styles or movements in architecture as post-modernist which do not involve a 'double-coding' of modernism with other codes, such as the 'high modernist post-modernism' of which he speaks in the same article.[157]

In addition to being foreign to architectural historians of post-modernism such as Jencks, such categorisations as the above, of

a 'high modernist postmodernism', may also be said to have
been made questionable by the fact that Jameson had begun his
1983 article on post-modernism in Foster's collection by arguing
that the post-modernisms mentioned by him there 'emerge as
specific reactions against the established forms of high modernism, against this or that dominant high modernism which con-
quered the university, the museum, the art gallery network, and
the foundations'.[158] Despite this claim, the post-modernisms
listed by Jameson in that article may also be said to contain a
variety of links with modernism, although here again the nature
of their links with the modern may not necessarily make them
into post-modernisms for such as Jencks. Jameson's list includes,
for instance, not only Robert Venturi's *Learning from Las Vegas*
on the 'pop' imagery of the Las Vegas strip[159] (but not his *Complexity and Contradiction*, in which some of the definers used by
Jencks to categorise post-modern architecture are more specifically foreshadowed[160]), but also both Andy Warhol's Pop Art
and the Photo-Realism, which are for Jencks as well as others
more representative of 'late modernism' than 'post-modernism'
proper.[161] While Jameson's definers also appear to be based here
on the assumption both that Venturi's (and Scott Brown and
Izenour's) *Learning from Las Vegas* had preferred populism to
high modernism, and that architectural post-modernism is in
general aimed at a rejection of 'high modernism' which involves
the deconstruction of the opposition of high and low culture in
the latter and a return to low or popular culture through the
utilisation of 'pop' images and techniques (as suggested,
moreover, by Hassan, following Fiedler),[162] Jencks's definers are
centred around a principle of 'double-coding' which none of the
above 'late modernist' works mentioned by Jameson specifically
mention or apply, and which, as explained below, will also mean
a rather different approach to the use of high and low codes from
that suggested by Jameson.

Jencks himself has referred critically to Jameson's use of the
term post-modern as an 'umbrella term to cover all reactions to
High-Modernism, . . . the levelling of distinctions between high
and mass culture and two of its significant features – pastiche
and schizophrenia' in his 1986 text entitled *What is Post-
Modernism?*[163] Earlier, in the Introduction to the second revised

and enlarged edition of his *The Language of Post-Modern Architecture* of 1978, Jencks had also written that post-modernism was trying to get over the 'elitism of Modernism', not by dropping it, but rather by 'extending the language of architecture in many different ways into the vernacular, towards tradition and the commercial slang of the street'.[164] Jencks continued: 'Hence the double-coding, the architecture which speaks to the elite and the man on the street.' Significantly, the double-coding of various codes in post-modern architecture is seen here not so much as eliminating the 'modernist' divide between the high and low culture, or as reducing the former to the latter as suggested by Fiedler and by those following him,[165] as using both to extend the language of modernism further and to a greater number of audiences. As projects such as that of the New State Gallery in Stuttgart by Stirling, Wilford and Associates show, the double-coding of high and low codes also does not necessarily mean the homogenisation of the two, but a juxtaposition of both which provides each with a new set of references as well as with a foregrounding of the original limits of their own codes.[166] Further to this, Jencks's 1980 list of definers for distinguishing the 'Post-Modern' from both the 'Modern' and the 'Late-Modern' sets up a contrast between the modernist divide between 'elitist' and 'for everyman' with the post-modernist's 'elitist *and* participative',[167] while he elsewhere suggests, as noted previously, that the double-coding of modernist and other codes in post-modernist architecture does not necessarily eliminate the divisions between high and low art, or replace the former with the latter, but is able to bring both different sets of codes together in a variety of new ways.

In addition to describing the place taken by popular images in post-modernist architecture in a way which does not accurately describe either post-modern architecture, or theories of post-modern architecture such as Jencks's, Jameson's identification of John Portman's Bonaventure Hotel in Los Angeles as 'post-modernist' in his 1984 article on 'Postmodernism, or the Cultural Logic of Late Capitalism' has also classified something as 'post-modernist' which Jencks and other architectural historians have described as either modernist or late-modernist. While Jameson's description of Portman's Bonaventure Hotel in his

2   John Portman, Bonaventure Hotel, Los Angeles, 1976, model;
illustrated in Charles Jencks, *The Language of Post-Modern Architecture*, 1st to
5th edns (London, 1987), p. 34, as an example of a 'Late-Modern' building

1984 article presents it as a 'full-blown' post-modern building which is in essence 'popular' (one of Jameson's definers for post-modern architecture, as seen previously), and yet also built on what he describes as a 'postmodern' creation of a 'decentering' 'hyperspace',[168] Jencks has described it as an example of 'Late-Modernism', and contrasted its exaggeration of the 'Modernist extension of space' with the more humanised space of that which is for him the typically post-modern building.[169]

Jameson's use of the word 'hyperspace' echoes, moreover, not the language of post-modernist architecture, but, as suggested earlier, that of Baudrillard. Hence Jameson had written of the hyperspace of Portman's Bonaventure Hotel that it had 'finally succeeded in transcending the capacities of the individual human body to locate itself, to organize its immediate surroundings perceptually, and cognitively to map its position in a mappable external world'. Earlier, in his 'The Orders of Simulacra', and prior to speaking of the non-intentional parody which 'hovers over everything', Baudrillard had referred to the growth of a 'hyperspace of representation where each is already technically in possession of the instantaneous reproduction of his own life',[170] as well as to a 'hyperrealism of simulation' characterised by 'the deconstruction of the real into details', the 'endlessly reflected vision' and the 'serial form' where 'all attention to the object is intercepted by its infinite diffraction into itself'.[171] While Jameson's use of the term 'hyperspace' may seem closer to Baudrillard's concept of the 'hyperreal', Baudrillard had also related the latter to the area of space when writing earlier in his contribution to Foster's 1983 anthology of articles on post-modern culture of that which he had termed the 'era of hyper-reality', that 'what was projected psychologically and mentally, what used to be lived out on earth as metaphor . . . is henceforth projected onto reality, without any metaphor at all, into an absolute space which is also that of simulation'.[172] Like Jameson's conception of 'postmodern' society Baudrillard's 'society of the simulacrum' is both neo-capitalist and high-tech as well as full of artifice and 'non-intentional' (or 'blank') parody. Later, as in, for example, his *America* of 1986, Baudrillard will also describe the culture of America and its 'parody' of other cultures as both the 'mirror of *our* [Europe's] decadence' and as 'hyperreal in its vitality'.[173] Whether Baudrillard, or Jameson, enjoy it or criticise it, the Portman Bonaventure Hotel and those like it are for Jencks, however, examples of the 'Late-Modern' and its exaggeration of space, rather than of the 'Post-Modern'.[174]

As suggested earlier, Jencks is, moreover, not alone in either his criticism or his description of the space used in buildings such as the Bonaventure Hotel as modernist. Prior to Jencks's formulations of his definers for post-modernism, Robert Venturi had suggested a new approach to the modernist use of space in his *Complexity and Contradiction* of 1966,[175] while, more recently, the German architectural historian Heinrich Klotz has also discussed the Bonaventure Hotel under the heading of 'Modern Architecture' rather than that of 'Postmodern Architecture'.[176] Although critical elsewhere of Jencks's distinction between 'Late-Modern' and 'Post-Modern' architecture,[177] Klotz also emphasises the characteristics in Portman's Bonaventure Hotel which had led Jencks to classify it as 'Late-Modern':

The Bonaventura Hotel in Los Angeles, with its five cylinders of reflective glass, appears to be more a space-travel terminal than an ordinary hotel – it is a kind of futurist anti-building whose splendor exceeds normal human sensibilities. The gridwork that indicates the stories produces nothing more than a checked surface of empty mirrors; a reminiscence of bygone concerns, it only emphasizes the building's superhuman scale.[178]

Further to this, Klotz compares the hotel with Hellmuth, Obata and Kassabaum's Equitable Building in St Louis of 1969–71, which he has previously described as 'reconfirming modern architecture in a striking new way': 'Like the glass block of the Equitable Building, the cylinders of the Bonaventura Hotel are reductionist shapes, primary stereometric figures. Here the aesthetic of elementary forms, which began with Gropius, reached new heights that made Gropius's first buildings seem childishly naive.'[179]

Klotz seems, moreover, to have been critical of Jencks's distinction between 'Modern' and 'Post-Modern' architecture largely because it has suggested to him not only a hard and fast opposition between post- and late-modern architecture, but that the modernist era is over.[180] Here, however, Klotz may be said to be overlooking both the fact that Jencks's dating of the 'Late-Modern', in, for example, his *Late-Modern Architecture* of 1980,[181] has described it as running concurrently with architectural 'Post-Modernism' from approximately 1960 on, and that Jencks has also acknowledged the possibility of late-modernist, as well as other modernist codes being double-coded with other codes in post-modernism.[182] Despite his criticism of Jencks's distinction between 'Late-Modernism' and 'Post-Modernism' in the early pages of his book,[183] Klotz also speaks later of a division in contemporary architecture between post-modern and high-tech architecture,[184] and includes within the latter, buildings like the Pompidou Centre, of which Jencks had spoken under the heading of 'Late-Modernism',[185] but which Jameson has again called 'postmodern'.[186] Later still, Klotz himself also uses the term 'late modern' to refer to the 'ultra-functionalist' aesthetic countered by post-modernism which many others have seen celebrated in 'high tech' architecture.[187]

Nine years after his description of Portman's Bonaventure Hotel in his *The Language of Post-Modern Architecture*, Charles Jencks has provided an illustration of how to misread Norman Foster's Hongkong Shanghai Bank as a 'Post-Modern' building – rather than as a 'Late-Modern' one – which might also be seen as providing at least some guidelines for the unravelling of any description of the Bonaventure Hotel as 'postmodern':[188]

Try to read Norman Foster's recently completed Hongkong Shanghai Bank as a Post-Modern building and you will get as far as the 'non-door' where the two escalators are shifted at an angle to accommodate the Chinese principle of *Feng Shui*. Is it contextual or related to the buildings surrounding it and the vernaculars of Hong Kong and China? Only in the most oblique sense that it is 'high-tech' and one side has a thin picturesque group of towers. Is it involved with the 'taste-cultures' of the inhabitants and users? Only in the subliminal sense that its 'skin and bones' suggest muscle power.

Jencks continues:

According to the permissive definitions of 'Nothing Post-Modernism' [Jencks's name for the sum total of the post-modernisms spoken of in Hal Foster's anthology of papers on the subject by Jameson, Baudrillard, and others[189]] it should be a member of this class, because it is a 'rupture'

3 Renzo Piano and Richard Rogers, Pompidou Centre, 1971–7; Jencks's caption to his illustration of this work in *What is Post-Modernism?* (London, 1986), p. 36, reads: 'The Modernist emphasis on structure, circulation, open space, industrial detailing and abstraction is taken to its Late-Modern extreme, although again often mis-termed Post-Modern.'

4 'Banking Hall', Norman Foster and Foster Associates, Hongkong Shanghai Bank, 1982–6; illustrated in Charles Jencks, *What is Post-Modernism?* (London, 1986), p. 41, as another example of a 'Late-Modern' building

with Modernism and fully committed to the tradition of the new. It is [also] the first radical 'multinational' building ... resolved by all the technologies of the post-industrial society, including of course the computer and instant world communication, and therefore according to the definitions of J. F. Lyotard and others[190] it should be a prime example of Post-Modernism. But it isn't, and if it were it should be a failure.[191]

Jencks concludes: 'No, it has to be judged as the latest triumph of Late-Modernism and celebrated for what it intends to be, namely, the most powerful expression of structural trusses, lightweight technology, and huge openspace stacked internally in the air.'[192]

In a postscript entitled 'Towards Radical Eclecticism' in the post-1978 editions of his *The Language of Post-Modern Architecture* Jencks had also made a distinction between 'Late-Modern' and 'Post-Modern' architecture in which he had stressed the point that while 'Late-Modern' architecture 'is an exaggeration of several Modern concerns such as the technological image of a building, its circulation, logic and structure', 'Post-Modern' architecture is 'double-coded' and an 'eclectic mix of traditional or local codes with Modern ones'.[193] In continuing to hold to this basic principle in defining the post-modern in his later works, Jencks has also continued his earlier criticisms of confusions of the late-modern with the post-modern as well as his criticisms of 'high-tech' architecture.[194]

Given the identification of late-modernist buildings with postmodernist architecture in Jameson's essays, and the identification of post-modernism with both post-industrialism and late-capitalism in them, it is perhaps not surprising that he has concluded his arguments about post-modernism by stating 'that the question of to what extent postmodernism may resist consumer capitalism must be left open'.[195]

Jameson's pessimism about post-modernism is, as suggested previously, also not lightened by either an explicit return to Lyotard's faith in the emancipatory power of the 'postmodernist' critique of 'metanarratives' or to a concept of post-modern avant-garde. Jameson's claim that post-modernism is characterised by the 'death of the old individual subject' in fact appears to make such a return to the concept of avant-garde even more difficult than Lyotard's suggestion in his 'Answering the Question: What is Postmodernism?' of 1982 that it is the 'work itself', rather than its author, which will define the rules by which it will proceed.[196] As seen previously, Jameson has also expanded Lyotard's criticisms of post-modern architecture as belonging to the 'culture of capitalism', and criticised the 'high modernist' belief that change might be brought about by aesthetic means alone more explicitly than Lyotard had done in his 1979 and 1982 texts on the post-modern.

In his scepticism of the power of any isolated aesthetic sphere Jameson will also be seen to be at one with Habermas, although his 'solution' to the impasse of aesthetic criticism (of 'an aesthetic of cognitive mapping of the world space of multinational capital' which will achieve 'a breakthrough to some as yet unimaginable new mode of representing this last', and in which 'we may again begin to grasp our positioning as individual and collective subjects and regain a capacity to act and struggle') will not adequately serve to describe that offered by Habermas, or make sense to those used to more accepted uses of the term 'aesthetic'.

Some of the problems with Jameson's characterisations of post-modernist architecture will be returned to later in chapter 4 with reference to works of post-modernist art and architecture. Put in brief here, they include the reduction of post-modernist architecture to one or two definers such as pastiche, and of post-modern pastiche to a form of 'blind' parody, as well as the reduction of post-modernist architecture to the criticism of 'high' modernism and the revival of 'popular' culture.[197]

Although he will be seen to differ from Jameson, in, for instance, his criticisms of the post-structuralist belief in the death of the subject which lies, in part at least, behind Jameson's explanation for the rise of post-modernist pastiche, the German philosopher and social theorist Juergen Habermas will also be seen to have criticised the use of pastiche in post-modernist architecture, and to have seen the latter as being antagonistic to both 'modernism' and the 'project of modernity'. Where Lyotard had separated his concept of a post-modernism critical of modern and modernist 'metanarratives' (including Habermas's 'consensus-ideal') from that of post-modernist architecture, and Jameson has concentrated much of his writing on the subject of post-modernism on a critique of post-modernist architecture as a symptom of 'late-capitalist' culture, Habermas will, moreover, be seen to have rejected both kinds of post-modernism because of what he perceives to be their joint antipathy to the 'project of modernity'. The discussion of what this project is, and of what the details of Habermas's critiques of post-modernism are, follows.

Juergen Habermas

Juergen Habermas's 1981 essay on 'Modern and Postmodern Architecture' begins by claiming that the use of the prefix 'post' in the word 'postmodernism' is symptomatic both of a desire in its protagonists to distance themselves from a past, and of an inability on their part to give the present a new name 'because we as yet have no answer to the discernible problems of the future'.[198] This last juxtaposition of the essence of the present with the solution of the problems of the future may, however, itself be seen as being symptomatic of Habermas's own particular approach to the 'postmodern', that it cannot simply reject the 'modern', or offer a new set of styles in lieu of modernism, to be able to speak for the future, but must first help to solve the present problems of society which are likely to continue into that future, and to complete, as he had put it in his earlier Adorno Prize lecture of 1980, the 'project of modernity' to 'enrich' the rational organization of everyday social life.[199]

Habermas had written of this 'project of modernity' in his 1980 Adorno Prize lecture:

The project of modernity formulated in the eighteenth century by the philosophers of the Enlightenment consisted in their efforts to develop objective science, universal morality and law, and autonomous art according to their inner logic. At the same time, this project intended to release the cognitive potentials of each of these domains from their esoteric forms. The Enlightenment philosophers wanted to utilize this accumulation of specialized culture for the enrichment of everyday life – that is to say, for the rational organization of everyday social life.[200]

Earlier Habermas had opened his lecture by attacking the post-modernist architecture shown in the Venice Biennale of 1980 as 'sacrificing the tradition of modernity in order to make way for a new historicism'.[201] While such statements may be criticised for their conflation of the post-modernist criticism of aspects of modernism with the rejection of the 'tradition of modernity' as such, Habermas had also gone on in his 1981 essay on modern and post-modern architecture to criticise post-modern architecture for providing an inadequate response to the problems of modernity and its project (there described as the control of the 'anonymous imperatives' of the 'system-world' which threaten to colonise the 'life-world').[202] Despite his qualification that it had at least 'taken up the unresolved problems which modern architecture has pushed into the background' such as 'the colonisation of the life-world through the imperatives of economic and administrative systems of activity which have become independent', the problem remained for Habermas that no post-modernism had yet provided any real answer to these concerns in his view, and even when suggesting that a new consensus should be established between architect and user.[203]

This last point will be returned to presently. Firstly, something more must be said about the relationship of Habermas's criticisms of post-modernism to the theses of his theory of communicative action.[204] Here, for instance, it should be noted that Habermas has both taken over the Weberian analysis of the growth of 'purposive rationality' and of the diminishment of 'value rationality' under modernisation which earlier 'Frankfurt School' theorists from Horkheimer to Marcuse had linked with a Lukacsian theory of 'reification' to speak of the 'instrumentalisation' of reason within the modernisation processes produced by industrial capitalism, and rejected the emphasis put by such as Adorno and Horkheimer on the need for, and ability of, individualistic 'value rationality' to counter the reifying effects of instrumentalised reason.[205]

To Habermas such individualistic forms of value-rationality are powerless if not also related to a concept of intersubjective communicative action, by means of which the superimposed 'values' of instrumental reason may be countered by a 'consensus-based' establishment of values. As Thomas McCarthy has written in the Introduction to Habermas's *The Philosophical Discourse of Modernity* of 1985: 'The key to Habermas's approach is his rejection of the "paradigm of consciousness" and its associated "philosophy of the subject" in favor of the through-

and-through intersubjectivist paradigm of "communicative action".'[206]

Although Habermas's *Philosophical Discourse of Modernity* also usefully points to the problems of self-referentiality involved in the 'deconstructionist' arguments of those from Nietzsche to Derrida and Foucault who have attempted to undermine the normative status of imposed values from a position 'beyond value' – where the defence of this position is itself value-laden[207] – it could also be said that Habermas's own belief in both the need for consensus about value to be established via the intersubjective path of communicative action and the 'anti-modern' character of all post-modernism may itself have the problem that it has appeared to have been established without such 'intersubjective' actions. Some disagreement with Habermas's attacks on post-modernism may at least be voiced by others over both his identification of the post-modernist criticism of modernism with a rejection of the 'project of modernity' and his identification of all post-modernisms with the criticism and rejection of modernism.[208]

As will be seen from the following chapter, the depiction by Jencks of architectural post-modernism as a 'double-coding' of modernism with other codes has seen it as not only incorporating some of the codes of modernism within its buildings, but as attempting to solve some of the problems of modernisation within modernity while still being attached to the latter. In contrast to this view, Habermas's 1980 and 1981 essays have described post-modernist architecture as being both anti-modernist and anti-modern, and even when it has been concerned with criticising the forces of modernisation which the 'project of modernity' is also supposed to criticise.[209] Habermas writes, for instance, in his essay of 1981 that both the 'neoconservatives' who wish to use a revival of old traditions to 'eradicate a culture antipathetic to their wishes', and those 'radical critics of growth' who 'see modern architecture as a symbol of the destruction caused by modernisation' are united by their desire to break from the modern,[210] and that 'those who would continue the uncompleted project of the modern are thus confronted by various opponents, who only agree in their determination to take their leave from the modern'.[211]

Amongst the problems raised by Habermas's attacks on post-modernist architecture here we have not just the problem that he has claimed without justification that all post-modernists are against both modernism and what he terms the 'project of modernity', but the problem that his use of the phrase 'the project of modernity' conceals the fact that it is in fact a 'post-modern' project in modern clothing in so far as it has also been concerned with criticising, and transforming, those negative elements of society which Weber and other forerunners of Habermas's theories had associated with elements of modernisation in modernity, and which post-modernist architects have also been concerned to reform through both the direct criticism of those forces and their criticisms of the functionalist aesthetics of modern architecture.

Despite this, Habermas criticises post-modernist architecture as being both against the project of modernity when it criticises modernism and as being anti-modernist when it criticises the project of modernity. For instance, although Habermas states in his 1981 essay that the experiments of architects like Lucien Kroll with establishing a community-based form of architecture – in which consultation and consensus between architect, builders and users are practised – represent a notable development,[212] he then proceeds to argue that these experiments, and their drive to free inhabitants from the differentiations and problems created by the conflicts between the forces of modernisation in the 'system world' and the 'life world', may also take on the appearance of being 'antimodernist'.[213] While Habermas's meaning is less than clear here, it would appear that he is assuming that any antipathy on the part of the post-modernist architect to the forces of modernisation which dominate the 'system world' will also entail an antipathy to the modernism born of that modernity,[214] just as he has elsewhere assumed that any criticism of modernism by post-modernist architecture may be read as a rejection of the project of modernity.

One other result of Habermas's designation of the consensus-architecture of Kroll as 'anti-modernist' is his suggestion that the attempts of post-modern architects to overcome the separations between agents which characterise modernity and its sub-divisions may also lead to an admiration for the banal and a lack of complexity. (Habermas writes with some colouration of his language towards a negative assessment of this architecture: 'Admittedly the longing for de-differentiated life-forms often gives these tendencies the appearance of an anti-modernism. Then they unite themselves with the cult of the vernacular ['des Bodenstaendigen'] and the admiration for the banal.') It is in this light that Habermas also sees the architecture of consensus as leading not to his form of consensus but to an 'anonymous' form of architecture in which the banal and the popular – the antitheses of high modernism – reign. (It is difficult to say to what extent this view of Habermas's may have been influenced by the misreadings by Jameson and others of post-modernist architecture as seeking to eliminate the divide between high and popular styles to reduce the former to the latter, but at least something of that idea might also be found here.) When Habermas then goes on to write that even when it 'refers to another *Volksgeist* than that which had its apotheosis in the monumentalism of Hitler's architecture' it has to pay the price of 'praising an anonymous architecture', we also have what appears to be an echo of Adorno's and Horkheimer's earlier comparisons of popular culture with the culture of fascism (Habermas's use of the word *bodenstaendig* also has similar connotations), and despite the fact that those comparisons were born of different presuppositions from those now used by Habermas himself, including the thesis (contradicted by both Habermas and post-modernist architects interested in increasing the communicative power of their buildings) that an autonomous (rather than a popular) sphere of aesthetic value was needed to counter the problems of modernity.[215]

In contrast to the impression given of his work in Habermas's essay, that it is contributing to a post-modernist drive towards an 'anonymous', populist form of 'anti-modernist' architecture, Lucien Kroll's account of his aims in his *The Architecture of Complexity* of 1983[216] describes his projects as having involved a deliberately fragmented participative design process involving clients, future inhabitants and architects known to Kroll. Further to this, the object of this involvement of a variety of persons is described as being 'to avoid a predictable, imposed outcome and to produce maximum variety and complexity, reflecting a range of individual choice within the community served by the buildings'. It is, moreover, 'Modern' architecture, and not his own, which Kroll sees as 'anonymous' when he describes the former as having been subordinated to a principle of mass construction in which the art of the craftsman had disappeared.[217]

While, ironically, in view of Habermas's criticisms of all post-modernism as rejecting modernism, Kroll himself has explicitly criticised those post-modernists who have 'tried to detach themselves from everything modernist',[218] he and his team have also been praised by Charles Jencks in the latter's *The Language of Post-Modern Architecture* of 1977 for having taken the process of 'participation in design' beyond the stage of a 'one-sided consultation with those being designed for' in their work on the Medical Faculty buildings for the University of Louvain[219] and to have pointed post-modernism in the right direction with their idea of a consensus-based architecture.[220]

To Jencks the buildings which resulted from Kroll's Louvain project also show not 'anonymity' but a 'complexity of richness and meaning, a delicate pluralism, that usually takes years to achieve and is the result of many inhabitants making small adjustments over time', and which even suggests that 'normality' and the 'silent majority' have been 'snubbed'.[221] Jencks even goes on to say here that 'By following only one mode of interaction in design, Kroll has actually precluded everyday impersonal architecture', and that one 'longs here for a judicious bit of the International Style'. He continues:

Post-Modernism accepts Modernism not only for factories and hospitals, but also for semiotic balance, for its place within a system of meaning. As soon as the system swings too far toward the idiosyncratic and *ad hoc*, it invites the return of the Neo-Classical, even 'Fascist Style', not for the 'rational' justifications which its adherents may proffer, but for reasons of signification and richness. Meaning consists in oppositions within a system, a dialectic in space or over time.[222]

Although Jencks also shows himself here as elsewhere to understand post-modernism as a 'double-coding' of modernism with other codes, Habermas's conviction that all post-modernisms may be described as both anti-modernist and anti-modern has continued to lead him to see their alternatives to modernism as being wholly antipathetic to the latter.[223] So too Habermas again went on to say in his 1982 article on 'Die Kulturkritik der Neokonservativen in den USA und in der Bundesrepublik' ('The Cultural Criticism of the Neo-Conservatives in the USA and in the Federal Republic of Germany'), published in his *Die neue Unuebersichtlichkeit* with his 1981 essay on modern and post-modern architecture, that his argument with post-modernism is that although it may be correct in pointing to the problems created by an increasing modernisation of culture in modernism itself, it has created as yet no alternative to modernism which he can find acceptable to 'fill the negative concept of the post-modern with positive content':

The postmodern is also the term for a debate which has been carried on in the field of architecture in recent years . . .[224] This was not accidental as it was exactly modern architecture which was, with its functionalist ideology, badly protected against the economic imperatives which post-war rebuilding brought with it, in the period, that is, in which the International Style could for the first time expand and make itself effective. The disaster of a simultaneously instrumentalised and overtaxed ['ueberforderten'] architecture has however to today produced no alternative, which did not either lead back into an uncreative historicism or itself feed from the creativity of an apparently superseded modernism.[225] Certainly no clear signals are to be heard today from the post-avant-garde art which has left the dreams of Surrealism [to reunite art and life] behind. But far and wide one can discover no productions which would fill the catchword of the postmodern – which remains caught in negation – with positive content.[226]

Clearly, it will be difficult to convince Habermas of any virtues in post-modernism so long as he believes its primary aim to be the negation or rejection of the 'project of modernity'. While Habermas has referred to both Jencks's *Late-Modern Architecture* and *The Language of Post-Modern Architecture* in his 1981 essay on 'modern and postmodern architecture' (although without giving any specific page references), he has, moreover, not specifically mentioned the Jencksian argument that post-modernist architecture stands in a 'double-coded' relationship to modernism, rather than in a solely adversary position to it, or argued specifically against it, but has continued to see all post-modernisms as a form of 'Lyotardian' deconstruction of the modern.

Habermas's *The Philosophical Discourse of Modernity* of 1985 also takes up this point in both referring to post-modernity as a concept connected with the work of Lyotard,[227] and in going on to divide it into two categories: firstly, the 'neoconservative' leave-taking from modernity which is directed 'not to the unchecked dynamism of societal modernization but to the husk of a cultural self-understanding of modernity that appears to have been overtaken'; and, secondly, an anarchist variety which advertises the end of the Enlightenment and 'the tradition of reason in which European modernity understood itself', but also 'farewells' modern society and culture 'in the same degree'.[228]

Whether, or how, Habermas might revise his negative view of post-modernism still remained to be seen when this book was completed. Ironically, as indicated above, Habermas's criticism of post-modernism also appeared at that point of time to be suited largely to the deconstructionist variety of post-modernism offered by Lyotard, although it could also be said to have shared Lyotard's own negative criticisms of post-modernist architecture.[229] Added to this, Habermas's acceptance of a deconstructionist and 'anti-modernist' form of post-modernism as the model for post-modernism in general meant that he could not attribute any positive role to the latter in his project for modernity, while the lack of clarity in his work over what form that completion could take also made the specific relation of architecture to any future completion of that project difficult to perceive.[230]

Habermas's continuing scepticism about post-modernism in the mid-1980s must, moreover, be noted when reading Ihab Hassan's recent claim that Habermas had modified his position on the post-modern debate in his interview in *The New Left Review* of May/June 1985, entitled 'A Philosophico-Political Profile', and that he now found 'certain affinities between the negative dialectics of Adorno, the archeologies of Foucault, and the deconstructions of Derrida'.[231] Further to this, Hassan's interpretation of Habermas's statement that he 'has no difficulties with the pluralism of interests' as meaning that Habermas was thereby pointing to 'the utopian promise of postmodernism, the promise of a society, if and when its time comes, that we will certainly call neither capitalist nor socialist', also appears to have projected Hassan's own understanding of post-modernism as representing both a pluralism of interests and a utopian and egalitarian vision of the future onto Habermas's discussion of the pluralism of interests.

In addition to the above, it should be noted that in neither of the passages referred to by Hassan has Habermas described his own position as that of a post-modernist (as always, the 'project of modernity' must be completed first), and was in fact speaking of 'post-structuralism' rather than of 'post-modernism' when speaking of Adorno, Derrida and Foucault.[232] Although the 'post-structuralists' may also be 'postmodernists' for Hassan, and although Habermas may sometimes apply some of the theories of the former to the latter, Habermas's distinction of Adorno from Derrida and Foucault in his interview because of Adorno's adherence to the 'project of modernity' also suggests that he was then not yet ready to agree with any post-modernist post-structuralism.[233]

It was in fact only when the question was put by Habermas's interviewers (Perry Anderson and Peter Dews) as to whether he believed 'that the shift away from the esotericism of high modern art to fusions of high and mass culture is a development to which the term "postmodernism" could be applied', and would such 'fusions' be a part of the emergence of the 'post-avant-garde art' alluded to in his *The Theory of Communicative Action*,[234] that Habermas was led specifically to discuss the issue of post-modernism.

In his reply to the above question Habermas began by referring to Peter Buerger's view of 'post-avant-garde art' that 'art after the failure of the surrealist revolt, the contemporary scene in general' is 'characterized by the juxtaposition of styles, which draw either on the formalist languages of the avant-garde, or on the inheritance of realistic or political–didactic styles and literatures'.[235] Here Habermas added that he 'would not interpret the contemporary scene in the sense of so-called post-modernism as a sign of the exhaustion or the "end" of modernism in art and architecture'. Again Habermas appeared loathe to sound a post-modernist death-knell for modernism, and had clearly not yet come to see post-modernism itself as entailing anything but such 'deconstructionist' acts.

Habermas's following sentences suggest, moreover, that with regard to the question as to whether he thought that the 'post-avant-garde art' of which he has spoken could be the same as the post-modern 'fusion of high and mass culture', there was no reason why, despite the failures of the past, the problem of finding a proper fusion of these two elements might find a modern (rather than a post-modern) solution. Although the question put by Habermas's *New Left Review* interviewers here had also directed the discussion of post-modernism in a certain direction by using the definition of post-modernism as aiming for an elimination of the distinctions between high and popular art as given in Jameson's previously quoted *New Left Review* article of 1984, Habermas's reply would also appear to cover every kind of post-modernism using that term. While Lyotard for one had supported the more critical and experimentalist aspects of the modernist avant-gardes in the name of a 'project of post-modernism', Habermas's final position here was that the project of modernity must still be completed in the name of modernity.

Conclusion

This chapter has looked at some of the major varieties of 'deconstructionist' theorisations of post-modernism (Hassan and Lyotard), the 'deconstructionist' critique of post-modernism (Jameson) and at the critique of post-modernism as a 'deconstruction' of the 'project of modernity' by Habermas. Other varieties of these theories which could be mentioned here (apart from the varieties of 'deconstructionist' art and architecture which will be referred to again in the following chapter) have included those developed by Hal Foster, a variety of literary theories,[236] and the development of the variety of post-modernist anthropology which had elicited the motto of this chapter's opening lines.[237]

Foster, the editor of the volume on 'postmodern culture' which had published both Habermas's 1980 Adorno Prize lecture and Jameson's 1982 lecture on 'postmodernism and consumer society' amongst others,[238] has also brought some ideas from those two thinkers together in an analysis of post-modernist art and architecture in an essay entitled '(Post)Modern Polemics'.[239] Here Foster combines terms and concepts taken from Habermas and Jameson to describe post-modernist architecture as a form of 'neoconservative postmodernism',[240] characterised by a return to ornament, pastiche and kitsch,[241] and both compares and contrasts its theoretical foundations to the 'poststructuralist postmodernism' which we have termed deconstructionist postmodernism.

In this essay 'poststructuralist postmodernism' also assumes for Foster (like many of the deconstructionist post-modernisms discussed previously in this chapter) the 'death of man', where 'man' is understood as the 'original creator' of unique artifacts as well as the 'centered subject of representation and history'. While Foster also tries to argue that 'neoconservative' postmodernism is closer to post-structuralist post-modernism than it thinks in using what he sees to be a normless and uncritical form of pastiche which brings with it the 'death of the subject', he does not, however, reflect on how his own analysis of pastiche as normless, uncritical, relative and associated with the idea of the 'death of the subject' might itself have followed from the very same view-point which he attributes to 'poststructuralist postmodernism', or from the 'poststructuralist' analysis of postmodernism given by Jameson, in which pastiche is described as both normless and as associated with a concept of the death of the subject.[242]

Contrary to Jameson's suggestions in his articles of 1983 and 1984, the term and device pastiche is itself, however, not specifically post-modern. To use it as if it were, and without acknowledgement of its use in earlier years to describe modern works from at least the Renaissance to twentieth-century forms of modernism, is also to conceal the fact that it may be being applied to post-modernism in a way which applies modernist or late-modernist traits to the other, and that some further distinctions may therefore have to be made between the modernist and post-modernist uses of such devices before labelling them as such.[243]

Foster's choice of the artist Julian Schnabel as an example of 'neoconservative postmodernism',[244] will also be seen in chapter 4 to have been of a painter whom others have chosen to categorise as deconstructionist rather than as post-modernist. Here it will also be possible to say that Foster, like Jameson, has projected characteristics of deconstructionist post-modernism onto architectural post-modernism by way of the application of categories and examples from the former to the latter, rather than by any empirically substantiated analysis.[245]

As suggested at the beginning of this Conclusion, many other 'deconstructionist' uses of the concept of the post-modern have already been attempted, and may be followed by others in the future in areas other than those to which that concept has been applied by the theorists already discussed in this work. P. Steven Sangren's article 'Rhetoric and the Authority of Ethnography: "Postmodernism" and the Social Reproduction of Texts' of 1988[246] draws attention, for instance, to the use of the term post-modern in articles on the interpretation of ethnographic writings in the volume *Writing Culture*.[247]

Few anthropologists or other professionals engaged in what current jargon terms 'cultural studies' can have failed to notice the recent proliferation of books and articles that analyze the rhetoric of ethnographic writing. This proliferation of a sort of 'meta-anthropology' is clearly part of the larger 'deconstructive' or 'postmodernist' fashion in literary criticism inspired by continental (mainly French) philosophy.[248]

Sangren, who appears to equate post-modernism with Deconstruction here, is also specifically referring in this passage to the use made of the word post-modern by Michael M.J. Fischer in his article 'Ethnicity and the Post-Modern Arts of Memory' in the volume *Writing Culture*,[249] and adds that Fischer 'equates postmodernism with skepticism regarding the grounds of authority'.[250]

Ironically, given the previous discussion of the various definitions of post-modernism offered in the recent literature on it, one comment on Sangren's paper by Goeran Aijmer[251] concludes by agreeing with Sangren's criticisms of the 'deconstructionist' anthropology which the latter has called 'postmodernist', by going on to describe that post-modernism in the terms of eclecticism and decorativeness used by some deconstructionist post-modernists to condemn the rival post-modernisms of Jencks and others. Although the charges of eclecticism and decoration made by Aijmer against the deconstructionist anthropology criticised by Sangren may have some point, especially if the latter term is to be understood in a more metaphoric sense than when applied to post-modernist architecture, they also suggest that he may be understanding post-modernism in a different sense from Sangren, and creating yet another new amalgam of meanings to be sorted out in the future.

Fischer himself, together with George E. Marcus and Stephen A. Tyler (two other contributors to the volume in question), suggests in a reply to Sangren on this[252] that their position may be 'poststructuralist',[253] but that their use of the term 'post-modern' with reference to anthropology was both with reference to 'a rather wide range of positions and problems' and 'a term in any case which many of us use ironically or tentatively to point to particular issues, or, alternatively, to explore the limits of a particular argument'.[254] Although presented as an 'alternative' strategy, this last phrase does appear to have some vestige still of the deconstructionist meaning attributed to their use of the term post-modern by Sangren, that it represented 'skepticism regarding the grounds of authority'. In addition to this, their commentary concludes by claiming, in what again appears to be a 'deconstructionist' manner, 'that postmodernism is not an "order-constructing ideology", but the deconstructive, parodic, entropic dissolution of power'.[255]

On the newness of the 'post-modern anthropology' spoken of here, it might further be suggested that it, like other forms of post-structuralist or deconstructionist post-modernisms, may also be termed late-modernist rather than post-modernist on the basis of several of its post-structuralist categories. Although Paul Rabinow begins his reply to Sangren by putting the question 'surely deconstruction and postmodernism are not the same thing', a problem here is not only that for some it is, but that it is not always made clear that deconstructionist post-modernism is not the only category of post-modernism available, or the agreed definition of post-modernism for all.[256]

Appendix

One of the interesting developments to arise together with the 'deconstructionist' theories of post-modernism discussed in this section has been the view of modernity presented in Marshall

Berman's *All That is Solid Melts into Air* of 1982. What is interesting here, and perhaps ironic, is that its view of modernity as that in which, in the words of Marx and Engels's *Communist Manifesto* of 1848, 'All that is solid melts into air', appears to attribute to the modern those characteristics which deconstructionist post-modernists and others have attributed to the post-modern.[257]

Just as the deconstructionist concept of the post-modern as a dissolution of the modern has had to be analysed critically in previous pages with regard, not least, to the construction of the concept or canon of the modern which accompanies such 'deconstructions', so too, however, must Berman's description of modernity as a 'melting of all that is solid' be viewed with care to see what 'constructions' are involved in his description of it as a 'de-construction' of the solid.

To begin, his claim that the phrase 'All that is solid melts into air' represents Marx's view of modernity reduces the latter to a phrase which, in Marx *and* Engels's *Manifesto*, refers critically to the constant but unproductive overturning of the 'modern' relations of production by the bourgeoisie.[258] That Marx both looked to the equally 'modern' proletariat to overturn those overturnings more productively and permanently, and continued to accept other aspects of what might now be called modernisation, including the need for progress in technology, is yet another important side to his concept of modernity which Berman appears to have avoided in his 1982 text.[259]

The *Manifesto* also clearly demonstrates the above points about the views of Marx and Engels in passages such as the following: 'Of all the classes that stand face to face with the bourgeoisie today, the proletariat alone is a really revolutionary class. The other classes decay and finally disappear in the face of modern industry; the proletariat is its special and essential product'.[260] Earlier in their text, Marx and Engels had also pointed to the union of the proletariat and modern industry by arguing that it was 'thanks to the railways' that the modern proletarians were able to achieve in a few years that for which the burghers of the Middle Ages had needed centuries.[261]

As Berman's later essay, 'The Experience of Modernity', makes clear, the thesis of his *All That is Solid Melts into Air* that modernity is characterised by the 'melting of solidity' had also contained, and concealed, the realisation that this may go together with the construction and conservation of a variety of both 'solid' and 'not so solid' institutions. So Berman writes in his later essay:

To be modern is to live a life of paradox and contradiction. It is to be overpowered by the immense bureaucratic organizations that have the power to control and often to destroy all communities, values, lives; and yet to be undeterred in our determination to face these forces, to fight to change their world and make it our own.[262]

Berman continues in a manner which qualifies his previous 'deconstructionist' image of modernity by making the latter contain within itself elements of both the molten and the solid: 'It [to be modern] is to be both revolutionary and conservative.'

While Berman also implies here that such 'modernism' is both 'modern' and 'anti-modern' at the same time, he is (like Habermas – if for very different reasons) not led into rejecting modernity, or modernism, for any 'post-modern' position.[263] Although some post-modernists have been led by a view of modernity similar to Berman's to speak of the need to reject it, Berman himself is content to remain within the terms of the modern, as he has described it, and to see it, rather than a new 'post-modernity', as being critical enough of the problems of the modern.

This, and a certain arbitrariness in the use of terms such as modern and post-modern in some of his writings, may also be noted when Berman is as critical as is Charles Jencks of the 'flat' and 'narrow' modernism of the International Style in architecture, but where Jencks opposes that modernism to the more complex double-coding of modernism with other codes in what he names 'Post-Modern' architecture, Berman opposes the modernism of the International Style to what he terms 'a modernism that knew how to accept and embrace'. Here it should further be pointed out, however, that Berman also finds the latter in the work of Robert Venturi, the architect whom Jameson has taken to be an archetypal post-modernist, and whom Jencks has also categorised as a pioneer in the field of the theory of contemporary post-modern architecture – if for different reasons from Jameson.[264]

Because Berman understands modernity as containing the

criticisms and tensions within it which Jencks attributes to his 'double-coded' post-modernisms and their 'dialogues' with modernism, he is also able to attribute to modernism the irony and ambivalence which Jencks has found in post-modernism, and to see the tensions which Jencks finds foregrounded in some post-modernisms in modernism itself. One result of this is, however, that Berman's 'predictions' for what he terms modernism seem to offer less hope for the development of any new, distinct trends:

It may turn out . . . that going back can be a way to go forward: that remembering the modernisms of the nineteenth century can give us the vision and courage to create modernisms of the twenty-first. This act of remembering can help us bring modernism back to its roots, so that it can nourish and renew itself, to confront the adventures and dangers that lie ahead. To appropriate the modernities of yesterday can be at once a critique of the modernities of today and an act of faith in the modernities – and in the modern men and women – of tomorrow and the day after tomorrow.[265]

While Jencks has praised Berman's *All That is Solid Melts into Air* in his article 'The Post-Avant-Garde' of 1987, it has been for showing how much of a modernist – rather than a post-modernist – Marx really was.[266] As the following chapter will show, Jencks's development of a theory of post-modernism which is alternative to the deconstructionist varieties of post-modernism discussed elsewhere in this chapter will also present post-modernism in the art and architecture of recent decades as a double-coding of modernism with other codes, and both modern deconstructionist theory and deconstructionist post-modernism as forms of late-modernism.

4

DOUBLE-CODED THEORIES

'Less is a bore' (Robert Venturi)

The architectural historian and critic Charles Jencks writes in the Introduction to the fourth, revised, edition of his *The Language of Post-Modern Architecture* of 1977, that when he had first written the book, 'in 1975 and 1976', the word and concept 'post-modernism' had only been used with any frequency 'in literary criticism', and that it was only later that he had realised it had been used there to mean 'ultra-Modern', and a 'philosophy of nihilism and anti-convention'.[1] Jencks went on to speak of his own use of the term: 'While I was aware of these writings, of Ihab Hassan and others, I used the term to mean the opposite of all this: the end of avantgarde extremism, the partial return to tradition and the central role of communicating with the public.[2] Jencks then added that his particular concept of post-modernism as involving a double-coding of one code with another had grown out of the 'contrary pressures of the movement': 'Architects who wanted to get over the Modernist impasse, or failure to communicate with their users, had to use a partly comprehensible language, a local and traditional symbolism. But they also had to communicate with their peers and use a current technology.'[3]

Later, in his *What is Post-Modernism?* of 1986, Jencks will also date his first usage of the term post-modern to describe double-coding as from around 1978, the date of the second revised and enlarged edition of his *The Language of Post-Modern Architecture* of 1977, and his use of the word 'post-modern' from the year 1975, in an article entitled 'The Rise of Post-Modern Architecture',[4] where, as he writes, he had used it 'as a temporising label, as a definition to describe where we had left rather than where we were going'.[5] Jencks's 1975 article had itself begun by suggesting that his title was 'evasive', and that if he knew what to call it, he would not be using the 'negative prefix "post"'.[6] Although Jencks had repeated this 1975 statement in the Introduction to the first edition of his *The Language of Post-Modern Architecture* of 1977[7] he has by the time of the second revised and enlarged edition of 1978 explicitly begun (as noted above) to define post-modern architecture as the more positive 'dual' or 'double' 'coding' of modernism with other codes or styles, and to use the term 'double-coding' to emphasise the way in which post-modern architecture is to be understood as a form of architecture which seeks to communicate messages to its users and observers through a variety of styles and devices.[8]

Despite Jencks's admission to using the prefix 'post' in a largely negative manner in his article of 1975, several of the arguments developed in it may also be said to point forward to his later theoretical statements on the nature of 'Post-Modern' architecture, and usage of that term. Not only, for example, does Jencks's 1975 article argue against those who would reduce architecture to the impersonal language of a machine aesthetic on the supposition or assumption that the contemporary age is essentially a machine age, but it also argues for treating architecture as an art which communicates with its users via a multiplicity of codes or messages. (As explained in a note earlier in this book, Jencks uses the term 'code' in his aptly named *The Language of Post-Modern Architecture* to refer to the fact that architecture is to be understood as sending out messages to its users in a similar way to other codes or speech acts, and then coins the word 'double-coding' to refer to the fact that post-modern architecture adds another code and set of messages to that of the modern style.) In answer, for instance, to a claim made by Peter Smithson that 'for the machine-supported present-day cities, only a live, cool, highly controlled, rather impersonal architectural language can deepen that base-connection, make it resonate with culture as a whole', Jencks had written in his 1975 article that 'if you want to "resonate with culture as a whole", then you'd better use a wide vernacular which includes all sorts of signs and traditional motifs'.[9]

Against the claims of modernists that they were using a 'universal' language in using 'impersonal' forms, Jencks also wrote in his 1975 article that 'the architect still believes he is providing universal identity with his articulated forms when he is really just giving identity within his own limited, historical code and one not shared by the majority of his clients'.[10] To counter this problem, Jencks's 1975 article suggests a new pluralism, including the social realism chosen by Tom Wolfe as an alternative to literary modernism,[11] and the 'social realism' demonstrated by Jane Jacobs in her criticisms of modernism. This is not only interesting for its echo (if unintentional) of Bernard Smith's 1944/5 use of the term 'post-modernism' to describe a new 'social realist' reaction to modernist abstraction, but for its reference to Jacobs, whose 1961 attacks on modernism will be described in Jencks's later works as having sounded the death knell for modernist architecture.[12]

Other alternatives to the impersonal language of modernism suggested by Jencks in 1975 had included in addition to his first alternative of '*Social realism*':

2. '*Advocacy planning and the anti-scheme*', by which both minority and majority interests are to be taken into account.[13]

3. '*Rehabilitation, restoration and preservation*', by which the conservation of old buildings is addressed.

4. '*Adhocism and collision city*', in which the symbolic complexity spoken of by Venturi is advocated as a way to achieving the social variety missing in modernist cities.

5. '*Ersatz or artificial cities*', of which Jencks writes: 'There had to be a popular, consumer reaction to modern architecture and ersatz is it. What the modern architect would not do with historical styles, ambience and mood, the speculator has been happy to do.'[14]

6. '*Semiotics and radical eclecticism*', under which Jencks writes that 'the most radical critique of functionalism and modern architecture as a single style has been made by those who used to be called Semiologists, and are now called Semioticians'.[15] Jencks adds here that 'the primary notion is that archi-

tecture is indeed a type of language and therefore all functions have to be put in a *specific code* before they can communicate'. This Jencks also illustrates by the 'lesson of the toilet bowl', in which it is shown that although the functionalist may think it a good example of form following function, other uses of it in, say, southern Italy as a cleaning tank for grapes, or in northern Greece as a fireplace, show that in other 'codes' it may be given other functions.[16] Jencks continues: 'functions are perceived through conventions which are above all historical and the relations between form and function are, for the most part, arbitrary, not natural'.[17] Returning to the theme of pluralism, Jencks adds that 'if the architect were trained in four or five different styles, then he could control the way his forms communicate with much greater effect', and 'a radical eclecticism would be born, reflecting the actual variety of the city and its subcultures'.[18] Although Jencks will not seek to break down the sub-divisions of industrial society attacked by Arthur J. Penty in his works of post-industrialism, there is also some echo here (as in the following point 8) of Penty's discontent with those sub-divisions as having affected, and made more specialised, the work of the modern architect.[19]

7. *'Radical traditionalism and piecemeal thinking'*. Here Jencks refers to Conrad Jameson's attacks on the 'pseudo-objectivity' of the so-called rationalism attributed by modern architects to their language,[20] and his alternative return to traditional forms as incorporating 'more positive meanings than an individual architect can possibly redefine'.[21]

8. *'Political reorganisation'*. Here Jencks writes that 'the final critique of modern architecture concerns the way it has allied itself with large scale enterprise whether it is in big business or big government', and that 'what is needed is a system of architectural *production* which returns to a scale similar to the pre-industrial past'. Jencks continues, 'This means small offices, where the architect is not alienated from design or his client, and smaller building commissions that can be handled by a few people.'[22]

In all of these eight points, Jencks's 1975 article may be seen to have foreshadowed many of the alternatives to modernist architecture which will be dubbed 'post-modernist' by both himself and others in later works, and to have developed ideas which are to be found not only in works since explicitly associated with post-modernism in architecture by some writers, such as Venturi, Scott Brown and Izenour's *Learning from Las Vegas* of 1972, on, for example, the semiotic character of the architectural building, but also in Venturi and others on the 'complexity' of good architecture.

Jencks himself writes in the revised and enlarged editions of his *The Language of Post-Modern Architecture* of 1977 that Venturi's *Complexity and Contradiction* of 1966 had set up a series of 'visual preferences in opposition to modernism' which had included complexity and contradiction versus simplification; ambiguity and tension rather than straightforwardness; 'both–and' rather than 'either–or'; doubly functioning elements rather than singly working ones; hybrid[23] rather than pure elements; and 'messy vitality' (or the 'difficult whole') rather than obvious unity.[24]

Venturi's 'Gentle Manifesto' in his *Complexity and Contradiction in Architecture* of 1966 had not only stated his preference for the richness of meaning created by 'complexity and contradiction' but had also criticised modernist architecture for its belief in Mies van der Rohe's dictum that 'less is more', and other 'one-dimensional' tenets:

I like complexity and contradiction in architecture. I do not like the incoherence or arbitrariness of incompetent architecture nor the precious intricacies of picturesqueness or expressionism. Instead, I speak of a complex and contradictory architecture based on the richness and ambiguity of modern experience, including that richness which is inherent in art.[25]

Venturi continued:

Architects can no longer afford to be intimidated by the puritanically moral language of orthodox Modern architecture. I like elements which are hybrid rather than 'pure', compromising rather than 'clean', distorted rather than 'straightforward', ambiguous rather than 'articulated', perverse as well as impersonal, boring as well as 'interesting', conventional rather than 'designed', accommodating rather than excluding, redundant rather than simple, vestigial as well as innovating, inconsistent and equivocal rather than direct and clear. I am for messy vitality over obvious unity. I include the non sequitur and proclaim the duality.

I am for richness of meaning rather than clarity of meaning; for the implicit function as well as the explicit function. I prefer 'both–and' to 'either–or', black and white, and sometimes gray, to black or white. A valid architecture evokes many levels of meanings and combinations of focus: its space and its elements become readable and workable in several ways at once.

But an architecture of complexity and contradiction has a special obligation toward the whole: its truth must be in the totality or its implications of totality. It must embody the difficult unity of inclusion rather than the easy unity of exclusion. More is not less.[26]

Venturi's own, now famous, reply to this last phrase from Mies van der Rohe was then that 'blatant simplification means bland architecture', and that 'Less is a bore.'[27]

Like Jencks after him, Venturi also mentions the work of such as Eero Saarinen and Alvar Aalto as breaking from the purism of early Modern Movement architecture, and praises them for introducing a new complexity which goes beyond subjective expressionism.[28]

Further to this, Venturi may be said to have at least prepared a way towards Jencks's definition of post-modernist architecture as a double-coding of modernism with other codes in having spoken not only of a 'double-functioning' element in complex and contradictory architecture pertaining to the particulars of use and structure,[29] but also of the 'double meanings' produced by the 'both–and' orientation of architecture which has not been bound by the tenets of the Modern Movement. Venturi goes on to write of the double meanings produced in complex and contradictory architecture:

Conventional elements in architecture represent one stage in an evolutionary development, and they contain in their changed use and expression some of their past meaning as well as their new meaning. What can be called the vestigial element parallels the double-functioning element. It is distinct from a superfluous element because it contains a double meaning. This is the result of a more or less ambiguous combination of the old meaning created by the modified or new function, structural or programmatic, and the new context. The vestigial element discourages clarity of meaning; it promotes richness of meaning instead.[30]

Although Jencks has not argued against clarity, he has generally agreed with Venturi's advocacy of richness rather than of paucity of meaning, and has used his own concept of 'double-coding' as a way towards illustrating the richness of meaning in that which he has termed 'post-modern' and 'post-modernist' architecture.[31]

Jencks had also continued his discussion of his use of the term 'post-modernism' in his *What is Post-Modernism?* of 1986, following his reference to his first usage of it in 1975, by adding that 'to this day' he would define post-modernism as he did in 1978[32] as *'double-coding: the combination of Modern techniques with something else (usually traditional building) in order for architecture to communicate with the public and a concerned minority, usually other architects.'*[33] Earlier in this same text Jencks had also defined post-modernism as that 'paradoxical dualism, or double coding, which its hybrid name entails: the continuation of Modernism and its transcendence',[34] and had added that 'there is no one Post-Modern style, although there is a dominating Classicism, just as there was no one Modern mode, although there was a dominating International Style'.[35] Further to this Jencks points out that he has also used thirty definers to distinguish the 'Post-Modern' from both 'Modern' and 'Late-Modern' architecture and that these cover a wide range of differences, over symbolism, ornament, humour, technology and the relation of the architect to existing and past cultures.[36]

The Language of Post-Modern Architecture

In contrast to the accounts given of it by such as Lyotard, Jameson and Habermas, the post-modernist view of architecture described by Jencks in his *The Language of Post-Modern Architecture* of 1977 and its subsequent editions is one which, although still critical of some of the more purist functionalist elements in modernist architecture, is not seen as rejecting 'modernism' or 'modernity' out of hand. As noted previously, Jencks's *The Language of Post-Modern Architecture* is, moreover, the text in which he introduces the concept of post-modernism as a hybrid or 'double' coding of modernism with other codes[37] and in the following pages of this chapter, Jencks's development of his concept of post-modernism as a double-cod-

5　The blowing up of the Pruitt-Igoe, from Charles Jencks, *The Language of Post-Modern Architecture*, p. 9

6 'High Rise', from Osbert Lancaster, *A Cartoon History of Architecture* (London, 1975), p. 191

ing of modernism with other codes will also be followed from his
The Language of Post-Modern Architecture of 1977 through to
his *What is Post-Modernism?* of 1986 and his *Post-Modernism:
the New Classicism in Art and Architecture* of 1987.[38]

To speak first of Jencks's *The Language of Post-Modern Architecture* of 1977, it is also relevant to the point made in the preceding section of this chapter on the connections between it and his
1975 essay to note that the first edition of his work of 1977 had
opened with a section on the death of modern architecture,
which Jencks had dated from the blowing up of parts of the
Pruitt-Igoe Housing Estate in St Louis on 15 July 1972 at 3.32
p.m. 'or thereabouts'.[39]

With a levity not appreciated by all disciples of the Modern
Movement Jencks had written:

it [Modern Architecture] expired finally and completely in 1972, after
having been flogged to death remorselessly for ten years by critics such
as Jane Jacobs ... Modern Architecture died in St Louis, Missouri on
July 15, 1972 at 3.32 pm (or thereabouts) when the infamous Pruitt-Igoe
scheme, or rather several of its slab blocks, were given the final *coup de
grace* by dynamite.[40]

Earlier, Osbert Lancaster had also used some grim humour in
concluding his *A Cartoon History of Architecture* of 1975 with a
cartoon showing a mother and pram being blown out of a block
of high rise apartments by an explosion and a page entitled 'HIGH
RISE' which concluded:

In addition, vertical living was soon found to be attended by certain
grave psychological effects. The fact of dwelling either below or above,
rather than alongside, one's neighbour, proved, not unforeseeably, to
be markedly discouraging to the community spirit, and the feeling of
isolation thus induced, combined with the absence of backyards,
encouraged the young to find a happy release from claustrophobic
boredom in enthusiastic vandalism. Nor was the prevalence of vertigo-
induced *angst* among the older generation in any way lessened by occasional mishaps due to an imperfect understanding, on the part of the
builders, of the exciting new structural methods and materials made
available by modern technology.

While Osbert Lancaster's history of architecture had concluded on a sorry note in describing the unintended dangers of

modern high rises, Jencks's *The Language of Post-Modern Architecture* has used the case of the intentional demolition of the Pruitt-Igoe as a beginning from which to discuss some more optimistic and 'post-modern' developments. Later, in his 1987 text on 'Post-Modernism', *Post-Modernism: the New Classicism in Art and Architecture*, Jencks will also go back to date both the demise of 'Modernism' and the rise of 'Post-Modernism' from the publication of Jane Jacobs's attack on modern architecture in her *The Death and Life of American Cities* of 1961 itself, and to admit that his previous dating had been 'symbolic' rather than accurate.[41] Jencks's 1977 witticism, that Modernism had 'gone out with a bang', had, however, not only been followed by his description of the rise of 'Post-Modern' architecture as the continuation and transformation of modern architecture, but had also been combined there with the more serious point that we were seeing the exit of that which was bad in the latter – of the anonymous, undecorated housing estates built without consultation with, or consideration for, the wishes of their inhabitants, and with little, if any, apparent understanding of the alienating effects of such buildings on them.[42]

Further to this, Jencks went on to note in his *What is Post-Modernism?* of 1986, that 'Modernism failed as mass-housing and city building partly because it failed to communicate with its inhabitants and users who might not have liked the style, understood what it meant or even known how to use it'.[43] Similarly, Jencks's *Post-Modernism: the New Classicism in Art and Architecture* of 1987 goes on to agree with Andreas Huyssen[44] that one of the reasons for the 'crystallisation' of post-modernism into an architectural movement during the mid-1970s was that architecture more than any other art form 'succumbed to the alienating effects of modernisation', and that there was a 'tragic, indeed fatal, connection between Modern architecture and modernisation which was more or less directly opposed by the Modern movement in the other arts'.[45]

Jencks had also added in his 1977 text that although the Pruitt-Igoe housing estate complex had been given an award by the American Institute of Architects when designed in 1951, it had produced a crime rate higher than other developments, and had been continuously vandalised. Its Purist style, 'meant to instil, by good example, corresponding virtues in the inhabitants', was at variance 'with the architectural codes of the latter'.[46] To Jencks, 'such simplistic ideas, taken over from philosophic doctrines of Rationalism, Behaviourism and Pragmatism proved as irrational as the philosophies themselves'.

Jencks's criticisms of the Rationalism espoused by modern architects here[47] will not lead him, however, to reject the 'Neo-Rationalism' of some post-modernist architects. Later, in his post-script on 'Post-Modern Classicism' to the later editions of his 1977 text, Jencks will speak, for example, of the Neo-Rationalism of such as Aldo Rossi as having helped to open the way to the development of the 'Post-Modern Classicism' which Jencks will see as having become the basis of the new 'public language of architecture'.[48]

In addition to criticising what he sees to be the faults of modernism, and to developing his understanding of post-modernism as a double-coding of modernism with other codes in his 1977 text, Jencks had gone on in it to speak of how architects may communicate missing values through the 'language of the local culture', and how this could lead to a variety of styles.[49] Here pastiche is, as seen in the previous chapter, also not 'blind' or empty of value as suggested by Jameson, but value-laden for Jencks.[50]

Although we have also seen Habermas criticise the post-modernist architecture defended by Jencks, the latter has not only defended the concept of consensus between architect and user, as in his previously cited defence of the work of Lucien Kroll, but has also written in his 1977 text that a way of preventing a post-modernist work which uses pluralist coding from degenerating into 'compromise and unintended pastiche' is through participatory design, where the designer is subjected to codes not necessarily his own 'in a way he can respect them'.[51]

Further to this, the variety of codes used in post-modern architecture is seen as leading to codings which may be read in different ways by a viewer, depending upon their own knowledge of visual languages,[52] while Jencks's point about the variety of codings used in post-modernism is also taken up in the third section of his 1977 work on 'Post-Modern Architecture', where an 'Evolutionary Tree' divides post-modern architecture into the six main traditions of 'Historicism', 'straight Revivalism', 'Neo-Vernacular', 'Ad Hoc Urbanist', 'Metaphor/Metaphysical' and 'Post-Modern Space'.[53]

Beginning with 'Historicism', Jencks covers works by such as Venturi, Portoghesi, Moore, Graves and Hollein, and styles from the 'radically eclectic' and the ornamental to 'post-modern classicism'. Paolo Portoghesi's *Casa Baldi* of 1959–61 is described here as 'an essay in free-form curves . . . reminiscent of the Borromini he was studying, yet also unmistakably influenced by Le Corbusier'.[54] Going on to describe it in terms of his concept of double-coding Jencks adds: 'Here is the schizophrenic cross between two codes that is characteristic of Post-Modernism: the enveloping, sweeping curves of the Baroque, the overlap of space, the various focii of space interfering with each other and the Brutalist treatment, the expression of concrete block, rugged joinery and the guitar-shapes of modernism.'[55]

Here too, then, is another 'end to modernism', preceding that of the blowing-up of the Pruitt-Igoe housing estate of July 1972, which Jencks had described in the opening of his book. The 'end' served to modern architecture by the early examples of post-modernist architecture is, however, not as violent as that served the Pruitt-Igoe by the dynamiters of 1972, because it is, to use Jencks's own term from 1978 on, a 'double-coding' of modernism with another style, of – in the case of Portoghesi's *Casa* – Le Corbusier plus Borromini.[56]

For all of Jencks's criticism of the modernist 'Rationalist' tradition which Habermas, for one, has seen as being basic to modernism,[57] such passages show Jencks to have presented post-modernism as the *preservation* as well as the *transformation* of modernism.[58] For this reason too, Jencks cannot be tagged with the 'anti-modernist' label which both Jameson and Lyotard, as well as Habermas, have attached to him in differing ways.[59]

In addition to describing post-modernist architecture as a double-coding of modernism with other codes in the second edition of his 1977 text,[60] Jencks, as mentioned earlier, has also gone on in later works to list thirty variables according to which 'Modern' (1920–60), 'Late-Modern' (1960–) and 'Post-Modern'

7   Portoghesi's *Casa Baldi*, 1959–61, from Charles Jencks, *The Language of Post-Modern Architecture*, p. 81

(1960–) architecture may be classified and periodised.[61] According to this table the eight 'Ideological' definers of the 'Post-Modern' are:

double-coding of style (in contrast to the 'Modern' 'one international style, or "no style" ' and to the 'Late-Modern' 'unconscious style');[62]
'popular' and pluralist (as opposed to the 'Modern' 'utopian and idealist' and the 'Late-Modern' 'pragmatic');
semiotic form (as opposed to the 'Modern' 'deterministic form, functional' and the 'loose fit' of the 'Late-Modern');
traditions and choice (in contrast to the 'Modern' *Zeitgeist*' and the 'Late-Modern' 'late-capitalist');
artist/client (as opposed to the artist as 'prophet/healer' of 'Modernism', or to the 'suppressed artist' of 'Late-Modernism');
elitist and participative (in contrast to the 'Modern' 'elitist/"for everyman" ' and the 'Late-Modern' 'elitist professional');
piecemeal (in contrast to the 'holistic' style of the 'Modern' and 'Late-Modern');
architect as representative and activist (rather than the 'Modern' architect as 'savior/doctor' or the 'Late-Modern' architect as one who 'provides service').

In addition to these 'ideological' definers, there are thirteen stylistic variables, the 'Post-Modern' being:

hybrid expression;
complexity;
variable space with surprises;
conventional and abstract form;
eclectic;
semiotic articulation;
variable mixed aesthetic depending on context; expression of content and semantic appropriateness toward function;
pro-organic and applied ornament;
pro-representation;
pro-metaphor;
pro-historical reference;
pro-humour;
pro-symbolic.

Finally Jencks lists the 'Design Ideas' of the 'Post-Modern' as including:

contextual urbanism and rehabilitation;
functional mixing;
'Mannerist and Baroque';
all rhetorical means;
skew space and extensions;
street buildings;
ambiguity;
tending to asymmetrical symmetry (Queen Anne Revival);[63]
collage/collision.[64]

While all of the above characteristics are contrasted by Jencks with characteristics of the 'Modern' and 'Late-Modern', such as the machine aesthetics of both, the anti-humour, anti-ornament and anti-symbolism of the 'Modern', and the 'unintended' humour and symbolism of the 'Late-Modern',[65] not all post-modernist architecture has proven to be as satisfactory as it might be for Jencks in its transformation of the 'Modern'.[66] Only with the emergence at the end of the 1970s, after the publication of the first edition of his *The Language of Post-Modern Architecture*, of a new 'post-modern classicism' will Jencks find, moreover, a new 'public' language for the post-modern architect to follow.

Post-script on post-modern classicism

Jencks's *The Language of Post-Modern Architecture* was first published just at the time when Stirling and Wilford and Associates' new Wuerttemberg State Gallery of 1977 to 1984 was being begun in Stuttgart, but the later edition of that work of 1984 contains a post-script on the 'new public language of architecture' – of post-modern classicism – as well as a specific reference to the Stuttgart Gallery.[67] This new 'public' language for post-modernism has not only occupied Jencks's attention for some years since,[68] but was also foreshadowed in certain respects in his 1977 work, in, for example, its emphasis on the need for architects to both communicate with a variety of publics and enable the latter to discuss architectural and other values in some manner akin to that which had characterised the old public sphere of classical times, the *agora* or *res publica*.[69]

To Jencks, writing in his 1984 post-script to his 1977 text, the post-modern classicism of the late 1970s still had some way to

8 Sculpture court, James Stirling, Michael Wilford and Associates' New Wuerttemberg State Gallery, Stuttgart, 1977–84, from Charles Jencks, *What is Post-Modernism?*, p. 17

go, but had already amounted to a consensus 'like the International Style of the Twenties', if with the difference that it was, as Jencks described it, a 'free eclectic manner to be used where it is appropriate on public buildings'. Here Jencks added that it is, therefore, 'not a totalistic style, the claim Nikolaus Pevsner made for the International one, and it exists as a genre, with other styles. In short it is the leading part of the pluralism which it supports as a necessary communicational device.'[70]

Before concluding his post-script of 1984 Jencks also returns to the opening theme of his 1977 text – the blowing up of the Pruitt-Igoe housing estate in St Louis – when he defends post-modern classicism as providing a style with which people would prefer to live,[71] and concludes with the statement that although 'Post-Modern Classicism' is only one style amongst several, it is the most public because of both its use of the language of classical architecture, and its desire to re-establish the public realm.[72]

Read together with its post-script of 1984, Jencks's 1977 text on the 'language of post-modern architecture' may also be seen to have moved from its initial critique of the aesthetic and social failures of the 'international language' of the Modern Movement to a vision – tempered by some warnings – of the possibility of a new 'post-modern' public language built from the 'double-coding' of modernism with classical and other codes.

All of these points are repeated in Jencks's other works of the 1980s on the post-modern, and in the new Introduction and Postscript to the fifth edition of his *The Language of Post-Modern Architecture* of 1987. Further to the above, some other new points are made in the 1984 and 1987 additions to Jencks's 1977 text which will also be developed in some of his later works, as when, for example, he speaks in the Introductions to the revised editions of 1984 and 1987, of the development of a new 'information society' in which 'instant communication', 'instant eclecticism' and 'overall mutual influence' will encourage further the development of the post-modern architecture described in the book.[73] Here the 'post-industrial' society is also seen as providing the basis for the growth of post-modernism rather than its undermining, and of a post-modernism largely different from that envisaged by Lyotard.[74]

Despite the many differences between Jencks and Lyotard which could be described again here, both concepts of post-modernism can, as Jencks himself points out later, in his 1987 text,[75] at least be said to be related to their author's acceptance of a need for the multiplication of discourses. Whereas for the relativist Lyotard a greater number of discourses was needed to challenge the 'meta-discourses' of modernity, for the pluralist Jencks the increase in discourses and codes provides, amongst other things, however, a greater choice for the double-coding of modernism with other codes.[76]

In contrast, further, to Lyotard's criticisms of post-modern architecture, the desire to 'live across time' shown by post-modern architecture and its use of a variety of codes also represents for Jencks an admirable drive to 'explore the universal language of architecture', as well as to be part of a larger, 'richer civilization', or 'world village'. Jencks returns to his understanding of post-modernism as a 'double-coding':

> The points lead immediately to what must be obvious to everyone: the style is hybrid, doubly-coded, based on fundamental dualities. Sometimes it stems from juxtaposition of new and old as in James Stirling's work; sometimes it is based on the amusing inversion of the old, as in the case of Robert Venturi and Hans Hollein; and nearly always it has something strange about it. In short, a highly developed taste for paradox is characteristic of our time and sensibility.[77]

As stated previously, many of the points made by Jencks in his 1977 text and its Introduction and Postscripts are also taken up and developed in his later works, and in the next section some of these points will also be looked at again with reference to the extension of Jencks's analysis of post-modern architecture to post-modern art in his 1986 work *What is Post-Modernism?*

What is Post-Modernism?

Jencks's *What is Post-Modernism?* of 1986 opens with an illustration of Carlo Maria Mariani's *La Mano ubbidisce all'inteletto (The Hand Submits to the Intellect)* of 1983 and a caption which again takes up his interest in the double-coding of modernism with other historical and specifically classical codes:

> For Modernists the subject of art was often the process of art; for Post-Modernists it is often the history of art. Mariani adapts eighteenth-century conventions, including even the 'erotic frigidaire', to portray his

allegory of autogenous creation: art painting itself. *The Hand Submits to the Intellect* recalls the Greek myth of the origins of painting and suggests that art today is still self-generated and as hermetically sealed as his ideal, claustrophobic space.[78]

Despite the implication of this last comment that both post-modernist art and modernist art are largely 'hermetically sealed' (which he will later dispel to some extent by suggesting that Mariani's work may also be seen to be satirising modernist

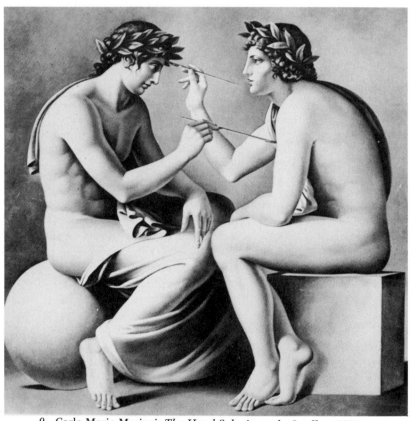

9   Carlo Maria Mariani, *The Hand Submits to the Intellect*, 1983, from Charles Jencks, *What is Post-Modernism?*, Frontispiece

10 Saul Steinberg, drawing from *The New World* (New York, 1965)

'hermeticism'[79]), Jencks's opening remark had made a clear distinction between the post-modern and the modern: 'For Modernists the subject of art was often the process of art; for Post-Modernists it is often the history of art.' What is interesting about Jencks's choice of this painting and his caption to it is, however, not only that the work is shown to demonstrate a return to the subject of the history of art missing in modernist art, but to have achieved a 'double-coding' of this return with the modernist interest in the process of art via its use of the story of the Greek Dibutade's, or 'Corinthian Maid's' 'invention' of the art of drawing in the act of outlining the shadow of her departing lover on a wall. Where modernism may well have chosen to have investigated the processes of art without such historical reference (take, for example, Saul Steinberg's numerous ironic drawings of drawings trying to draw themselves), post-modernism is shown to have 'double-coded' the modernist interest in the process of art with a historical context, and to have clothed it with that which Jencks has described elsewhere as the 'public' language of classicism.[80]

As Jencks's *What is Post-Modernism?* of 1986 goes on to suggest by way of its extension of Jencks's earlier arguments about post-modern architecture to the visual arts, one of the results of the post-modernist interest in placing modernism into a historical context has also been that it has been able to reflect on and extend modernism in ways which the latter could never do itself. By using works such as Carlo Maria Mariani's 'The Hand Submits to the Intellect' in which the modernist theme of self-reflection is joined to both the language of classicism, and to the Greek story of the origins of painting, post-modernism is, for instance, not only presented by Jencks as being attached to modernism in a doubly coded way which prevents its treatment of the modern from being too antipathetic or destructive, but is also presented as a way out of the modernist impasse of being concerned with depicting a type of self-reflection which had been detached from both the history of art and the more objective gaze of future artists or observers.

Post-modernism, as the art which has followed something defined by it as modernism, is at least able to depict modernism from outside itself, or 'alongside' itself, as a distinctly different tradition, and in a way which the various different modernisms of the past were not able to do themselves. Again the works which Jencks will describe as 'post-modernist' will have both this 'double-coded' relationship to the modern and some historical perspective on the latter. Whether they treat the modernist work in a symbolic, realistic or humorous manner will be up to the artist, although many will, because of their double-coding of the modern work with another, also imply some criticism of those modernist works which did not double-code their message with something else.

It is here too, moreover, that irony and parody, as devices involving the dual-coding of codes in art and literature, may also be used in a post-modern manner when used to double-code the modern with another code; although it should also be made clear that not all post-modern dual-coding need be ironic or parodic, just as not all 'dual-coded' irony or parody may be post-modern in a Jencksian sense if it does not encode a modernist 'code' with another.[81]

Prior to Jencks's 1986 text, Achille Bonito Oliva's *Transavant-garde International* of 1982 had presented 'post-modern' art as 'overturning the idea of progress in art which was formerly geared toward conceptual abstraction' and as 'going back to older styles as well as forward'. Further to this Bonito Oliva wrote of transavantgardism that it had also 'included craft and other arts excluded by the modern avant-garde'; had 'returned value to the image' while also being aware of the problematic character of representation; played with meaning so that it often used irony; countered the analytic character of modern art with a new synthetic character; replaced the 'puritanical' elements in modernism by a new opulence, decorativeness and plurality of styles; and had gone beyond nihilism towards a more open cultural exchange, interbreeding and eclecticism.[82]

Although Jencks's 1986 text has criticised the concept of 'trans-avantgarde',[83] his 1987 article on the 'post-avant-garde' to which reference was made in the previous section on Marshall Berman, had described the 'post-avant-garde' as giving up many of the goals of the old modernist avant-gardes and of substituting 'the new shock of the old of Mariani' for the 'old "shock of the new" of Duchamp'.[84] While Mariani's painting might also be seen as continuing some of the traditions of modernism, such as its interest in the processes of art, its return to the language of classicism and to its historical and humanist perspectives has also helped to make something new of both the modern and the classical traditions for Jencks.

Further to this, Jencks's 1986 comments on Mariani's more satirical *Costellazioni del Leone (School of Rome)* of 1980–1[85] also show that a work may still comply with his criteria of post-modernism while using parody, pastiche and satire together with a classical code. Where Jameson had suggested that because of the normlessness of post-modernist pastiche, critical parody, or satire, was not to be found in post-modernism, Jencks finds numerous examples of these other devices in Mariani's depiction of contemporary art dealers and artists in classical dress, and also indicates that the norm or ideal by which Mariani's satire works may be found in his evocation of the classical in his pastiche both of Raphael's *School of Athens* of 1510 and of some of Raphael's later classicistic admirers.[86]

While Jencks's 1986 text also recognises differences between post-modernist art and architecture,[87] one of the threads which connects the post-modern art discussed in his text with that of post-modern architecture (apart from its polemical classification of modernist and post-modernists into puritan reformers and non-puritan counter-reformers[88]) is again the use of the language of classicism, and it is this which is also the theme of the section in which Jencks is able to spend some time and space on the illustration of James Stirling and Michael Wilford and Associates' *Neue Staatsgalerie* in Stuttgart of 1977–84. As noted previously, this was a work which had only just been begun when Jencks's *The Language of Post-Modern Architecture* was first published in 1977, and Jencks's 1986 text is one of the first monographs on post-modernism written after its completion in 1984 to discuss it in some detail.

To Jencks, Stirling and Wilford and Associates' new State Gallery at Stuttgart is not only an admirable example of the new post-modern use of the language of classical architecture for a public building, but has also juxtaposed the modern with the classical in a manner which is post-modern in both its 'double-coding' of the modern with the classical and its use of such varied 'tropes' as ornament, colour, historicism and irony. Thus the modern invention of the car park is shown by Jencks to have been hidden ironically, but also aesthetically, beneath a classical superstructure by Stirling and his associates, and also to be revealed by that structure in a 'foregrounding' of its modernist elements where some of its blocks have been removed to form both the aesthetic illusion of a classical ruin outside, and the functional ventilation of the car park within.[89] Here modern functionalism and a post-modern-classical aestheticism both ironise and support each other – the latter preventing the former from degenerating into any purist form, and the former saving the latter from the appearance of any unselfcritical elitism.[90]

In addition to juxtaposing classical and modernist codes, Stirling's Stuttgart State Gallery also offers Jencks the example of the post-modern creation of another new 'public sphere' or '*res publica*'. In particular, the sculpture court is seen as acting as such a sphere or realm in being based on the arenas of classical Greece and Italy, and in the channelling of the public through it – from one part of the gallery to another – by means of a curvilinear walkway.[91] Again the classical is, however, also seen to have been juxtaposed with the modern in what Jencks suggests is 'an allegory of a schizophrenic culture', by the introduction of a bright orange revolving door into the arena's sunken Doric portico.[92]

While Jencks has some fun here in depicting modern culture as 'schizophrenic',[93] his 1986 text also proceeds to an extended critique of the 'deconstructionist' definition of post-modernism as an anarchic or nihilistic movement, as given by Ihab Hassan and by some of the contributors to Hal Foster's 1983 collection of essays on 'postmodern' culture. To Jencks, as seen previously, this view of post-modernism has attributed to it characteristics of 'Late-Modernism', and in a confused and confusing manner.[94] Jencks concludes, moreover, that it is in fact necessary to redefine as mostly 'Late' that which 'Davis, Goldberger, Foster, Jameson, Lyotard, Baudrillard, Krauss, Hassan and so many others often define as "Post" ': 'It [the post-modernism presented by the above] is mostly "Late" because it is still committed to the tradition of the new and does not have a complex relation to the past, or pluralism, or the transformation of western culture –

11 Carlo Maria Mariani, *The constellation of Leo*, 1980–1; in Charles Jencks, *What is Post-Modernism?*, p. 24

12   Raphael *School of Athens*, 1510, Vatican, Rome

13   View of part of the exterior of James Stirling, Michael Wilford
and Associates' New Wuerttemberg State Gallery, Stuttgart,
1977–84; from Charles Jencks, *What is Post-Modernism?*, p. 16

a concern with meaning, continuity and symbolism.'[95] Ironically it is therefore those post-modernisms which have most wanted to 'deconstruct' the modern and the late-modern which Jencks sees as being closer to the latter than the doubly coded – attached but also transformative – relationship to modernism of the post-modernist art and architecture praised in his texts.

Interestingly, in view of his previous connections between post-modern architecture and post-industrial society,[96] Jencks adds, following his reading of the Hongkong Shanghai Bank as a 'Late-Modern' building,[97] that 'the concept of Post-Modernism is often confused with Late Modernism because they both spring from a post-industrial society'. As suggested in his previous discussions of the post-industrial society, Jencks has also recognised that the latter is one in which many of the older elements of industrial and modern society continue to exist alongside the new 'post-industrial' technologies and service industries,[98] and appears here to regard the presence of a post-industrial sphere as being akin to a 'necessary' but not to a 'sufficient' cause of the development of the post-modern.[99]

Following his criticism of the confusion of post-modernism with late-modernism because of their common post-industrial bases, Jencks also accuses Lyotard of having elided the two terms (the *post-industrial* and the *post-modern*) in the beginning of his *The Post-Modern Condition* when he wrote that the object of his study 'is the condition of knowledge in the most highly developed societies'. Jencks adds here that although there is a connection between the post-industrial and the post-modern it is not the 'simple and direct one that Lyotard implies'.[100]

As mentioned previously, in the section on Jameson in chapter 3, Jencks had also written in his 1986 text[101] that because Foster's Hongkong Shanghai Bank is the 'first radical "multinational" building' with parts fabricated in several countries, and 'resolved by all the technologies of the post-industrial society, including . . . the computer and instant world communication', it should, 'according to the definitions of J.F. Lyotard and others', be a 'prime example of Post-Modernism . . . But it isn't, and if it were it would be a failure.'[102] As also suggested previously, in chapter 3, although Lyotard had not exactly equated the post-industrial and the post-modern (because, for one thing, he had tried to maintain a view of the post-modern as a force which should be directed towards the criticising of capitalism together with an equation of both post-modern architecture and some elements of the post-industrial society with capitalism) others, such as Jameson, have.[103] Further to this, Lyotard, as Jencks is aware,[104] had also defended the avant-garde or 'experimental' elements of 'High Modernism' against the concept of post-modernism put forward by Jencks, and had, like Hassan and others, also based his central concept of post-modernism as the critique of selected 'metanarratives' of modernity, such as capitalism, on the late-modern deconstructionist belief that all philosophies could be treated as discourses to be deconstructed as well as on the modern Marxian criticism of capitalism.[105]

Later, Jencks will not only repeat his criticisms of the late modern character of Hassan's and Lyotard's 'postmodernisms' in his *Post-Modernism: the New Classicism in Art and Architecture*,[106] but will also go on to criticise the new 'deconstructionist' architecture of the 1980s as 'late-modernist' in several articles published following that work.

Jencks's criticisms of 'deconstructionist' architecture

Not only are 'high-tech' buildings such as Norman Foster's Hongkong Shanghai Bank a form of 'Late-Modern' architecture contemporaneous with, but also very different from, 'Post-Modern' architecture for Jencks, but the 'Deconstructionist' forms of architecture of such as Bernard Tschumi, Rem Koolhaas, Peter Eisenman, Zaha M. Hadid and Frank O. Gehry have also been categorised by him in some recent articles as 'Late-' rather than 'Post-Modern'.

Jencks writes, for instance, in his 1988 article, 'Deconstruction: the Pleasure of Absence':

If there really is a 'Neo-Modern' architecture, as many architects and critics have been quick to claim, then it must rest on a new theory and practice of Modernism. The only such development to have emerged in the last 20 years – known as Deconstruction or Post-Structuralism – takes Modernist elitism and abstraction to an extreme and exaggerates already known motifs, which is why I would continue to call it 'Late'.[107]

As Jencks goes on to note, one of the modernist abstractionist

traditions called upon by at least some so-called 'Deconstruc-
tionist' architects in recent years has been, moreover, that of the
Russian Constructivists of the 1920s, and to the extent that a
recent exhibition of 'Deconstructionist' architecture, organised in
1988 by Philip Johnson and Mark Wigley, has joined the terms of
'Deconstruction' and 'Constructivism' together to speak of
'Deconstructivism'[108] to describe the work of Frank Gehry,
Daniel Libeskind, Rem Koolhaas, Peter Eisenman, Zaha M.
Hadid, Coop Himmelblau and Bernard Tschumi.[109]

While the linking of Constructivism with Deconstruction may
seem paradoxical if both terms are understood in a literal sense,
Mark Wigley's essay on 'Deconstructivist Architecture' in the
text of the same name by himself and Philip Johnson claims that
Deconstruction is 'often misunderstood as the taking apart of
constructions', and goes on to state that a 'deconstructive architect is ... not one who dismantles buildings, but one who
locates the inherent dilemmas within buildings'.[110] Wigley continues: 'The deconstructive architect puts the pure forms of the
architectural tradition on the couch and identifies the symptoms
of a repressed impurity. The impurity is drawn to the surface by
a combination of gentle coaxing and violent torture: the form is
interrogated.'[111] To connect this with Constructivism Wigley
adds: 'To do so, each project employs formal strategies developed by the Russian avant-garde early in the twentieth century.
Russian Constructivism constituted a critical turning point
where the architectural tradition was bent so radically that a
fissure opened up through which certain disturbing architectural
possibilities first became visible.'[112]

Charles Jencks's *Architectural Design* Interview with Peter
Eisenman of 1988[113] not only takes up the question of to what
extent Deconstructionist architecture is 'Constructivist',[114] but
also raises the issue of the relationship between Deconstruction
and 'Post-Modernism'.[115] Here Jencks suggests not only that 'the
Post-Structuralists don't want to be called Post-Modern by and
large',[116] but that if the 'Deconstructionist' Eisenman is a 'Post-
Modernist' in any sense it is only in the sense of 'Hassanian-
Post-Modernism'.[117] To Jencks's aside that Eisenman has even
slipped out of this role, Eisenman replies in what is to Jencks a
typically 'Deconstructionist', and not truly 'Post-Modernist'

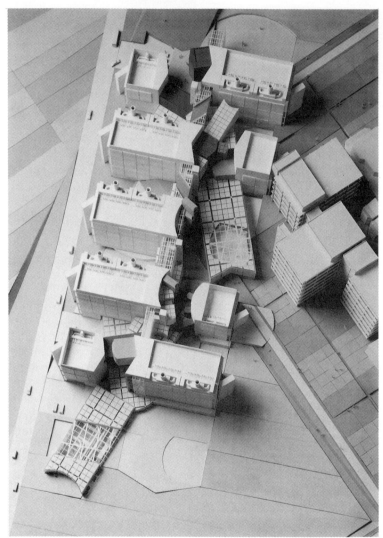

14 Peter Eisenman, Biocenter for the University of Frankfurt, 1987, Site
Model A, illustrated in Philip Johnson and Mark Wigley, *Deconstructivist
Architecture* (New York, 1988), p. 57

manner, that 'being slippery ... is the trait of a post-modernist'.[118]

As Jencks has also suggested in his interview with Eisenman, many other architects designated 'Deconstructionist' have wished, however, to distance themselves from post-modernism. One of the architects dubbed a 'Deconstructivist' by Johnson and Wigley, Bernard Tschumi, has written, for example, in his contribution to the *Architectural Design* edition on 'Deconstruction in Architecture' on his Parc de la Villette project, Paris,[119] that 'it might be worthwhile ... to abandon any notion of a Post-Modern architecture in favour of a post-humanist architecture, one that would stress not only the dispersion of the subject and the force of social regulation, but also the effect of such decentering on the entire notion of unified, coherent, architectural form'. Tschumi continues in a manner echoed by Wigley's description of Deconstruction in architecture: 'It also seems important to think, not in terms of principles of formal composition, but rather of questioning structures, that is, the order, techniques and procedures that are entailed by any architectural work.'[120]

Tschumi's Parc de la Villette project (a project discussed by Jacques Derrida in a paper entitled 'Point de folie – maintenant l'architecture'),[121] had also been described by him as encouraging 'conflict over synthesis, fragmentation over unity, madness and play over careful management'.[122] Although Tschumi goes on to say that in subverting some ideals 'sacrosanct to the Modern period' it could also be 'allied to a specific vision of Post-Modernity', he had continued to differentiate it from that architecture which had emphasised the immanence of meaning in architectural structures.[123]

Not only has Jencks (by contrast) stressed the importance of a complexity of immanent and obvious meanings in post-modernist architecture, but he has, as seen previously, also followed Venturi in arguing for *both* complexity *and* contradiction rather than for the preferences for fragmentation *over* unity, and conflict *over* synthesis, recommended by Tschumi, and it is also here, as well as in the criticisms by Tschumi and others of the post-modernist architecture preferred by Jencks, that we may find a basis for their divergence.

While Jencks had not yet formulated his concept of post-

modernism as a double-coding of modernism with another code
in the early to mid-1970s when Hassan's writings on deconstructionist post-modernism were developing, he has, as seen from
his list of thirty definers distinguishing the 'Post-Modern' from
the 'Modern' and 'Late-Modern', since used it to contrast his
concept of post-modernism with those forms of architecture
which he sees as being as 'Late-Modern' as Deconstructionist
theory itself.[124] One of the definitions given by Jencks of 'Late-
Modernists' there, that they 'keep alive the Modernist values
through an elaboration of the previous language', rather than by
a 'double-coding' of it with another as in post-modern architecture, would also appear to describe both the 'Deconstructivist'
resurrection of Constructivism, and the 'Deconstructivist' or
'Deconstructionist' architect's elaboration of Deconstructionist
theory.[125]

In contrast to 'deconstructionist' post-modernism, Jencks, as
noted already, has not only maintained his belief in the need to
transform the modern by a 'double-coding' of it with other
codes, which also preserves some of it in some way, but has also
insisted on the affirmation of values lost in some modernist
practices, rather than the relativisation of value. With regard to
this latter point, Jencks has also argued from his *The Language
of Post-Modern Architecture* onwards for the restoration of
architectural values lost by the modernist extension of space and
abolition of ornament, and concluded his 1986 text by emphasising the fact that the role of the post-modernist critic must be the
evaluation of works and the making of distinctions forbidden by
the relativism entailed by the theories of such as Lyotard:

> the examples from the past are objective standards against which we can
> measure Post-Modernism; artistic traditions may be more widely
> defined than scientific ones but distinctions of value can still be defined
> objectively. Right-wing critics such as Roger Scruton, left-wing critics
> such as Fuller, and liberals such as Ernst Gombrich agree on this and on
> condemning the relativism that Lyotard's position entails.[126]

Peter Fuller's criticisms of both deconstructionist post-modernism and Jencks will be included in the following chapter.[127]
Before turning to that chapter, the following sections will complete this analysis of Jencks and his work with a discussion of his

1987 book *Post-Modernism: the New Classicism in Art and Architecture* and of its arguments for seeing the post-modernist revival of the language of classicism as one of its more valuable developments.

Post-modernism and the new classicism in art and architecture

The question of value with which Jencks's *What is Post-Modernism?* of 1986 had ended is again returned to by Jencks in his *Post-Modernism: the New Classicism in Art and Architecture* of 1987 and with the statement that Jencks's own 'values and prejudices' are with what he terms the emerging 'Post-Modern Classicism'.[128] As Jencks's Preface indicates by pointing to the distinction which can be made between post-modernism presented as a break with the past and as a negation of modernism, and the post-modernism which seeks to 'reweave' modernism with strands of Western humanism, this 'Post-Modern Classicism' will also be one which will be understood as double-coding the language of classicism with modernism, rather than as breaking from it.[129] Later Jencks will also list the 'Four Traditions of Post-Modern Classical Architecture' of the years 1960–85 as 'Fundamentalist Classicism' (which includes Aldo Rossi, Matthias Ungers and Leon Krier's later work), 'Revivalist Classicism' (the Getty Museum to the AT&T), 'Urbanist Classicism' (including Stirling's Stuttgart Gallery) and 'Eclectic Classicism' (Robert Venturi, and Charles Moore and others).[130]

Prior to listing these categories of post-modern classical architecture Jencks had again taken up the question of post-modernism in the visual arts, and had divided post-modern classical art of the period 1960–85 into the five major traditions of 'Metaphysical Classical', 'Narrative Classical', 'Allegorical Classical', 'Realist Classical' and 'Classical Sensibility'.[131] While Carlo Maria Mariani is classified as 'Metaphysical Classical', Ron Kitaj, Peter Blake and David Hockney are categorised as 'Narrative Classical'. In contrast to Hal Foster and others who have seen Julian Schnabel as an archetypal post-modernist (and 'neoconservative') artist,[132] Jencks does not, however, choose to include him amongst his list of post-modernist classicists.[133] Indeed,

15   Julian Schnabel, *Winter*, 1982 (plates, bondo, frames, antlers, plaques and oil on wood), from Achille Bonito Oliva's, *Transavantgarde International* (Milan, 1982), p. 45

Schnabel's broken tea-cups and alienated faces seem much better suited as an illustration of the deconstructionist post-modernism which Jencks has elsewhere described as 'Late-Modern'. Despite the classification of Schnabel by Hal Foster as a 'neoconservative' post-modernist in his essay on 'poststructuralist' and 'neoconservative' post-modernists,[134] Schnabel has, moreover, recently been included in the list of deconstructionist artists published in numbers 3/4 of volume 4 of *Art & Design* 1988, and has also been related to Baudrillard's search for 'something beyond the vanishing point: a hyper-simulation which would be a type of disappearance beyond disappearance' by the critic Kim Levin.[135]

Compared with Schnabel, the 'post-modern' works illustrated by Jencks, such as Mariani's classicist allegories, Blakes's ironies or Stone Roberts's painstakingly detailed realist works, all demonstrate an interest in 'building up' the art work from either a multiplicity of metaphorical levels (as in Mariani), or a mixture of modernist and classical allusions as in Blake's *The Meeting*, in which allusions are to be found to classical art as well as to Courbet and Hockney, or a plethora of realistic detail as in Roberts, rather than in the 'deconstruction' of images as with Schnabel's broken crockery, or the reduction of metaphor to a single modern theme such as alienation. While there may be some who will find more than this in the work of Schnabel, others may maintain that the style and themes of his work remain late-modernist in their often neo-expressionistic treatment of the subject of alienation.[136]

Clearly the concept of post-modernism chosen by a particular theorist will also play some role in the selection of works to be categorised as post-modernist by them. In the case of Schnabel, for instance, some may well wish to categorise him as a post-modernist if they understand post-modernism, as Suzi Gablik has, as 'anything goes',[137] or if they understand it as aiming at the 'deconstruction' of other discourses, or at the depiction of the 'death of the subject'.[138] If, however, we are to follow Jencks and his concept of post-modernism as the double-coding of modernism with other codes, such as the language of classicism and its humanist values, then it will be more difficult to categorise Schnabel as a post-modernist.

As this text has tried to illustrate, the development of a variety of definitions and theories of post-modernism since the early years of this century, and the development in recent years of at least two major different philosophic approaches to post-modernism, as either the deconstruction of certain modernist

16 Peter Blake, 'The Meeting', or 'Have a Nice Day Mr Hockney', 1981–3; illustrated in Charles Jencks, *What is Post-Modernism?*, pp. 4–5

17 Gustave Courbet's *'Bonjour, Monsieur Courbet'*, 1854

discourses (in favour of the retention of the (late-modern) discourse of deconstruction), or as the double-coding of modernism
with other codes, also show that there will be a variety of ways of
categorising artists and artifacts as post-modern, and a variety of
theories of post-modernism for artists themselves to follow.
Problems will arise, however, not only if this variety is ignored,
and the 'late-modern' nature of deconstructionist theories not
taken into consideration, but if the variety of different presuppositions used to describe something or someone as post-modern
are misunderstood, and distinguishing adjectives such as
'deconstructionist' or 'double-coded' are not accurately or consistently applied to the particular post-modernism in question.[139]

18 Classical works such as this 'Crouching Aphrodite' from the
Archeological Museum of Rhodes may also be found echoed in the figure
of the 'teenybopper' on skates placed by Blake to the side of his Hockney

While the application of a distinguishing adjective may be most easily justified where the author of the theory or work in question has used such an adjective and demonstrated an accurate understanding of its meaning, cases may also arise where, even without specific agreement from the author in question, one or other of the distinguishing adjectives noted in this text might help to either explain the character of the particular theory or work more fully, or save it from being used as an example of post-modernism in general where it is clearly not in harmony with the aims or ideas of all other 'post-modernisms'. One example of something which could be differentiated as 'deconstructionist' post-modernism in art to avoid the latter situation may, moreover, be found in Robert Rosenblum's *The Dog in Art from Rococo to Post-Modernism* of 1988 and its illustration of Philip Taaffe's *Chi-Chi Meets the Death of Painting* of 1985, in which the image of the dog 'Chi-Chi' confronting a spectral image of itself is repeated in several 'mirror-images' placed vertically above each other.[140] Aware of the irony of Taaffe painting about the 'death of painting', but unconcerned to specify Taaffe as a 'deconstructionist' post-modernist, or as belonging to some similar category, on that account, Rosenblum describes the artist as demonstrating 'a cynicism typical of a younger generation confronting the void, but, like the rest of us, making hay while the sun is still shining'.[141]

Not only might theorists of post-modernism such as Jencks object to such a statement being used to cover the types of post-modernism for which they have sought to argue, but Rosenblum's choice of Taaffe's and others' repetitive or mechanically reproduced images of the dog in his section on 'the dog in post-modernism' evoke both late-modernist Pop Art works, such as Warhol's repetitive images, and earlier modernist works such as Duchamp's famous *Nude Descending a Staircase* and the variations on it.[142]

Similarities between Taaffe's use of serial images and the work of such as Warhol may also lead the spectator to recall Jean Baudrillard's use of Warhol's work to illustrate his theses about the 'death of the original' and the 'end of representation' in his description of the present age of simulation in his 'The Orders of Simulacra'.[143] Where Taaffe's dog Chi-Chi confronts a spectral

19 Philip Taaffe's
*Chi-Chi Meets
the Death of
Painting*, 1985
(Collection Peter
Brams) in Robert
Rosenblum's *The
Dog in Art from
Rococo to Post-
Modernism*
(New York,
1988), p. 112

image of itself in several vertically depicted stages of reproduction, Baudrillard had spoken in his section on 'The Hyperrealism of Simulation' in his 'The Orders of Simulacra'[144] of the 'deconstruction of the real into details', the 'endlessly reflected vision' and the 'serial form', where 'all attention to the object is intercepted by its infinite diffraction into itself', and where the 'seduction is possibly that of death, in the sense that for sexual beings, death is possibly not nothingness, but simply the mode of reproduction anterior to the sexual'. Prior to this, Jacques Derrida's essay on the artist Valerio Adami had also begun with the note that Adami's works ICH and CHI (CHIMERE for the whole) had received their names from Derrida's text on Adami's drawings 'After *Glas*'.[145] Whether death, reproduction or illusion be taken as the central theme of Taaffe's painting, its 'deconstruction' of the image into several spectral 'mirror-images' of itself might easily be seen to echo several of the themes of 'deconstructionist' texts, such as those referred to above, as well as some of the techniques of late-modernist painting, rather than the precepts of some of the other types of post-modernism discussed previously in our text.[146]

Returning to Jencks's 1987 book on 'Post-Modernism', it will be clear from his opening chapter on 'The Values of Post-Modernism' that the value of the post-modern for him will not lie primarily in the deconstruction of other images or other canons, but in the 'double-coding' of them with other values. In addition to being described as 'halting the wanton destruction of cities', post-modernism as understood by Jencks is also presented as having instituted positive laws for growth in at least one city and to have returned rather than abolished the human presence.[147] Jencks adds:

Contrary to common belief, Post-Modernism is neither anti-Modernist nor reactionary. It accepts the discoveries of the twentieth century – those of Freud, Einstein and Henry Ford – and the fact that two world wars and mass culture are now integral parts of our world picture, but doesn't make from this an entire ideology. In short, as its name implies, it acknowledges the debt to Modernism but transcends the movement by synthesising it with other concerns.[148]

In an expansion on this Jencks also writes that the common element in the eclecticism of post-modernism of the 1970s was its assault on the notion of a stable category such as high art, good taste, classicism or modernism,[149] but that its move towards a pluralism in taste also encompassed a return to ornament and a variety of styles, concepts and values.[150]

Like all movements, post-modernism has, Jencks adds, produced both bad and good art. Not to make such an admission could even imply that values were not being applied as claimed. How the good is to be distinguished from the bad does, however, pose a problem when one of the tenets of the movement is that a pluralism of tastes be encouraged. Nevertheless, Jencks's text suggests that it should be possible to say that, within the range of the works produced, some will approximate more closely than others the interweaving of the modern with the classical codes which constitute the new public language of post-modernism. Further to this, Jencks had also spoken in the conclusion of his *What is Post-Modernism?* of 1986 of being able to use examples from the past (in which a shared symbolic order such as that aimed for in his post-modern classicism is achieved) as 'objective standards' against which the post-modernist work may be evaluated.[151] Choosing these examples may, of course, be value-laden in some way or another, but, as with other post-modern enterprises in which participation between architect and user is encouraged, discussion of these more concealed or less obvious values should also be possible. Jencks returns to the conclusion of his 1986 text early in his 1987 book when he adds that the idea of being able to find 'objective standards' from the past against which 'present efforts can be measured' is welcome in a pluralist era which tries to 'avoid making judgements of relative worth'. Jencks continues: 'Where absolute values have lost credibility, tradition and the historical continuum replace them as the new departure points.'[152]

While Jencks will continue to argue against Lyotard that pluralism need not mean the abolition of all previously established values, but the acceptance of a variety, he also goes on to write later in his 1987 work that 'since our metaphysics is not shared, since, as he [Lyotard] puts it, "the grand narratives" of religion, social emancipation, progress and science have been relativised, there is no possibility of a shared world view', and that 'The implication of this for aesthetics, and particularly urban aesthetics, is a plural language.'[153] Although Jencks may still be described as a pluralist rather than as a relativist of Lyotard's kind, he adds that it is, moreover, here that the arguments 'of so many Post-Modern theorists', including himself, 'come into agreement with Lyotard'.[154]

It is also against the background of such arguments that Jencks goes on in his 1987 text to write against too great an integration of the modern and the classical and to present Stirling, Wilford and Associates' new State Gallery in Stuttgart not just as an integration of modernism and classicism, but as a 'fractured' interweaving of a variety of styles with the modern and the classical:

> The most feasible style for an open society is not the integrated ones of Modernism and Neoclassicism – nor even the monolithic mode of Ricardo Bofill. Rather it is one that acknowledges our fragile position of departure, where we have left the certainties of an integrated Christian culture, where we gain a certain identity from the past but are dependent on, and enjoy the fruits of, a fast-changing technology. Our sensibilities have been formed by these fragmentations and discontinuities but, far from disliking the heterogeneity which they entail, we enjoy the resultant hybrid aesthetic for its continuity with our daily life. By contrast, integrated systems can seem artificial and constricting.[155]

Jencks continues with specific reference to the new Stuttgart State Gallery:

> It is to this Post-Modern condition that the Stuttgart Museum speaks directly and with a kind of fractured beauty. On the main street side the classical harmonies prevail as they are enveloped within a Schinkelesque wall architecture of sandstone set against travertine – and concrete! Romanesque arches and windows, Egyptian cornice, rustication and the classical set of motifs – rectangle and circle are so subtly absorbed into the overall grammar that we hardly notice the eclecticism. A particularly strong opposition emerges – the essential dichotomy between Traditionalism and Modernism – which Stirling dramatises without attempting to resolve.[156]

Not only is post-modernism shown to have refused to create any false synthesis of the modern with the classical here, but it is also shown to have openly revealed to us its thinking on this score, together with its historical awareness of the importance of preserving, if not synthesising, both the past and the present. As

Jencks continues: 'Neither [Traditionalism nor Modernism] can win, nor can there be a transcendent Hegelian synthesis. There is simply the juxtaposition of two world views with the ironic reversal of both: the Modernist high-tech mode has been used as symbolic ornament, while the traditional rustication functions to clothe the volumes.'[157] Like Lyotard, Jencks does not see post-modernism as attempting an Hegelian synthesis of any kind here. Unlike Lyotard's post-modernism, however, Jencks's variety does not aim at a dialectic where we are always left at the second stage of the Hegelian dialectic of thesis, antithesis, synthesis – at, that is, the stage of antithesis, deconstruction or permanent criticism. What we appear to have instead with Jencks is a variation on an older, perhaps appropriately classical, Socratic form of dialectic in which two (or more) positions may comment upon and expand or change each other, but without the supersession of both (or all) into one 'homogenised' synthesis. Stirling's Stuttgart State Gallery is also a good example of this appropriately classical 'dialogue' or 'conversation'[158] between differing forms because it shows us the different, often contrasting, character of those forms, while using all of them to create a new 'whole' but sometimes also 'disharmoniously harmonic' structure, as spoken of by Jencks in the first of his new 'rules' for the post-modern.[159]

Before listing these rules in summary, Jencks concludes the tenth chapter of his *Post-Modernism: the New Classicism in Art and Architecture* by returning to the question of the values brought by 'Post-Modernism':

Post-Modern work shows some very real gains over Modern architecture. With Venturi, Moore, Isozaki and Stirling it has returned to a representational language which uses various, even divergent codes to appeal to different tastes and to send different messages. This variety recognises in a positive way the pluralism of an agnostic culture and yet still seeks a 'difficult unity' in attempting to synthesise such commonly held values as the continuity of history and urban context, the anthropomorphic image and the sensual response to form and colour.[160]

Jencks's concluding rules for the new 'Post-Modern Classicism' read in summary:[161]

1.   Disharmonious harmony (or 'dissonant beauty').

2.   Pluralism (both cultural and political).

3.   Urbane urbanism (or contextualism – the idea that new buildings should both fit into and extend the urban context).

4.   Anthropomorphism (ornament suggestive of the human body).

5.   'Historicist' subjects, including the relation between past and present, *anamnesis* or 'suggested recollection' and 'an out-break of parody, nostalgia and pastiche', which Jencks goes on to describe in this instance as 'the lesser genres with which Post-Modernism is equated by its detractors'.[162]

6.   A return to content (again with a pluralism of narratives rather than just one single story line).

7.   Double-coding, and the use of irony,[163] ambiguity and con-tradiction.[164] Jencks also writes with regard to this rule that irony and ambiguity were 'key concepts in Modern literature and Post-Modernists have continued using these tropes and methods while extending them to painting and architecture', and adds that the idea of double-meaning and the *'coincidentia oppositorum'* ultimately goes back to Heraclitus and to Nicholas of Cusa. (Here it may be noted that Jencks has also referred in his 1986 *What is Post-Modernism?* to one of the modernist painters most keen on using such 'double-codings', René Magritte, as a precursor of some post-modernist painting.[165] One of the major differences between the modern and post-modern uses of irony and parody, as implicitly suggested in Jencks's work, is, however, that with the latter, post-modern usage of them, modernism itself may become the object of the post-modernist's parodic, ironic or historicising reflection.[166]) Jencks concludes his seventh rule on double-coding by adding that it 'can, of course, be used in an opposite way to emphasise the disjunctions, as, for instance, Stirling and Salle employ it; but however the method is articulated it acknowledges the simultaneous validity of opposite approaches and different tastes'.[167]

8.   'When several codes are used coherently to some purpose they produce another quality sought by Post-Modernists, *multivalence.*' To Jencks, the multivalent work 'reaches out to

the rest of the environment, to many adjacent references, and to many different associations'.

9.   A complex relation to the past (which Jencks also describes as a precondition for the resonance of the 'multivalent' work) or *tradition reinterpreted.*

10.   The elaboration of *new rhetorical figures* as a way to renew past conventions. (These include double-coding, irony, eclectic quotation and many other devices already mentioned by Jencks, and constitute an example of text in which double-coding, irony and eclectic quotation, or pastiche, are brought together.)[168]

11.   The *'return to the absent centre'*. This follows Jencks's reference at the conclusion of his discussion of the previous point, to a 'return to humanism, but without the full and confident metaphysics which supported it in the Renaissance', and continues:

It is portrayed both consciously by Arata Isozaki as a comment on the decentred nature of Japanese life ... and unselfconsciously by James Stirling at Stuttgart, Michael Graves at the Humana Building, Ricardo Bofill at Montpellier and just about every Post-Modern architect who makes a central plan and then doesn't know what to put in the honorific place. This paradox is both startling and revealing: a desire for a communal space, a perfectly valid celebration of what we have in common, and then the admission that there is nothing quite adequate to fill it.[169]

(Jencks had also previously made reference to the ironic absence of any sacred object in the centre of the 'public sphere' of Stirling's Stuttgart Gallery, where instead of some divine symbol we have a functional, if also aesthetically designed, drain. Jencks's discussion with Stirling about the nature of the centre of his *agora* had, however, suggested to him that while such 'absences' might be seen by some to designate a sense of loss, for others they might express a sense of acceptance of the humanist secularisation of the sacred.[170])

Here, as elsewhere in his 1987 text, Jencks had also referred to those 'late-modernist' theories of post-modernism which speak of the 'death of the subject itself' and to the 'deconstructionist' symbolisation of an absent centre by architects such as Arata Isozaki.[171] In contrast to the 'late-modernist' theory of the 'death of the author', which he explicitly criticises in his 1987 text as tending to 'overemphasise the role played by traditions and dissolve the synthesising power of the individual',[172] Jencks's own post-modernism remains characterised by a 'return' of some kind or another to both 'the absent centre' and to the subject. Jencks not only speaks in the conclusion of his discussion of his eleventh rule of the way in which the various meanings given to the architecture of post-modernism by its users or observers show the latter to have returned some meaning to the 'absent centre', and to be themselves the 'presence at the absent centre',[173] but also writes in his conclusion proper that for the modernist things may fall apart, and 'the centre not hold', but that post-modernism offers the dialectical answer to this, that 'Things fall together, and there is no centre, but connections.'[174]

Although the goal of post-modernism may not be the raising of itself to a source of universal laws or values,[175] Jencks's post-modern subject is again presented here as being capable of both making new connections out of the older values of the past and asserting the possibility of a plurality of new values.[176] The way in which Jencks's theories – of both the subjects of post-modernism and of the post-modern forms created or observed by them – differ from those of others will also be pursued in the following chapter of this text in its discussions of Frampton, Portoghesi and Fuller.

5

ALTERNATIVE THEORIES

'Anything goes'?

We have just seen in chapter 4 how the architectural historian and critic Charles Jencks has described a number of architects as 'Post-Modern' by using a variety of definers, including that of double-coding. While Jencks has provided a great variety of definers and classifications to cover the variety or 'pluralism' of styles which can be found in post-modern architecture, not all of those architects themselves have, however, always agreed with Jencks's definitions, or philosophy, or even, in some cases, with the description of their works as post-modern.[1] Although several of the refusals of these architects to be termed post-modern will be seen to have arisen from their disagreement with, or misunderstanding of, a particular interpretation of post-modernism (whether it be Jencks's or someone else's), some further knowledge of the varieties of theories of architecture now in use may be gained by reading what these architects have said of their own work as well as the commentaries on them by others which are coloured by different presuppositions from those which Jencks has described himself as using.[2]

One other historian of post-modern architecture, Heinrich Klotz, has suggested, for instance, only ten main definers of post-modern architecture against the thirty suggested by Jencks – of 'Regionalism, Fictional representation, Seeing building as an art, Multiplicity of meanings, Poetry, Improvization and spontaneity, History and irony, Contextualism, Pluralism of style', and 'Fiction as well as function'.[3] Despite Klotz's suggestion that his larger purpose was not incompatible with Jencks's in describing it to be 'to illustrate the thesis that postmodern architecture

150

needs to be seen as a revision of modernism',[4] Jencks himself has been seen to have explicitly disagreed with some of the more specific definers used by Klotz to describe the particular forms to be taken by that revision,[5] so that some differences in both their approach to the post-modern, and in that of those using their works to define the post-modern, may be expected.

Kenneth Frampton

One other view of post-modernism which has already been alluded to in chapter 4 is that of Kenneth Frampton, who, as noted previously, has presented a theory of architecture in Hal Foster's collection of essays on 'Postmodern Culture' which sees the ideal contemporary architecture as 'an architecture of resistance' which will distance itself from both the 'Enlightenment myth of progress' and the 'reactionary, unrealistic impulse to return to the architectonic forms of the preindustrial past'.[6]

In addition to developing these arguments in his essay 'Towards a Critical Regionalism' in Foster's 1983 collection of essays on 'Postmodern Culture', Frampton has also criticised the philosophy behind the exhibition of architecture organised by Paolo Portoghesi for the Venice Biennale of 1980 in a paper entitled 'Some Reflections on Postmodernism and Architecture',[7] and written that he wishes to counter the 'power of Anglo-American hegemony in the field of so-called postmodern architecture, ideologically recognized and polemicized as such in Charles Jencks's influential book, *The Language of Post-Modern Architecture*'.[8] Frampton adds that he also wishes to use the term 'critical regionalism' in order 'to evoke a real and hypothetical condition in which a critical culture of architecture is consciously cultivated in a particular place, in express opposition to the cultural domination of hegemonic power',[9] and continues: 'It is, in theory at least, the critical culture, which while it does not reject the thrust of modernization, nonetheless resists being totally absorbed and consumed by it.'[10]

Frampton's 1986 criticisms of both Jencks's works on post-modernism and the concept behind Paolo Portoghesi's organisation of the exhibition of post-modern art under the title 'The Presence of the Past, the End of Prohibition' in the Venice Biennale of 1980,[11] also suggest that neither of these critics have represented his form of 'critical' architecture. Despite this implication, Jencks, as seen previously, has been critical, with Portoghesi, of at least some of the dominating features of the modernisation which underlie both modern and post-modern architecture, and which have sometimes even appeared to be celebrated in works of 'Late-Modern' 'High-Tech' architecture.[12]

Not only had Jencks begun his *The Language of Post-Modern Architecture* of 1977 with the suggestion that the alienating elements in modernism were to be a target of post-modernism, but he had also written a decade later, in his article on 'The Post-Avant-Garde' of 1987, that 'Post-Modern architecture, more than Post-Modernism in the other arts, is faced with such clear failures of Modernism as the bi-monthly blowing-up of inoperable housing estates, and this is why it has faced the "death of Modernism" so directly.' Jencks continued, 'Modernisation, the destructive/constructive forces of urban renewal and capitalism are nowhere so apparent as in the environment.'[13]

Here, as elsewhere, Jencks has clearly set the post-modern up as a cure for the injurious effects of modernisation, and supported at least something of the avant-garde critical role which Frampton suggests to be necessary in architecture.[14] As stated previously, in chapter 4, both modern and post-modern architecture may have developed in a post-industrial society in which the forces of modernisation are still at work, but the presence of those forces is not a 'sufficient' explanation of the post-modern (or of its power to criticise them) for Jencks.[15]

Paolo Portoghesi

John Blatteau's 'Architectural Self-Portrait' for the exhibition 'The Presence of the Past' which Paolo Portoghesi organised for the 1980 Venice Biennale was sub-titled 'It is again possible to learn from tradition and to connect one's work with the fine and beautiful works of the past.' This return to tradition, and to the 'fine and beautiful works of the past', has, however, not been the only theme of Portoghesi's work on post-modernism, and Portoghesi, like Jencks, has also seen post-modernism as arising from a dissatisfaction with 'modernity'.[16]

Hence the opening chapter of Portoghesi's book, *Postmodern: the Architecture of the Postindustrial Society* of 1982, on 'What is the Postmodern?', points out that the term 'postmodern' should not be thought of 'as a label designating homogeneous and convergent things', but that 'its usefulness lies, rather, in its having allowed us temporarily to put together and compare different things arising from a common dissatisfaction with that group of equally heterogeneous things called modernity'.[17] Portoghesi continues by going even further than Jencks towards seeing post-modernism as a break with modernism: 'to put it another way, the Postmodern is a refusal, a rupture, a renouncement, much more than a simple change of direction'. Here Portoghesi may even be said to be moving closer towards Lyotard than Jencks, and it is indeed Lyotard to whom he turns for support for his view that 'the fundamental principles of architectural modernity' have been 'unhinged' when he writes:

The crisis of theoretical legitimation, which Jean-François Lyotard calls the 'scarce credibility of the great *Récits*', and the fact that today we must confront the problem of the meaning 'without having the possibility of responding with the hope of the emancipation of Mankind as in the school of the Enlightenment, of the Spirit, as in the school of German Idealism, or of the Proletariat, by means of the establishment of a transparent society', has unhinged the fundamental principles of architectural modernity, consisting of a series of equations which have never been verified except through insignificant small samples. These are the equations: useful=beautiful, structural truth=esthetic prestige, and the dogmatic assertions of the functionalist statute: 'form follows function', 'architecture must coincide with construction', 'ornament is a crime', and so on . . . In place of faith in the great centered designs, and the anxious pursuits of salvation, the postmodern condition is gradually substituting the concreteness of small circumstantial struggles with its precise objectives capable of having a great effect because they change systems of relations.[18]

Following this, Portoghesi also specifically returns to Lyotard to connect the post-modern questioning of older 'récits' of modernity as described by Lyotard with that of the post-modernist architect's questioning of modernism:

The collapse of the great summarizing discourses that propose unitary interpretations and programmatic prophecies (it is the incredulity toward them that qualifies the Postmodern position, according to Lyotard), makes the strategy of listening obligatory, and the intellectuals can regain a specific role in the self-interrogation of real society as regards its desires and objectives.

Despite his reference to Lyotard here and elsewhere, Portoghesi continues by speaking of the restitution of the role of the subject to the community of its users:

The architect's interest in history and in the recycling of forms and traditional compositional systems should also be seen in relation to this self-interrogation, to this census of still valid or confirmable conventions, to the restitution of the role of the subject to the community of its users, after the long parenthesis of the claim of this role by the 'technicians of form', made legitimate by the theory of the Modern Movement.[19]

Here Portoghesi may also be said to have been somewhat more optimistic than Lyotard about the 'postmodern' possibilities of the post-industrial society, and even to have suggested that the 'postmodern condition' produced by the 'postindustrial' had led to the present post-modern revival of tradition.[20] Although Portoghesi, like Jencks, is critical of many of the effects of modernisation, he is thus (and also like Jencks) not totally pessimistic about the presence of the post-industrial as a base for the post-modern.

To Portoghesi, as for Jencks, the post-industrial society is a society in which the 'new electronic technology' has turned our age into an age of information and communication. As a consequence, architecture has become, so Portoghesi writes,

an instrument of the production and transmission of communicative models, which have for a particular society a value analogous to that of laws and other civil institutions, models whose roots lie in the appropriation and transformation of the places of the earth, and which have for centuries played the part of confirming and developing the identity of places (of cities) and of communities.[21]

Portoghesi continues: 'The result of the discovery of the sudden impoverishment produced in architecture by the adoption of technologies and morphologies separated from places and traditions has been the reemergence of architectonic archetypes as precious instruments of communication.'[22]

To Portoghesi the 'new conservatives' are, moreover, not those who return to the artistic traditions of the past to counter the effects of modernisation let loose in modernism, but those who act as the 'guardians of modernity at any cost'.[23] Portoghesi continues:

Unable to refute the radical criticisms of the tradition of the new, they speak of an incomplete project of modernity that must be continued; they pretend to ignore the fact that in order to really change, the essential premises of the modern project, and not its last consequences, must be debated once more. And they refuse to admit that continuity with the great tradition of modern art lies today more in the courage to break with the past (which in this case is precisely what was modern yesterday), than in keeping its surviving traces on ice.[24]

Here it is also Habermas and those others who have defended the 'project of modernity' against the post-modernists whom they had termed neo-conservatives who are seen, ironically, to be the real 'neo-conservatives'. In contrast to Lyotard (that other critic of Habermas as a defender of the 'metanarratives of modernity'), Portoghesi, like Jencks, will, however, also defend post-modern architecture, and its historicism, as a way forward out of the problems of modernity (and of modernisation) into a new post-modern condition.

Portoghesi had also written in his Introduction that 'A kind of new renaissance is . . . being outlined which intends to recover certain aspects of the past, not to interrupt history, but to arrest its paralysis', and goes on to add to his above arguments that his text 'accuses the modern city of being the product of an alliance between bureaucracy and totalitarianism', and singles out the great error of modern architecture not in its use of post-industrial forces, but 'in the break of historical continuity'.[25] Portoghesi also goes on to write of the new post-modern architecture as an architecture of communication in terms similar to those used by Jencks, if with some greater emphasis on the 'imagistic' quality of its buildings: 'The Postmodern in architecture can . . . be read overall as a reemergence of archetypes, or as a reintegration of architectonic conventions, and thus as a premise to the creation of an *architecture of communication*, and architecture of the image for a civilization of the image.'[26]

In addition to sharing Jencks's belief in the interaction of post-industrial technologies with post-modernist architecture, and in the goal of achieving greater communication, Portoghesi has also appeared to agree with Jencks's belief in the capacity of post-modernist classicism to restore at least some of the values missing from modernism by providing some exempla of past historical conventions against which the new may be constructed and evaluated. Portoghesi writes:

Classicism is not a style, but a way of looking at architecture as one of man's institutions. It is no longer understood as the art of a perfect and balanced society to be nostalgically evoked, but as a way of thinking about architecture that makes use of certain historical invariants of the collective memory, of the possibility of agreeing by referring to a patrimony of conventions . . . shared critically by society.[27]

Portoghesi also writes of the new architecture that it is 'certainly closer to the majority of the people than that technocratic architecture which arose from the crisis of the Modern Movement because it constantly borrows from a common patrimony', and goes on to relate it to a new set of 'universal values': 'It is inalienable and stamped on the minds of everyone through the common experience of historical space, because it makes an appeal to conventions of universal value corresponding not to ideological superstructures, but to permanent characteristics of the perception and appropriation of space.'[28]

Whether all the characteristics of the 'perception and appropriation of space' may be regarded as 'permanent' while still allowing for some variations between the individual agents involved in that same 'perception' and 'appropriation' may, of course, be questioned, although it may also be countered that Portoghesi need not mean that all of these factors be regarded as permanent in the sense of preventing change or variation. Indeed, in addition to going on to speak of 'the return to symmetry and repetition' as symptomatic of the return to older conventions, Portoghesi also suggests that this allows greater freedom of choice to the individual architect than the 'intolerant and authoritarian prohibition' of these conventions by such as Bruno Zevi in his *The Modern Language of Architecture*.[29]

Portoghesi proceeds to quote from a manifesto of the Polish

union Solidarity, criticising the 'totalitarianism' of twentieth-century architecture:

Totalitarianism, the principle feature of 20th century architecture, is not only the result of socio-political systems. Blind faith in progress, the mythology of science and technology, the huge numbers involved in the increasing population, pluralism confused with chaos, all this has created the belief that man himself does not know how he must dwell and live. And that in its place it is up to architecture to know ... The architecture of our century opposes ideology to life, projects to reality. Instead of making our profession a task more and more complicated and further removed from reality, an architectural continuity must be recovered which searches for new fundamental architectural ideas such as style, method and dogma.[30]

Portoghesi himself writes with reference to the need for a new 'postindustrial' concept of the city in his chapter on 'The Post-industrial City: Between Zeal and Indolence', that 'our cities have ... lost the capacity to express the values of society, collective wishes, and the role of institutions'.[31] Earlier, Portoghesi's concern with the capacity for post-modern architecture to return to basic human values had also been reflected in a chapter on Aldo Rossi's *Teatro del Mondo* from the Venice Biennale of 1980 and what he saw to be its comments on the 'meaning of the human condition'. Here, however, he had also gone on to follow André Gorz in writing that 'society will never be "good" by virtue of its organization, but only by reason of the spaces of autonomy, self-organization and voluntary co-operation that it offers to individuals'.[32] It is also in this spirit that Portoghesi proceeds to interpret Alain Touraine's call for 'spaces without norms' as a call for 'spaces in which people will be able to recognize their aspiration to the development of a free personality', but also to a 'new intensity of social relationships';[33] the norms which are absent from the 'spaces without norms' being the norms of the 'bureaucratic apparatus' of which Portoghesi had also spoken in the beginning of his book as one of the causes of the problems of the modern city.[34]

Portoghesi continues in a more optimistic vein than either Touraine or Baudrillard on the fate of the post-industrial city:

We live in the information age, and we will learn to read the city as a system of signs, a whole of possible itineraries, from the daily itinerary to the contemplative one of the tourist. These routes must intertwine not by chance, and act on the city with the cautiousness of the farmer who carries out his grafting, making diversity possible in continuity.[35]

Having said this, Portoghesi also goes on to complain of the 'total pessimism' of 'certain communist intellectuals' about the survival of intellectual work, and to see this as yet another symptom of problems which are to be challenged in the new post-industrial society.[36]

Although Portoghesi's call on thinkers like Lyotard and Touraine might appear to give his theory of post-modernism a different direction from Jencks's, most of his ideas, including his basic call for post-modern architecture to be seen as a way of returning both aesthetic and ethical values to modernity which have been lost by the modernist break with history, are not incompatible with those of Jencks, and even echo and expand many of the thoughts put forward in Jencks's 1977 work.[37]

While Portoghesi's work is also interesting from the point of view of this survey of the varieties of theories about the post-modern and the post-industrial for its combination of a variety of concepts of both the post-modern and the post-industrial, and from that body of post-modernist theory which we have termed deconstructionist as well as from the theories of post-modern architecture of Jencks, it should however be noted that the search for a post-modernist set of values has not only followed in the divergent tracks laid down for it by such as Lyotard and Jencks, or sought to bring them together as in the writings of Portoghesi, but has also produced a rejection of both of these schools of thought and a suggestion of an ideal form of post-modernism which is independent of them from the critic Peter Fuller.[38]

Peter Fuller

Peter Fuller's essay 'The Search for a Postmodern Aesthetic' is but one work by him which has opposed an ideal post-modern aesthetic to already existing theories of post-modernism, as well as to the modernisms which have been rejected, criticised or reformed by the latter.[39] In it Fuller wrote critically of both modernism and existing post-modernist alternatives after having offered a critique of Loos's famous 'modernist' dictum that ornament was a crime:

Of course much has changed since Loos' day; indeed the concerns of Loos, and many of his contemporaries, seem almost quaint in the era of the new electronics. None the less, I believe that many of the most significant and destructive Modernist assumptions are built into those design movements which are commonly described as 'Post-Modernist'.[40]

Fuller continued: 'A genuinely "postmodern" design aesthetic will not be possible until those assumptions have been examined and eradicated. Indeed, the constructive tasks facing designers today are ... essentially *conservationist* and *recuperative*.'

Fuller's essay also specifically related the above tasks to Ruskin's call for the artist to 'go to Nature in all singleness of heart',[41] while his *Theoria: Art, and the Absence of Grace* of 1988 went on to suggest that 'Ruskin's critical enterprise', his search for value in art, had made him into the 'first post-modernist'.[42] In addition to making this latter claim, Fuller's *Theoria* argued that Ruskin, in volume II of his *Modern Painters* of 1846, had drawn a 'distinction between what he called *aesthesis* and *theoria*'. While the former was described as ' "mere sensual perception of the outward qualities and necessary effects of bodies" or "the mere animal consciousness of the pleasantness" to which such effects can give rise', the latter was defined 'as the response to beauty of one's whole moral being'.[43]

Although Fuller's Ruskin is also 'post-modern' in the sense of some of Jencks's post-modernists in valuing ornament against structure, the ornament most valued by him is not that of the classical arts, but of the Gothic.[44] Further to this, Fuller's ideal post-modernism not only appears still to exist only in its past Ruskinian 'prototype' and not in present reality, in contrast, for example, to the 'Post-Modern Classicism' described by Jencks, but Fuller had also gone on in his *Theoria* to criticise explicitly both Lyotard's and Jencks's criteria for the post-modern.[45] What is common to both for Fuller was, moreover, their apparent approval of a relativity of values and/or codes:

The post-modernists began to say that the certainties of modernism – its meta-narratives, in Jean-François Lyotard's overused phrase – could only be replaced by self-conscious incredulity about everything. Post-modernism knows no commitments: it takes up what one of its leading exponents, Charles Jencks, once called a 'situational position' in which 'no code is inherently better than any other'.[46]

While Fuller's description of Lyotard's position may be accepted, the projection of its relativism onto Jencks's variety of post-modernism must be questioned, and not only on the basis of Jencks's 1986 alignment of himself with Fuller on the question of value, but also because of Jencks's own criticisms of Lyotard's relativism and attempts to support some specific values whilst also arguing for a pluralism of codes.

Here it should however also not be forgotten that differences between Fuller and Jencks include Jencks's development of an ideal 'public' language for post-modernism which is classical rather than Gothic; is based on actual recent developments in architecture; involves the 'double-coding' of modernism with other 'codes'; and is not based on the Ruskinian premisses of Fuller's ideal post-modernism. As Fuller's essay 'Towards a New Nature for the Gothic' makes clear, he, furthermore, had regarded the dual-coding of modernism with something else in the post-modernism defended by Jencks as continuing the ills of modernism rather than as overcoming them, and as constituting, therefore, something which was for him a less than ideal post-modern alternative to the modern.[47] In addition to making it clear that any post-modernism which is antipathetic to the dual-coding of modernism with other codes may not be truly 'post-modern', Jencks has seen Fuller's ideal post-modernism as not being truly post-modern in asking for little more than a return to pre-modern values.

Despite the fact that Fuller's presentation of his ideal post-modernism as one which will both reject the modernist relativisation of values and restore the Ruskinian value of 'rediscovering the aesthetic and spiritual meanings in nature' had involved a return to what may be described as pre-modern values,[48] his application of those pre-modern values to the post-industrial had created an amalgam of ideas which, although ambiguous, was, however, not wholly backwards-looking. In his article entitled 'Art and Post-Industrialism', for example,

Fuller had suggested that the computer world of the second industrial revolution was both here to stay and in need of the assistance of the arts,[49] while he had also gone on in an interview entitled 'Towards a Fuller Meaning of Art' to present his ideal post-industrial society as one which was to see post-industrial technology free people for a greater and more meaningful involvement in the production of art: 'Fully automated production, the electronic revolution, has made Morris's Utopia a much more practical and feasible proposition.'[50]

While the second edition of Jencks's *The Language of Post-Modern Architecture* of 1977 had described Daniel Bell's concept of the post-industrial society in terms which are to some extent similar to Fuller's description of the post-industrial as freeing people for a richer aesthetic life,[51] his later works had spoken of how the computer could be put to use in the actual design of buildings and their environment[52] so that the process of design itself is shared with the machine in a manner not necessarily approvable by Morris. Here it is however interesting to note that Fuller's essay 'The Search for a Postmodern Aesthetic' had also suggested both that a new (post-modernist) aesthetic will be based on an 'imaginative response to nature', and that it is 'just here that the higher mathematics, physics and new information processing procedures, associated with advances in computer technology, can help'.[53] Fuller continued: 'Of course, a new aesthetic will spring out of new beliefs, not out of a new technology; but like Modernism itself, the post-modern structures and patterns will be informed and shaped by new technologies.'

Although Fuller added that these latter beliefs will also be 'expressive of very different sorts of values' (from modernism), and will be 'of traditional and conservative values' which will 'emphasize our sense of belonging to and unity with the Nature of which we are a part', his juxtaposition of contemporary post-industrial technology with the values of Ruskin and Morris here not only brought him further forward than Penty, who – in his antagonism to the industrial uses of machinery he saw around him and in the absence of any other present or future alternative to them – could see no other way to go forward than to go back to a 'pre-industrial' form of 'post-industrialism',[54] but again produced a new if still somewhat enigmatic juxtaposition of 'pre-modern' aesthetics with some selected ideas from more recent post-industrialist theory.

In so far as Fuller's common denominator for his ideal post-industrial and post-modern societies was the Ruskinian values which were to inform them, there also appeared to be no problem for him in seeing the post-modern and the post-industrial as being potentially wholly complementary rather than as either wholly or partially antagonistic to each other, as is the case in some other theories of post-modernism. When or whether such an ideal harmony of the post-modern and the post-industrial is ever to be achieved in practice, and what this would look like in detail, is, however, still to be seen, and was not fully outlined in Fuller's work before his untimely death in April 1990.

Despite its incompleteness, Fuller's work on post-modernism, like Jencks's, has been important because, not least, of its insistence that the question of value be a part of the post-modern aesthetic. Although Habermas has discussed the need for a new intersubjective achievement of consensus on values which would also see an interconnection of the ethical and aesthetic spheres,[55] his simultaneous defence of the project of modernity and criticism of post-modernism has, as seen previously, not suggested any future form or role for the latter in the establishment of new values. While Habermas might also find Fuller's values insufficient for the battle against the negative forces of modernisation,[56] and regard his criticisms of modernism as another 'rejection of the project of modernity',[57] there would seem, however, to be no necessary reason why those criticisms (like those of Jencks and of others like him criticised by Habermas) might not also lead to the suggestion of some further alternative values for the post-modern which could assist in analysing and resolving at least some of the problems of modernity which it had been the task of the 'project of modernity' to resolve.

Conclusion

As Fuller's moves towards pursuing the question of value in post-modernism suggest, there is still much to be done in this field because of the relativist bases of many of the deconstructionist varieties of post-modernism which still proliferate and the silencing of questions of value which has resulted from them.[58] In addition to the deconstructionist theories of post-modernism discussed in chapter 3, one of the contributors to the programme *State of the Art*,[59] Victor Burgin, for instance, has continued the attack on what Jameson and others have described as the modernist valorisation of high art, and described post-modernism as bringing the end of what he sees as the concept of art as a 'sphere of "higher" values, independent of history, social forms and the unconscious'.[60] Here a deconstructionist view of post-modernism as abolishing the 'great divide' between high art and mass culture is also contrasted to the 'Greenbergian' concept of modernism as one in which the avant-garde will ' "keep culture moving" by raising art to "the expression of an absolute in which all relativities and contradictions would be either resolved or beside the point" '.[61]

Value is not necessarily excluded altogether from the post-modern here, but does appear to be reduced, or at least restricted, to what Burgin describes in the concluding lines of his *The End of Art Theory* as a 'critical understanding of the modes and means of symbolic articulation of our *critical* forms of sociality and subjectivity'. While Burgin seeks to place art and art theory back into a context where they are not conceived of as autonomous fields of value, their own resulting value appears to be understood to rest largely in their critical, and deconstructionist functions, rather than in the establishment of any new specific values relevant to the variety of spheres to which they are said to belong. Although many deconstructionist post-modernists have thought such a depiction of the post-modern to be sufficient, both Fuller and Jencks have been seen to have suggested in their different ways that such deconstructionist views need to be replaced by a concept of art which will see it as aspiring to some specific positive values, rather than just to claiming the truths of others to be relative to their value judgements.

Here we might also suggest that with all enquiries into the values espoused by post-modernists it should be asked:

1.   What do they mean by the word 'value'?
2.   What do they mean by the particular value they espouse (to

begin, how would they define the particular value they
support)?

3.   What are their targets?
4.   What are their goals?
5.   What are their arguments for the above, and how well
     argued are they?
6.   What consequences (intended and unintended) could their
     values have in the future?
7.   What are the values which we are using in evaluating the
     above, and how well grounded are they?

Not all of the answers to these questions will, of course, be
immediately obvious. Although the title of John Fekete's *Life
After Postmodernism* suggests that it may be yet another rejection of post-modernism in general, Fekete's own project is described as seeing post-modernism open up the question of value
again by going beyond that which he calls 'the positivist–
modernist tradition, with its antinomic "fact–value" structure'[62]
so that 'the postmodern paradigm shift may place value-theoretical interventions into positions of far greater esteem'.[63] Fekete,
moreover, not only presents himself as wanting to encourage a
deconstruction of the fact–value opposition which will show our
explanation of facts to have involved a value-based interpretation of some kind, but also describes his overall goal in terms
similar to some 'Lyotardian' post-modernists as being to achieve
'an emerging intertextual discursive field in which the point of
view of value orientation may disseminate, in which value commentary may take the form of an intervention, and in which a
value-theoretical approach may hold greater attractions than the
representations of the onto-epistemological tradition'.[64]

In addition to the problems already found in the Lyotardian
view of the post-modern outlined in earlier chapters, problems
for the future development of the concept of the post-modern
here may include ones arising from the intended or unintended
restriction of the concept of value to the value-judgements of
those proposing or defending certain values, including the
revival of a relativist fallacy that the existence of a variety of
different value-judgements may be said to mean that no one
value can be said to be more correct or valuable than another.[65]

Further to the above it might also be asked with regard to Fekete's arguments why the shift away from the 'fact–value' distinction should be called post-modernist in the first place.[66] Not only has the so-called positivist insistence on the distinction been challenged by modernists such as the members of the early Frankfurt School as well as by Habermas,[67] but, as Fekete himself acknowledges,[68] one recent contribution to this debate has been made by the sociologist and social theorist Anthony Giddens, who has also offered several criticisms of the post-structuralist theory to which at least some of Fekete's arguments have been aligned.[69]

Giddens writes, for instance, of the post-structuralist decentring of the subject that

> Structuralist and post-structuralist accounts of the decentring of the subject are inevitably closely tied to the versions of language and the unconscious associated with structuralist linguistics and its influence. The detour needed to recover the 'I' is not only taken very largely through language, but is in addition filtered through a particular theory of language as well. If we regard language as situated in social practices, and if we reject the distinction between consciousness and unconscious followed by the structuralist and post-structuralist authors, we reach a different conception of the human subject – as agent.[70]

As in his *The Constitution of Society* of 1984, Giddens also relates his subject to the contexts which may constrain or enable action: 'In speaking of the contextuality of action, I mean to rework the differentiation between presence and absence. Human social life may be understood in terms of relations between individuals moving in time–space, linking both action and context, and differing contexts with another.'[71] If all of these factors were to be considered in a post-modern theory of the subject, then the latter would, moreover, also have to be seen in the context of the factors of both agency and constraint of the society in which it develops and acts, and not just in terms of the one or the other factor stressed by some of the theories of the post-modern discussed in earlier chapters, although some might also wish to argue counterfactually (as has Giddens himself in his recent *The Consequences of Modernity*) that a post-modern society would see the transformation of such factors in some way.

As seen previously, there are now a great variety of theories of the post-modern as well as of post-industrial society. To describe the dissolution of the 'fact–value' distinction as post-modern not only needs some explanation of why, or how, it comes after, rejects or transforms the *modernist* challenges to that opposition, but also how the post-modernism which it represents relates to, or contrasts with, other active forms of post-modernism, including those which have been critical of relativism.[72] To some post-modernists, as seen earlier, only a 'post-relativist', rather than a 'neo-relativist', set of theories will, furthermore, be truly 'post-modern'.

Failure to distinguish between the deconstructionist post-modernisms and the other forms of post-modernism we have discussed here has also appeared to lead to the rejection of post-modernism as a whole by some who might have been more sympathetic to it had they been made more aware of its different varieties and possibilities.

Andreas Huyssen's claim in his 'Mapping the Postmodern' that it is 'somewhat baffling that feminist criticism has so far largely stayed away from the postmodernism debate', answers its own question by adding that the latter 'is considered not to be pertinent to feminist concerns',[73] although his own conception of what constitutes that debate might also be said to have led him, like others, away from both the discussion of some post-modernisms which are of potential use to feminist theoreticians as well as from a fuller account of the many different varieties of post-modernist architecture in which women practitioners and theoreticians have already played significant roles.[74] Despite the above problems it may, however, be said that it was none the less true that at the time at which Huyssen's essay was written there had not yet developed any substantial body of theory which might be termed either 'feminist post-modernism', or 'post-modernist feminism'.

Clearly, the concept of the latter form of post-modernism has also been of concern to at least some feminist theoreticians. Whilst a feminist post-modernism could wish to turn post-modernism towards specifically feminist issues by questioning further some of the assumptions of modern theory on the place of women in the family or the work-place, and from the specific points of view of women, a post-modernist feminism might well be understood as having the task of questioning some of the dominant feminist theories of the modern period as well as the variety of modern theories on which some of them have been based, such as, for instance, structuralist Marxism and Deconstruction.

While there is already a move away from the deconstructionist diminution of the subject in recent feminist theory, some feminist theorists moving in this direction have also identified post-modernism with what we have specified as deconstructionist post-modernism, and criticised it not only for its failure to provide an adequate theory of the woman subject as agent,[75] but also for its elimination of difference between subjects in a way which they believe threatens the concepts of gender difference developed in feminist theory as a basis for both theory and practice. E. Ann Kaplan, for instance, has suggested in her article 'Feminism/Oedipus/Postmodernism: The Case of MTV', in her *Postmodernism and its Discontents* of 1988, that the break-down of difference suggested in many theories of post-modernism might threaten the feminist establishment of its categories of 'difference'.[76] What again needs to be spelt out here, however, is that the type of post-modernism being spoken of in this instance is only one particular type of post-modernism, and not the only variety already available.[77] In so far, for example, as the post-modernism of Jencks has suggested a return to the subject, together with some awareness of the constraints upon it, that post-modernism at least may be seen to be offering some new possibilities for women as well as for men to take on the role of rational agents in the post-modern and post-industrial worlds.[78] What such a theory also implies, however, is that the all too uncritical acceptance of ready-made ideologies – of either a modernist or post-modernist kind – will not be a feature of the thoughts or actions of such rational agents.

Here too some further distinctions between the post-modernisms discussed in this and previous chapters may also be made by the reader. While some post-modern theories have clearly revived or continued older ideologies, despite their claims to a critical questioning of the 'metanarratives of modernity', others have offered much that is new in terms of both their questioning of previous theories and their more positive suggestions for the establishment of new values, including that of the use of the new post-industrial technologies to achieve a greater rational communication between subjects. To achieve the latter goal it is, however, also clear that we shall need both to understand as well as is possible what the various post-modernisms have been saying (both overtly and covertly), and to lay the ground-work for the more explicit description of their nature and goals in the future. No plea for the return of value to post-modern culture or post-industrial society will be able to be heard if we do not also value both the accurate rather than the merely 'playful' interpretation of discourse, and the logical development of concepts and arguments. It cannot be the case, moreover, that 'anything goes' in the interpretation of post-modernist texts, and even when a text appears to be stating that claim as a principle.[79]

It was in the belief that the literature on post-modernism of recent years had created a need for a critical reading of its various, and often contradictory, claims and assumptions that this book was begun. Although it will end with only some of the recently published literature on the subject discussed in depth, it is hoped that its readers will continue the work of clarifying some of the many confusions and misleading or unclear distinctions made in the literature on the post-modern, as well as the task of developing some of the more potentially valuable ideas to be found in it. In line with the general aims of this work to provide an overview of the development of the most influential concepts of post-modern and of its related concepts to date, and a critical guide to both their interpretation and the interpretation of other theories based upon them, the following Conclusion will offer a summary of some of the major theories of the post-industrial and the post-modern discussed throughout the preceding text, and some concluding comments on the problems of defining and evaluating them.

6

CONCLUSION AND SUMMARY

'The future is not what it was.'

We have now come to a stage in the history of the use of the term post-modern where it is not only necessary for the post-modernist theorist to define his or her own use of the terms 'modernism' and 'post', but where it would also seem necessary for the term to be defined against, or with at least some reference to, the many other definitions of that term, and of its related concept of the post-industrial society, which are still in use.

As seen previously, earlier uses of the term post-industrial, and contributions to the development of contemporary theories of it, have included the following:

1914 Ananda K. Coomaraswamy and Arthur J. Penty's *Essays in Post-Industrialism: a Symposium of Prophecy concerning the Future of Society*. While Coomaraswamy's contribution was entitled 'The Religious Foundation of Art and Life', Penty's was on the unsuitability of industrial products for architecture and the impossibility of forming any new architecture from them.

1917 Penty's *Old Worlds for New: a Study of the Post-Industrial State*, in which he criticised the sub-divisions of labour of industrial society and argued for a return to the precepts of pre-industrial Guild society.[1]

1922 Penty's *Post-Industrialism*, in which he returns to his earlier criticisms of the sub-divisions of industrial society and also criticises those socialists who have concentrated on the capitalist rather than the industrial effects of society.

169

1958 David Riesman's depiction of post-industrial society as a new 'leisure society'.

1959 Daniel Bell's use of the term 'post-industrial society' in a series of lectures in Salzburg to denote a society 'which has passed from a goods-producing stage to a service society'.[2]

1962 Bell's paper 'The Post-Industrial Society: a Speculative View of the United States in 1958 and Beyond', in which Bell turns his attention to the role played by intellectual technology and science in social change.

1968 Amitai Etzioni's description of the post-modern society as one characterised by the 'radical transformation of the technologies of communication, knowledge and energy that followed World War Two'.

1969 Alain Touraine's text, *The Post-Industrial Society, Tomorrow's Social History: Classes, Conflicts and Culture in the Programmed Society* and his use of the term post-industrial to describe a new type of 'technocratic' or 'programmed' society.[3]

1970 Zbigniew Brzezinski's discussion of a 'technetronic' society dominated by the new technologies and electronics of the post-war years, in his *Between Two Ages: America's Role in the Technetronic Era.*

1970 Alvin Toffler's picture of future society as one dominated by both new technologies and their effects in his *Future Shock* of 1970.[4]

1973 Daniel Bell's *The Coming of Post-Industrial Society* and his description of post-industrial society as characterised by changes in: (1) the economic sector – the change from a goods-producing to a service-economy; (2) occupational distribution – the pre-eminence of the professional and technical class; (3) axial principle – the centrality of theoretical knowledge as the source of innovation and of policy formulation for the society; (4) future orientation – the control of technology and technological assessment; (5) decision-making – the creation of a new 'intellectual technology'.[5]

1980 André Gorz's description of the post-industrial society in his *Farewell to the Working Class: an essay on Post-Industrial Socialism* (Paris 1980 and London 1982) as one in which workers will, ideally, be able to work in their own freely chosen time.

1986 Peter Fuller's suggestion of a new concept of post-industrialism in which Morris's idea of utilising machinery to leave men and women free for artistic creation is applied to the new computer technologies.

Many other uses of the idea of the post-industrial could, of course, be given here, and some of these have also been referred to in the text or notes of previous chapters. A summary would, however, not be a summary if it reproduced every statement, and some selection has been made in both the above list and the one which follows on the basis of either the originality of the definitions discussed in earlier pages, or their importance for the development of the major concepts studied in this work. As seen earlier, many recent theories of the post-modern have also specified their own understanding of how the post-industrial society may be described.

Uses of the terms post-modern and post-modernism and their understandings of the post-industrial discussed in previous pages of this text have included:

1934 Federico de Onis's use of the term 'postmodernismo' to describe the Spanish and Latin-American poetry of 1905–14 which had reacted against the 'excesses' of modernism.

1939 Arnold J. Toynbee's use of the phrase 'the Post-Modern Age' to describe the period from 1914 onwards.

1942 Dudley Fitts and H. R. Hays's translation of the term 'postmodernismo' to describe the Latin-American poetry of both before and after Dario's death in 1916 which had reacted against the decorative excesses of (Symbolist) modernism.

1945 Bernard Smith's 'post-Modernism' of the 1940s, understood, amongst other things, as a new 'social-realist' reaction to modernist abstraction.

1945 Joseph Hudnut's 'post-modern house', describing the

(ultra-modern) prefabricated house of the then immediate future.

1946 D. C. Somervell's description of Arnold J. Toynbee's 'Post-Modern Age' as stretching from the year 1875 on.

1954 Arnold J. Toynbee's use of the term 'post-Modern' to describe the age, from *circa* 1875 on, which saw the decline of the 'Modern' middle classes and the rise of a new Western proletariat as well as the growth of other non-Western nations and their proletariats, non-Christian religions, cults and new 'post-Modern' sciences.

1959 C. Wright Mills's use of the phrase 'a post-modern period' in his *The Sociological Imagination* to describe a new 'Fourth Epoch' which he saw as succeeding 'The Modern Age' and as being characterised by the collapse of the latter's Enlightenment ideals.

1959 Irving Howe's 'Mass Society and Postmodern Fiction', in which he spoke of the new mass society as eliminating many of the moral and aesthetic bases on which modernism and its classics had been based.

1960 Harry Levin's 'What Was Modernism?' and contrast of the post-modern fiction which he saw to be popularising the achievements of the more experimental modernists with the innovatory nature of the latter.

1965 Leslie Fiedler's use of the term 'post-Modernist literature', to describe a new interest in the future nature of human-kind in contemporary writing, and use of the term 'post-modernist' to describe some of the 'counter-cultures' of the 1960s in which the more mystical, anti-rational and anti-Protestant beings of the future were becoming evident.

1966 and 1967 Nikolaus Pevsner's 'post-modern style' to describe a new expressionism and extremism in architecture, as well as both a new 'eclecticism' and 'contradiction of form and function'.[6]

1968 Amitai Etzioni's description of the 'post-modern period' as one characterised by the 'radical transformation of the tech-

nologies of communication, knowledge and energy that followed World War Two'.

1969 Leslie Fiedler's suggestions that 'Post-Modernist literature'
had 'crossed the gap' between high and popular culture and
expanded the popular, and that this development had also
raised the question of what form a new 'Post-Modernist criticism' might take.

1971 Ihab Hassan's 'postmodernism' to describe a variety of
aesthetic, literary, technological and philosophic deconstructions of the canons of modernism and increase in 'indetermi-
nancy'.

1975 Charles Jencks's use of the term 'Post-Modern' to describe
a move away from the Modern Movement in architecture, but
also some of the new criteria for architecture developed in his
later works.[7]

1976 Daniel Bell's attack on modernism and on post-modernism
understood in Fiedler's sense as a new irrationality in his *The
Cultural Contradictions of Capitalism*, and contrast of both to
the principles of the Protestant ethic underlying earlier forms
of modern Western society.[8]

1977 Charles Jencks's *The Language of Post-Modern Architecture* and its description of a new multivalence of styles and
codes in architecture.

1977 Robert Stern's description of the three principles of post-
modernism as being 'Contextualism', 'Allusionism' and
'Ornamentalism'.[9]

1977 Michael Koehler's periodisation of 'postmodernism' from
1970 on and contrast of it to late-modernism.[10]

1978 The second edition of Charles Jencks's *The Language of
Post-Modern Architecture*, and the description of 'Post-
Modern' architecture as a double-coding of one code with
another.

1979 Jean-François Lyotard's *The Postmodern Condition* and
the description of the 'postmodern' as the deconstruction of
the meta-narratives of modernity, and of the post-industrial

society as a techno-scientific society which is also aligned in some respects with the meta-narratives of capitalism, and, hence, in need of some post-modernist criticism.[11]

1980 Jencks's tabling of differences between the 'Modern', the 'Late-Modern' and the 'Post-Modern', and development of his idea of 'Post-Modern Classicism'.

1980 Robert Stern's distinction in his 'The Doubles of Post-Modern' between a 'schismatic' post-modernism that argues for a break with Western humanism and a 'traditional' post-modernism that argues for a return to its traditions.[12]

1980 Paolo Portoghesi's organisation of the exhibition of post-modern architecture in the Venice Biennale of 1980 under the title of 'The Presence of the Past', and defence of post-modern 'historicism'.[13]

1980 Habermas's Adorno Prize lecture and its attack on both the post-modernist architecture shown in the Venice Biennale of 1980 as turning its back on the 'project of modernity', and on the 'neo-conservatives' who 'push the blame' for the problems of modernity onto cultural modernism.

1981 Habermas's 'Modern and Postmodern Architecture' essay, and the extension of his 1980 attack on post-modernist architecture.[14]

1981 Jean Baudrillard's description of post-modernity in his 'On Nihilism' as the 'destruction of meaning'.

1982 Lyotard's 'Answering the Question: What is Postmodernism?', and the development of a notion of 'postmodern sublime', as well as the suggestion that post-modernist architecture has thrown out the experimental elements of modernism and developed its capitalist aspects.

1982 Paolo Portoghesi's book, *Postmodern: the Architecture of the Postindustrial Society*, in which he points out, amongst other things, that the term 'postmodern' should not be thought of 'as a label designating homogeneous and convergent things', but that 'its usefulness lies, rather, in its having allowed us temporarily to put together and compare different things [including the return to history and classical tradition] arising from a common dissatisfaction with that group of equally heterogeneous things called modernity', and in which he describes the post-industrial society as a society in which the 'new electronic technology' has turned our age into an age of information and communication.

1983 Fredric Jameson's use of the term 'postmodernism' to attack post-modernist architecture as part of the culture of capital, and projection of a Baudrillardian concept of modern parody onto the pastiche of post-modern architecture.

1984 Fredric Jameson's projection of the term 'postmodernist' onto John Portman's late-modern Bonaventure Hotel and description of the post-industrial society as 'late capitalist'.

1984 Andreas Huyssen's development of ideas such as that found in Fiedler that 'postmodernism' attempts to cross the modernist divide between high and low art (also found in Hassan, and in Jameson where it is also related to his identification of post-modern architecture and the 'pop culture' of capitalism).

1984 Hal Foster's suggestion that there are two forms of 'postmodernism': 'neoconservative' (Humanist) 'postmodernism' and 'post-structuralist' 'postmodernism', but that both assume some death, or deconstruction, of the subject.

1984 Heinrich Klotz's *The History of Postmodern Architecture*, and his description of post-modern architecture as 'fiction as well as function'.

1986 Jencks's development of his criticisms of Hassan, Lyotard, Jameson and Foster as presenting descriptions of postmodernism which in fact describe the 'Late-Modern'.

1987 Jencks's rules for 'Post-Modern Classicism'.

1988 Peter Fuller's development of his criticisms of both deconstructionist and double-coded 'post-modernism' in his *Theoria*, and suggestion of a more ideal post-modernism which would take up the Ruskinian value of 'theoria'.[15]

Further details of all of the concepts of post-modernism summarised above, and of their concepts of the post-industrial, can
of course be found, together with details of theories of both the
post-modern and the post-industrial not summarised here, in
the chapters preceding this Conclusion.

As also suggested in previous pages, many of the more recent
concepts of post-modernism may be placed in the broader categories of 'deconstructionist', 'double-coded' and 'ideal' post-
modernisms. Within these categories, deconstructionist post-
modernism may be said to have criticised modernist value
systems of various kinds (for Hassan, the old canons of modernism; for Lyotard, the 'metanarratives' of modernity – of capitalism, progress and consensus; for Jameson the 'culture of capital';
for Burgin, Greenberg's valorisation of high modernist art; or for
Fekete that which he terms the 'modern' 'fact–value' distinction), as well as some other rival forms of post-modernism which
they have seen to be antipathetic to theirs. Further to this, and in
opposition to many of the deconstructionist theories outlined
above, Charles Jencks's theory of post-modernism as a double-
coding of modernism with other codes has presented the post-
modern as both incorporating and transforming modernism,
while ideal post-modernisms such as Fuller's have expressed
dissatisfaction with both of the above sets of theories and looked
to the future establishment of values which are both 'post' the
'modern' and all earlier theories dubbed post-modern.[16]

While a purpose of this text has been to point to as many
specific differences between the various uses of post-modernism
and post-industrial as is possible in the space available, it has
also been necessary to suggest these three broader categories in
order to point to the major philosophical differences between
many of the theorists concerned, and to alert the attention of
those who have up to now spoken of post-modernism as based
on but one *Weltanschauung* to the very wide differences in
philosophy between many of those now using the same term.[17]

Again it cannot be emphasised enough that in discussing any
theory of the post-modern or post-industrial it will be necessary
to try to determine both the specific way in which the 'modern'
or the 'industrial' is understood and the specific meaning given
the prefix 'post', as well as to specify the different definers used

by a theorist or practitioner for the designation of a work or theory as 'post' the modern or the industrial. Sometimes it may, of course, not be easy or even possible to pin a theory of the post-modern or the post-industrial down to any specific understanding of its various components if its theorist has not been aware of the need to make his or her use of them clear, or consistent. In such instances it may, moreover, be the case that the theory of the post-modern or the post-industrial offered by such theorists will be of little value to others wishing to define or understand either the nature or the possibilities of these concepts. Here it should also be acknowledged that not every theory of the post-modern or the post-industrial will be as clearly explained as another, or present a theory which goes beyond other theories, or be of as great a use as others in explaining contemporary society, or in predicting or planning the future.

Given the above, some may also wish to take note of Frank Kermode's conclusion to his *History and Value* of 1988 on the confusions surrounding the term post-modernism when used to describe a new historical period and his suggestion that if something is to have value, then we must have the ability 'so to construct history that the valued object stands out from the unvalued and belongs to a totality of literature rather than to an archive of hopelessly diverse documents'.[18]

As suggested elsewhere in this work, theories of the post-modern and the post-industrial have, despite their many differences, also now come to form a body of literature in which not only the modern, modernism, modernisation or modernity have been defined as phenomena or traditions of the past to be criticised or transformed, but new ideals or goals set for the future. While much, if not all, of the literature on the post-modern and the post-industrial has been of this kind, it is, however, still up to ourselves to understand and evaluate both the new ideals or goals set up by its various authors and their evaluations of the past.

While I have done as much as was possible in the time and space available to me to both criticise and clarify some of the confusions surrounding the definition of the post-modern, and of the related concept of the post-industrial, I have also been aware that because of the still burgeoning literature on these subjects, some readers may wish to carry on the task of hunting down presuppositions and tying them up into appropriately labelled sacks as a part of the process of understanding and evaluating the theories in question for themselves.[19] I have, therefore, also attempted to lay down some ground-rules for the definition of the post-modern and the post-industrial (such as, most basically, the clear definition of the meaning of all of the terms involved in these concepts), as well to give examples of the most influential definitions and theorisations of them, or of those definitions or theories which have offered some different or distinct or significant understanding of them or of the works they describe; and together with some critical analysis of the logic of their arguments.[20]

Given that it must now be left to the reader to make his or her own decisions about which concepts to use, and about how to use them, I have also tried to stress both the importance of maintaining a broad awareness of the many different definitions of the post-modern and the post-industrial which exist, and the need for the individual user to be aware of the continuing usefulness of the clear and logical development of any chosen application. Making 'offers no-one can understand' cannot, after all, be the best way for anyone to proceed who wishes to introduce a new, or even old, idea or criticism of any kind. While some may agree that it has unfortunately been characteristic of many of the 'deconstructionist mafias' of the past (to vary the motto of chapter 3 just a little) that offers have been made which few, if any, could really understand (or defend in any logical manner), I am hopeful that the clarity of at least some writers on the subject of the post-modern and its values[21] may finally ensure an informed discussion of the more important issues raised by the many theories of the post-modern discussed here, and enable readers to choose theories which will lead to the establishment of values which are worth having, rather than of ones which are not.[22]

If this book can be said to have its own view on the usefulness of the concepts of the post-modern and the post-industrial discussed in it, it is, furthermore, that those concepts have been particularly useful not only when leading us to question ideologies which have been carried forward into this century from the last (rather than when adding new and often even more questionable ones which will need to be demythologised in the future), but also, as in the case of Charles Jencks and some others, when returning or restoring the idea lost in some late-modern theory of the importance of the subject as someone who is both able to make up their own mind about the ideas and values of the day, and willing and able to communicate these to others.

As suggested in previous pages of the text, although many recent late-modern theories of the post-modern have been presented by their protagonists in a confused and often logically questionable manner, others may hence be seen to have given some hope that both the undervaluation of communication in some aspects of modern and late modern art and life may be challenged, and that some other values may be communicated and agreed upon in the future which will be of benefit to its inhabitants.[23] The statement quoted at the beginning of this chapter,[24] which may also be used to describe the changes in our view of the future produced by the theories just discussed, that 'the future is not what it was', might then even sound quite optimistic.

Notes

Preface

1 Wolfgang Welsch, it should be added, has claimed in his *Unsere postmoderne Moderne* (Weinheim, 1988), pp. 12f., in a passage brought to my attention by Charles Jencks, that the word post-modern was also used as early as the 1870s by the British artist John Watkins Chapman and in 1917 by Rudolf Pannwitz. Given that little was heard of these usages before Welsch's claim (and that Chapman was to be remembered as a painter of genre pictures with titles such as *The Mischievous Model* and *Wooed but not Won*), it is, however, now hard to attribute any great significance to them in the history of the term. As will become clear in the following text, so long as there has been the word modern and the prefix post there has been the possibility of someone speaking of the post-modern, just as the existence of the words industrial and post has made the use of the word post-industrial possible. That with which the following text will be largely concerned is the analysis and history of the more significant uses of those terms for theories of the post-modern and the post-industrial developed in this last century as a critique of existing modern culture or society and/or as a blueprint for the present or the future.

2 While some such as Habermas (see also note 5 below and chapter 3) have suggested that the term post-modernism indicates that the concept has no real identity of its own, it should also be noted that that term now covers several different types of reaction to the modern and that this latter factor now also acts as a common denominator for the post-modern as a generic term.

3 See also the Introduction and following chapters for further discussion of this point. As will be seen in the latter, some uses of the concepts post-modern and post-industrial also see them as breaking less radically from the past than others.

180

4 See also the explanation of the use of the term deconstructionist post-modernism given in the Preface's description of chapter 4.

5 Although he has been one of the strongest critics of post-modernism, the German philosopher and social theorist Juergen Habermas is included in chapter 3 because of both the critical discussion given of his work in that of Lyotard and of his own negative conception of post-modernism as a deconstruction of what he has termed 'the project of modernity'. Other uses of the term post-modern discussed in this section include the recent use made of it in some ethnographic theories, while an appendix to the chapter will also deal with the depiction of modernity in the work of Marshall Berman.

6 As explained in the following piece of text it is also important to note here that Jencks describes the 'Late-Modern' and 'Post-Modern' as running concurrently from 1960 on, and that new developments such as 'Deconstructivist' architecture need not necessarily be post-modern just because they have sprung up at a time in which post-modern architecture is still being built and discussed.

7 See Charles Jencks, *Late-Modern Architecture* (London and New York, 1980), p. 32.

8 See, for example, Jencks's *What is Post-Modernism?* (London 1986), pp. 35ff.

9 With regard to film it should, for instance, be possible to trace the usually deconstructionist post-modernist theories used so far for such analyses by using the Index to find the discussion of the theorists named or used as authorities in those analyses, such as Baudrillard or Jameson, or the concepts borrowed from them, such as 'hyperreality' or 'normless pastiche'. (And see also chapter 1, note 4, on the designation of these words as 'tracers'.) Because this text has also been written so that others may use it to trace the origins of theories or applications of the post-modern and post-industrial not specifically discussed in its pages, it has furthermore used the notes as a way of making connections between the theories being discussed, or their more recent applications, so that these notes should also be regarded as being as important as the text itself, and referred to where possible to gain the maximum information about a particular subject. While some readers may prefer not to have so many notes (although no-one, of course, will make them read them if they do not wish to), to have brought all of the pieces of information contained in them into the text would not only have made the latter less readable, but would also have made the cross-

referencing to particular concepts and ideas through the Index much less precise.

10 Several notes have also been added since the completion of the text of this work on books published after its completion which give some indication of how this work might be used in a reading of others recently published on the subject of the post-modern.

11 Because this book develops several ideas on the problems of defining post-modernism which I presented in a paper on the topic of innovation and tradition in the post-modern to the eleventh International Congress in Aesthetics in Nottingham in 1988 I should also like to take this opportunity to thank the delegates to the latter, and its organisers, for the many helpful comments which were made by them there or in later correspondence. In addition, I should like to thank Professor J. Mordaunt Crook, whose *Dilemma of Style* provides such an elegant discussion of the post-modern in architecture and other related issues, for reading and providing comments on parts of this study; Charles Jencks for his generosity in discussing some of the ideas presented here on his work, and for allowing the reproduction of illustrations from the latter; all others who have in some way contributed thoughts on this subject or comments on the text which follows (some of whom are also specifically named in notes to the appropriate points in the text); Churchill College Cambridge for the Overseas Fellowship which made the completion of the manuscript possible; the Architecture and Planning Branch Library of the University of Melbourne, the British Library and the University Library, Cambridge; my friends and family for their continuing support; and, last, but not least, my editor Judith Ayling, copy-editor Jenny Potts and others at Cambridge University Press who provided their invaluable professional assistance.

Introduction

1 See, for instance, vol. VI of the *Oxford English Dictionary* (Oxford, 1933), p. 573, or the new second edition (Oxford 1989), vol. IX, pp. 947–8, for the various ways in which the term modern has been used in English. Page 947 of the latter also gives an 1864 usage of the term when meaning 'of or pertaining to the present and recent times as distinguished from the remote past' which takes it back to the Renaissance period: 'The close of the 15th century is universally

recognised as ... the starting-point ... of Modern, in distinction from Mediaeval, history.'

2 See again the entry on the word modern in the *Oxford English Dictionary*, 2nd edn, vol. IX, pp. 947–8, and also the entry on modernisation in the *International Encyclopedia of the Social Sciences*, ed. David L. Sills, volume X (London and New York, 1968), pp. 386–409. The concept of modernisation is sometimes also used with reference to the work of Max Weber, Weber having spoken, for example, in his *Economy and Society* (ed. Guenther Roth and Claus Wittich (Berkeley, Los Angeles and London, 1978), vol. I, p. 436) of 'the possibility of rationalising the method of production, which is basic to all modern rational technology, or the possibility of systematically organising a commercial enterprise along the lines of a rational business economy, which is the foundation of modern capitalism' in contrast to the craft-orientated economy of India. But see also Habermas on what he understands to be the misuse of Weber's concept to refer to conditions other than those of modern Western societies and their forms of rationality, in his *The Philosophical Discourse of Modernity* (translated Frederick Lawrence, Oxford and Cambridge, 1987), pp. 2–3.

3 Further discussion of the types of dialectic relevant to this issue is given later, in chapter 4.

4 See also note 9 to the Preface on the way in which the use of certain authorities and their concepts by an author or artist may provide clues to the earlier theories being used in an application.

1 Defining the post-modern

1 See Dick Hebdige, *Hiding in the Light: on Images and Things* (London and New York, 1988), pp. 181ff.

2 See, for example, Ihab Hassan, 'The Question of Postmodernism', in Harry R. Garvin (ed.), *Romanticism, Modernism, Postmodernism (Bucknell Review*, vol. 25, no. 2), (London and Toronto, 1980), p. 120; and Wallace Martin, 'Postmodernism: Ultima Thule or Seim Anew?', in Garvin, *Romanticism, Modernism, Postmodernism*, p. 145.

3 See the discussion of Lyotard's attack on post-modernist architecture in chapter 3. Ironically, the term 'anything goes' (see also chapter 5, note 79) may more accurately describe Lyotard's relativistic stance, although even here a close analysis of his position will show that not everything 'does go', and especially when he is speaking of

targets of his post-modernism which he has described as modernist 'metanarratives'.

4 See the previous note and the following section on Lyotard in chapter 3. The spelling of the term post-modernism without its hyphen is often an indication that the user is following deconstructionist post-modernist theories, although some editorial intervention may also be responsible. (And see note 20 on other reasons for the form 'postmodernism'.) Other 'tracers' (to use a term suggested to me by Charles Jencks to refer to words or concepts from which the origins or theoretical underpinnings of a particular use of the term post-modern may be traced) include the designation, following Jameson, of the Portman Bonaventure Hotel as post-modern rather than as late-modern, the use of concepts such as 'hyperreality' or 'normless pastiche' (and see also the Preface, note 9), and, as suggested in note 10 below, the use, following Hassan, of the concept of indeterminacy. As with all tracings of ideas, other factors involved in the use of similar ideas, such as chance or misunderstanding, will also have to be taken into account, although in most cases there will be other factors involved, such as a direct reference to an author or to his or her other ideas, which may support the use of a 'tracer' in the above manner.

5 Hebdige, *Hiding in the Light*, p. 183.

6 See the section on Lyotard in chapter 3.

7 See Jean Baudrillard, 'The Ecstasy of Communication', in Hal Foster (ed.), *Postmodern Culture* (London, 1985), p. 130. (Because Foster's text was originally published in 1983, although with the title *The Anti-Aesthetic: Essays on Postmodern Culture* and in Port Townsend, Washington, its original publication date will be referred to in the text as 1983.)

8 Jean Baudrillard, 'The Orders of Simulacra', translated by Philip Beitchmann in Jean Baudrillard, *Simulations* (New York, 1983), p. 128.

9 Baudrillard, *Simulations*, p. 83 and pp. 103ff.

10 See chapter 3 on Hassan and the preceding note 4 on the way in which both the spelling of the term post-modernism and the use of certain concepts (such as 'indeterminacy') may act as 'tracers' back to the main theories being followed.

11 See Baudrillard, *Simulations*, p. 111, and the pages on Jameson and his projection of Baudrillard's analyses of modernism onto what Jameson terms 'postmodernism' in chapter 3. Guy Debord's *Society of the Spectacle* (Detroit, 1983) had also accused capitalism of producing a society in which the image of the commodity was

dominant, and for Jameson, as will be seen in chapter 3, post-modern society is also essentially a late-capitalist society.

12 Hebdige, *Hiding in the Light*, p. 195.

13 Ibid. The usage of terms such as decentring will also be discussed in chapters 3 and 4.

14 Hebdige, *Hiding in the Light*, p. 195.

15 See chapters 3 and 4 for further discussion of this point. Hebdige is not altogether uncritical of Baudrillard's attitudes to contemporary society and its culture (see, for example, Hebdige, *Hiding in the Light*, p. 176, and p. 253, n. 6), but does take over many of Baudrillard's characterisations of the latter for his depiction of the post-modern and from either Baudrillard himself (see Hebdige p. 253 for examples of his reading of Baudrillard) or from other readers of Baudrillard such as Frederic Jameson. (See, for example, Hebdige, *Hiding in the Light*, top of p. 254.)

16 See chapter 4 for a detailed discussion of Jencks's views. Hebdige's discussion of the theories of post-modernism also revolves in general around the figures of Lyotard, Baudrillard, Habermas and Richard Rorty, rather than theorists of post-modern architecture such as Jencks.

17 Mike Featherstone's introductory essay to the special issue of *Theory, Culture & Society* on post-modernism of June 1988 (vol. 5, nos. 2–3, pp. 195–215), 'In Pursuit of the Postmodern: an Introduction', also provides a list of 'definers' of post-modernism on its p. 203, which brings together several different schools of thought about the subject without always making their separate identities clear. As with many recent anthologies on post-modernism, the collection of diverse articles which follows adds to, rather than subtracts from, the confusion about the definitions of the term being used. Rather than take the time and space necessary for an extended critique of the essays collected by Featherstone (and of others in similar anthologies) this study will attempt to give as clear an account as is possible of the main sources and meanings of the term post-modernism in the hope, as suggested previously, that this will assist the reader in making his or her own analysis of the many descriptions of the term which have been made so far, and which may be made in the future.

18 See the *Oxford English Dictionary Supplement* (Oxford, 1982), vol. III, p. 698, or the *Oxford English Dictionary*, 2nd edn (Oxford 1989), vol. XII, p. 201. The dictionary's coverage of the history of the term is not only limited by the space allotted it, but by its omission of texts such as those by Charles Jencks on post-modern architecture.

Other uses of the terms post-modern and post-modernism omitted in the *OED* entry will be covered in following pages of this text and repeated in summary at its conclusion.

19 Here the dictionary refers to its previous definition of the term modern (in vol. II of the supplement to the 1st edn, p. 993; or the 2nd edn, vol. IX, p. 948) as being 'of a movement in art or architecture, or the works produced by such a movement: characterised by a departure from or a repudiation of accepted or traditional styles and values'. As noted earlier, the derivation of the word modern from the Latin for 'today' or 'just now', is given in vol. VI of the *OED*, 1st edn, p. 573, and may also be found in the new, second, edition, in vol. IX, pp. 947–8.

20 See chapter 4 for further details of Jencks's theories. The term 'double-coding' is used by him from at least 1978 on (in the 2nd edn of his *The Language of Post-Modern Architecture*), and refers to how the post-modern building may use both a 'Modern' code (described as a code because it, like other architectural styles, is understood as sending out messages to its users in a similar way to other codes or speech acts) and at least one other style or code (such as, for example, the classical codes used in Stirling, Wilford and Associates' new Stuttgart State Gallery). While Jencks uses the hyphenated term 'Post-Modern' from at least 1977 on, and then together with the term 'Post-Modernism', Hassan, Lyotard, Jameson and other recent critics will be seen to have spoken of 'postmodernism'. One other form of the word 'post-Modernism' has also been used by Leslie Fiedler (in 1965) and by Bernard Smith (in 1945), while Arnold J. Toynbee had used the spelling 'post-Modern' from at least 1954 on. Sometimes the particular form taken by the word has also been influenced by the form taken by it in the language from which it has been translated (such as, for example, Spanish, French or German) in which hyphens are not used, although, as pointed out in the preceding note 4, it may also follow, in other instances, from the particular canon of post-modernist theory being supported by the user in question. Except where quoting from a particular usage, this text will use the form given in the *OED* of the hyphenation 'post-modern' as being the most correct form for usage in English.

21 See the previous note 19.

22 Hudnut had used the term in 1945 in an article entitled 'the post-modern house' in the *Architectural Record*, vol. 97 (May 1945), pp. 70–5. The article was also published in the *Royal Architectural Institute of Canada Journal*, vol. 22 (July 1945), pp. 135–40. (See also note 25 below.)

23 The relationship of post-modern architecture to late- or ultra-modern architectural styles will be discussed again in chapters 3 and 4. To my knowledge, no self-professed post-modern architect of recent times has described the prefabricated house as post-modern on that basis alone. When Charles Jencks illustrates his partly pre-fabricated *Garagia Rotunda* of 1977 in the fifth edition of his *The Language of Post-Modern Architecture*, p. 120, he describes it as 'Architecture as prefabrication plus cosmetics'. And see also Lucien Kroll's condemnation of the prefabricated house as a product of modernism in his *The Architecture of Complexity* of 1983, translated by Peter Blundell Jones, (London, 1986), p. 10.

24 The *OED* is quoting p. 119 of Joseph Hudnut's *Architecture and the Spirit of Man* (Harvard, 1949). The misleading nature of the *OED*'s entry on Hudnut's usage of the word post-modern may also be reflected in Frank Kermode's interpretation of its 1949 usage in his *History and Value* (Oxford, 1988, p. 129) to refer to 'a kind of architecture that came later than, and reacted against, the Modern Movement in that field.'

25 See the previous note 22 for details of Hudnut's 1945 article. It was a slightly different version of that article that was published by Hudnut in his *Architecture and the Spirit of Man*, pp. 108–19, under the same title of 'the post-modern house'.

26 Hudnut, 'the post-modern house' 1945, p. 75; and 1949, p. 119.

27 Hudnut had begun his 1945 article with the words: 'I have been thinking about that cloud burst of new houses which as soon as the war is ended is going to cover the hills and valleys of New England with so many square miles of prefabricated happiness' (see Hudnut, 'the post-modern house' 1945, p. 70).

28 Hudnut, 'the post-modern house', 1949, p. 108.

29 Ibid.

30 Ibid.

31 Toynbee's descriptions of the 'post-Modern Age' in the post-war (1954) volumes of his *A Study of History* also characterise it as 'collective industrial' in a way which makes it seem fixed in a stage prior to the post-industrial as described by Bell and others in more recent years. (See chapter 2 for details of Bell's use of the term post-industrial and chapter 4 for details of Jencks's concepts of both the post-modern and post-industrial.)

32 See Charles Jencks's *What is Post-Modernism?* (London, 1986), p. 14. Jencks also refers to Hudnut in a 'Foot-Note' to the Introductions of the 1978 and following revised editions of his *The Language of Post-Modern Architecture* of 1977 as having made what 'appears to be' the 'first use of Post-Modern in an architectural context'. See

Jencks's *The Language of Post-Modern Architecture*, 4th revised enlarged edn (London, 1984), p. 8. Unless specified otherwise, this will be the edition referred to under the rubric of 'Jencks, *Language of Post-Modern Architecture*' in later notes. (The page numbers of the 1984 edition also correspond largely to those of 1978 up to its p. 132, to those of 1981 up to its p. 146, and to those of 1987 up to its p. 164, but see also chapters 3 and 4 for references to the different Introductions and Post-scripts.)

33 See Hudnut, 'the post-modern house', 1945, pp. 72–3. Hudnut had, however, also added on p. 73 with regard to the 'harlequinade' of styles used in the suburbs that he thought 'that that adventure is at an end'.

34 See Hudnut, ibid., p. 73. One of the criteria for post-modernism suggested by Jencks (see chapter 4) is that it give meaning to its techniques and motives.

35 See chapter 4 for details of Jencks's views on post-modernism. Jencks has also criticised modern architecture's belief in the 'myth of the machine aesthetic'. See, for example, his 1975 article 'The Rise of Post Modern Architecture' in the *Architectural Association Quarterly*, vol. 7, n. 4, p. 6: 'What is modern architecture based on? Why . . . the myth of the machine aesthetic, an abstract language, geometry and good taste.'

36 Although Gropius had also experimented with prefabricated housing in America, Hudnut had defended him and other founders of the Modern Movement in architecture for their ideals, while also criticising those who had 'distorted' the latter into a 'cold and uncompromising functionalism' in his 1945 article, 'the post-modern house', pp. 73–4. In addition to such statements, Hudnut's 1949 collection of essays also contains passages where he defends the 'modernist dictum' that 'form follows function'. (See Hudnut, 'the post-modern house', 1949, p. 113 and p. 13.)

37 Toynbee's use of the term post-modern will be discussed more fully presently. In being used as early as 1939 it predates Hudnut's usage rather than the other way around as suggested by the *OED*. Even earlier uses of the term will, however, also be dealt with in this chapter in following pages.

38 See Arnold J. Toynbee, *A Study of History*, vol. V (London, 1939), p. 43.

39 *A Study of History by Arnold J. Toynbee*, abridged by D. C. Somervell (Oxford, 1946), p. 39.

40 As suggested in the text, the first use of the term 'post-Modern' to denote the period from 1875 on in Toynbee's own *A Study of*

History is only to be found in the post-war volumes published in 1954. When used in Somervell's abridgement to describe the period from 1875 on the term 'Post-Modern' is also followed by a question-mark.

41 See note 40 above.

42 Somervell's abridgement was completed in 1946 and approved by Toynbee. The use of the term 'Post-Modern' in the abridgement with a question-mark may mean that Somervell thought that this was the direction which Toynbee's work was taking in the post-war years.

43 Toynbee, *A Study of History*, vol. VIII, 1954, p. 338. Toynbee also makes some references to Western architecture on pp. 374–5 of vol. VIII, and describes the 'sky-scrapers' of the twentieth century as 'Modern Neo-Gothic'. Previously (see, for example, Somervell, *A Study of History*, pp. 507–8, or Toynbee, *A Study of History*, vol. VI, 1939, pp. 60–1), Toynbee had also attacked both the 'Gothic revival' in 'modern' architecture as a decadent archaism, and (Somervell, *A Study of History*, pp. 446–7 or Toynbee *A Study of History*, vol. V, 1939, p. 482) the modern commercialisation of art. Both were signs of decay for Toynbee, who also went on to con demn the 'Futurist' destruction of the heritage of the past as equally damaging. (See, for example, Somervell, *A Study of History*, p. 519, or Toynbee, *A Study of History*, vol. VI, pp. 115ff.)

44 See Charles Jencks *Post-Modernism: the New Classicism in Art and Architecture* (London, 1987), p. 13, and also Jencks's Foreword to his *What is Post-Modernism?* of 1986, p. 3.

45 See also Toynbee *A Study of History*, vol. IX, p. 235.

46 Ibid., p. 421.

47 Ibid.; and see the 'Compulsory Preface' of *1066 and All That* for the line quoted by Toynbee. The 'end of History' ironically referred to as such by Sellar and Yeatman was marked in their text by the rise of America to 'top nation' status after the end of the Great War of 1914–18: 'America was thus clearly top nation, and History came to a.'

48 See Toynbee, *A Study of History*, vol. IX, p. 436. A 'pessimistic' view of history has also been ascribed to Jean Baudrillard in more recent times. Douglas Kellner, for example, has described Baudrillard as preaching a 'nihilism' which is 'without joy, without energy, without hope for a better future'. See Douglas Kellner, 'Post-modernism as Social Theory', in *Theory, Culture & Society*, vol. 5, nos. 2–3 (June 1988), p. 247. Baudrillard also writes in his 'The Orders of Simulacra', in *Simulations*, p. 111, of the 'new age of the

simulacrum', that 'It is the end of a history in which successively, God, Man, Progress and History itself die to profit the code, in which transcendence dies to profit immanence.' Baudrillard adds (ibid., p. 112) that 'In its indefinite reproduction . . . the system puts an end to the myth of its origin and to all the referential values it has itself secreted along the way.'

49 Toynbee *A Study of History*, vol. IX, p. 436, takes the British historian Edward Gibbon as an exemplar of the optimistic view of modern history and the French writer Paul Valéry as an exemplar of the pessimist. Toynbee adds (ibid., p. 438) that 'pessimism . . . was no more proof than optimism against the possibility of being refuted by events'. Toynbee continues (ibid., p. 439): 'The pessimist's error of mistaking dawn for nightfall may be rarer than the optimist's error of mistaking sunset for noon' – but is still 'an error'.

50 Ibid., p. 441.

51 See Oswald Spengler, *The Decline of the West*, translated by Charles Francis Atkinson (London, 1971), p. 507. In contrast to Spengler, Toynbee had written of the role of the individual in society in the 1946 D. C. Somervell abridgement of his *A Study of History*, pp. 576–7, that the 'source of action' is 'in the individuals'. (And see also the text referred to in note 50 above as well as Toynbee's specific criticisms of Spengler's belief in the omnipotence of necessity on, for example p. 168 of vol. IX of his *A Study of History*.) Here it is also interesting to note that Rudolf Pannwitz's 1917 use of the term 'post-modern' (as referred to by Wolfang Welsch, *Unsere postmoderne Moderne* (Weinheim, 1988), pp. 12f.) had occurred in a work entitled 'Die Krisis der europaeischen Kultur' ('The Crisis of European Culture'), published just prior to Spengler's *Decline of the West* and had been used to describe a type of human who was outwardly tough but inwardly decadent. By contrast to Toynbee, Jean Baudrillard's contribution to Hal Foster's *Postmodern Culture*, his essay 'The Ecstasy of Communication', concludes (p. 133) in a pessimistic as well as fanciful manner on the agency of the human subject: 'He can no longer produce the limits of his own being, can no longer play nor stage himself, can no longer produce himself as a mirror. He is now only a pure screen, a switching center for all the networks of influence.'

52 See C. Wright Mills, *The Sociological Imagination* (Harmondsworth, 1983), pp. 184ff. Mills characterises the 'Fourth Epoch' as one in which the liberalism and socialism 'born of the Enlightenment' have both 'virtually collapsed as adequate explanations of the world'; 'the ideas of freedom and of reason have become moot'; and

'increased rationality may not be assumed to make for increased reason.'

53 See Leslie Fiedler, 'The New Mutants', in *Partisan Review* (1965), p. 508, or in *The Collected Essays of Leslie Fiedler*, vol. II (New York, 1971), pp. 379–400. Just prior to this passage Fiedler had been referring to the influence of science fiction on Wilhelm Reich, Buckminster Fuller, Marshall McLuhan and ('perhaps') Norman O. Brown as well as on writers such as William Golding, Anthony Burgess, William Burroughs, Kurt Vonnegut Jr, Harry Matthews and John Barth. The passage quoted by the *OED* had continued: 'but rather in coming to terms with the prophetic content common to both; with the myth rather than the modes of Science Fiction'. Fiedler had then proceeded (*Collected Essays*, p. 382) to describe that myth as 'quite simply the myth of the end of man', and, more specifically, as the idea of turning humans into newly irrational, and even 'barbaric' beings, or, that is, 'the new mutants', and had then also gone on to speak at length of the new 'post-modernist' irrationality, cultism and antipathy to the precepts of the Protestant work ethic which he found to be already evident in the 1960s. (See also the pages on Daniel Bell's use of this latter depiction of the post-modern in the following chapter and the notes on Fiedler in chapter 3.) Later, in an article published in *Playboy* in December 1969 entitled 'Cross the Border – Close the Gap', Fiedler also spoke of 'Post-Modernist' literature as closing the gap between 'High' and Pop literature to align itself with the latter and its subversive (parodistic and other) forms as the culture of the present, and of the need created thereby for a new 'Post-Modernist criticism', able to make judgements 'about the "goodness" and "badness" of art quite separated from distinctions between "high" and "low" with their concealed class bias'.

54 In *Encounter*, vol. 26, no. 4 (April 1966), p. 73. Here Kermode was referring, however, largely to Fiedler's use of the term, and did not entirely agree with Fiedler's assessment that something so new was happening in literature.

55 Nikolaus Pevsner's December 1966 remarks were made in *The Listener* (29 December 1966), p. 955, following a discussion of the buildings of Churchill College Cambridge and referred to architecture of the 1950s and 1960s which Jencks and others have since described as 'late-modern'. Pevsner's second article in *The Listener* (5 January 1967), pp. 7–9, was, however, to include some buildings in his new category which Jencks will at least classify as both late-modern and post-modern, such as Eero Saarinen's TWA Terminal

and Jorn Utzon's Sydney Opera House. (See, for example, the entries on Saarinen and Utzon in Charles Jencks, *The Language of Post-Modern Architecture*, and in his *Architecture Today* (London, 1988), as well as the latter's 'evolutionary trees' of 'Late-Modernism' and 'Post-Modernism' on its pp. 20 and 110.)

56 Although clearer than some of the other quotations, it should be noted that this is again a reference to a particular view of post-modernism, and not one which can be generalised to cover all forms of post-modernism.

57 Michael Koehler's ' "Postmodernismus": ein begriffsgeschichtlicher Ueberblick" is published in *Amerikastudien*, vol. 22, no. 1 (1977), pp. 8–18. An editorial note to Koehler's article on its p. 8 also refers the reader to the next article in the journal by Gerhard Hoffmann, Alfred Hornung and Ruediger Kunow, ' "Modern", "Postmodern" and "Contemporary" as Criteria for the Analysis of 20th Century Literature', in *Amerikastudien*, vol. 22, no. 1 (1977), pp. 19–46, for further bibliographic information.

58 Hoffmann, Hornung and Kunow, ' "Modern", "Postmodern" and "Contemporary" ', p. 45, list the following papers by Olson: 'The Act of Writing in the Context of Post-Modern Man' of 1952; 'The Present is Prologue' of 1955; 'Definitions by Undoings' of 1956; and 'Equal, That Is, To the Real Itself' of 1958. Koehler, ' "Post-modernismus" ', p. 11, also sees Olson as following Toynbee in dating the post-modern from the last quarter of the nineteenth century. (See also the following notes on Toynbee in this chapter.) The reference given by Koehler for Harry Levin's usage is his 'What is Modernism?' in the *Massachussetts Review* of 1960, for Howe his 'Mass Society and Postmodern Fiction' in the *Partisan Review* of 1959, and for Fiedler his 'The New Mutants' in the *Partisan Review* of 1965. While Howe's essay is summarised as describing the new mass society as eliminating many of the moral and aesthetic bases on which classical modernism had been based, Levin's text is described as contrasting the ('postmodern') fiction which he saw to be popularising the achievements of the more experimental modernists of earlier times with the more innovatory nature of the latter. Both are thus seen by Koehler to have used the term post-modern in a negative manner to mourn the demise of modernism. (Further reference to Perreault, whose use of the term occurred in articles in the *Village Voice*, New York, will be made presently.)

59 Amitai Etzioni's *The Active Society: a Theory of Societal and Political Processes* (London and New York, 1968) describes the modern period as having 'ended with the radical transformation of the tech-

nologies of communication, knowledge and energy that followed World War Two', and dates the onset of the 'post-modern period' at 1945. Later Etzioni also goes on to claim that the post-modern is similar to the 'late-modern' in some important respects, but still gives some differences, such as that just quoted, by which other theorists will also come to classify the 'post-industrial' society as different from the 'industrial' society. (And see also chapter 2 on these subjects.)

60 This article has recently been republished in Hassan's *The Post-modern Turn* (1987); see also the section on Hassan in chapter 3.

61 The issue of the journal was entitled 'Modernism and Postmodernism: Inquiries, Reflections and Speculations' and was vol. 3, no. 1 (Autumn 1971). Cohen is quoted by Koehler, ' "Post-modernismus" ', p. 14, as saying that 'The issue was planned as an attempt to deal with contemporary avantgarde movements' and that Cohen had decided on the term 'post-modern' 'as the best way to distinguish them from past movements of the avant-garde'. Other journals mentioned by Koehler as having used the term 'post-modern' include *Boundary 2* of 1972, *Triquarterly* of autumn 1973 and spring 1975, the *Journal of Modern Literature* of July 1974, the *New York Drama Review* of March 1975, and the *Hudson Review* of autumn 1973.

62 The *OED* entry referred to earlier was, of course, dealing with uses of the term in English. Although Koehler is also able to suggest that the word post-modernism may have entered the English language through the translation of the term 'postmodernismo' in Dudley Fitts's 1942 anthology of contemporary Latin-American verse, it has already been seen in this chapter that an even earlier use in English of the term post-modern (if not of post-modernism) can be found in the early (1939) volumes of Arnold Toynbee's *A Study of History*, which Koehler has not mentioned in his survey. Because of these complications, a revised list of the most significant uses of the terms post-modern and post-industrial will be given at the conclusion of this text. As suggested above, and as stated in the notes to the Preface, other claims for terms being prior to de Onis's, such as that made for John Watkins Chapman's in the 1870s, should also be able to show that the use was of some influence or significance.

63 See Koehler ' "Postmodernismus" ', p. 10, and Federico de Onis, *Antologia de la poesia española e hispanoamericana (1882–1932)* (Madrid, 1934), pp. xviii–xix. I should also like to take the opportunity here to thank Dr Michael Hoskin, Fellow of Churchill College Cambridge, for his assistance with the translation of these pages.

64 See Dudley Fitts, *Anthology of Contemporary Latin-American Poetry* (London and Norfolk, Conn., 1947), p. 609, or the 1942 edn, p. 601.

65 Ibid., 1947, p. xix. (Koehler makes no mention of Hays, and attributes the use of the term 'postmodernism' in Fitts's anthology to Fitts alone.)

66 Fitts's Preface, ibid., also acknowledges his debt to Federico de Onis.

67 Epigraph to Fitts's anthology, translated by John Peale Bishop.

68 Fitts, *Anthology of Contemporary Latin-American Poetry*, p. xi.

69 See the preceding pages on Hudnut. While Hudnut's 'post-modern' house may be understood as representing an exaggeration of the functionalist ideas of the modern International Style, the 'post-modernismo' of which de Onis and Fitts speak is presented by them as a reaction to an excessively decorated form of Modernism. In consequence, both Hudnut's and de Onis and Fitts's concepts of post-modernism may now be understood as being similar in their evocation of a lack of decoration, and in this both will also be seen to be very different from contemporary applications of the term post-modernism to architecture where post-modern architecture is understood as countering the lack of decoration of the modern International Style.

70 See also note 69 above. The quotation 'less is more' is from Mies van der Rohe.

71 See Koehler, ' "Postmodernismus" ', pp. 16f., and also the earlier discussion of the use of the term modern to cover this period in the Introduction and its first note.

72 Jencks writes of this quarrel in his 'The New Classicism and its Emergent Rules', in *Architectural Design*, vol. 58, nos. 1/2 (1988), Profile 70, p. 24, that it may also be said to have led to the 'struggle between Modernists of all brands that is still with us today'; and see also on this and other issues relating to the definition of modernity and modernism, Matei Calinescu's *Five Faces of Modernity* (Durham, N.C., 1987). This work, which I saw only after completing the body of this manuscript, also has an interesting discussion of de Onis on modernism and post-modernism, as well as of the avant-garde. Calinescu's final (1986) chapter on post-modernism is, however, rather more problematical in its apparent conflation (following Linda Hutcheon), on its p. 285, of the double-coding which I described as a characteristic of literary parody in my *Parody/Meta-Fiction* (London, 1979) (a book used by Hutcheon together with several other works for her work on both parody and post-modern-

ism, though not referred to by Calinescu) and the double-coding of which Charles Jencks speaks with reference to post-modern architecture. (And see also chapter 3, note 37, and chapter 4, note 81, for further criticism of this conflation.)

73 But see also the earlier discussion of Toynbee's usage of the term post-modern to describe the post-1914 years in 1939, and the post-1875 period in his later texts.

74 Koehler, ' "Postmodernismus" ', p. 16: 'diese "Postmoderne" schliesst den Modernismus schon in seiner ganzen Dauer ein'. As noted previously, Koehler, however, has only made mention of Toynbee's post-World War Two dating of the 'Post-Modern Age' as being from 1875 on, and has made no mention of Toynbee's earlier 1939 dating of it as being from 1914 onwards.

75 See the previous pages on Toynbee for further discussion of his views, as well as both the discussion of Toynbee's views on Modernist art in the pages on Bernard Smith's use of the term 'post-Modernism' at the end of this chapter and the following note 76.

76 In addition to condemning both 'futurist' and 'archaic' types of art of the Modern and 'Post-Modern' (that is, for him, post-1875) periods in his *Study of History*, Toynbee was also to put Frank Lloyd Wright's 'Mayan-style' Imperial Hotel in Tokyo in the same class of archaic art as nineteenth-century Pre-Raphaelite painting in his later article 'Art: Communicative or Esoteric?', in the collection *On the Future of Art*, introduced by Edward F. Fry (New York, 1970), p. 18. While Toynbee condemned such historicising art as esoteric in a way which suggests that he might also have been antipathetic to much of the post-modernist architecture of recent years, he had also both criticised the role played by modern specialisation in the creation of such esotericism and argued for an increased valuation of communication in much the same way as some 'historicising' (and other) post-modernist architects and architectural theorists have done, and in a way which suggests that even if he were not to agree with the solutions provided by the latter, he had agreed with their analyses of the problems of both modernity and modernism. (And see also chapter 2 on Arthur J. Penty's criticisms of modernist specialisation and chapter 4 on the writings of Charles Jencks on post-modernist architecture.)

77 See Koehler, ' "Postmodernismus" ', p. 16, note 17.

78 See Koehler, ibid., p. 17.

79 See the section on Hassan in chapter 3.

80 Koehler sometimes shifts from speaking of 'postmodernism' to

speak of either the 'postmodern' or 'postmodernity' without fully defining the differences between these terms.

81 See, for example, the pages on Jencks in this chapter and in chapters 3 and 4.

82 See Koehler, ' "Postmodernismus" ', p. 17, and following.

83 See the pages on Jencks in both the Preface and in chapter 4 on this. Jencks is, however, unlike Koehler in seeing the late-modern and post-modern as running concurrently from the 1960s on; where Koehler, as explained in the following paragraphs of the text, sees the latter as developing largely from the time when the other has worn itself out. As suggested elsewhere, it may also be because others have assumed the post-modern architecture of which Jencks has spoken to have followed the late-modern from the 1960s on, rather than to have run concurrently with it, that they have accepted Jameson's designation of Portman's 1970s Bonaventure Hotel as post-modern.

84 Like several other German critics (including Habermas) Koehler also appears to have taken up some of the ideas put forward by Peter Buerger in his *Theory of the Avant-Garde* (Manchester and Minneapolis, 1984). Like Buerger (and Habermas after him) Koehler chooses, for instance, the Surrealists and Dadaists as representative of the modern avant-garde (instead of, say, the Russian Constructivists of the 1920s), and then goes on to speak somewhat arbitrarily of the modern avant-garde as having died out with the demise of these chosen groups. For further discussion of the concept of the avant-garde, and a critique of the restrictiveness of the Buerger view on it, see also the following chapters 3 and 4.

85 See note 80, above.

86 Namely the attribution to Fitts rather than to Hays of the use of the term 'postmodernism' in Fitts's 1942 anthology; the dating of Toynbee's usage of the term 'post-Modern' at 1947; and the interpretation of Hassan's periodisation of 'postmodernism'.

87 Although Charles Jencks's influential book *The Language of Post-Modern Architecture* only appeared first in 1977, the year in which Koehler's article was published, he had used the word post-modern in an architectural essay of 1975 (see note 35 to this chapter), while other uses of the term had, as noted previously, also been applied to architecture in earlier years by both Joseph Hudnut (in 1945) and by Nikolaus Pevsner (in the 1960s). Like Koehler, several other commentators on the concept of the post-modern have also continued to ignore or avoid architectural uses of the term, especially when writing of either literature or French literary theory, although it has also

been suggested by others that architecture is the area where the term has been most clearly defined and used, and especially when applied to architecture of the 1960s and after, which has consciously shared some of the precepts of the concepts in question.

88 Apart from the missing architectural references mentioned in note 87 above, Koehler's survey has been seen by Hans Bertens (in his essay, 'The Postmodern *Weltanschauung* and its Relation to Modernism: an Introductory Survey', in Douwe Fokkema and Hans Bertens (eds.), *Approaching Postmodernism* (Amsterdam and Philadelphia, 1986), pp. 9–51) to have omitted references to the American poet Randall Jarrell's use of the term in a review of Robert Lowell's *Lord Weary's Castle* of 1946, and to John Berryman's use of it following Jarrell as well as several later uses. (See Fokkema and Bertens, *Approaching Postmodernism*, pp. 12ff.)

89 And see also Preface note 1 on Wolfgang Welsch's claim about the use made of the term in the 1870s by the artist John Watkins Chapman. Koehler's references to the use of the term 'postmodernism' in visual art criticism include that to John Perreault mentioned previously, and to Brian O'Doherty's May–June 1971 edition of *Art in America*, in which he had put the question 'What is Post-modernism?'. Koehler adds, however, that the question was largely rhetorical, as O'Doherty could give 'no satisfactory answer'. (See Koehler, ' "Postmodernismus" ', p. 13.)

90 Bernard Smith provided this information when I asked him in April 1989 about his use of the term 'post-Modernist'. As noted previously, Arnold J. Toynbee had used the term 'Post-Modern' in vol. V of his *A Study of History* of 1939, p. 43, to describe the period following World War One, while he later wrote it in the form 'post-Modern' in the 1954 volumes of his study to refer to the new 'post-middle class' age following the year 1875. Although written before the publication of these later volumes of Toynbee's study, Smith's 'post-Modernism' also appears to be dealing with a 'post-bourgeois' set of artists, in so far as all of those listed by Smith had some connection with communist or socialist beliefs, while their art was concerned with the depiction of workers and the impoverished and their conditions, rather than with what was understood to be a middle-class way of life.

91 See, for example, Bernard Smith, *Place, Taste and Tradition* (Oxford, 1979), p. 277.

92 Ibid., p. 255.

93 See Smith, ibid., pp. 270–1.

94 See Toynbee, *A Study of History*, vol. V, p. 482.

95 Later, in April 1989, after writing an attack on contemporary post-modernism (see the following note 99), Smith claimed that he had used the word 'post-Modernism' in 1944/5 because the art to which it was applied appeared to be doing something different from other modernist works. (And see also the following note 98.)

96 See the previous pages on Toynbee for further explanation of this point.

97 While Koehler has also claimed (' "Postmodernismus" ', p. 9) that the use of the prefix 'post' had become more frequent following its use in the term 'post-war' (dated by the *OED* from 1908), one other use of the prefix 'post' in art criticism had been the use of it in the term 'Post-Impressionism' from around the same time.

98 The styles of Counihan, Bergner and O'Connor had, as Smith has noted, combined elements of modernist Expressionism with subject matter typical of Social Realism. For Smith (conversation of April 1989) their 'post-Modernism' had therefore seemed to be doing something different from 'other forms of Modernism'. By the time of Smith's *Australian Painting 1733–1970* (Oxford, 1962) (see pp. 233–9 of the 2nd edn of 1971) the Social Realism discussed above is, however, being described as something which 'as a creative trend in Australian art barely survived the war' and the post-war years as ones which 'did not favour a realistic approach to art'.

99 Smith could not at first recall having used the term 'post-Modernism' in his 1945 text when asked about it in April 1989, and had by then also used it in a review of Peter Fuller's *Theoria* (in *Australian Society* (March 1989), p. 41) to write that 'a central weakness of post-modernism has been to treat tradition as a load of old junk to be dismissed or ruthlessly exploited'.

100 Here it should, however, also be noted that Smith's final target in his 1944/5 work was not simply modernist abstraction but the fascism of the time and its aesthetics. Hence Smith concluded his 1945 book (*Place, Taste and Tradition*, pp. 280–1) by quoting from Melvin Rader's attack on fascist aesthetics in his *No Compromise* of 1939: 'It is important to remember that there is a tradition, embodied in the works of men like Ruskin, Morris, Wright, Gropius, and Mumford, which insists upon the democratic functional and collective nature of art.'

101 See the pages on Achille Bonito Oliva's theory of the 'transavant-garde' in chapter 4.

102 Koehler, ' "Postmodernismus" ', p. 13.

103 See chapter 4 for further discussion of this point.

104 See also the later discussion of Achille Bonito Oliva's criteria for the 'transavantgarde'.

2 Defining the post-industrial

1 See Daniel Bell, *The Coming of Post-Industrial Society* (Harmondsworth, 1976), pp. 33ff. Other works on the post-industrial society which discuss the history of the term include Krishan Kumar's *Prophecy and Progress: the Sociology of Industrial and Post-Industrial Society* (Harmondsworth, 1978).

2 Bell adds in *The Coming of Post-Industrial Society*, p. 37, that he had coined the term in 1959 unaware of the earlier uses of the term by Penty and Riesman.

3 See Bell, ibid., p. 39.

4 Orage was editor of *The New Age* between 1907 and 1922.

5 The volume was published in 1914 in London.

6 For further details of this collection, and of the partnership between Penty and Coomaraswamy, see Roger Lipsey, *Coomaraswamy: his Life and Work* (Princeton, 1977), chapter 9.

7 Arthur J. Penty, *Post-Industrialism* (London, 1922), p. 45. Penty continued: 'Other arts are being extinguished by the competition of mechanical processes of one kind or another. The market for painting has been ruined by cheap reproductions; music has to compete with the gramophone; the stage with the cinema.' Earlier, in his *Old Worlds for New* (London, 1917), pp. 157ff., Penty had also condemned effects of the industrial sub-division of labour on the profession of the architect, including the 'enslavement' of the architect to 'middlemen' such as the surveyor and estate agent.

8 Arthur J. Penty, *The Elements of Domestic Design* (Westminster, 1930), p. 2.

9 Penty had also written in his *Post-Industrialism*, p. 42, that 'there is no temperament about machine work. It can reproduce things of good proportion, of pleasing colour and design. But the temperament will be missing. It eludes the machine.'

10 Penty, *The Elements of Domestic Design*, p. 4. Penty had specifically included Norman architecture in his category of the 'primitive', but also praised (ibid., p. 3) what he saw to be a vernacular Renaissance architecture in which elements of the primitive had been linked to the classical. Penty also saw the revival of such vernacular architecture to have been encouraged by the Queen Anne movement (of the 1870s on), which, he added, had led to 'everything that is vital in architecture at the present day – the Domestic Revival, the Arts and Crafts Movement, and the Neo-Renaissance movement'. Later (ibid., p. 5), Penty also wrote that 'old work should be studied' and that 'we must resist all attempts to overthrow tradition, but insist that it be interpreted in a more liberal

spirit, while simultaneously new ideas which meet with our approval should be incorporated in tradition'. Penty continued, 'It will thus be "by fusing new with old we shall effect a real growth", and re-establish in our midst a new and common tradition'.

11 See, for example, the passages quoted above, and Penty, *Post-Industrialism*, p. 149, where he praises the Arts and Crafts movement for bringing into existence 'a number of craftsmen who knew what they were about', to pave the way 'for the revival of craftsmanship on a wider scale'.

12 See, for example, Penty, ibid., p. 148. Although Penty criticises the Arts and Crafts movement here for their overconcentration on the 'decorative crafts', he does acknowledge that a reason for this was the lack of funds to undertake other projects.

13 See, for example, Ananda K. Coomaraswamy, *The Arts and Crafts of India And Ceylon* (London and Edinburgh, 1913), p. 34. As noted earlier, Max Weber's description of modernity in his *Economy and Society* which he worked on between 1910 and 1914 (Weber, *Economy and Society*, ed. Guenther Roth and Claus Wittich (Berkeley, Los Angeles, and London, 1978), p. 436), had also specifically contrasted the craft-orientated economy of India with both modern rational technology and its method of production and with modern capitalism. (See the Introduction, note 2.) The word 'villagism', which is, for example, used with reference to Coomaraswamy's work by Lipsey, *Coomaraswamy*, p. 114, also denoted a return to pre-industrial divisions of work.

14 Penty refers, for example, to Coomaraswamy's *The Indian Craftsman* on the Indian guilds in his *Old Worlds for New*, p. 47. For Penty the Guilds had two main functions: 'One of them was that of mutual aid; the other was the safeguarding of the standard of production against commercial abuses.'

15 See Penty's Preface to his *Post-Industrialism*, quoted in the following piece of text.

16 Penty, ibid., p. 14.

17 This issue will be returned to in the section on Fredric Jameson in chapter 3 in the passages on his use of Ernest Mandel's theories to argue that the post-industrial society is simply a 'late capitalist' society. Although many recent theorists of post-industrial society have not denied that it is also a capitalist or late-capitalist society, they have followed Penty in recognising that the term post-industrial relates that phenomenon not just to the capitalist aspects of industrialism but to other even more specifically industrial issues such as the divisions of labour and the role of machines in those divisions.

18 See Penty, *Post-Industrialism*, pp. 49–50.

19 Ibid., p. 13. Penty also relates his 'interesting discovery' here to his reading of Max Beer's *History of British Socialism*.

20 Lipsey, *Coomaraswamy*, p. 117, quotes Sir Herbert Read's *Art and Industry* of 1934 as having described Penty as an 'extreme reactionary' and in the same breath as Read had called another friend of Coomaraswamy, Eric Gill, an 'enlightened critic of the industrial system'. (Read quotes a passage from a piece written by Penty for *The Criterion*, vol. 13 (1934), p. 368, in which Penty criticises Gill for advising architects, artists and craftsmen 'to throw in their lot with industrialism'.) Lipsey himself criticises Penty (*Coomaraswamy*, p. 113) for believing in the impossibility of the emergence of a new architecture from the new industrial materials as being 'absurdly anachronistic', and sees Penty as 'missing the signs' of the new architecture 'on the horizon', although it could equally be suggested that Penty had simply disliked the signs he saw. (See also the previous discussion of Penty's views on architecture.) While Penty's criticism of the modernist admiration for the machine has been shared by some recent post-modernist artists and architects, he might not have necessarily approved of their moves away from 'simplicity', or of their 'double-coding' of the modern with other codes, where the use of the modern also entails the use of modern materials and divisions of labour as well as of a modern style.

21 See also note 17 in this chapter.

22 Boris Frankel's *The Post-Industrial Utopians* (Oxford and Cambridge, 1987), p. 8, follows Bell in describing Penty as a follower of Morris and Ruskin (see the following note 23), but also goes on to contrast Penty to both Rudolf Bahro and Peter Fuller, as well as to 'other admirers of craft society', by describing the latter as 'wishing to go forward beyond capitalism rather than backwards'. While there is some truth in this claim (see also chapter 5 on Fuller) one of the problems here is, however, that, as elsewhere in his book, Frankel has suddenly moved from speaking of industrial society to speaking of capitalist society, so that it remains unclear as to how exactly Penty's *post-industrialism* contrasts with the views of others on *industrialism*. One other recent discussion of Penty, Mark Swenarton's chapter, 'A.J. Penty and the Building Guilds', in his *Artisans and Architects: the Ruskinian Tradition in Architectural Thought* (London, 1989), pp. 167–88, also points to the mixture of conservative and socialist ideas in Penty's thought, as well as to what Swenarton describes as Penty's later interest in the ideas of fascism (which Penty saw as being more true to some – though not all – of the ideas of Guild Socialism than communism). While

analysing Penty's architectural as well as socialist ideas, Swenarton makes, however, no mention of either Penty's *Elements of Domestic Design* of 1930 or his books on post-industrialism.

23 See, for example, Arthur J. Penty, *Old Worlds for New*, pp. 57ff., where he emphasises the point that the real issue of industrialism is the sub-division of labour which leads to the misuse of the machine. Further to this, Penty also writes on pp. 157ff. of his *Old Worlds for New* on the profession of architecture, of how architecture is 'incompatible with industrialism' because of the sub-divisions of labour encouraged in the latter. (And see also note 7 of this chapter.)

24 See Bell, *The Coming of Post-Industrial Society*, p. 37. Later, on p. 39, Bell also describes the use of the term post-industrial in the work of Keniston and Goodman of 1971 as denoting a new anti-material-ism in the youth of the time and adds that Goodman's belief that there is a 'turn toward "a personal subsistence economy", independent of the excesses of a machine civilization' is 'close to Penty's view of the artisan guild society'.

25 Penty's reference to Ruskin on pages 79–80 of his *Old Worlds for New* (at the conclusion of its chapter on the 'Division of Labour') had been, moreover, to Ruskin's observations in his *The Stones of Venice* on the divisive effects of the division of labour on the human being.

26 Bell, *The Coming of Post-Industrial Society*, p. 37, moves from his mention of Riesman to Penty.

27 See Penty, *Old Worlds for New*, pp. 176f. Penty also wrote on p. 91 that 'To use machinery as a slave is impossible for a people who treat it as a divinity.' Later, in his *Post-Industrialism* of 1922, p. 57, Penty added that his criticism of machinery had 'not been directed against machinery as such, but against its unrestricted use and the deliberate ignoring of its social and economic consequences', but that his criticism of the sub-division of labour 'which lies behind the misapplication of machinery' was unqualified.

28 See Riesman's essay 'Leisure and Work in Post-Industrial Society', in E. Larrabee and R. Meyersohn (eds.), *Mass Leisure* (Glencoe, Ill., 1958), pp. 363–85; and Bell, *The Coming of Post-Industrial Society*, pp. 37f. While differing from Penty in several ways, Riesman is, however, not entirely uncritical of the new 'leisure society'.

29 See Bell, *The Coming of Post-Industrial Society*, pp. 449ff.

30 Some of these other contemporary theories will be discussed presently. As noted previously (in chapter 1), Amitai Etzioni's 1968 description of the 'post-modern period' had also included the 'rad-

ical transformation of the technologies of communication, knowledge and energy that followed World War Two' in its list of definers for that period.

31 See Bell, *The Coming of Post-Industrial Society*, pp. 38–9. On pp. 52–3 Bell also criticises Amitai Etzioni's 1968 text for having implied that the post-modern period had seen a 'radical transformation of the technologies of communication' and of 'knowledge' without adequate evidence. Despite Bell's criticisms of Etzioni, the latter had suggested at least two characteristics of the post-industrial society which Bell develops further in his work: namely, the decline of the power of business (compare Etzioni, *The Active Society*, p. 528, with Bell, *The Coming of Post-Industrial Society*, p. 344) and the rise of secularism (Etzioni, p. 603, and Bell, p. 477). While Bell will see both of these to be characteristic of the post-industrial society (he writes (ibid., p. 344) on business and production that its power will be surpassed by that of government as well as science), he will also see both modern and post-modern society as characterised by a lack of values, where Etzioni had looked to the post-modern to establish new values through acts of consensus. (See Etzioni, ibid., pp. vii and 432ff., and also the following discussion of Bell on post-modernism.)

32 Alvin Toffler's *Future Shock* (London, 1970), describes the future society as 'super-industrial' rather than 'post-industrial', but characterises it as dominated by technology in much the same way as Etzioni had characterised the 'post-modern period'. In addition to describing the society of the future as one dominated by new technologies, Toffler had also spoken of it as dominated by cults and sub-cults, as suggested by both Etzioni, *The Active Society*, p. 603, and Leslie Fiedler in his 1965 essay 'The New Mutants'. (And see also both chapter 1 on Fiedler and the following passages and notes on Bell and Fiedler.)

33 Fiedler's 1965 essay had also named McLuhan as one of the new post-modernist writers. (See p. 191, n. 53.) McLuhan's major works include his *The Mechanical Bride: Folklore of Industrial Man* (New York, 1951); *Explorations in Communication*, with E. S. Carpenter (Boston, 1960); *The Gutenberg Galaxy: the Making of Typographic Man* (Toronto, 1962); *Understanding Media: the Extensions of Man* (New York, 1964); *The Medium is the Massage: an Inventory of Effects*, with Quentin Fiore (New York, 1967); and *War and Peace in the Global Village*, also with Quentin Fiore (New York, 1968). Here it should also be noted that McLuhan's concept of the 'global village' is very different from the pre-industrial villages praised by

both Coomaraswamy and Penty. This is so for one thing because although the 'global village' may be understood as bringing people of all nations into contact with each other through the media of the electronics industry, it may also be seen as increasing rather than reducing the sub-divisions of labour characteristic of industrial society.

34 Baudrillard himself has tended not to use the term 'postmodernism' with any frequency (although his 'On Nihilism' of 1981 (*On the Beach*, vol. 6 (spring 1984)) describes post-modernity as the process of the 'destruction of meaning'), but has been published in collections on that subject and been described as a 'postmodernist' by others. (See, for example, the blurb to the English translation of his *Amérique* (London and New York, 1988).) As discussed further in following chapters, McLuhan's descriptions of the 'global village' have been taken over by Ihab Hassan to describe what he terms 'postmodernism', while the term 'the world village' is also used by Charles Jencks in some of his descriptions of post-industrial society.

35 See Baudrillard, 'The Orders of Simulacra' in *Simulations*, translated by Philip Beitchmann (New York, 1983), pp. 119, 123 and 126.

36 See 'Requiem for the Media', in Baudrillard, *For a Critique of the Political Economy of the Sign*, translated by Charles Levin (St Louis, 1981), p. 177.

37 See note 36 above.

38 See Baudrillard, 'The Ecstasy of Communication', in Hal Foster (ed.), *Postmodern Culture* (London, 1985), pp. 126–34.

39 Baudrillard, 'The Ecstasy of Communication', p. 127. Baudrillard also goes on, on p. 128, to speak of this era as 'an era of hyper-reality'. (The latter is, moreover, a concept which has been taken up by others to characterise the 'postmodern', and will be returned to in chapter 3.) Baudrillard further describes this concept in this essay by claiming that 'what used to be lived out on earth as metaphor . . . is henceforth projected onto reality, without any metaphor at all, into an absolute space which is also that of simulation'.

40 See Baudrillard's 'The Implosion of Meaning in the Media and the Implosion of the Social in the Masses', in Kathleen Woodward (ed.), *The Myths of Information: Technology and Postindustrial Culture* (London, 1980), pp. 137–48.

41 See, for example, McLuhan's 'Dialogue' with G.E. Stearn in *McLuhan: Hot and Cool*, ed. Gerald Emanuel Stearn (Harmondsworth, 1968), p. 336.

42 See Jean Baudrillard, 'Design and Environment', in Baudrillard, *For*

a Critique of the Political Economy of the Sign, p. 199. (On pp. 186ff. Baudrillard also describes the modern obsession with the sign as a 'legacy of the Bauhaus'.)

43 Baudrillard, 'Requiem for the Media', p. 164.

44 Douglas Kellner's article 'Postmodernism as Social Theory', in *Theory, Culture & Society*, vol. 5, nos. 2–3 (June 1988), pp. 247ff., also describes Baudrillard as the 'first high-tech social theorist' and as reproducing 'certain trends of the present age which he projects into a simulation model of postmodernism as the catastrophe of modernity.' Kellner's more recent book on Baudrillard, his *Jean Baudrillard: from Marxism to Postmodernism and Beyond* (Oxford and Cambridge, 1989), also admits, however (on p. 120), that Baudrillard's 'On Nihilism' was to date the only text in which he had presented his own theory as one of post-modernity.

45 See the sections on Lyotard and Jameson in the following chapter.

46 Dick Hebdige, *Hiding in the Light: on Images and Things* (London and New York, 1988), p. 195.

47 Some of these points will be returned to again in following passages. Richard Kearney's *The Wake of Imagination* (London, 1988), pp. 380ff. also runs together several different definitions of the post-industrial in speaking of the 'post-industrial' society, 'to use Daniel Bell's term', as 'governed' by the 'means of communication'. As will be seen presently, Bell's major definer for the post-industrial society is, however, very different from this latter more technologically deterministic one.

48 Touraine's conclusion to his post-1968 text specifically asks sociologists to be effective in introducing social change, although without seeming altogether optimistic about whether or how they will accept his challenge. André Gorz's later *Farewell to the Working Class: an Essay on Post-Industrial Socialism* of 1980 (translated by Mike Sonenscher (London, 1982)) also contains both a utopian conclusion and pessimistic passages such as (p. 73): 'Progress has arrived at a threshhold beyond which plus turns into minus. The future is heavy with menace and devoid of promise. The forward march of productivism now brings the advance of barbarism and oppression.' While Gorz does still regard the individual as being able to break out of that oppression, his individual is conceived as being a member of the 'non-class of non-producers' of post-industrial society. Although the possibility for action would still appear to make Gorz's position less pessimistic than Baudrillard's, Gorz may also be seen to be following here a Marcusean opposition (see Gorz, ibid., p. 85) between production and freedom which is

also to be found in Baudrillard's many criticisms of the 'spectre of production' (see, for example, Baudrillard's *The Mirror of Production* (St Louis, 1975)). In the end, Gorz's ideal post-industrial society is largely one in which the workers will be free to work in their own 'freely chosen time'. (Gorz, *Farewell to the Working Class*, p. 144.)

49 See Alain Touraine, *The Post-Industrial Society, Tomorrow's Social History: Classes, Conflicts and Culture in the Programmed Society*, translated Leonard F. Mayhew (London, 1974), p. 3. On page 69 Touraine also suggests that the term 'technocracy' owes something to Georges Gurvitch's concept of 'techno-bureaucracy' (from his *Industrialisation et technocratie* (Paris, 1949), pp. 179–99), by which Gurvitch (a commentator on both Marx and Saint-Simon) had indicated 'the connection of technocracy with bureaucracy and with technicism'.

50 Touraine, *The Post-Industrial Society*, p. 3.

51 Ibid., p. 10.

52 Ibid., p. 27.

53 Ibid., p. 49.

54 Ibid., pp. 55–6.

55 See the previous note 48.

56 See Bell, *The Coming of Post-Industrial Society*, p. 14 and following.

57 Penty, *Post-Industrialism*, p. 13, and see also the following note 128 on Arnold J. Toynbee's 1954 depiction of the 'post-Modern Age' as one characterised by a new growth of scientific knowledge.

58 See, for example, Penty, *Old Worlds for New*, pp. 145ff., and Penty, *Post-Industrialism*, pp. 61ff.

59 Bell's Preface is dated March 1973. Although it begins with a reference to Arnold J. Toynbee and to his work on the history of world civilisation (see Bell, *The Coming of Post-Industrial Society*, p. ix), it makes no specific mention of Toynbee's use of the term 'post-Modern'. In so far as Toynbee had used that term in the post-war volumes of his *A Study of History* to describe a post-middle-class age, or proletarian age, he had, however, used it in a sense very different from Bell's usage of the term 'post-industrial' to describe the growth of white-collar work over blue-collar work.

60 See Bell, *The Coming of Post-Industrial Society*, p. 13.

61 See Bell, ibid., p. x. Bell also refers here specifically to Marx.

62 Bell also explains here (ibid., p. xi) that he is trying to use a new kind of conceptual analysis, 'of axial principles and structures', used as 'a way of "ordering" the bewildering number of possible

perspectives about macro-historical change'. Bell adds (p. 10): 'The idea of axial principles and structures is an effort to specify not causation (this can only be done in a theory of empirical relationships) but centrality', and that this may also be understood as searching for a principle of organisation or 'energizing principle' such as Marx did when suggesting that the production of commodities was the axial principle of capitalism, or Weber, the process of rationalisation. With regard to the use of the word 'determining' in the passage quoted from Bell's Preface, it should also be noted that Bell goes on to write on *The Coming of Post-Industrial Society*, p. 13, that the post-industrial society will not determine the way in which individuals will act, but 'pose questions' for them and the rest of society.

63　Ibid., p. x.

64　Bell gives a brief description of industrialism, in *The Coming of Post-Industrial Society*, pp. ix–x.

65　Bell also speaks of the concept of the post-industrial society in his Conclusion (ibid., p. 487) as the social-theoretical construction of an 'ideal type'.

66　Ibid., p. xi.

67　Ibid., p. 36.

68　Ibid.

69　See Bell, ibid., p. 37.

70　See Bell, ibid., p. 214.

71　See the pages on Lyotard in chapter 3.

72　See Bell, *The Coming of Post-Industrial Society*, pp. 382–3.

73　Jean-François Lyotard, *The Postmodern Condition: a Report on Knowledge*, translated by Geoff Bennington and Brian Massumi (Manchester, 1984), p. 45.

74　Ibid., p. 46.

75　Bell, *The Coming of Post-Industrial Society*, p. 14.

76　See Bell, ibid., pp. 14ff.

77　Bell also admits (ibid., p. 134) that his figures for his first two points tend to conceal the amount of service work done by women in the past, and are in general based on the employment of male workers.

78　Anthony Giddens refers in his essay 'The Perils of Punditry: Gorz and the End of the Working Class', in his *Social Theory and Modern Sociology* (Stanford, 1987), pp. 282ff., to Ulf Himmelstrand's redefinition of the 'working class', which Gorz claims to be 'disappearing', by means of the inclusion in it of white-collar and service workers whom Bell and other theorists of post-industrial society have excluded from the 'traditional' working class. Here the point could also be made that not all of the types of service work included by Bell in his post-industrial society necessarily involve the theoretical knowledge which he goes on to describe in his third point as the 'axial principle' of the post-industrial society.

79 See Bell, *The Coming of Post-Industrial Society*, p. 43.

80 I have previously discussed this topic in my *Marx's Lost Aesthetic* (Cambridge, 1984), and in an article on 'The Concept of the Avant-Garde: from the Modern to the Post-Modern', in *Agenda* 1/2, Melbourne (August 1988), pp. 23–4. The most accessible editions of works by Saint-Simon in English are still *The Political Thought of Saint-Simon*, edited by Ghita Ionescu (Oxford, 1976) and Keith Taylor's selection of works by Saint-Simon, *Henri Saint-Simon (1760–1825): Selected Writings on Science, Industry and Social Organisation* (London, 1975). To Saint-Simon, his 'avant-garde' of scientists, industrialists, engineers and artists was to both 'appreciate a new idea' and 'defeat the forces of inertia', and to 'contribute greatly to the prosperity of manufacturers by the designs and models with which they furnish artisans' (see Ionescu, *The Political Thought of Saint-Simon*, p. 132), or by making products of use as well as of aesthetic value (see Ionescu, ibid., p. 233, and Taylor, *Henri Saint-Simon (1760–1825)*, p. 194).

81 See Bell, *The Coming of Post-Industrial Society*, pp. 212ff.

82 See Ionescu, *The Political Thought of Saint-Simon*, p. 233.

83 See his 'Lettres d'un habitant de Genève à ses contemporains', in Taylor, *Henri Saint-Simon (1760–1825)*, p. 71.

84 See Ionescu, *The Political Thought of Saint-Simon*, pp. 221–2.

85 See Walter Benjamin's ninth 'Thesis on the Philosophy of History', in *Illuminations*, edited by Hannah Arendt, English translation of 1968 by Harry Zohn (New York, 1969), pp. 257–8. The major section on post-modernism in Dick Hebdige's *Hiding in the Light*, pp. 180–1, opens with not just one but two representations of the 'Angel of History'.

86 Despite Lyotard's criticisms of the military connotations of the concept of avant-garde (referred to later in chapter 3, note 100), at least some elements of the Saint-Simonist concept of avant-garde will be seen to have been retained in his work, including his implicit attribution of an avant-garde role to the work of those 'deconstructing' the 'meta-narratives' of modernity.

87 See Ken'ichi Tominaga, 'Post-Industrial Society and Cultural Diversity', in *Survey*, vol. 16, no. 1 (Winter 1971), pp. 68–77. Other contributions to this volume included Daniel Bell's 'Technocracy and Politics'; Jean Floud's 'A Critique of Bell'; Peter Wiles's 'A Com-

ment on Bell'; François Bourricard's 'Post-Industrial Society and the Paradoxes of Welfare'; and Giovanni Sartori's 'Technological Forecasting and Politics'. A continuation of Bell's contribution, entitled 'The Post-Industrial Society: the Evolution of an Idea', was subsequently published in the next edition of the journal, vol. 17, no. 2 (Spring 1971), pp. 102–68.

88 Tominaga, 'Post-Industrial Society and Cultural Diversity', p. 68, claims that Saint-Simon had coined the term industrial society in 1821. Various other dates have been given for the first use of this term, Barry Jones having suggested, for example, in his *Sleepers Wake! Technology and the Future of Work* (Melbourne, 1982), p. 2, that Auguste Comte's periodical *L'Industrie* had coined the word *industrialisme* in 1816. Keith Taylor, however, writes in his selection of works by Saint-Simon (*Henri Saint-Simon (1760–1825)*, p. 47) that Saint-Simon (to whom Comte was at one time secretary) had introduced the term 'industrial' in 'the early years of the Restoration' to refer to any member of any of the productive classes, and that while after 1820 the term 'industrial' was applied by Saint-Simon only to those doing practical work in farming or industry, he had also used the term in this sense as early as 1815 in an unpublished manuscript entitled 'Aux Anglais et aux Français qui sont zélés pour le bien public'. (See Taylor, ibid., pp. 47 and 59.)

89 See Tominaga, 'Post-Industrial Society and Cultural Diversity', p. 69.

90 Ibid. Bell's characterisation of the post-industrial society as a 'meritocracy' (*The Coming of Post-Industrial Society*, p. 43) may also be compared with Saint-Simon's famous tenet of 'to each according to his abilities'. (See Ionescu, *The Political Thought of Saint-Simon*, p. 28.) Although Bell gives a twentieth-century definition of 'merit' as involving IQ plus effort, Saint-Simon's use of the term 'abilities' could also be said to have implied that their presence had been proven by something like that which is now termed merit.

91 Tominaga, 'Post-Industrial Society and Cultural Diversity', p. 69. Tominaga also refers to Saint-Simon here, although his quotation from the latter gives only a glimpse of the range of ideas to be found in Saint-Simon which could be related to more recent theories of the post-industrial society.

92 See Daniel Bell, 'Technocracy and Politics', p. 2. Bell's contribution contains material later published in his *The Coming of Post Industrial Society*.

93 Bell, 'Technocracy and Politics', p. 3.

94 Bell, *The Coming of Post-Industrial Society*, p. 115.

95 Ibid.

96 Bell also goes on here to speak of how for 'analytical purposes' one can still divide societies into pre-industrial, industrial and post-industrial, although he adds that they are 'of course, ideal-type constructions'.

97 Bell, *The Coming of Post-Industrial Society*, p. 344. He had also written (ibid., p. 128) that 'the growth of technical requirements and professional skills makes education, and access to higher education, the condition of entry into the post-industrial society itself'.

98 Marx's 1845 and 1858–62 notes from Babbage's *On the Economy of Machinery and Manufactures* of 1832 are housed in the Institute for Social History in Amsterdam, and include several excerpts from Babbage's chapters on the divisions of labour.

99 See the Preface to the first edition of Babbage's *On the Economy of Machinery and Manufactures* (London, 1832).

100 See, for example, the *Dictionary of Scientific Biography*, edited by Charles Coulston Gillispie (New York, 1970), vol. I, p. 355; and *Charles Babbage and his Calculating Engines: Selected Writings by Charles Babbage and Others*, edited and with an Introduction by Philip Morrison and Emily Morrison (New York, 1961), pp. xvi–xvii.

101 See, for example, Anthony Hyman's *Charles Babbage: Pioneer of the Computer* (Oxford, 1982), p. 48; and also Babbage's chapter on 'Calculating Machines' on pp. 173ff. of his *The Exposition of 1851* (London, 1851), new (1968) impression of the 2nd edn of 1851, on the relationship of these two machines.

102 See paragraph 459 of the fourth enlarged edition of 1835 of Babbage's *On the Economy of Machinery and Manufactures*.

103 See especially Babbage's chapter on the divisions of mental labour in his *On the Economy of Machinery and Manufactures*. Although Babbage had combined his advocacy of an increased division of labour with his support for the 'union of scientific theory and industrial practice' (see Hyman, *Charles Babbage*, pp. 103ff.), Penty had specifically criticised both the industrial sub-division of labour 'to increase the output and reduce the cost of production of certain articles by subdividing a trade into a great number of separate branches' as 'eulogized by Adam Smith in *The Wealth of Nations*' in his *Old Worlds for New* (pp. 74ff.), and, as noted earlier, the sub-division of the professions as leading to too much specialisation. By contrast to Penty, both Babbage and Saint-Simon had admired the work of Adam Smith.

104 See paragraphs 460 and 461 of the fourth edition of Babbage's 1832 text. Both iodine and bromine were to be used in photography as well as in chemistry and medicine.

105 The *Encyclopaedia Britannica*, 30 vols., 15th edn (Chicago, 1982), Micropaedia, vol. 1, pp. 705–6, begins its entry on Babbage by describing him as a 'Mathematician and inventor who originated the modern automatic computer' and concludes by noting not only that he had 'published papers on mathematics, statistics, physics and geology', but had also 'assisted in establishing the modern postal system in England', had 'compiled the first reliable actuarial tables' and 'invented the speedometer and the locomotive cowcatcher'.

106 Bell, *The Coming of Post-Industrial Society*, p. 25.

107 Ibid., p. 27. Although the edition of the *Encyclopaedia Britannica* referred to above opens its entry on Babbage by describing him as the 'inventor who originated the modern automatic computer' (see the above note 105), its entry on Felix Bloch makes no mention of his contribution to the same.

108 Despite the relevance of Babbage's recognition of the economic and scientific importance of the divisions of mental labour to the development of those sectors which Bell and others have termed 'post-industrial', no theorist or historian of the concept of the latter has, to my knowledge, included Babbage in the canon of 'post-industrial thinkers'. Rather, his arguments for the increased division of labour have led some commentators to discuss him in the context of Frederick Winslow Taylor's development of the concept of scientific management, and of his attempts to produce the maximum efficiency and productivity in the workplace. See, for example, Barry Jones, *Sleepers Wake!*, pp. 85–6. (Jones also follows Harry Braverman's interpretation of Babbage in the former's *Labor and Monopoly Capital* of 1974 to some extent here.) Bell had written in both 1971 and 1973 that the advent of Taylorism had also meant a reversal of the Saint-Simonist prophecy for an age in which men would administer things and not people, in that now the things began 'to ride' the men (*The Coming of Post-Industrial Society*, pp. 351–2); and Penty (*Post-Industrialism*, pp. 58ff.) had also criticised the principles of scientific management for carrying Adam Smith's system to its 'logical conclusion'. To Babbage, however, the machine was to help give order to work but was not to oppress the worker, Babbage's ideal rules for the factory (*On the Economy of Machinery and Manufactures*, 1835, p. 293) having demanded, for example, that they were 'conduce to the general benefit of all the persons concerned' and were to 'interfere as little as possible with the free agency of each individual'.

109 See also the earlier discussion of the first of Bell's definers of the post-industrial society.

110 By contrast, C. Wright Mills's *The Sociological Imagination* of 1959 had been critical both of the 'grand theories' of sociology and of science in his section on the post-modern period. (See Mills, *The Sociological Imagination* (Harmondsworth, 1983), pp. 186–7.) Mills's argument in his latter critique that science had not eradicated irrationality in other spheres is, however, to some extent comparable to that taken up by Bell in the Coda to his 1973 text and in his 1976 work, when he attacks the irrationalisms of modern and postmodern culture, although Bell also sees the causes for the latter largely in the loss of the ethical elements of capitalism.

111 See, for example, Daniel Bell, *The Cultural Contradictions of Capitalism* (New York, 1976), p. 75.

112 See Habermas's Adorno Prize lecture on 'Modernity – an Incomplete Project', in Foster, *Postmodern Culture*, p. 6.

113 See Bell, *The Coming of Post-Industrial Society*, p. 477; and Bell, *The Cultural Contradictions of Capitalism*, p. 21. Arthur Penty had also criticised machine production as having 'created an atmosphere antipathetic to religion' in his *Post-Industrialism* of 1922, p. 48, and had seen capitalism as the 'financial aspect' of industrial machinism in that same work (ibid., p. 147).

114 See Habermas, 'Modernity – an Incomplete Project', p. 7. Jonathan Arac's Introduction to his *Postmodernism and Politics* (Minnesota and Manchester, 1986), pp. xviff.) also correctly identifies the misreading of Bell made in Habermas's text. By contrast, Andreas Huyssen's essay 'Mapping the Postmodern' (in his *After the Great Divide: Modernism, Mass Culture and Postmodernism* (Bloomington, In., 1986, and London, 1988), pp. 203ff. of the latter) joins Habermas in claiming that Bell blames modernism for the crises of contemporary capitalism. While Huyssen differs from Habermas in acknowledging Bell's identification of modernism and postmodernism, the inclusion of the latter in the argument that Bell blames modernism for the crises of contemporary capitalism does nothing to correct the original errors of Habermas's argument.

115 See also the essays in Habermas's *Die neue Unuebersichtlichkeit* (Frankfurt am Main, 1985). In it (on p. 12) Habermas's essay on modern and post-modern architecture of 1981 defines the term 'post-industrial' in terms of the expansion of the service sectors of industrial capitalism at the expense of the directly productive realm, rather than in terms of the axial principle of theoretical knowledge given by Bell in his 1973 work.

116 See again Bell, *The Coming of Post-Industrial Society*, p. 477 (quoted in part in the following text); and Bell, *The Cultural Con-*

tradictions of Capitalism, p. 21. Although Habermas does not mention it in his attack on Bell, it is also interesting to note with regard to his reading of the latter that Bell had attacked him just prior to his 1980 lecture, in a 1979 essay entitled 'Liberalism in the Post-industrial Society' (see Bell, *The Winding Passage: Essays and Sociological Journeys 1960–1980* (Cambridge, Mass., 1980), pp. 242–3), and for suggesting in his *Legitimation Crisis* that we need not a 'liberal theory of society orientated primarily to individuals', but a form of ' "public law" that will represent universal, generalizable interests'. To Bell the 'fundamental fallacy' in Habermas's argument is 'the idea, derived from the Enlightenment, that there can be such a unitary phenomenon as a set of universal, generalizable interests'. See also chapter 3 for further details of Habermas's theories and, in particular, of his argument against both Bell and Lyotard for the need to complete the Enlightenment 'project of modernity'. While Bell would appear to have been on the same side as Lyotard when criticising Habermas's 'consensus' theories his complaint against them is based on very different premises from Lyotard's in arguing, for one thing, for the retention of the idea of the importance of the individual.

117 See Bell, *The Cultural Contradictions of Capitalism*, p. 21. To make yet another comparison with Penty, it may be recalled that his 1917 work had also argued for a revaluation of work rather than for an escape from it.

118 Bell, ibid., p. 28.

119 Ibid., p. 52. Whether Bell's prediction about the longevity of this type of post-modernism will be correct or not cannot yet be said, although it has (for better or worse) at least survived the fifteen or so years since Bell first published these words.

120 Ibid., p. 51.

121 The essay appeared in *Art, Politics and Will: Essays in Honor of Lionel Trilling*, edited by Quentin Anderson, Stephen Donadio and Steven Marcus (New York, 1977), pp. 213–53, and was later republished in Bell's *The Winding Passage*, pp. 235–302, from which quotations will be taken here.

122 See the previous references to Fiedler in chapter 1 and Bell's reference to Fiedler's essay 'The New Mutants' in his 1977 essay 'Beyond Modernism, Beyond Self' in his *The Winding Passage*, p. 292. Unlike some who have taken up Fiedler's descriptions of post-modernism, Bell is clearly critical of that which he sees Fiedler to be describing under the rubric of the post-modern.

123 See L. A. Fiedler's *The Collected Essays of Leslie Fiedler* (New York,

1971), vol. II, pp. 392–3, and the previous reference to the *Oxford English Dictionary*'s citation of Fiedler's use of the term 'post-Modernist literature' in chapter 1.

124 See Fiedler, *Collected Essays*, p. 389, and chapter 1, note 53, as well as note 125 below.

125 Bell, *The Cultural Contradictions of Capitalism*, p. 118. Fiedler's characterisations of post-modernism as cultist and hedonistic are also echoed in Ihab Hassan's characterisation of the post-modern of 1971. (See chapter 3 and its section on Hassan.) Earlier Arnold J. Toynbee had also referred to the growth of a 'post-Christian' age, in which other religions, cults and secular movements would displace Christianity from centre stage in the civilisation of the West (see, for example, the ninth volume of his *A Study of History* (London, 1954), pp. 618ff., as well as the reference to this argument in chapter 1). (As seen previously, Bell was familiar with both Toynbee's *A Study of History* and with Fiedler's 1969 essay, as well as with other associations of the post-modern with the rise of cultism such as Etzioni's and Toffler's.)

126 Bell, *The Coming of Post-Industrial Society*, p. 476.

127 Bell, ibid., p. 478.

128 Bell, *The Winding Passage*, p. 301. Earlier, in 1971, Ihab Hassan had described the modern as 'antinomian' and the post-modern as characterised by 'counter-cultures', whilst also emphasising links between the two movements. (This was, moreover, in an essay in which, as will be seen in chapter 3, Hassan names Fiedler as one of the founders of 'postmodern criticism', a subject also discussed by Fiedler in his 1969 essay.) Prior to Hassan, Arnold J. Toynbee had spoken of the 'Antinomianism of Late Modern Western Historians' and 'The Repudiation of the Belief in a "Law of God" by Late Modern Western Minds' as ironically being accompanied by the development of a 'post-Modern' scientific obsession with the laws of Nature as well as of the new social sciences of psychology, anthropology, political economics and sociology. See Toynbee's *A Study of History*, vol. 9, chapter 11, pp. 173ff. (Toynbee also sometimes uses the terms 'Late Modern' and 'post-Modern' inter-changeably in this chapter, as on, for example, its p. 189, where he speaks of an 'intellectually anarchic Late Modern and post-Modern Age'.) While Toynbee speaks critically of both antinomianism and the growth of modern social science in this chapter, Bell's contrast of modernist/post-modernist culture with post-industrial society suggests a somewhat clearer distinction between the antinomianism of the former and the scientific character of the latter, as well as a

preference for the latter. Here it should also be noted that in many theories of post-modernism and post-industrialism an understanding of the particular concept of science used, and of its interpretation by the theorist in question,. may also be important. Ihab Hassan's understanding of post-modern science as being exemplified by such early twentieth-century theories as Heisenberg's 'Uncertainty Principle' (see Ihab Hassan, 'Culture, Indeterminacy, and Immanence: Margins of the (Postmodern) Age', in Hassan, *The Postmodern Turn: Essays in Postmodern Theory and Culture* (Columbus, Oh., 1987), p. 57) is, for example, not only based on Hassan's understanding of the post-modern as something characterised by an 'indeterminacy' which allows of a variety of points of view rather than any one truth or certainty, but also his particular interpretation of Heisenberg's uncertainty principle as something which puts forward a similar concept of indeterminacy to his own.

129 Bell, *The Coming of Post-Industrial Society*, p. 478.
130 Bell, *The Winding Passage*, pp. 289ff.
131 Bell, *The Cultural Contradictions of Capitalism*, p. 29.
132 See, for example, ibid., p. 52.
133 See chapters 4 and 5 for an account of these other 'post-modernisms'.

3 Deconstructionist theories

1 Quoted by Steve Woolgar in a discussion of 'postmodern' anthropology, in *Current Anthropology*, vol. 29, no. 3 (June 1988), p. 430. (And see also the Conclusion of this chapter for further details of that discussion.)
2 Christopher Norris, *The Deconstructive Turn* (London and New York, 1983), p. 6.
3 Ibid.
4 See, for instance, the following discussion of Ihab Hassan's 'deconstruction' of certain 'modernist' canonisations of authors and styles, and Jean-François Lyotard's critique of what he has termed the 'metanarratives of modernity'.
5 Different types of deconstructionist post-modernism will be discussed in the various sections of the chapter which follow. Because Derrida has also been seen as a critic of structuralism, many of the ideas described as deconstructionist in the following pages may also be found to be described by others as post-structuralist. (See, for example, the pages on Hal Foster's article on post-modernism in the conclusion of this chapter.) As will be seen by the time of the

Conclusion to this chapter, the latter will also deal with some deconstructionist critiques of post-modernism as well as with what will be generally described as deconstructionist theories of the post-modern.

6 Jacques Derrida, *The Truth in Painting*, translated by Geoff Bennington and Ian McLeod (Chicago and London, 1987), p. 19. This work also contains an article written by Derrida in 1975 on the painter Valerio Adami, about whom Lyotard has also written. (See Derrida, *The Truth in Painting*, pp. 151–81.) A recent interview made with Derrida by Christopher Norris, entitled 'Jacques Derrida: in Discussion with Christopher Norris', in *Architectural Design*, vol. 58, no. 1/2 (1989); Profile 77, Deconstruction II, pp. 6–11, also gives some further definition of Deconstruction with particular reference to Deconstruction and architecture, and quizzes Derrida on his reluctance to describe his deconstructionist philosophy as either modern or post-modern.

7 See Norris, *The Deconstructive Turn*, p. 169.

8 Ibid., p. 106.

9 Ibid., pp. 3ff.

10 Ibid., p. 6. Norris also begins his section of Christopher Norris and Andrew Benjamin, *What is Deconstruction?* (London and New York, 1988), p. 7, with the statement that 'To "deconstruct" a text is to draw out conflicting logics of sense and implication, with the object of showing that the text never exactly means what it says or says what it means.' Problems which arise here include, however, the legitimation of arbitrary interpretations of texts which may not only be misleading in their choice of the 'logics' of the text which are to be drawn out, but which must themselves appear to go against their own theory of deconstruction to claim that their choices, and interpretations, are correct.

11 The inclusion of Habermas in this chapter is more problematic as he clearly does not agree with the majority of tenets of Deconstruction (see the section in this chapter on his theories), but has none the less taken over some of the 'deconstructionist' critiques of post-modern architecture (of, for example, Lyotard and Jameson), and seen both post-modern architecture and Lyotard's post-modernism as attempting to 'deconstruct' the 'project of modernity'. Habermas's comments on post-modernism have, however, also been included in this chapter because his own work has been a target for attack in Lyotard's 1979 and 1982 texts on the post-modern.

12 Ihab Hassan writes in a section on Lyotard in the conclusion of his *The Postmodern Turn: Essays in Postmodern Theory and Culture*

(Columbus, Oh., 1987), p. 222, that although beginnings 'are always dim', we know 'that the postmodern debate drifted from America to Europe'. In notes to this Hassan adds that the Milwaukee and New York City conferences on 'postmodernism' (of 1976 and 1978) were attended, respectively, by Jean-François Lyotard and Julia Kristeva, and that the Milwaukee conference attended by Lyotard in 1976 entitled 'Postmodern Performance' had also led to the publication *Performance in Postmodern Culture* of 1977. An even earlier conference on 'Postmodernity and Hermeneutics', at Binghamton, New York, in 1976 was, Hassan notes (p. 231), also published in *Boundary 2*, vol. 4, n. 2 (Winter 1976).

13 See also the earlier reference in chapter 1 to Baudrillard and Hassan. Hassan himself suggests of Lyotard in his 1987 text, when speaking of the transmission of his ideas on post-modernism to the latter, that Lyotard had already been 'congenial to indetermanences'. (See Hassan, *The Postmodern Turn*, p. 222.) Earlier Jean-François Lyotard had also discussed 'deconstruction' in modern art in the interview published in his *Driftworks*, edited by Roger McKeon (New York, 1984), entitled 'On Theory', of 1970. (See Lyotard, *Driftworks*, pp. 26ff.) Deconstruction in art is not only dated from the beginnings of the twentieth century in this interview by Lyotard, but is also related to both the work of Picasso in another *Driftworks* piece, entitled 'The Connivance of Desire with the Figural' of 1971 (Lyotard, *Driftworks*, p. 64), and to political revolution (of proletariat against capital) in his 'Notes on the Critical Function of the Work of Art' of 1970, in Lyotard, *Driftworks*, p. 79.

14 See Michael Koehler, '"Postmodernismus": ein begriffsgeschichtlicher Ueberblick', *Amerikastudien*, vol. 22, no. 1 (1977), p. 11.

15 This article has recently been republished, together with several other more recent essays by Hassan in his *The Postmodern Turn* of 1987. That work also concludes with an extensive bibliography of works on post-modernism, and includes a list of Hassan's own works on the subject.

16 See Charles Jencks, *Post-Modernism: the New Classicism in Art and Architecture* (London, 1987), p. 18. Jencks adds, however, that 'even then the term, like its inconsistent capitalisation, wasn't clearly defined', and, as Jencks had pointed out elsewhere (in, for example, his *What is Post-Modernism?* (London, 1986), pp. 6–7), Hassan was still largely concerned with what could also have been called 'Late-Modernism'.

17 Jencks's writings on post-modernism will be dealt with in more

detail in chapter 4. As he also pointed out in his 1987 discussion of Hassan, Hassan's concept of post-modernism as 'subversive in form and anarchic in its cultural spirit' was part of a view of post-modernism which represented the 'antithesis of what was going on in the Post-Modern Movement in architecture at that time'. (See Jencks, *Post-Modernism: the New Classicism in Art and Architecture*, p. 19.)

18 See note 17 above. Jencks also writes in his 1987 text (*Post-Modernism: the New Classicism in Art and Architecture*, p. 19) that only one of Hassan's definers of post-modernism, of 'Participation', was relevant to post-modern architecture, and that other definers such as 'Pataphysics/Dadaism, Play, Chance and Anarchy' were also inaccurate for post-modern literature.

19 Hassan, *The Postmodern Turn*, p. 26.

20 Ibid., p. 30.

21 Ibid. Hassan's listing of Burroughs as a post-modernist here may also recall Leslie Fiedler's description of him as such in his 1965 essay 'The New Mutants'. (See both chapters 1 and 2 as well as the following discussion of Hassan's 1980 comments on Fiedler.) Hassan, *The Postmodern Turn*, pp. 31–2, also goes on to name Fiedler, together with George Steiner, himself, Hugh Kenner, Susan Sontag, Richard Poirier and John Barth as part of the history of 'Postmodern criticism'. Although a reference to Fiedler's concept of postmodern criticism (see, for instance, the end of note 53 of chapter 1) may help to explain Steiner's inclusion here, it might also be noted that Hassan is specifically referring to the Steiner of the essay 'The Retreat from the Word' and that that is a work in which Steiner had in fact both questioned the application of the scientist's concept of indeterminacy to culture and concluded by asking that more clarity and stringency of meaning be restored to our use of words. (See George Steiner, *Language and Silence: Essays 1953–1966* (London and New York, 1967).)

22 See also note 26 and its related text on parody as a device which has been used in several centuries for different purposes.

23 Hassan, *The Postmodern Turn*, pp. 33ff.

24 See ibid., pp. 40–4. Sontag's essay 'Against Interpretation' does not itself describe the 'post-modern' as such, but has often been included in the canon of post-modernist texts since Hassan's inclusion of it in his.

25 See also the previous note 21 and the comments on Fiedler in both chapters 1 and 2. As noted in the latter chapter, Daniel Bell also appears to follow Fiedler's characterisation of post-modernism as

involving the rise of a new emphasis on irrationality whilst also listing 'antinomianism' as one of the major characteristics of post-modernism. And see also chapter 2 for references to both Bell and Fiedler as well as to Arnold J. Toynbee's description of the late-modern growth of antinomianism and its effects.

26 I have previously discussed the subject of parody in my *Parody/Meta-Fiction* (London, 1979), as well as in some more recent articles on both parody and pastiche in post-modernism, and will suggest some ways of differentiating the modernist and post-modernist uses of parody later in this study. As will be seen in the section on Jameson in this chapter, he has taken parody to be characteristic of modernism rather than of post-modernism, despite following Hassan in some of his characterisations of post-modern-ism, but has then also projected a Baudrillardian concept of 'blank' or 'blind' parody from Baudrillard's critiques of the modern onto post-modernist pastiche. When other critics have followed Hassan in naming parodistic (and meta-fictional and self-reflexive) authors such as Beckett, Barth or Borges as post-modern some confusion has arisen for those who have previously known these authors as modernists, and especially when parody itself has been renamed post-modern in order to describe them as post-modern, and treated (as when named modern by Jameson) without regard for the fact that it is but a device which has been used for some centuries, and for several different purposes.

27 See also chapter 2 on Baudrillard and McLuhan.

28 See the Introduction to this book as well as chapter 1.

29 This issue will also be taken up again in later chapters.

30 Hassan's list of definers for 'Modernism' and 'Postmodernism' sum-marised earlier clearly mixes elements of the modern, modernisa-tion and modernism together with 'postmodernism'.

31 See, for example, Jencks, *What is Post-Modernism?*, p. 28, and Stephen Bann's pages on Finlay's Versailles project in *Art & Design*, vol. 4, no. 5/6 (1988), pp. 38–9.

32 See both chapter 1 and chapter 4 on this.

33 Hassan had also earlier suggested that post-modernist 'technolog-ism' may see matter 'disappearing into a concept', but does not explain the connection between this statement and his predictions for a transformation of artistic abstraction into concreteness further. The nature of post-modernist as opposed to late modernist art will be discussed further in both this chapter and the next.

34 See note 18 above.

35 This is, however, not so obviously the case in the 1980 list set up by

Hassan which will be quoted presently, and which Jencks (see also the previous note 18 and the following discussion of Hassan's 1980 list) may be said to have followed when discussing the term 'Participation' in his 1987 work.

36 Baudrillard will also be seen to have presented a comparable description of parody, while Jameson's concept of post-modernist pastiche as 'blind parody' will be seen to have attributed some similar characteristics to the latter. (See the following discussion of Jameson.)

37 See also chapter 1 note 20 for a preliminary explanation of Jencks's use of the term 'double-coding', and the discussion in chapter 4 of the seventh of Jencks's eleven rules in his *Post-Modernism: the New Classicism in Art and Architecture* for an instance of his relating of irony to double-coding. I have also discussed the way in which irony and parody may offer more than one message to the decoder in my *Parody/Meta-Fiction* of 1979, and will discuss this issue again, with reference to Jencks's concept of 'double-' or 'dual-coding', in chapter 4. With reference to Calinescu's 1986/7 discussion of post-modernism, the description of literary parody as a duplication of textual codes cannot necessarily be equated with the more metaphorical description of architectural post-modernism as a 'double-coding' of modernism with other 'codes' by Jencks, as suggested by both Matei Calinescu (*Five Faces of Modernity* (Durham, N.C., 1987), p. 285) and Linda Hutcheon (in, for instance, her *A Poetics of Postmodernism: History, Theory, Fiction* (New York and London, 1988), chapter 2). Indeed, a form of 'undistributed middle' (of the type of 'all cats are four-legged, all dogs are four-legged: therefore all dogs are cats – and vice versa') would appear to be concealed in any argument that 'all parody is dual-coded, all post-modernism is dual-coded: therefore all parody is post-modern and all post-modernism is parodic', because such arguments have overlooked not only the metaphoric character of the undistributed term 'dual-coded' in the second premiss, but also the fact that the characteristic of 'dual-codedness' does not exhaust the character of either parody or post-modern architecture (just as 'four-leggedness' does not exhaust the nature of either cats or dogs), but is, in both cases, only one essential characteristic amongst many. Parody, for one thing, has been defined since the times of classical rhetoric as specifically having some comic effect (as well as being both 'beside' and 'opposite' its target, as pointed out, for example, in Rose, *Parody/Meta-Fiction*, p. 33), where post-modern architecture does not necessarily or even frequently aim at a comic result. Hutcheon's

further argument (in Hutcheon, *A Poetics of Postmodernism*, p. 34) that post-modern architects have rarely linked their work with parody (despite her argument that they should) because they understand it as 'ridiculing imitation', also overlooks Jencks's description of parody in his *The Language of Post-Modern Architecture*, p. 93 as a device characterised by wit as well as by a use of cliché and convention, which he describes as 'aspects of communication which are essential to Post-Modernism'. Despite some similarities in the functions of the dual-coded parody and dual-coded post-modern building to increase the number of 'codes' being sent out, it should also be noted that parody, in contrast to post-modernism, is a device rather than a period term, and one which is to be found from ancient to 'post-modern' times. (And see also chapter 4 note 81 and following related notes on this subject.)

38 Jencks's writings will be discussed in greater detail in chapter 4. Earlier Robert Venturi, Denise Scott Brown and Steven Izenour's *Learning from Las Vegas* of 1972 (revised edn (Massachusetts, 1988), p. 161), had also claimed that irony could be 'the tool with which to confront and combine divergent values in architecture for a pluralist society and to accommodate the differences in values that arise between architects and clients'.

39 See Hassan, 'The Question of Postmodernism', in Harry R. Garvin (ed.), *Romanticism, Modernism, Postmodernism* (*Bucknell Review*, vol. 25, no. 2) (London and Toronto, 1980), p. 117. Hassan's 'Toward a Concept of Postmodernism' in his *The Postmodern Turn* p. 94 later acknowledges Koehler's contributions to this history of the term and repeats Koehler's error in dating Somervell's summary of Toynbee's *A Study of History* from 1947 rather than from 1946.

40 See Hassan, 'The Question of Postmodernism', p. 118, and the following notes on Fiedler. As Hassan explains in a note to his 1980 essay, on p. 125, it, like others in the collection, was part of a forum on the question of 'Postmodernism', organised by Hassan at the Modern Languages Association in New York in December 1978. The later essay entitled 'Toward a Concept of Postmodernism' is in many ways another version of the above essay (in it Hassan adds the names of both Lyotard and Jencks to the pantheon of post-modernists), and is to be found in Hassan's *The Post-Modern Turn* of 1987, pp. 84–96.

41 Hassan, 'The Question of Postmodernism', p. 118. Although Jencks also writes in his *What is Post-Modernism?* of 1986 (in an echo of Andreas Huyssen's description of Fiedler in his 1984 essay 'Map-

ping the Postmodern', in Huyssen, *After the Great Divide: Modernism, Mass Culture and Postmodernism* (Indiana, 1986, and London, 1988), p. 194) that 'virtually the first positive use of the prefix "post" ' was by the writer Leslie Fiedler in 1965 'when he repeated it like an incantation and tied it to current radical trends which made up the counter-culture', Jencks further describes it as an anarchic use of the term which is very different from his own use of it. (See Jencks, *What is Post-Modernism?*, pp. 3–4.) Not unlike Jencks, Daniel Bell (see chapter 2) had also read Fiedler's 1965 essay as presenting an essentially negative picture of post-modern culture, although he had, in contrast to Jencks, not suggested any more positive meaning or reference for the concept.

42 See Hassan, 'The Question of Postmodernism', p. 120.

43 This is discussed further in chapter 4.

44 Despite Hassan's criticisms of his emphasis on the 'anarchic' elements in his concept of post-modernism here, 'neo-gnostic' could also refer to an anti-logical way of thinking. In this case, the nature of Hassan's 'dialectic' would also be unlike either the Socratic or Hegelian dialectics. What it is, is, in any case, not made clear.

45 Hassan also refers here to Richard E. Palmer's discussion of the difference between post-modernism as a contemporary artistic tendency, and post-modernity, as a cultural phenomenon, 'perhaps even an era of history' in his 'Postmodernity and Hermeneutics', *Boundary 2*, vol. 5, n. 2 (Winter 1977), pp. 363–93.

46 See Hassan, 'The Question of Postmodernism', p. 123.

47 Such as, for example, the parody described in Hassan's 1971 list.

48 See also the previous notes on Jencks in this chapter and chapter 4.

49 I have also investigated some aspects of the way in which structuralist and post-structuralist theories have 'canonised' certain characteristics of modern parody – such as the intertextuality, discontinuity and reflectivity on the role of the author which may be found in the latter – as part of their own canons of theory, and then fed those characteristics back into other parodistic works to describe them as structuralist or post-structuralist, in my *Parody/Meta-Fiction* of 1979. Hassan's description of 'self-reflective' authors such as Joyce, Beckett and Barth as post-modernist, even though they have previously been described by some other critics as typical of *modernist* meta-fictional writing, may also be seen to follow from his extension of structuralist categories derived from modernist parodistic and/or meta-fictional works, and help explain why there is now much apparent confusion amongst critics as to whether to call these writers modern or post-modern, and why many such authors

may turn up in both 'canons'. As may be seen from other passages of my text, I myself would prefer to describe as 'post-modern' those works which, following Jencks, may be said to have clearly 'double-coded' something which they have defined as modern with something else to present the new work as something consciously 'post' in the sense of 'after' the modern.

50 It may also be no accident that the title of Hassan's *The Postmodern Turn* echoes that of Christopher Norris's *The Deconstructive Turn* of 1983. Although Norris uses the adjective 'deconstructive' for Deconstruction, here I have tried to avoid using it because of the more recent usage of the adjective 'deconstructive' in Johnson and Wigley's 1988 exhibition of 'Deconstructive Architecture', in which the word 'Deconstructive' was used to evoke both *Deconstruc*tion and Construct*ivism*. (See also the pages on Deconstructionist architecture in chapter 4.)

51 Unfortunately, Hassan does not suggest here what this new 'post-modern' 'accommodation between art and society' might be. His distinction between the 'older' avant-gardes and both post-modernism and modernism may also be questioned when we recall that he has previously used Dadaism as one of the characteristics of post-modernism.

52 Hassan, 'The Question of Postmodernism', pp. 124–5.

53 See Hassan's 'Pluralism in Postmodern Perspective', published in *Critical Inquiry*, vol. 12, n. 3 (1986), and republished in Hassan, *The Postmodern Turn*, pp. 167–87.

54 See also my *Parody/Meta-Fiction*, pp. 167ff.

55 Hassan, *The Postmodern Turn*, p. 173.

56 Ibid., p. 180. This is also a subject with which Richard Kearney has dealt in his *The Wake of Imagination* (London, 1988), but on the basis of a deconstructionist approach to the subject of the post-modern which also takes over elements from Lyotard and Jameson of which Hassan himself has been critical. (See the following note 62 on Hassan's criticisms of Lyotard and Jameson.)

57 See Daniel Bell, *The Coming of Post-Industrial Society* (Harmondsworth, 1976), pp. 52–3 and the previous entries on Etzioni.

58 But see also the following note 62 for reference to some of Hassan's disagreements with those who have followed him.

59 Gillian Rose's claim in her 'Architecture to Philosophy – the Post-modern Complicity', on pp. 362–3 of the special issue on post-modernism of the journal *Theory, Culture & Society*, vol. 5, nos. 2–3 (June 1988), that 'The debate between Juergen Habermas and Jean-François Lyotard . . . has taken over Jencks's terminology into

social theory and philosophy' seems to overlook the line of transmission which moves from American literary critics such as Hassan
to Lyotard, as well as differences between the uses of the term by
Jencks and Lyotard. Although Lyotard himself has recently stated
in an interview with Christine Pries of 6 May 1988, entitled
'Sublimity is that which Cannot be Consumed' ('Jean-François
Lyotard. Die Erhabenheit ist das Unkonsumierbare. Ein Gespraech
mit Christine Pries am 6.5.1988'), in *Kunstforum*, vol. 100
(April/May 1989), p. 358, that the word 'postmodernism' has come
'in principle from architecture', he will be seen in the following text
to have claimed in 1979 that the term 'postmodern' had come from
recent American sociology and criticism, while the history of the
usage of the term itself is, as seen in chapter 1, also much more
complicated than his 1988 statement would appear to suggest.

60 Jean-François Lyotard, *The Postmodern Condition: a Report on
Knowledge*, translated by Geoff Bennington and Brian Massumi
(Manchester, 1984), p. xxiiif.

61 Although Amitai Etzioni had used the term 'post-modern' in 1968 to
suggest a transformation of the technologies of communication and
knowledge (see the notes on Etzioni in the preceding chapters),
Michael Koehler for one has noted that Etzioni's term had not
caught on in sociological circles as much as Daniel Bell's use of
the term 'the post-industrial society'. (See Koehler, ' "Postmodernismus" ', p. 13.)

62 Hassan later criticises both Lyotard and Jameson in the chapter
entitled 'Prospects in Retrospect' of his *The Postmodern Turn* of
1987, and is also critical of too deconstructionist an approach to
post-modernism when he writes (p. 216) that 'deconstruction
threatens to engulf postmodernism in its ironies, threatens to
neutralize its utopian will'. Here too, however, Hassan continues to
defend some of his earlier characterisations of post-modernism, and
also praises Baudrillard's contribution to Hal Foster's *Postmodern
Culture*, as 'problematizing the postmodern condition in terms . . .
adequate to itself'. (See Hassan, *The Postmodern Turn*, p. 221 and
also note 13 above.)

63 See Lyotard, *The Postmodern Condition*, pp. 71ff.

64 See also the section on Habermas in this chapter. Habermas had not
named Lyotard himself as a neo-conservative in this work, although
he had described Daniel Bell (some of whose ideas are used by
Lyotard in his 1979 work) as such (see also the preceding chapter),
and had spoken of a line leading from Bataille via Foucault to Derrida in France as representing a 'young conservative' tradition

whose members 'on the basis of modernistic attitudes . . . justify an irreconcilable antimodernism'. (See Habermas's 'Modernity – an Incomplete Project', in Foster, *Postmodern Culture*, p. 14.)

65 Lyotard, *The Postmodern Condition*, p. 3.

66 Lyotard concludes this statement (ibid.) by adding that 'the general situation is one of temporal disjunction which makes sketching an overview difficult'.

67 Later, in his 'Apostille aux récits' of 1984, in his *Le Postmoderne expliqué aux enfants* (Paris, 1986), pp. 37ff., Lyotard himself will suggest that he perhaps put too much emphasis on the 'genre narrative' in his *The Postmodern Condition* of 1979.

68 Lyotard, *The Postmodern Condition*, p. 4.

69 See Lyotard, ibid., pp. 3–4.

70 See also the following note 73 on Lyotard's relationship to this concept. Some modernist literature may also be said to have taken over the concept of the alienation of the worker suggested by Marx and extended it into concepts of the alienation and even 'death' of the subject as such via Sartre, Beckett and other 'post-Marxian' modernist writers made aware of Marx's idea by the publication of his 1844 manuscripts earlier this century.

71 Lyotard's treatment of scientific knowledge and discourse as commodities of the post-industrial society further suggests them to have been reified or turned into things. (I have also discussed the metaphorical nature of Marx's concept of reification and its progeny in a paper entitled 'Myth in Modern and Post-Modern Theory: from Marx's Theory of Commodity Fetishism to Theories of Reification in Critical and Post-Modernist Theory', in F.J. West (ed.), *Myth and Mythology* (Canberra, 1989), pp. 35–49.)

72 Lyotard, *The Postmodern Condition*, p. 6; and see also its p. 45.

73 See also Lyotard's reference, ibid., p. 7, to the way in which post-industrial scientific knowledge may 'undergo an exteriorization with respect to the "knower" and an alienation from its user'. Lyotard uses these terms here even though he later goes on, on p. 13, to criticise Marx's critique of alienated society as having been used 'in one way or another' as an aid in 'programming the system' in both liberal and communist countries. Although Lyotard excludes his own former group, *Socialisme ou Barbarie*, and the early Frankfurt School, from which he has borrowed some arguments, from this latter process, as offering critical models in opposition to it (ibid., p. 13 and p. 37), both of these groups could also be said to have used the 'metanarrative' of alienation in their work, as in, for example, the critiques of the Frankfurt School of the

dominance of the principles of instrumental reason (Adorno and Horkheimer) or performance (Marcuse) which may also be found to be echoed in Lyotard's criticisms of the 'metanarratives' of progress and performativity. (And see also the text relating to note 77 below.)

74 See Lyotard on this, ibid., pp. 16, 60f. and 65f.

75 Ibid., pp. 17ff.

76 See Lyotard, ibid., pp. 46ff. Lyotard refers on these pages specifically to Luhmann's 'hypothesis' that 'in postindustrial societies the normativity of laws is replaced by the performativity of procedures', but it might again be recalled here that the dominance of the 'performance principle' had also been one of the targets of Marcuse's writings.

77 Ibid., p. 60. Some comparison with Hassan's view that post-modern science is characterised by indeterminacy (see chapter 2, note 128) might also be made here.

78 Ibid., p. 66.

79 Ibid., p. 67.

80 See Hassan, *The Postmodern Turn*, pp. 222–3. And see also P. Steven Sangren's article on 'Postmodernism and the Social Reproduction of Texts', in *Current Anthropology*, vol. 29, no. 3 (June 1988), pp. 405–35 for a critique of the way in which many deconstructive analyses of 'hegemonic' discourses appropriate power to their own analyses in an equally and sometimes even more hegemonic manner than those they claim to be against. Further to this Sangren also goes on (on p. 416) to criticise the deconstructionist implication that society can be read as a text, and that textual analyses can be sufficient to describe or analyse all of its various aspects.

81 See Lyotard, *The Postmodern Condition*, p. 79. Lyotard's 1982 text (here translated by Régis Durand) deals more specifically with aesthetic matters than his 1979 text. Jencks refers to Lyotard's statement in, for example, his *What is Post-Modernism?* of 1986.

82 Lyotard, *The Postmodern Condition*, p. 71.

83 As the chapter on Jencks will show, Lyotard's characterisation of his theory here is not easily defensible when actually related to the details of Jencks's arguments.

84 Lyotard, *The Postmodern Condition*, p. 76. Lyotard also states that Jencks's 'postmodern architecture' is not to be confused with what he has called the 'postmodern condition' in an article entitled 'Représentation, présentation, imprésentable', published in German under the title 'Vorstellung, Darstellung, Undarstellbares' in the volume *Immaterialitaet und Postmoderne* (Berlin, 1985), pp. 91ff.

85 More details of this text will also be given in the following section on Habermas.
86 Lyotard, *The Postmodern Condition*, p. 72.
87 Where Lyotard, ibid., translates Lyotard's text as speaking of the 'uncompleted project of modernism' here, the French text (see Lyotard, *Le Postmoderne expliqué aux enfants*, pp. 13ff.) suggests it should be the phrase 'the ... project of the modern', as used by Habermas.
88 Lyotard, *The Postmodern Condition*, p. 72. Lyotard's last description of Habermas's theories may even be said to make the latter sound like a follower of Arthur Penty. Habermas's comments on the splintering of the totality of life refer, however, not just to any increased sub-division of labour, but to the separation of spheres like that of religion, culture, the arts and moral values in modernity. Although Habermas and Bell have been seen to disagree on other matters, both may be said to have taken this idea up from Weberian theory, and to have criticised the effects described by it. (And see also the following section on Habermas.)
89 See also the preceding note 64 and the following section on Habermas.
90 Lyotard, *The Postmodern Condition*, p. 72.
91 As suggested by Lyotard's earlier comments on Habermas and Adorno, one of Habermas's criticisms of Adorno has been that the latter had placed too much hope in the ability of the aesthetic sphere to encourage the implementation of the values which he saw as being threatened by the 'instrumental reason' characteristic of modernisation. While criticising Habermas, Lyotard's 1982 text also explicitly defends Adorno, as in Lyotard, *The Postmodern Condition*, p. 73.
92 Ibid., pp. 72–3.
93 Ibid.
94 Ibid., p. 82.
95 Ibid., p. 81.
96 See the interview with Mariani entitled 'Carlo Maria Mariani. An *Art & Design* interview by Hugh Cumming', in *Art & Design*, vol. 4, nos. 5/6 (1988), 'The New Modernism: Deconstructionist Tendencies in Art (London, 1988), p. 22. (Mariani is, however, responding here specifically to a question about modern art.) On p. 23 he is also quoted as saying that he thinks of himself 'as a modern artist who is anti-modern at the same time', but see also the discussion of Mariani in chapter 4.
97 See the review of Lyotard's *Que Peindre? Adami, Arakawa, Buren* (Paris, 1988) by James MacFarlane entitled 'Jean-François Lyotard

on Adami, Buren and Arakawa', in *Art & Design*, vol. 4, nos. 3/4 (1988), pp. 77–80.

98 With regard to the designation of artists such as Adami, Buren and Arakawa as deconstructionist, see, for instance, the *Art & Design* volume entitled 'The New Modernism: Deconstructionist Tendencies in Art', vol. 4, nos. 3/4 (1988), and especially John Griffiths's 'Deconstructionist Tendencies in Art', pp. 53–60; and see the previous note 13 for Lyotard's earlier statements on deconstruction and art.

99 Lyotard, *The Postmodern Condition*, p. 82.

100 See chapter 4 for further discussion of the concept of avant-garde and of its place in post-modernist theory. Although Lyotard has stated in both his 'Defining the Postmodern' translated by Geoffrey Bennington in *ICA Documents*, nos. 4/5 (1986), pp. 6–7 (and see Lyotard's 1985 'Note sur les sens de "post"', in Lyotard's *Le Postmoderne expliqué aux enfants*, pp. 119–26) and his 1988 interview in *Kunstforum*, vol. 100, p. 356, that he does not like the military associations of the concept of 'avant-garde', the 'experimental' aspects of modernism defended by him in his 1982 text have been described by others as 'avant-garde', while he himself has also compared the modernist avant-gardes with aspects of the post-modern. See, for instance, Lyotard's 'Defining the Postmodern', where he suggests on pp. 6–7 that the modernist avant-garde had not only been responsible for the 'investigation of the presuppositions implied in modernity', but that this was similar to the function of the 'post' of post-modernity in both *ana*-lysing and *ana*-mnesing in the sense of reflecting on the problems of modernity.

101 James MacFarlane's, 'Jean-François Lyotard on Adami, Buren and Arakawa', p. 80, suggests that Adami (who is, as noted earlier, also discussed by Derrida in his *Truth in Painting*) is presented by Lyotard in his *Du Peindre* not only as evoking a nostalgia for a lost 'sacred tenderness' but as presenting the world as devoid of human agency in a way which also seems to bring his work closer to the ideas of post-structuralist theory than to those of post-modernism as understood, for example, by Jencks as able to fill the role of a 'post-avant-garde'. (This last concept is also discussed further in chapter 4.)

102 See Robert Hughes's essay on 'The Decline and Fall of the Avant-Garde', in Gregory Battcock (ed.), *Idea Art* (New York, 1973), pp. 184–94.

103 Ibid.

104 See, for example, Lyotard's 'Apostille aux récits' of February 1984 in

his *Le Postmoderne expliqué aux enfants*, p. 38, in which he suggests that the project of modernity is not just incomplete (as suggested by Habermas) but dead, and destroyed by the 'capitalist techno-science' which appeared to be keeping it alive. (Daniel Bell, it may be remembered, had blamed 'post-ethical' capitalism – though not science – for the problems of modern culture, but had not gone so far as to suggest that that culture as a whole was dead.)

105 From 'Immaterialien. Konzeption' in *Immaterialitaet und Postmoderne*, pp. 75ff.

106 See Lyotard's 'Apostille aux récits', in his *Le Postmoderne expliqué aux enfants* (Paris, 1986). Later, on p. 359 of his 1988 *Kunstforum* interview referred to previously, Lyotard states that he now believes that it is modernism and its emancipatory ideals (and not modernity) which are no longer possible.

107 See the comments on Baudrillard in chapter 2. Baudrillard's claim in his 'On Nihilism' (*On the Beach* (Spring 1984)) that post-modernity is the 'destruction of meaning' could even be said to have radicalised and then projected the 'deconstruction' of meaning of deconstructionist post-modernism onto post-modernity itself.

108 The term 'post-Baudrillardian' is used here to designate the projection of Baudrillard's analyses of late-modernism and late-capitalism onto the post-modern rather than a break from Baudrillard.

109 See Lyotard, *The Postmodern Condition*, p. viii.

110 Ibid., pp. viiff.

111 Ibid., p. xvi. But see also both the following paragraph of text and the previous note 106.

112 See Lyotard, ibid., p. 71, and the previous discussion of this statement. On pp. 73f. Lyotard had also attacked those who would 'suspend artistic experimentation for the sake of security and unity', and those like the 'transavantgardists' (with whom Jencks is also linked by Lyotard on p. 76) who would 'liquidate the heritage of the avant-gardes'.

113 Ibid., p. 76; quoted in full in the previous section.

114 Ibid., p. xviii.

115 Ibid. On Lyotard, *The Postmodern Condition*, p. xvii, Jameson also agrees with Habermas that the 'postmodernist repudiation of modernist values' may involve 'the explicit repudiation of the modernist tradition' from a new 'conservative standpoint', and goes on to describe the pioneers of modernist architecture as being by contrast 'revolutionary'. Despite this, Jameson does not believe that a return to high modernism is possible, or that its aesthetic form of revolution was sufficient. (And see also Jameson's praise for

Habermas's defence of modernism against post-modernism in his 1984 essay, 'The Politics of Theory', in Jameson, *The Ideologies of Theory: Essays 1971–1986*, vol. II: *The Syntax of History* (London, 1988), p. 107f.)

116 Fredric Jameson, 'Postmodernism, or the Cultural Logic of Late Capitalism', in *New Left Review*, no. 146 (July–August 1984), p. 55.

117 Ibid., p. 55, and see also its p. 85. As suggested in the previous section on Lyotard, he has also criticised the production of knowledge in the post-industrial society through the language of Marx's criticisms of capitalist industrial society, though without making this move as explicit as here.

118 See chapter 2 for the background to this point. The capital-making elements in Bell's post-industrial society are, for instance, only a part of the axial principles controlling the more significant changes from the industrial to the post-industrial sciences and technologies and service areas of work for Bell. As even Arthur Penty's use of the term post-industrial suggested at the beginning of the century, the term itself focuses attention on the industrial relations and modes of manufacture of society rather than on the capitalist factors traditionally studied by many Marxists. Only if the term used by Bell was 'post-capitalist' rather than 'post-industrial' (and see chapter 2 for Bell's explicit rejection of the term 'post-capitalist') would there be any point in discussing the society in question in terms of claims for it not to be capitalist, although even here the prefix 'post' in the term post-capitalist might not necessarily be used to suggest a total break with modern capitalism.

119 Jameson, 'Postmodernism, or the Cultural Logic of Late Capitalism', p. 79.

120 Ibid., p. 55, and see also p. 85.

121 Ibid., p. 80.

122 Ibid., p. 84. Again we have here a problem found in much 'post-structuralist' Marxist theory, that statements are made about the general alienation, reification or 'overdetermination' of subjects without explanation of how the critic has become free enough from those alienations to make his or her criticisms or analyses of them.

123 Jameson, 'Postmodernism and Consumer Society', p. 113 (in Foster, *Postmodern Culture*, pp. 111–25), is said by him to have been based on a talk given in 1982 as a Whitney Museum Lecture.

124 Here it may also be noted that while Jameson shares and extends Lyotard's and Habermas's condemnations of post-modernist architecture, he also sets up no clear alternative post-modernism to counter the latter.

125 Hassan, *The Postmodern Turn*, pp. 232–3.
126 Jameson, 'Postmodernism, or the Cultural Logic of Late Capitalism', p. 57.
127 See, for example, the description of Jencks's 'thirty definers' of postmodernism in chapter 4 and the following note 144.
128 See also Jameson, 'The Politics of Theory: Ideological Positions in the Postmodernism Debate' (1984), in Jameson, *The Ideologies of Theory*, p. 105, where Jameson writes that the 'complacent play of historical allusion and stylistic pastiche (termed "historicism" in the architecture literature) is a central feature of postmodernism more generally'.
129 Jameson, 'Postmodernism, or the Cultural Logic of Late Capitalism', p. 65.
130 Ibid. Jameson writes here: 'the advanced capitalist countries are now a field of stylistic and discursive heterogencity without a norm'.
131 Jameson, 'Postmodernism and Consumer Society', p. 114.
132 Jameson had also written on p. 54 of his 'Postmodernism, or the Cultural Logic of Late Capitalism', that it had been from 'architectural debates' that his own conception of post-modernism 'initially began to emerge'. As will be seen, many of Jameson's 'definers' for post-modernist architecture appear, however, to be much more closely related to those of 'deconstructionist' post-modernism than to those of post-modernist architecture as described by its theorists.
133 See Baudrillard's 'The Orders of Simulacra' in Baudrillard *Simulations*, translated by Philip Beitchmann (New York, 1983), pp. 150ff. Michael Newman's discussion of parody in his article 'Revising Modernism, Representing Postmodernism', in *ICA Documents*, nos. 4/5 (London, 1986), p. 48, also appears to take up a Baudrillardian view of it when he writes that 'the difference between modernist and postmodernist parody' is a shift from 'a strong to a weak form of nihilism'. Earlier, Susan Sontag had written in her 'Against Interpretation' of 1964, (a work included by Hassan in his 'canon' of post-modernist works of criticism) that parody (together with both abstraction and decoration) 'was a flight from interpretation'. (See Sontag, *Against Interpretation and Other Essays* (New York, 1978), p. 10; and see also the earlier note 26 in this chapter on Baudrillard's and Jameson's descriptions of 'blind parody'.)
134 See Baudrillard's *For a Critique of the Political Economy of the Sign* of 1972, translated Charles Levin (St Louis, 1981), p. 110.
135 Baudrillard, ibid., had also stated 'that art no longer contests anything if it ever did'.

136 'The Precession of Simulacra', in Baudrillard, *Simulations*, p. 72.
137 Jameson, 'Postmodernism, or the Cultural Logic of Late Capitalism', pp. 66ff.
138 Ibid., p. 71.
139 See the previous discussion of Lyotard on the 'sublime'.
140 Jameson, 'Postmodernism and Consumer Society', pp. 114–15.
141 Ibid., pp. 115–16.
142 Jameson, 'Postmodernism, or the Cultural Logic of Late Capitalism', p. 63. Jameson explicitly chooses to use what he terms the 'historicist' formulation of the notion of the death of the subject, which he describes as the disappearance of the 'old bourgeois autonomous ego', rather than 'the more radical idea' that such a subject 'never existed in the first place', but may still be said to be using an idea typical of some late-modern post-structuralist theory (including some interpretations of Althusserian theory) in using the former.
143 The special case of Deconstructionist architecture will be looked at in the following chapter on Jencks's work on the architectural theories of post-modernism.
144 I have discussed different aspects of the concept of pastiche in my *Parody/Meta-Fiction* of 1979, pp. 43ff.; and in the articles 'Parody/Post-Modernism', *Poetics*, vol. 17 (1988), pp. 49–56; 'Post-Modernism Today: some Thoughts on Charles Jencks's "What is Post-Modernism?" ', in *Reasons to be Cheerful* (Melbourne, 1987), pp. 1–6; and in a more recent paper entitled 'Post-Modern Pastiche' for the *British Journal of Aesthetics*. As also noted in *Parody/Meta-Fiction*, the term pastiche, when applied to works of art, has been described as deriving from the term *pasticcio analogen* and as the 'compilation of motives from several works'. In French criticism it has been used as a synonym for parody, but in English-language texts it has also sometimes been used to refer to a form of 'counterfeit'. Confusing these different meanings of pastiche, or adding value judgements to the description of its functions, has also led to descriptions of pastiche in art and architecture as forgeries or fakes by those who are not necessarily, or consciously, following Jameson, as can be seen, for instance, in the collection of uses of the term given in the *OED*. As also noted in Rose, *Parody/Meta-Fiction*, p. 43, L. Albertsen is at least one authority on the concept of pastiche who has recommended that it should be separated from that of counterfeit, while HRH The Prince of Wales's more recent *A Vision of Britain* (London, 1989), p. 73, also refers to people using the word 'pastiche' disparagingly, and adds: 'They mean "fake" or a direct copy, something utterly unimaginative. But there's nothing "fake"

about building in an established tradition, or in trying to revive one.' Further to these comments, it should also be noted that pastiche understood as a compilation of artistic or architectural elements may be found in several modern and *pre-modern* periods of both art and architecture, and, *contra* Jameson, in both satiric works of art and in earlier architecture, while Jencks himself (in his *The Language of Post-Modern Architecture*, p. 128) has also distinguished between the 'vague pastiche', or 'weak eclecticism', of some 'pre-post-Modern' works and the strong eclecticism of what he describes as 'Post-Modern' architecture. As is the case with parody, pastiche may in general be described as a device which has been used for several different purposes in a number of different periods by a variety of artists and architects, and a post-modern use of it one which uses it for some specifically defined post-modern purpose such as the 'dual-coding' of a modern style or work of art with another.

145 See, for instance, Jameson, 'The Politics of Theory: Ideological Positions in the Postmodernism Debate' (1984), in his *The Ideologies of Theory*, p. 110, where he describes Jencks as a 'propostmodernist antimodernist'.

146 See also note 144 above on 'pastiche'. The *OED*'s entries on *pasticcio* and *pastiche* make it clear that the concept of pastiche as a compilation of motifs from various works of art was in use in English from at least the early eighteenth century, while J. Mordaunt Crook's *The Dilemma of Style: Architectural Ideas from the Picturesque to the Post-Modern* (London, 1987), points to the use of pastiche in both post-modern architecture and in earlier styles. When Jencks makes a distinction between the 'strong eclecticism' of the post-modern and the weak eclecticism preceding it, his distinction also affirms the fact that eclecticism is something which has existed in art and architecture well before the advent of the post-modern.

147 Jencks's *What is Post-Modernism?*, p. 38, has also criticised Jameson and others for having committed a 'category mistake' in confusing 'Late-Modernism' with 'Post-Modernism'.

148 See Hassan, *The Postmodern Turn*, pp. 220–1. It is also in his note to this statement on pp. 232–3 that Hassan criticises Jameson's 1984 essay on post-modernism 'as pressed down by the yoke of ideology'.

149 See Hassan, ibid., p. 221, and chapter 1 for the passages from Toynbee on the similar subjectivity of optimistic and pessimistic views of history.

150 Jameson writes this in another article of 1984, entitled 'The Politics of Theory: Ideological Positions in the Postmodernism Debate', in his *The Ideologies of Theory*, p. 105. Jameson's listing of a category called 'high modernist postmodernism' (despite his other statements that post-modernism of Jencks's kind has set itself up in opposition to high modernism) bears no clear relation to Jencks's categories and also appears, as in Jameson's interpretation of Portman's Bonaventure Hotel, to have confused a late-modernist form of architecture with post-modernism. While Jencks describes postmodernism as a double-coding of modernism with other codes, he has not seen late-modern architecture as undertaking such a double-coding, but, rather, as simply extending the language of modernism.

151 See also chapter 4 on this last topic.

152 See Charles Jencks, *The Language of Post-Modern Architecture*, revised enlarged editions 1978ff. (London), p. 128 (referred to previously in notes 144 and 146), and also the conclusion of Jencks's more recent article on 'The Bank as Cathedral and Village', in *Architectural Design*, vol. 58, nos. 11/12 (1988), p. 79, on the advantages of eclecticism which demonstrates oppositions and contradictions, as well as continuities, over the 'nostalgic' use of pastiche. From a different point of view, Jencks argues in his interview with Peter Eisenman, in *Architectural Design* Profile 72, vol. 58, nos. 3/4 (1988), p. 54, that nostalgia can also be 'radical'.

153 See also the following section on Habermas as well as chapter 4 for further discussion of this issue.

154 See also Jencks, *The Language of Post-Modern Architecture*, pp. 130–1, and chapter 4 below.

155 Ibid. (1984 and other post-1978 editions), pp. 131–2.

156 Jameson, *The Ideologies of Theory*, p. 110.

157 To Jencks such 'high modernism' is not necessarily 'post-modernist' if it has not double-coded the modern with something else.

158 Jameson, 'Postmodernism and Consumer Society', p. 111.

159 Ibid.

160 While Venturi, Scott Brown and Izenour's *Learning from Las Vegas* of 1972 had suggested some ideas included by Jencks in his writings on post-modernism, it had not explicitly developed the idea of double-coding which Jencks will see as being central to the postmodern (and which was in part at least foreshadowed by some of the concepts in Venturi's *Complexity and Contradiction in Architecture*), and had also been criticised by Jencks for not having formulated the standards by which images from mass culture or 'schlock'

could be used for new post-modern purposes, as well as for other matters. See Jencks on Venturi in Jencks, *The Language of Post-Modern Architecture*, pp. 87–8, and also the discussion of both in chapter 4.

161 See, for example, Jencks's 1987 analysis of the association of 'Pop' and post-modernism in his *Post-Modernism: the New Classicism in Art and Architecture*, p. 18. Jencks first of all takes the association of the two back to both Leslie Fiedler's use of the prefix 'post' to describe 'all the mini-movements against the centre' (Jencks also says 'support', as Andreas Huyssen has implied in his discussion of Fiedler's 1965 essay in his 'Mapping the Postmodern' of 1984, in Huyssen, *After the Great Divide*, p. 194) and to Tom Wolfe's use of Las Vegas and its sign artists to criticise the formalism of modernism. Of Warhol's Pop Art Jencks adds that it was 'aimed simply at the commercial success of Modernism and aimed to supplant it with a blatant form of exploitative cynicism'. While Pop Art may be seen as a reaction to modernism which paves the way towards post-modernism, it is, however, not yet fully post-modern in Jencks's sense of a double-coding of modernism with something else. Here it may also be noted that, in contrast to Jencks's depiction of post-modernism in his 1987 text as double-coding the modern with the classical, Fiedler's 1969 article had argued that post-modernism had crossed the divide between high and pop culture not only by expanding the latter, but also by leaving the use of classical and humanistic myths and traditions to the former.

162 Jameson, 'Postmodernism, or the Cultural Logic of Late Capitalism', p. 54. Denise Scott Brown's 'Reply to Frampton', in *Casabella* (May/June 1971), pp. 39–46, also suggests this to be a misreading of *Learning from Las Vegas* (Frampton having argued amongst other things that it condoned the pop culture it described) when it points out (p. 45) that the architects and their works are still 'part of a high art, not a folk or popular art, tradition'. Like Hassan, however, Jameson appears to have accepted the thesis found by the former in Fiedler's 1969 essay, that post-modernism may be described as an elimination of the divide between high and pop culture which also results in the expansion of the latter.

163 See Jencks, *What is Post-Modernism?*, p. 34.

164 See the Introduction to the second revised and enlarged edition of Jencks's *The Language of Post-Modern Architecture* (2nd edn), p. 8.

165 See also Andreas Huyssen, *After the Great Divide*. While Huyssen, like Hassan, refers to Fiedler's essay 'Cross the Border – Close the Gap' as well as to his 'The New Mutants', he sometimes also

appears to read Fiedler's injunction to 'cross the divide' between high and popular culture in the light of Peter Buerger's description of the goal of the 'classical' (Surrealist) avant-garde as being to reunite the two spheres, rather than, as implied in Fiedler's essay, to replace high with pop culture (see, for example, Huyssen, *After the Great Divide*, p. 165). At other times, however (as ibid., pp. 187f.), Huyssen clearly associates Fiedler with the equation of post-modernism and pop, and also reads Scott Brown, Venturi and Izenour's *Learning from Las Vegas* (and via Frampton – see also note 162 above) in the same light. The variations in Huyssen's presentation of Fiedler may, moreover, be said to explain the uncertainty of his page 194 where he writes both that Fiedler's 'call to cross the border and close the gap between high and mass culture . . . can serve as an important marker for subsequent developments within postmodernism' and that 'Fiedler's populism reiterates precisely that adversarial relationship between high art and mass culture'.

166 See chapter 4 for further discussion of Jencks's views on the Stuttgart Gallery.

167 See Charles Jencks, *Late-Modern Architecture* (London and New York, 1980), p. 32.

168 Jameson, 'Postmodernism, or the Cultural Logic of Late Capitalism', pp. 80ff.

169 See Jencks, *The Language of Post-Modern Architecture*, p. 35, and *Late-Modern Architecture*, pp. 15 and 70. The *OED*'s reference to the *Journal of the Royal Society of Arts* statement on post-modernists 'who have substituted the body metaphor for the machine metaphor' might also be recalled here. In addition, it may be noted that Arthur J. Penty had criticised the influence of Palladio's popularisation of the idea of the 'big scale' over that of the Vitruvian concept of scale in his *The Elements of Domestic Design* (Westminster, 1930), p. 3.

170 Baudrillard, 'The Orders of Simulacra', in Baudrillard *Simulations*, p. 149.

171 Ibid., pp. 138ff. Baudrillard also refers on p. 147 to Lyotard with reference to the idea that 'the hyperreal transcends representation'.

172 Baudrillard, 'The Ecstasy of Communication', in Foster, *Postmodern Culture*, p. 128. Baudrillard's 1977 analysis of the Pompidou Centre in his 'The Beaubourg-Effect: Implosion and Deterrence', in *October* (Spring 1982), pp. 3–13, might also be seen as a model for Jameson's analysis of the Bonaventure Hotel. Although Baudrillard was again depicting characteristics of *modern* consumer culture in his essay, and not a consciously proclaimed

post-modern condition as described by Jameson, his characterisation of the Pompidou Centre and its visitors is – given both the origins of much of Jameson's terminology in Baudrillard's works and the late-modern character of both the Pompidou Centre and Portman's Hotel – not surprisingly similar to many of the comments later made by Jameson on the 'hyper-space' of the latter. In addition to seeing that the picture of the post-modern presented by Jameson is at least partly based on Baudrillard's characterisations of the modern and late-modern, it might also now be the time and place to ask how arguments such as Baudrillard's in his 1977 'Beaubourg-Effect' that the crowds visiting the Pompidou Centre were actually showing their hatred of it by unintentionally wearing it out ('The Beaubourg-Effect', p. 9) could ever have been taken seriously. Not only may we also see visitors to the Parthenon in Athens in a similar light – not to speak of the many kamikaze motorists destroying it and themselves with their petrol exhaust fumes from below – but Baudrillard's translation of the unintentionally destructive effect of the crowds on the Centre into an unintentional maliciousness on their part both reduces the individuals in those crowds to a machine-like mass with one unspoken and yet united purpose and fails to ask the question which a post-modern architect might ask, of why the late-modern Centre had not been built to cope with such situations.

173 See Jean Baudrillard, *America*, translated by Chris Turner (London and New York, 1988), p. 104.
174 See also Jencks's *Current Architecture* (London, 1982) on both late- and post-modern architecture. Jencks's 1980 list of definers for the 'Modern', 'Late-Modern' and 'Post-Modern' in his *Late-Modern Architecture* also date the latter two as running concurrently from the 1960s on. One reason why some observers of 1970s buildings such as the Bonaventure Hotel have assumed it to be post-modern may also be because of the date, or newness of it, although Jencks's chronology of the 'Late-Modern' makes it clear that this style is also to be found in the same years as that with which the 'Post-Modern' has been associated.
175 See Venturi, *Complexity and Contradiction*, pp. 71ff., and the previous reference to that text with reference to Jameson and Jencks.
176 See Heinrich Klotz, *The History of Postmodern Architecture*, translated by Radka Donnell from *Moderne und Postmoderne: Architektur der Gegenwart* (Braunschweig and Wiesbaden, 1984; Cambridge, Mass., and London, 1988), p. 65.
177 Ibid., p. 5.

178 Ibid. Although Klotz follows Jencks rather than Jameson in describing Portman's Bonaventure Hotel as 'modernist' rather than postmodernist, the spelling which he gives of it as 'Bonaventura' rather than 'Bonaventure' (as used by Jencks and others) is the same as that given by Jameson in his 1984 article.

179 Klotz, ibid., p. 5.

180 Ibid.

181 See Jencks, *Late-Modern Architecture*, p. 32.

182 Klotz, *The History of Postmodern Architecture*, p. 5, also refers to the use of high-tech elements in Stirling's Stuttgart Gallery together with the neo-classical as an example of a 'postmodernist' use of high tech. Again the point which must be made here is, however, that it will be the 'double-coding' of those 'high tech' elements with others which will start to make the building in question a post-modern one for Jencks.

183 Klotz, ibid., pp. 5ff.

184 Ibid., p. 128.

185 See, for example, the Postscript 'Late Modernism and Post-Modernism', in Jencks's *Modern Movements in Architecture*, 2nd edn (Harmondsworth, 1985), pp. 379–81; and Jencks, *What is Post-Modernism?*, p. 36, where his caption to his illustration of the Pompidou Centre reads: 'The Modernist emphasis on structure, circulation, open space, industrial detailing and abstraction is taken to its Late-Modern extreme, although again often mis-termed Post-Modern.' In the preceding pages 33–4 of this work Jencks had also written on this last point that some of these misinterpretations were based on the assumption that 'Post-Modern meant *everything* that was different from High-Modernism', and 'That such architects were against the pluralism, ornament and convention of Post-Modernism was missed.'

186 Jameson, 'Postmodernism, or the Cultural Logic of Late Capitalism', p. 81. Baudrillard had also described the Pompidou Centre as an example of the invasion by advertising of the public spaces of architecture in his essay 'The Ecstasy of Communication', pp. 129–30; and see also the previous note 172 on Baudrillard's 1977 essay on the Pompidou Centre.

187 See the conclusion to Klotz's *The History of Postmodern Architecture*, p. 421. J. Mordaunt Crook has also described post-modernism as 'Post-Functional' in his *Dilemma of Style*, p. 265, and referred on p. 310 to Peter Eisenman's use of the term in 1976, while Jencks has emphasised the fact that post-modernism also adds something new to the functionalist aesthetic of the Modern Movement in double-coding the modern with some other style.

188 Jameson's description of the Bonaventure Hotel as 'postmodern' has been echoed by others writing on post-modernism, such as, for instance, Mike Featherstone in his 'In Pursuit of the Postmodern: an Introduction', in the special issue on post-modernism of *Theory, Culture & Society*, vol. 5, nos. 2–3 (June 1988), p. 200; and the geographer M.J. Dear in an article entitled 'Postmodernism and Planning', in *Environment and Planning D: Society and Space*, vol. 4 (1986), pp. 367–84, discussed further in the following note 237.

189 See Jencks's *What is Post-Modernism?*, p. 30. Jencks also sums up Jameson's view of post-modernism here as using it as an 'umbrella term to cover all reactions to High-Modernism ... the levelling of distinctions between high- and mass-culture and two of its "significant features" – pastiche and schizophrenia'.

190 As seen previously, Lyotard does not explicitly or exactly equate the post-industrial and the post-modern but Jameson does when speaking of architecture such as Portman's Bonaventure Hotel as 'postmodern'.

191 Jencks, *What is Post-Modernism?*, p. 38.

192 Ibid.

193 Jencks, *The Language of Post-Modern Architecture*, pp. 133ff.

194 See, for example, Jencks's article 'The Battle of High-Tech: Great Buildings with Great Faults', in *Architectural Design*, vol. 58, no. 11/12 (1988), pp. 19–39.

195 See Jameson, 'Postmodernism and Consumer Society', p. 125 and also Jameson's combination of that essay with his 1984 article 'Postmodernism: the Cultural Logic of Late Capitalism', in his 'Postmodernism and Consumer Society', in E. Ann Kaplan (ed.), *Postmodernism and its Discontents* (London and New York, 1988), pp. 13–29. As in his essay for Foster's 1983 volume, Jameson concludes this latter article by saying that the question of whether postmodernism will resist 'the logic of consumer capitalism' must be left open.

196 See also the previous section on Lyotard. The conflict between theories of avant-garde agency and the alienation of agency do not just belong to the mid or late twentieth century. As I have tried to show in my *Marx's Lost Aesthetic* (Cambridge, 1984), p. 96, it is also one which is to be found in the writings of Marx. The repetition of this conflict in recent 'post-structuralist' Marxism, where the agency of subjects is problematised by theories borrowed from Lacan via Althusser of their supposed 'interpellation' into ideology, may also be described as producing an even more extreme version of the contradiction between theories of alienation and agency in the work of Marx. Nor is it resolved by Jameson, who, while apparently

consistent in speaking of an assumed correlation between the 'death of the old individual subject' and the 'imitation of dead styles' in post-modernism, does not relate either the differences in imitation which he does acknowledge to exist in the latter or his own apparent ability to stand apart from post-modern architecture to criticise it to any agency of the individual subject, or to any other such concept which might serve to explain their existence.

197 See, for example, Jameson's 1982 description of Venturi and also his 1984 essay, 'The Politics of Theory', in Jameson, *The Ideologies of Theory*, p. 112, where Jameson congratulates Jencks for asserting that 'postmodern architecture distinguishes itself from that of high modernism through its populist priorities'.

198 Juergen Habermas, 'Moderne und postmoderne Architektur', in Habermas, *Die neue Unuebersichtlichkeit* (Frankfurt am Main, 1985), p. 11.

199 See Habermas's 'Modernity – an Incomplete Project', p. 9.

200 Ibid.

201 Ibid., p. 3.

202 Habermas, *Die neue Unuebersichtlichkeit*, pp. 23ff. In summary, Habermas uses the term 'system world' here to refer to the forces of both the market place and government which he deems to have 'colonised' the 'life-world' in modern times and to have made the establishment of communicative interaction more necessary for its inhabitants.

203 Ibid., p. 27.

204 This is particularly necessary given the somewhat misleading description of Habermas as developing ideas of 'Marxist rationality' by some writers on post-modernism. (See, for example, Ihab Hassan, *The Postmodern Turn*, p. 223.) Frank Kermode's description of Habermas in his *History and Value* (Oxford, 1988), p. 134, as 'favouring a return to Modernist rationality' again tells us only some of the story of this thinker. Although Habermas criticises those who would give up the project of modernity for something called post-modernity, his own project may be described as wanting to expand earlier 'modernist' analyses of rationality (such as those by the early Frankfurt School) to include intersubjective communicative action as a means to achieving rational consensus. (And see also the discussion of this issue in the text which follows.)

205 See Habermas's *Theory of Communicative Action* of 1981 (English translation of vol. 1 by Thomas McCarthy (Boston, 1984), pp. 398–9) and also Martin Jay's suggestion in his chapter on Habermas in his *Marxism and Totality: the Adventures of a Concept from Lukacs to*

Habermas (Oxford, Cambridge and California, 1984), pp. 462–509, that Habermas differs from the early Frankfurt School in both the limitation of instrumental reason (Jay, ibid., p. 506) to a sub-sphere of system integration, rather than to (Jay, ibid., p. 467) an all-dominant force over nature, and in his designation of an intersubjective form of reason, rather than an individual-based form of value rationality, as a way to its control.

206 See Juergen Habermas, *The Philosophical Discourse of Modernity*, translated by Frederick Lawrence (Oxford and Cambridge, 1987), p. x.

207 See, for example, Habermas, ibid., pp. 185ff. on Adorno and Derrida and pp. 276ff. on Foucault. In the latter section Habermas writes (p. 276) that Foucault's genealogical historiography 'follows the movement of a radically historicist extinction of the subject and ends up in an unholy subjectivism', and (p. 279) that 'Foucault's historiography can evade relativism as little as it can ... acute presentism', and that 'His investigations are caught exactly in the self-referentiality that was supposed to be excluded by a naturalistic treatment of the problem of validity.'

208 Although sympathetic to many of Habermas's ideas (such as, for instance, his criticisms of Bell), Andreas Huyssen has also criticised him (in Huyssen, *After the Great Divide*, pp. 174–7) for being blind to 'attempts to steer modernity in different and alternative directions'.

209 See, for example, Habermas *Die neue Unuebersichtlichkeit*, pp. 12f.

210 Ibid. The conclusion of Habermas's 1980 Adorno Prize lecture, 'Modernity – an Incomplete Project', pp. 14–15, had also spoken of distinguishing the 'young conservatives' (from Bataille via Michel Foucault to Jacques Derrida) from the 'premodernism' of the 'old conservatives' and from the 'postmodernism' of 'neoconservatives' such as Daniel Bell who had, according to Habermas's understanding of them, blamed cultural modernism for the ills of modernity. (See also the previous note 64 as well as the previous criticisms of Habermas's misreadings of Bell.)

211 Habermas, *Die neue Unuebersichtlichkeit*, p. 15.

212 Ibid., p. 27.

213 Ibid. Habermas writes here: 'Freilich gibt die Sehnsucht nach entdifferenzierten Lebensformen diesen Tendenzen oft den Anstrich eines Antimodernismus.' ('Admittedly the longing for de-differentiated life-forms often gives these tendencies the appearance of an anti-modernism.')

214 Martin Jay has written in his contribution to *Habermas and Modernity*, ed. Richard J. Bernstein (Oxford and Cambridge, 1985), on 'Habermas and Modernism' (p. 133), that the abandonment of the 'unfulfilled project of modernity' would mean for Habermas 'a loss of hope in the creative reappropriation of aesthetic rationality into an increasingly rationalized everyday life'. Jay also questions how the latter will be achieved (on pp. 133–9), while Habermas argues in his reply to him (on pp. 199–203) that aesthetic judgements will need to be based on criticisable claims about the harmony, authenticity and success of expression in the work of art, and goes on to agree with a 1983 claim by Albrecht Wellmer (who has elsewhere, in his *Zur Dialektik von Moderne und Postmoderne* (Frankfurt am Main, 1985), also described post-modernism as helping in the destruction of reason) that the validity claim made in aesthetic discourse 'stands for a *potential* for "truth" that can be released only in the whole complexity of life-experience'. Following Wellmer, Habermas concludes that 'the work of art, as a symbolic formation with an aesthetic validity claim, is at the same time an object of the life-world experience in which the three validity domains [of cognitive–instrumental, moral–practical and aesthetic–expressive rationality] are unmetaphorically intermeshed'.

215 See, for example, Thodor W. Adorno and Max Horkheimer's *Dialectic of Enlightenment* of 1944, translated by John Cumming (London, 1986), for their criticisms of popular culture. Adorno has since been criticised by Habermas for putting too much faith in an alternative sphere of art autonomous from both the popular realm and that of instrumental reason. Habermas's reduction of the consensus-based architecture favoured by many post-modernists to 'anonymous' architecture also appears to reduce the latter to the 'anonymity' which Habermas has seen as characterising the instrumental imperatives of the 'system-world'.

216 See Lucien Kroll, *The Architecture of Complexity*, translated by Peter Blundell Jones (London, 1986).

217 Ibid., p. 10. Arthur Penty's complaints about modern architecture and support of the Arts and Crafts attempts to revive the art of a non-anonymous 'craftsmanship' might be recalled here, although it should also be remembered that he had preferred the plain and primitive in architecture to the over-decorated.

218 Kroll, ibid., p. 11.

219 Built for the University of Louvain, the Medical Faculty buildings in question were erected at Woluwé-St Lambert in Brussels. And see also Kroll, *The Architecture of Complexity*, pp. 35ff., for his description of the project.

220 Jencks, *The Language of Post-Modern Architecture*, pp. 104ff.

221 Ibid.

222 Ibid., p. 106. (It should also be noted here that Jencks has used the term 'neo-classicism' to refer to modern rather than post-modern classicism.)

223 One of the other, unverbalised, problems with Kroll's Louvain project for Habermas might also have been that it had the appearance of a 'deconstructed' building site in many photographs. As the German architectural historian Heinrich Klotz writes in his history of post-modern architecture (*The History of Postmodern Architecture*, p. 392): 'The facades of the Louvain dormitory look as if a storm has blown away parts of the siding. Never before had such a large building looked so much like a temporary shack pieced together from salvaged scrap.' By contrast to Klotz, Jencks writes in his caption to the photograph of Kroll's Louvain project used in his 1977 text (*The Language of Post-Modern Architecture*, p. 106) that the variety of detail 'simulates the piecemeal decisions which take place over time and give identity to any old city'.

224 Habermas refers here in his *Die neue Unuebersichtlichkeit*, p. 49, to *Der Architekt* of February 1982.

225 Habermas appears to be suggesting here that if post-modernism does use modernism it is to borrow from it while claiming to supersede it, and even though Jencks's concept of 'double-coding' for one does not necessarily claim that post-modernism 'supersedes' modernism when it encodes it with other codes. Habermas's 1982 essay also appears, however, to link uncritically the 'young conservative' Arnold Gehlen's concept of 'post-history' and its belief that the innovations of cultural modernism are now over with 'post-modernism', and to project the former's perceived pessimism about completing the 'project of modernity' onto the latter. (See, for example, Habermas *Die neue Unuebersichtlichkeit*, pp. 48–9.)

226 Habermas *Die neue Unuebersichtlichkeit*, p. 49. The German from which I have translated this last sentence reads: 'aber weit und breit entdeckt man keine Produktionen, die das in Negation verharrende Schlagwort der "Postmoderne" mit positivem Gehalt ausfuellen wuerden'. Although it might sound less clumsy to translate the last lines as referring to 'the negative catchword of the postmodern' (as in, for example, Russell A. Berman's translation of the article in Richard J. Bernstein (ed.), *Habermas and Modernity* (Oxford and Cambridge, 1985), p. 90), this would, I believe, lose Habermas's reference to the aim of the post-modern (as he understands it) as being to 'negate' the tradition of the modern. Strangely, the Berman translation referred to above also compresses the passage translated

in full in our text to a few lines and substitutes the word 'post-modernism' for 'postmodern' at the end. (The English translation of Klotz's history of post-modern architecture also speaks with reference to Habermas of the 'project of modernism', on, for example, *The History of Postmodern Architecture*, p. 14, but with specific reference to modernist architecture. To Klotz, the 'completion' or 'resolution' of this 'project' is, moreover, to liberate modernism from its 'dogmatic fixation with' and 'falsification by' functionalism.)

227 Habermas, *The Philosophical Discourse of Modernity*, p. xix.

228 Ibid., pp. 3–4.

229 Martin Jay's chapter, 'Habermas and Postmodernism', in his *Fin de Siècle Socialism and Other Essays* (New York and London, 1988), pp. 137–48, also tends to speak of deconstructionist post-modernism as the measure for all post-modernisms when discussing Habermas's writings on the subject. (See, for example, its p. 138.)

230 See also the previous note on Habermas's criteria for aesthetic 'validity claims'. While Habermas gives no concrete example of an acceptable claim there, his 1981 essay on modern and post-modern architecture ends by following its statement that post-modernism has been right to take up the criticism of those forces of the 'system-world' which have 'colonised' the 'life-world' with the claim that modern architecture had at least developed as a 'tradition' from the 'happy and unforced coalition of the aesthetic wilfulness of constructivism with the purposiveness of a strict functionalism' (in Habermas *Die neue Unuebersichtlichkeit*, p. 28). Given Habermas's article had been written for an exhibition of what had been understood by him to be essentially modernist works, this conclusion is not surprising, but is also not very illuminating about why that tradition should be praised over others more critical of the 'colonising' powers of the forces of modernisation.

231 Hassan, *The Postmodern Turn*, pp. 224–5.

232 See the Habermas interview, 'A Philosophico-Political Profile', *New Left Review*, vol. 151 (May/June 1985), pp. 81–2. Habermas begins this part of the interview by saying that 'condemnation' is not the appropriate word for his attitude towards 'post-structuralism', but goes on to distinguish Adorno from Derrida and Foucault because of Adorno's adherence to what Habermas has elsewhere described as the completion of the 'project of modernity'.

233 See also note 232 above on Habermas's contrast of Adorno to Derrida and Foucault.

234 Habermas, 'A Philosophico-Political Profile', p. 93.

235 Ibid.

236 These are too numerous to mention here in detail, and have been discussed or listed by Hassan and others in recent surveys of the field (see, for instance, Hassan, *The Postmodern Turn*). More general theorists of post-modernism who follow one or other of the theorists mentioned here include Dick Hebdige, while Terry Eagleton's 'Capitalism, Modernism and Postmodernism', in *New Left Review*, no. 152 and in Eagleton's *Against the Grain: Essays 1975–1985* (London, 1986), has also presented post-modernism as something based on an 'unpolitical' 'fragmentation of the self'.

237 Some geographers cum urban planners, such as M.J. Dear, might also be mentioned here as having taken over both a variety of elements from 'deconstructionist postmodernist' critiques of post-modern architecture and the philosophy of deconstructionist analysis itself. Dear's essay 'Postmodernism and Planning' accepts, and confuses, moreover, several different definitions of post-modernism, so that, for instance, Portman's Bonaventure Hotel is spoken of as an archetypical post-modernist building on the same page as Jencks is referred to as having defended post-modernist architecture, even though, as seen previously, Jencks has not discussed Portman's building as a post-modern, but as a late-modern building. Further to this, little explicit distinction is made by Dear between deconstruction and post-modernism, or between deconstructionist varieties of post-modernism and 'deconstructionist' criticisms of post-modernist architecture such as Jameson's, or Jencks's views on post-modernism – while Jameson's characterisations of post-modernist architecture as dominated by both pastiche and hyperspace are taken over as characteristic of post-modernism in general. (And see also the note on David Harvey in chapter 6.)

238 Foster's 1983 volume on post-modern culture included essays by Foster ('Postmodernism: a Preface'), Habermas ('Modernity – an Incomplete Project'), Kenneth Frampton ('Towards a Critical Regionalism: Six Points for an Architecture of Resistance'), Rosalind Krauss ('Sculpture in the Expanded Field'), Douglas Crimp ('On the Museum's Ruins'), Craig Owens ('The Discourse of Others: Feminists and Postmodernism'), Gregory L. Ulmer ('The Object of Post-Criticism'), Fredric Jameson ('Postmodernism and Consumer Society'), Jean Baudrillard ('The Ecstasy of Communication') and Edward W. Said ('Opponents, Audiences, Constituencies and Community').

239 This essay has been published in *New German Critique*, vol. 33 (1984), *Perspecta*, vol. 21 (1984) and in Foster, *Recodings: Art Spec-*

tacle, Cultural Politics (Washington, 1985), pp. 121ff. Here Foster both takes over the term neo-conservative from Habermas to apply to post-modernist architecture (and also follows Habermas's interpretation of Daniel Bell as a neo-conservative), and applies categories from Jameson's critiques of post-modernist architecture such as pastiche to it.

240 Foster's use of the term neo-conservative here echoes Habermas's use of it in his 1980 lecture, as published by Foster in 1983, to describe what Habermas thought to be Daniel Bell's critical attitude to modernism, but when attached to post-modernist architecture appears to reduce what was developed as a new body of architectural theory to the terminology of political diatribe without any discussion of either the actual political positions of the protagonists in question or of their views on what is referred to in Habermas's use of the term neo-conservative to describe the projection of the ills of modernisation onto modernism. Further to this, the unintended, or intended, association of Bell with what Foster terms neo-conservative post-modernism through the combination of Habermas's term for him with the latter also presents problems in that Bell was not associated with the architectural post-modernism which Foster includes in that category.

241 Foster, *Recodings*, pp. 121ff.

242 As suggested previously, the association of post-modernist pastiche with normlessness and a concept of the 'death of the subject' in both Jameson and Foster might also be described as involving a form of category error by means of which two different categories – architectural pastiche and pastiche understood as normless – are equated without regard for their differing meanings or sources.

243 See also note 242 above.

244 See Foster, *Recodings*, p. 122.

245 To Foster 'neoconservative postmodernism', in consequence, 'does not argue with modernism in any serious way', while its historicism reduces the classical to 'pop' and the art-historical to pastiche and 'kitsch'. As will be seen in the following chapter, this juxtaposition of terms from Habermas and Jameson on post-modernism may, however, itself be described as a reductionist account of historicist post-modernism which has overlooked many of its aims and effects to reduce them to but one or two. As with several other critics who have chosen to describe post-modern architecture and its critics as 'conservative' (as, for example, has Steven Connor in his recent *Postmodernist Culture: an Introduction to Theories of the Contemporary* (Oxford, 1989)), the imposition of a term which is largely

political in its connotations (see also the previous note 240) does little to assist the establishment of an accurate account of the cultural theories in question.

246 See P. Steven Sangren, 'Rhetoric and the Authority of Ethnography: "Postmodernism" and the Social Reproduction of Texts', in *Current Anthropology*, vol. 29, no. 3 (June 1988), pp. 405–24, and the 'Comments' to it on pp. 424–35. (I should also like to take this opportunity to thank Professor J. A. Barnes for drawing my attention to this volume, and for taking the time to discuss some of its points.)

247 *Writing Culture: the Poetics and Politics of Ethnography*, edited by James Clifford and George E. Marcus (Berkeley, Los Angeles, and London, 1986). Of the eleven essays contained in this volume three have the word post-modern in their title: (1) Stephen A. Tyler, 'Post-Modern Ethnography: from Document of the Occult to Occult Document', pp. 122ff.; (2) Michael M. J. Fischer, 'Ethnicity and the Post-Modern Arts of Memory', pp. 194ff.; and (3) Paul Rabinow, 'Representations are Social Facts; Modernity and Post-Modernity in Anthropology', pp. 234ff.

248 Sangren, 'Rhetoric and the Authority of Ethnography', p. 405.

249 See note 247 above.

250 Sangren, 'Rhetoric and the Authority of Ethnography', p. 405. Zygmunt Bauman's *Legislators and Interpreters: on Modernity, Postmodernity and Intellectuals* (Oxford and Cambridge, 1987) also describes the post-modern as characterised by the interpretation rather than the legislation of values whilst referring to the work of Clifford Geertz and other anthropologists of influence on the rise of that which has been termed post-modern anthropology. (See, for example, Bauman, *Legislators and Interpreters*, p. 5.) Further to his essentially deconstructionist conception of post-modernism as the disavowal of the legislation of absolute value, Bauman has also followed Fredric Jameson in characterising post-modern art as eclectic and as pastiche (Bauman, *Legislators and Interpreters*, p. 130) and post-modern society (p. 193) as a consumer society. Later, in an article entitled 'Sociological Responses to Postmodernity', in *Thesis Eleven*, no. 23 (1989), pp. 35–63, Bauman sets up an alternative 'sociology of postmodernity' to both the 'postmodern sociology' which he sees as merely reflecting post-modernity and its uncertainties and those modern sociologies which have treated the post-modern as an aberration of the modern system. Despite his positing of an alternative to the post-modern sociology which is said to simply reflect the post-modern and its indetermanences, Bauman's view of post-modernity as entailing the latter appears

still to be based largely on the view of it offered by deconstructionist post-modernism.

251 In *Current Anthropology*, vol. 29, no. 3 (June 1988), pp. 424–5.

252 *Current Anthropology*, vol. 29, no. 3 (June 1988), p. 426.

253 Ibid.

254 Ibid. (Marcus's contributions to *Writing Culture* had been entitled 'Contemporary Problems of Ethnography in the Modern World System' and 'Afterword: Ethnographic Writing and Anthropological Careers'.)

255 Ibid. The particular use made of the term parody in this sentence may also be said to be typical of much deconstructionist theory.

256 As Maryon McDonald suggests, in another commentary on Sangren's paper, (*Current Anthropology*, vol. 29, no. 3 (June 1988), p. 429), the structuralist and post-structuralist theories used by the 'postmodern anthropologists' referred to by Sangren have already had an input into 'modern' anthropology, although we must also be careful here to distinguish between specific structuralist and post-structuralist ideas as well as between both of these and the varieties of post-modernism. One relatively succinct definition of the difference between structuralism and post-structuralism is also given by Christopher Norris in his *The Deconstructive Turn*, p. 164. Having spoken of the role played by Derrida's deconstruction of the concept of structure in the development of post-structuralism from structuralism, Norris describes this as having made the idea of 'structure' give way to that of 'structuration' (which should not, by the way, be confused with the sociologist and social theorist Anthony Giddens's very different use of that term), and depicts the latter as an 'activity which recognized no proper or constitutive limits to the production of meaning in and around the multiple codes of the text', although he also goes on to refer to Jonathan Culler's *The Pursuit of Signs* of 1981 as seeing deconstruction as the 'upshot' of structuralism.

257 See the beginning of Suzi Gablik's *Has Modernism Failed?* (New York and London, 1984), p. 11, for a description of the transition from modernism to post-modernism as a new terrain 'in which the limits of art seem to have been reached, and overturning conventions has become routine', and see also the note on David Harvey's *The Condition of Postmodernity* in chapter 6 on his use of Berman's 1982 descriptions of modernity for his argument that both modernity and post-modernity demonstrate a flux characteristic of capitalist society.

258 See Karl Marx and Friedrich Engels, *Manifesto of the Communist*

Party, translated by S. Moore, edited by F. Engels (Moscow, 1966), pp. 44–8.

259 I have also discussed some of these issues in my *Marx's Lost Aesthetic*.

260 Marx and Engels, *Manifesto*, p. 55.

261 Ibid., p. 54.

262 See Berman, 'The Experience of Modernity', in *Design After Modernism*, edited by John Thackara (London, 1988), p. 35.

263 As seen previously, Habermas remains critical of both deconstructionist and post-modernist approaches to modernity.

264 See Berman, 'The Experience of Modernity', pp. 43ff., as well as the other discussions of Venturi in both this chapter and the next.

265 Berman, ibid., p. 48.

266 See Charles Jencks, 'The Post-Avant Garde', in *The Post-Avant-Garde: Painting in the Eighties* (London, 1987), p. 16. As suggested previously, the view of modernity with which Berman's text associates Marx may also be said to have been coloured by Berman's deconstructionist view of the same. (Berman's 'The Experience of Modernity' also includes both Marx and Nietzsche in its pantheon of modernist theoreticians.) Despite this, we might still agree with Jencks that Marx was a modernist in the sense that that term may also be used to describe some of the 'productivist' ideas shared by some of the modernist Constructivist avant-gardes of the nineteenth and early twentieth centuries with both Marx and Saint-Simon (a point I discuss at greater length in my *Marx's Lost Aesthetic* of 1984). Here we should, however, also remain aware of the many different possible applications and meanings of the terms modern and modernist, and in particular, of the difference between this last use of them with reference to 'productivist modernism' and Berman's.

4 Double-coded theories

1 See Charles Jencks, *The Language of Post-Modern Architecture* (1977), fourth, revised, enlarged edition (London, 1984), p. 6. Jencks also writes in a note to the fifth edition of 1987, that the different editions of that book may be said to have shown 'to a degree' what the 'Post-Modern Movement' looked like at three different stages: in the early 1970s, when it was more 'pluralist'; by the late 1970s, when it was more 'eclectic'; and in 1987 'as it looks in its third classical stage'.

2 Ibid. This description of post-modernism as connoting the end of

'avant-garde extremism' may also be contrasted with Pevsner's use of the term post-modern to describe a new extremism and 'neo-expressionism' in architecture, and compared with Robert Stern's 1980 description of traditional post-modernism (see chapter 6, note 12).

3 Ibid. And see also chapter 1 note 20 for a preliminary explanation of Jencks's use of the term 'double-coding' as involving the use by post-modern architects of at least two styles, understood as codes which send out messages (or communications) to their users in a similar way to other codes or speech acts.

4 Jencks writes in his *What is Post-Modernism?* (London, 1986), p. 14, that this article ('The Rise of Post Modern Architecture') was published twice in 1975: once in Eindhoven in July 1975, in a volume entitled *Architecture – Inner Town Government*, and again in the *Architecture Association Quarterly*, vol. 7, no. 4 (October/December 1975), from which passages will be quoted in this text.

5 Charles Jencks, *What is Post-Modernism?*, p. 14. Jencks also suggests here that his 1975 use of the term post-modern was, 'except for an occasional slip here and there', by Philip Johnson or Nikolaus Pevsner, the first time it had been used in an architectural context since Joseph Hudnut. Jencks also gives a brief history of the use of the term post-modern in notes to the Introductions to the revised editions of his 1977 text, and in a note to the 1985 Postscript to his *Modern Movements in Architecture* of 1973 (2nd edn, Harmondsworth, 1985).

6 Jencks, 'The Rise of Post Modern Architecture', p. 3.

7 See the Introduction (dated September 1977) to the first edition of Jencks's *The Language of Post-Modern Architecture* (London, 1977), p. 7.

8 See also note 3 above on Jencks's understanding of the term 'double-coding', and the exposition (in the following piece of text) of his 1975 article for an explanation of the origins of his use of the term 'code'. The beginnings of the concept of dual or double-coding is already to be found in the first edition of Jencks's *The Language of Post-Modern Architecture* (1977), in its discussions of post-modern architecture as involving a 'pluralism' (or 'multivalence') of styles and codes, but the term itself is first used in the beginning of that work in the Introduction to the second edition of 1978, where it is used to explain the 'hybrid' appearance of post-modern buildings, the way in which they 'speak on two levels at once', to both an elite of architects and local inhabitants, and the inclusion of modernist codes in them. Jencks has also continued to hold to these defini-

tions, as witnessed, for example, by his *Post-Modernism: the New Classicism in Art and Architecture* (London, 1987), p. 282, and his *Architecture Today* (London, 1988), p. 111. As suggested in the text relating to this note, the description of post-modern architecture as involving a multiplicity of codes (or messages) also relates to Jencks's understanding of it as a form of architecture which communicates with its users in a variety of ways.

 9 Jencks, 'The Rise of Post Modern Architecture', p. 4.

10 Ibid., p. 5. Jencks also suggests on this page, in an interesting foreshadowing of Tom Wolfe's *From Bauhaus to Our House* (London, 1981), and of some of Jencks's own later arguments, that Wolfe's attacks on the modern novel could also be applied to modern architecture.

11 See Jencks, 'The Rise of Post Modern Architecture', p. 6, and also note 10 above.

12 See the following pages on Jencks's 1977 text. Jacobs's 1961 text, *The Death and Life of Great American Cities*, had also been mentioned in Robert Venturi, Denise Scott Brown and Steven Izenour's *Learning from Las Vegas* of 1972 (see the revised edition (Cambridge, Mass., and London, 1988), p. 81).

13 See Jencks, 'The Rise of Post Modern Architecture, p. 7.

14 Ibid., p. 9.

15 Jencks continues here (Ibid., p. 10): 'This laborious terminology underscores the fact that although semiology is about communication, its practitioners have made it rather difficult. Nevertheless they have clarified, once and for all, several important facts about architecture as a sign system.' One other architectural critic to use the concept of architecture as a source of meanings, Robert Venturi, had, as seen previously, also understood good architecture as presenting a complexity of meanings in his *Complexity and Contradictions in Architecture* (New York, 1966), although he had not used the term post-modern for it.

16 Jencks, 'The Rise of Post Modern Architecture, p. 10.

17 Ibid. Jencks's semiotic approach to architecture as presenting a variety of different codes will also be important to the development of his concept of post-modernism as a 'double-coding' of modernism with other codes which may, like other linguistic encodings, speak or send out meanings to a variety of different audiences, and may also be seen to have contributed to the ease with which he is later able to apply similar categories and criteria to both architecture and the visual arts, and to see both as offering a multiplicity of levels of meaning. On this topic Jencks has also written in chapter 6 of his

Towards a Symbolic Architecture: the Thematic House (London, 1985), p. 228, that 'Architecture like all art is multi-layered in a way that allows different paths to be found through its web of meanings. Hence one defence of symbolic design is its interest for the beholder: it encourages a dynamic reading and the invention of new interpretations.'

18 Jencks, 'The Rise of Post Modern Architecture, p. 10. Jencks adds (p. 11) that 'If semiotics has shown that form doesn't follow function, or vice versa, it has also shown that the duality is based on convention.' (And see also the previous discussions of Jencks's concept of 'radical eclecticism'.)

19 See the previous discussion of Penty in chapter 2.

20 Jencks, 'The Rise of Post Modern Architecture', p. 11.

21 Ibid., p. 12.

22 Ibid. Jencks's reference here to a 'pre-industrial' working situation might also be compared with Arthur Penty's use of the word 'post-industrial' to refer to pre-industrial working conditions operative prior to the modern 'machine-age'. (See also point 6 in the text related to this note and the previous discussion of Penty in chapter 2.) Later Jencks will refer to contemporary society as 'post-industrial' in the more contemporary sense of a computer-based service society, while also maintaining his belief that architect and client should be able to maintain suitable contact. (See also the following note 73 on some of Jencks's various comments on the concept of the post-industrial society.)

23 See also the previous note 8. Jencks himself uses the term 'hybrid' in his 1978 Introduction to his *The Language of Post-Modern Architecture* to describe the complexity of codes in post-modern architecture, and it is later also used by Hassan in his writings on the post-modern, as in, for example, his previously quoted essay of 1986. Just as Jencks will be seen to have taken over at least one or two ideas from deconstruction in his later works, it may also be said that deconstructionist post-modernists such as Hassan have taken over or at least shared some of the definers used for post-modernist architecture by Jencks and others in their later writings, so that some interactions as well as differences between these two bodies of post-modern theory may also be noted.

24 See Jencks, *The Language of Post-Modern Architecture* (1978ff.), p. 87. Jencks adds that Venturi had also provided 'two more important contributions' with his interest in 'pillaging from disregarded historical work' and his 'plunge into Pop Art'. As suggested previously, Venturi, Scott Brown and Izenour's *Learning from Las*

Vegas had also been concerned with the semiotic aspects of architecture, or, to put this in terms also used by Jencks, the use by the
architect of different 'codes', while Venturi's *Complexity and Contradiction in Architecture* of 1966 had also spoken of liking architecture which expressed a richness of meaning.

25 Robert Venturi, *Complexity and Contradiction in Architecture*,
p. 22. It is also interesting to note Venturi's criticism of expressionism in architecture here given Nikolaus Pevsner's attack on the
same in his discussions in 'Architecture in our Time: the Anti-
Pioneers', *The Listener* (29 December 1966 and 5 January 1967) of
what he had termed the 'post-modern style'. (See also the note on
Pevsner in chapter 1 and note 2 in this chapter.) While Pevsner had
included some 'neo-expressionist' works in his new category of
'post-modernist' architecture in his 1966 article, his second article on
the subject, of January 1967, had also given both 'eclecticism' and
the 'contradiction' of form and function as definers of the post-
modern. (See *The Listener*, 5 January 1967, pp. 7–9.) Although
some contemporary post-modernists have foregrounded the inter-
relationship of form and function by contrasting the two, others
have tabled their protest against the Modern Movement's valorisation of function over form by arguing for the equal valuation of
both. See, for example, the first of Rob Krier's '10 Theses on Architecture', in *Rob Krier on Architecture*, translated by Eileen Martin
(London and New York, 1982), p. 5: 'FUNCTION, CONSTRUCTION AND
FORM are of equal value and together determine the architecture.
None should have priority over the others.'

26 See Venturi, *Complexity and Contradiction*, pp. 22ff.

27 Ibid., p. 25.

28 Ibid. and following. As mentioned previously, Pevsner's *Listener*
articles of December 1966 and January 1967 had, however, included
both 'neo-expressionism' and Saarinen in the same category of
'post-modernism' and been critical of them. Further to this, Jencks
speaks critically in the Appendix to the Introduction to the second
edition of his *The Language of Post-Modern Architecture* of 1977
(London, 1978), p. 8, of what he calls Pevsner's use of the phrase
'post-modern-style' to attack those he (Pevsner) had called 'neo-
expressionist', and himself categorises many of the latter as 'late'
rather than 'post' modern.

29 See Venturi, *Complexity and Contradiction*, p. 38.

30 Ibid., p. 44. Venturi adds here that 'It [the vestigial element] is a
basis for change and growth in the city as manifest in remodelling
which involves old buildings with new uses both programmatic and

symbolic (like palazzi which become museums or embassies), and the old street patters with new uses and scales of movement.'

31 It should also be noted that Venturi does not use the term 'post-modern' in either of the texts referred to here, and that Jencks, while developing some of his ideas, is critical of others.

32 As stated in note 8, the *concept* of double-coding is already to be found in the first edition of Jencks's*The Language of Post-Modern Architecture* of 1977, in its description of the pluralist or multivalent use of styles in post-modern architecture, but the term itself is first emphasised in the beginning of that work in the Introduction to the second edition of 1978.

33 Jencks, *What is Post-Modernism?*, p. 14. (Please note that all references made in this work to Jencks's *What is Post-Modernism?* are to its first edition of 1986, but that readers are also recommended to see its later editions for further comments by Jencks on the subjects treated in it, as well as for indications of how his work on the post-modern is now developing into other areas such as psychology and social economics.)

34 Ibid., p 7.

35 Ibid., p. 23. John Perreault's description of post-modernism as quoted by Koehler (Michael Koehler, ' "Postmodernismus": Ein begriffsgeschichtlicher Ueberblick', *Amerikastudien*, vol. 22, no. 1 (1977), p. 13) had also claimed that 'Post-modernism is not a particular style, but a cluster of attempts to go beyond modernism', but not with any particular reference to architecture, and, too, without providing any common denominator or precept.

36 Jencks, *What is Post-Modernism?*, p. 23. Jencks also refers here to his listing of these definers in his *Late-Modern Architecture* (London and New York, 1980), p. 32. (See also the following discussion of these definers.) Earlier Jencks's Postscript to his *Modern Movements in Architecture* of 1973 (2nd edn, Harmondsworth, 1985), p. 373) had also described post-modernists as 'a group of architects who have evolved from the preceding movements because they have seen the inadequacies of Modernism both as an ideology and language'.

37 See the previous note 8 and its related text.

38 Other works by Jencks will also be referred to where possible, although readers will have to analyse for themselves works by Jencks which had not yet appeared when this text went to press, such as, for instance, the third edition of his *What is Post-Modernism?* and a new work on 'The Post-Modern World', in which subjects from economics through to psychology were to be covered. (And see also chapter 6 note 22.)

39 Jencks, *The Language of Post-Modern Architecture*, p. 9.
40 Ibid.
41 Jencks, *Post-Modernism: the New Classicism in Art and Architecture*, p. 27.
42 Jencks, *What is Post-Modernism?*, p. 15, also refers to the collapse of Ronan Point, an English tower block of housing, after an explosion in 1968, as another 'death-blow' to modernism.
43 Ibid., p. 19.
44 Jencks refers here to Andreas Huyssen's article 'Mapping the Postmodern', in *New German Critique*, no. 33 (Autumn 1984), pp. 13–16, a piece later republished in Huyssen, *After the Great Divide. Modernism, Mass Culture and Postmodernism* (London, 1988), pp. 178–221.
45 Jencks, *Post-Modernism: the New Classicism in Art and Architecture*, pp. 26–7.
46 Jencks, *The Language of Post-Modern Architecture*', p. 10.
47 And see also Jencks's *Late-Modern Architecture* of 1980, pp. 131ff., for a criticism of modernist 'Rationalist' beliefs.
48 Ibid., pp. 147ff. Heinrich Klotz has written in his *The History of Postmodern Architecture*, translated by Radka Donnell (Cambridge, Mass., and London, 1988), p. 210, that Rationalism 'has proved to be the most successful response to functionalism in Europe', and (p. 263) that Rossi, as one of its initiators, had also agreed that the 'decisive fault of functionalism lies in its opposition to communication'.
49 Jencks, *The Language of Post-Modern Architecture*, pp. 37f.
50 See the previous discussion of this in the section on Jameson in chapter 3.
51 Jencks, *The Language of Post-Modern Architecture*, p. 88. Jencks's defence of both a concept of consensus and a concept of the public sphere also distinguishes him from Lyotard who has attacked both concepts as well as Habermas's defence of them.
52 See Jencks, *The Language of Post-Modern Architecture*, pp. 42ff., on this, where he also uses a 'duck-rabbit' to illustrate how two codes may be contained in one image or object, and elicit several different readings. Later, in his 1987 book on 'Post-Modernism' (Jencks, *Post-Modernism: the New Classicism in Art and Architecture*, p. 271), Jencks will take this point up again in commenting on the variety of different readings given the new State Gallery in Stuttgart by its visitors – some of the younger of these having seen it as a German version of the Pompidou Centre, while older visitors saw it as a revival of Graeco-Roman architecture, or of the classicism of Schinkel.

53 Jencks, *The Language of Post-Modern Architecture*, pp. 80ff.

54 Ibid., pp. 81–2.

55 Ibid. It is also worth noting that Jencks's use of the term 'schizophrenic' here to describe post-modernism differs from both Hassan's and Fredric Jameson's in referring to a *conscious*, rather than to an unconscious and pathological state (see also the Introduction to the second edition of 1978 of Jencks's *The Language of Post-Modern Architecture*, p. 6), and in being used as a metaphor for the post-modernist use of two codes, or sets of codes.

56 Ironically, Portoghesi's *Casa Baldi* was built in the same decade as the *Pruitt-Igoe*, if some years after it. Because of the several different types of post-modernist architectures listed by Jencks – of 'Historicism', 'Straight Revivalism', 'Neo-Vernacular', 'Ad Hoc Urbanist', 'Metaphor/Metaphysical' and 'Post-Modern Space' – it is difficult to describe any one building as the first post-modernist building. Several, however, are, like Portoghesi's house, seen as having contributed to the evolution of these post-modern traditions from the modern. (Although the Introductions to the fourth and fifth editions of Jencks's 1977 text – 1984, p. 7, and 1987, p. 8 – go on to describe Michael Graves's Portland Building of 1982 as the 'first major monument of Post-Modernism, just as the Bauhaus was of Modernism, because with all its faults it still is the first to show that one can build with art, ornament and symbolism on a grand scale and in a language the inhabitants understand', they also add that Jencks's 1977 text will show that it was 'not the first building to do so'.)

57 Habermas has written in his 1981 essay on modern and post-modern architecture that the modern architecture which developed out of 'the organic as well as the rationalistic beginnings of a Frank Lloyd Wright and an Adolf Loos, and which has come to fruition in the most successful works of a Gropius and Mies van der Rohe, Corbusier and Alvar Aalto, is still the first and only united and widely influential style since the days of classicism; . . . is born of the spirit of the avant-garde; . . . has continued the line of tradition of occidental Rationalism, and was itself strong enough to create models, . . . to become classical itself and to found a tradition'. (This is a summary of my translation of Habermas, *Die neue Unueber-sichtlichkeit*, p. 15, in Rose, 'Habermas and Post-Modern Architecture', *Australian Journal of Art*, vol. 5 (1986), pp. 113–19.)

58 Jencks will also be criticised by some more radical critics of modernism for not being critical enough of the latter. See, for example, the section on Peter Fuller in the following chapter.

59 While Lyotard has been seen to have accused Jencks of having thrown out the experimental, avant-garde elements from modernism, Jameson has been seen to have both attacked post-modernist architecture as part of the 'culture of capitalism', and described Jencks as a 'propostmodernist antimodernist' in his essay 'The Politics of Theory', in *The Ideologies of Theory: Essays 1971–1986* (London, 1988). Although a later essay by Jameson of 1985, entitled 'Architecture and the Critique of Ideology' (in Jameson, *The Ideologies of Theory*, p. 59), agrees that the architecture of post-modernism may remain 'in some kind of parasitic relationship with the high modernism it repudiates', Jameson's use of the adjective 'parasitic' indicates that his is still a much more negative view of the relationship of post-modernism to modernism than Jencks's.

60 See Jencks, *The Language of Post-Modern Architecture* (2nd edn), p. 131, as well as the Introductions to both this and later editions. Jencks's *The Language of Post-Modern Architecture*, p. 90, and *What is Post-Modernism?*, p. 15, also point out that the postmodernist architect had usually been trained by a modernist, and was (like himself) a modernist before moving on to 'Post-Modernism'.

61 Jencks has published his table of differences between the 'Modern', 'Late-Modern' and 'Post-Modern' in his *Late-Modern Architecture* (London and New York, 1980), p. 32, and in the work referred to in the following passages, his 'Essay on the Battle of the Labels Late-Modernism vs Post-Modernism', in *Architecture and Urbanism*, Extra Edition (Tokyo, January 1986), entitled 'Charles Jencks', p. 213.

62 Jencks also writes in his 'Essay on the Battle of the Labels Late-Modernism vs Post-Modernism', p. 227, that 'Post-Modernists' may be distinguished from 'Late-Modernists' because the former 'doubly-code their buildings in all sorts of ways – with historical, commercial or vernacular layers of meaning – because they try to communicate with various groups through a particular use of their codes'.

63 See also Jencks, *The Language of Post-Modern Architecture* (1st edn 1977), p. 93, for a description of the 'Queen Anne Style' of the late nineteenth century as 'the last great attempt to merge different styles, and incorporate disparate material'. It might also be recalled here that Arthur J. Penty had praised the Queen Anne movement for its revival of the 'vernacular' (see note 10 to chapter 2), although it should also be noted that Penty had both prized simplicity above decoration and criticised the modern materials which are now still

being used by some post-modernists in their revival of older and 'vernacular' styles.

64 Jencks, 'Essay on the Battle of the Labels Late-Modernism vs Post-Modernism', p. 213. By contrast to Jencks, Heinrich Klotz lists only ten main characteristics of post-modernism (Klotz, *The History of Postmodern Architecture*, p. 421) – of 'Regionalism', 'Fictional representation', 'Seeing building as an art', 'Multiplicity of meanings', 'Poetry', 'Improvization and spontaneity', 'History and irony', 'Contextualism', 'Pluralism of style', 'Fiction as well as function'. Jencks has moreover not agreed with Klotz's emphasis on fiction as a definer, having written in his 'Essay on the Battle of the Labels', p. 235: 'whether the "fictional" approach towards Post-Modernism is a sufficient definition I would doubt, just as I find historicism, polychromy, facadism, ornamentalism (or whatever 'ism) a vast reduction'. Jencks continued: 'It is very obvious, but nonetheless worth stating since all these critics miss the point, that architectural movements require multiple definers – at least more than ten – and something like an evolutionary tree.'

65 See Jencks's 'Essay on the Battle of the Labels', p. 213 or Jencks, *Late-Modern Architecture*, p. 32, for the full list of contrasts and comparisons between the 'Modern', the 'Late-Modern' and the 'Post-Modern'.

66 The post-script to the 1987 edition of Jencks's *The Language of Post-Modern Architecture* is also particularly critical of works calling themselves post-modern which have not come up to the standards of the best works of that tradition.

67 See the fourth edition (1984) of Jencks, *The Language of Post-Modern Architecture*, pp. 147ff.

68 Jencks's earliest monograph on post-modern classicism, his *Post-Modern Classicism – The New Synthesis* was published first as a special issue of *Architectural Design* in London in May/June 1980, while his *Post-Modernism: the New Classicism in Art and Architecture* was published first in 1987.

69 See, for example, Jencks's discussion of the work of the Krier brothers and others in Jencks, *The Language of Post-Modern Architecture*, pp. 108ff., where Jencks writes of their revival of the idea of the public realm that they had taken the view that the 'planner, architect or market researcher *intervenes* to bring about those values he supports, but ... within a democratic, political context where his values can be made explicit and debated', and the following discussion of Jencks's comments on the need for architecture to participate in the construction of a new public sphere in his post-

script of 1984. Although the subject of the public sphere was also the topic of Habermas's 'Habilitationsschrift' (his *Strukturwandel der Oeffentlichkeit* (Darmstadt, 1962)), and is echoed in some of his more recent writings on the need for 'communicative action', he has not so far acknowledged or discussed this aspect of Jencks's writings on post-modernism. (Habermas's 1962 text had not yet appeared in English when this book was completed, but a translation of a 1964 encyclopaedia article by Habermas on 'The Public Sphere' was published in the journal *New German Critique* (Autumn 1974), pp. 49–55. In the latter Habermas begins by arguing that 'By the "public sphere" we mean first of all a realm of our social life in which something approaching public opinion can be formed', and where 'access is guaranteed to all citizens'. And see also Habermas's 1976 essay, 'Hannah Arendt: on the Concept of Power', in Juergen Habermas, *Philosophical-Political Profiles*, translated by Frederick G. Lawrence (Cambridge, Mass., and London, 1985), pp. 173–89 for a discussion by him or her related concepts.)

70 Jencks, *The Language of Post-Modern Architecture*, p. 147.
71 Ibid., p. 160.
72 Ibid., p. 164. Jencks adds in this conclusion to his post-script of 1984 that it is obvious that architecture alone cannot achieve the goal of establishing a genuinely new public realm 'since', as he writes, 'the *res publica* is established by social and political action', but, he adds, architecture must none the less 'represent this realm and build for it in a comprehensible way'.
73 Jencks's descriptions of the concept of the post-industrial society have also varied somewhat through the various editions of his *The Language of Post-Modern Architecture*, from, for instance, his description in the Introductions of 1978 and 1981 (p. 7) of Daniel Bell's idea of the post-industrial society as implying that 'some fortunate Westerners could escape laborious toil altogether', through his 1984 description (*The Language of Post-Modern Architecture*, p. 8) of post-modern society as having a 'city-based identity' while also being part of the 'world-village' with its 'instant communication', 'instant eclecticism' and 'overall mutual influence' (as well as having a new faculty of production more geared to change and individuality than previously which has been aided by the new technologies stemming from the computer) to his 1987 (5th edn of the 1977 volume) description of the post-industrial society as one in which, in addition to the preceding, 'most people are engaged in office and home, not factory work, and a host of information technologies have now made production more personalised and aimed at world

and local tastes'. (Jencks also goes on here, however, to describe the computer in a way which may have pleased Babbage, as 'symbolic of the fruits of modern technology'.) Previous to this 1987 text, Jencks had also written in his *What is Post-Modernism?* of 1986, p. 27, that the 'influence of the international media, so emphasised as a defining aspect of the post-industrial society' has helped make art a part of the world village and its cosmopolitanism, and increased the number of movements breaking off from modernism, while his *Post-Modernism: the New Classicism in Art and Architecture* of 1987 has claimed (p. 330), that the computer has helped 'make us conscious of the assumptions behind a building', while 'analytical scholarship within the art world has also increased this consciousness'.

74 See the previous chapter for discussion of Lyotard's arguments on the sometimes antagonistic relation of the post-industrial to the post-modern as well as for his criticisms of post-modern architecture. With regard to Jencks's conception of the relationship of both modernism and post-modernism to the industrial and the post-industrial, it may also be noted that Jencks, *The Language of Post-Modern Architecture*, p. 5, tells his readers that post-modernists are still partly modern in terms of both 'sensibility' and the 'use of current technology', and goes on in his 1987 text (*Post-Modernism: the New Classicism in Art and Architecture*, pp. 346–7) to state sensibly that 'A Post-Industrial society . . . still depends fundamentally on industry no matter how much its power structure and economy have moved on to the next level of organisation – computers, information exchange and a service economy'.

75 Jencks, *Post-Modernism: the New Classicism in Art and Architecture*, p. 271.

76 See, for example, Jencks, *The Language of Post-Modern Architecture*, p. 5.

77 Ibid.

78 Jencks, *What is Post-Modernism?*, Frontispiece.

79 See Jencks, *Post-Modernism: the New Classicism in Art and Architecture*, pp. 51–2, where he writes: 'Both hands are submitting to both intellects: the past paints the present, the present the past. The implication is that art and culture are created from nothing except themselves, but this interpretation of auto-invention remains *just* an implication, even if it is an apt satire on Modernist hermeticism.'

80 See, for example, the post-script on post-modern classicism in the 1984ff. editions of Jencks's *The Language of Post-Modern Architecture* for his discussion of the public character of post-modern classi-

cism. Mariani himself has said of his *The Hand Submits to the Intellect* in an interview published in *Art & Design* in 1988: 'The theme is the artist. The laurels symbolise the glory of the artist. The artist paints here the intellect (the head) and also the spirit. And the figures look at each other as they would in a mirror and the image reflects that. It's the same image. It's a visionary concept. It's not traditional.' (See Hugh Cumming, 'Carlo Maria Mariani. An *Art & Design* Interview by Hugh Cumming', in *Art & Design*, vol. 4, nos. 5/6 (1988), p. 18.)

81 As noted earlier, I have discussed the 'dual-coded' nature of modern literary irony and parody in my *Parody/Meta-Fiction* (London, 1979), a work also used by Linda Hutcheon in her work on parody and post-modernism. I also argued in note 37 of chapter 3, however, against Hutcheon's suggestions that the dual-coding which occurs in parody is equatable with that of the dual-coding which occurs in the post-modernist architecture described by Jencks and that this also allows us to equate parody with post-modernism, that such arguments fail to take into account both the particular nature of Jencks's use of the term 'double-coding' for architecture, and the fact that other factors are involved in the constitution of both the parody as parody (such as the production of a comic or ironic effect) and of the post-modern building. Rather than describing parody as either inherently modern or post-modern, it should be recognised that it is essentially a device, used from ancient to modern times, which can be used for different purposes, but which has retained certain characteristics (such as both its double-coded structure and comic effect) no matter in which 'period' it appears, so that, moreover, it has continued to be recognised as parody in the next.

82 See Achille Bonito Oliva's *Transavantgarde International* (Milan, 1982), pp. 44ff. These pages also contain a criticism of Lyotard, who, it will be remembered, had attacked both Jencks and Bonito Oliva in his 1982 text for throwing out the experimental elements from modernism and attempting to liquidate the heritage of the avant-gardes'. (See Lyotard, *The Postmodern Condition*, p. 73.) Achille Bonito Oliva had in his turn criticised Lyotard for not defining an active role for the artist, despite his recognition of the need to change the modern. (See Bonito Oliva, *Transavantgarde International*, pp. 44f.)

83 See Jencks, *What is Post-Modernism?*, p. 23. It should also be noted that Jencks uses the term 'post-avant-garde' to refer to a 'post-modern' form of avant-garde rather than to the impossibility of

having a post-modern avant-garde as suggested, for example, by some recent critics from Peter Buerger to Rosalind Krauss. (See, for example, Peter Buerger's comments on the death of the avant-garde in his *The Theory of the Avant-Garde* (Manchester and Minneapolis, 1984); and Rosalind Krauss's *The Originality of the Avant-Garde and Other Modernist Myths* (Cambridge, Mass., and London, 1986).) I have also argued elsewhere (in an article on 'The Concept of Avant-Garde: from the Modern to the Post-Modern', in *Agenda*, 1/2 (1988), pp. 23–4), that the use of the term avant-garde by certain modernist artists does not mean that it cannot be used by 'Post-Modernist' artists for other purposes and goals – and especially given the fact that none of the modernist avant-gardes have so far exhausted (or fully represented) the meanings given the term by Saint-Simon, as described, for example, in chapter 2.

84 See Jencks's 1987 essay 'The Post-Avant-Garde', p. 17.

85 See Jencks, *What is Post-Modernism?*, pp. 24 and 27.

86 See Jencks, ibid. (For Jencks, Raphael's *School of Athens* is, following Michael Greenhalgh, also the 'locus classicus' of classicism.) Further comments on Mariani's works are also made by Jencks in his 1987 book on 'Post-Modernism', with some minor adjustments to his interpretation of Mariani's *The Hand Submits to the Intellect* so that it is also seen as satirising modernism to some extent. (See Jencks, *Post-Modernism: the New Classicism in Art and Architecture*, pp. 51–2.) One other work which Jencks discusses in his 1986 text as juxtaposing the modern with the classical is Peter Blake's *'The Meeting'* or *'Have a Nice Day, Mr Hockney'*, in which Courbet's *The Meeting* is not only used as the basis for the depiction of a meeting between the three 'Pop' artists – Blake, Hockney and Hodgkin – but a classical Crouching Aphrodite (see, for example, that of Rhodes) is transformed into a teenage model on roller skates. Jencks had also written in his *What is Post-Modernism?*, p. 23, that post-modern art can be dated roughly from 1960 and from the succession of departures from modernism – from Pop Art, Hyperrealism, Photo Realism, Allegorical and Political Realism, New Image Painting, the 'Transavantgarde', Neo-Expressionism and a 'host of other more or less fabricated movements'.

87 See, for example, Jencks, *What is Post-Modernism?*, p. 14, where he writes that 'Post-Modernism, like Modernism, varies for each art both in its motives and time-frame.' It should also be mentioned here, however, that not all have appreciated the art works chosen by Jencks as representative of 'Post-Modernist' art. Anne Gregory's review of Jencks's 1987 book on post-modernism, in which Mariani

and other 'Post-Modern Classicists' are featured, concludes, for instance, with the pithy, if also somewhat 'fast', comment that 'This "art" is simply unworthy of serious critical attention; and, like fast food that has been quickly consumed, . . . it will pass.' (In *Modern Painters*, vol. 1, no. 1 (Spring 1988), pp. 96–7.)

88   This metaphor is carried through Jencks's text and is used to pillory some of the more orthodox followers of the Modern Movement as old 'Puritans'.

89   See Jencks, *What is Post-Modernism?*, p. 16. One year earlier Jencks had written in an article dealing with the completed Gallery in Stuttgart that 'since Modernists made a fetish of structural honesty, Post-Modernists accentuate the fact that all art entails deceit' (see Charles Jencks, 'Translating Past into Present: Post Modern Art and Architecture', in *Country Life* (21 November 1985), pp. 1620ff.). Later Jencks wrote in his *Post-Modernism: the New Classicism in Art and Architecture*, p. 177, that 'Post-Modern architecture inherited from Modernism two character traits: irony and classicism. But it displayed these characteristics rather than repressed them.'

90   The design of the stair-well in the Architectural Library of Jencks's 'Thematic House' in Lansdowne Walk, London, may also be said to have used the modernist trick of showing how it does its craft together with the post-modernist drive towards using its craft for both function and decoration, and for decoration which combines the modern with other historical codes; the revelation of the different layers of material in the stair-well also having created a decorative, even *art-deco* classical pattern. (See the illustration of the stair-well in the section on 'The Architectural Library' in Jencks's *Towards a Symbolic Architecture: the Thematic House* (London, 1985), pp. 175–83, as well as the previous note 17 on this text.)

91   See Jencks, *What is Post-Modernism?*, p. 17.

92   Ibid. Jencks even continues on in another caption describing the 'Acropolis' perched on top of the Gallery car park (ibid.) to see this juxtaposition of contrasting codes as a further aspect 'of the discontinuous pluralism which Lyotard and others see as a defining aspect of Post-Modernism'. This is, however, practically the only time in his 1986 text that Jencks suggests Lyotard's definition of postmodernism to be of any use. Later in his *Post-Modernism: the New Classicism in Art and Architecture*, p. 271, Jencks again uses Lyotard's claim that *The Post-Modern Condition* evolves from 'the battle between . . . different language games, none of which has absolute authority' to describe the different 'language games' used

in reading the different codes found in the new Stuttgart State Gallery, but is elsewhere in that work (on, for example, p. 12) again critical of Lyotard's account of the post-modern.

93 Although Jencks has previously used the term 'schizophrenic' in a metaphoric and non-pathological sense to describe the 'hybrid' nature of post-modernist architecture, he appears in this passage to be referring to modern culture and its more pathological characteristics.

94 See Jencks, *What is Post-Modernism?*, p. 34, on this. Jencks also goes on here to criticise those 'like Rosalind Krauss' who define post-modernism 'in terms of what it is not'.

95 Ibid., p. 38.

96 See the previous note 73 and its related text.

97 See the section on Jameson in chapter 3.

98 See again the previous note 73.

99 That is to say that although post-modern architecture may be seen to have arisen from a post-industrial society, the presence of the post-industrial society is not regarded as the only necessary condition for the development of the post-modern.

100 Jencks, *What is Post-Modernism?*, p. 39.

101 Ibid., p. 38.

102 Ibid.

103 See the section on Jameson in chapter 3.

104 Jencks, *What is Post-Modernism?*, p. 42, specifically criticises Lyotard for having confused post-modernism with a late modernist revolutionary form of avant-garde.

105 See the discussion of this in the Introduction and section on Lyotard in chapter 3.

106 Jencks, *Post-Modernism: the New Classicism in Art and Architecture*, p. 12.

107 See Charles Jencks, 'Deconstruction: the Pleasure of Absence', in *Architectural Design*, Profile 72, 'Deconstruction in Architecture', vol. 58, nos. 3/4 (1988), p. 17.

108 See Mark Wigley's essay 'Deconstructivist Architecture', in Philip Johnson and Mark Wigley, *Deconstructive Architecture* (New York, 1988), p. 16: 'The projects can be called deconstructivist because they draw from Constructivism and yet constitute a radical deviation from it.' I have avoided using the adjective 'deconstructive' as a synonym for 'deconstructionist' elsewhere in this text because of this recent use of the term to relate it specifically to certain types of 'deconstructionist' architecture.

109 See, however, 'Peter Eisenman: an *Architectural Design* Interview

by Charles Jencks', in *Architectural Design*, vol. 58, nos. 3/4 (1988), Profile 72, 'Deconstruction in Architecture' (London, 1988), p. 58, for an account of Eisenman's disagreement with the use of the term 'Deconstructivist' for his work.

110 Wigley, 'Deconstructivist Architecture', p. 11.

111 Ibid.

112 Ibid. Despite such claims by Wigley it should also be noted that the Constructivists of the 1920s have been understood by other interpreters of their work as providing bases for both the functionalist and organic aesthetics of modernism and as being the 'avant-garde' of the experimental modernism of the Bauhaus.

113 See note 109 above.

114 See Jencks, 'Peter Eisenman: an *Architectural Design* Interview', p. 58, and also note 112 above.

115 See especially Jencks, ibid., pp. 53ff.

116 Ibid., p. 53, and see also the following comments on Tschumi.

117 See Jencks, ibid., p. 54. Hal Foster's essay, '(Post)Modern Polemics' (in Hal Foster (ed.), *Recodings: Art, Spectacle, Cultural Politics* (Washington, 1985), pp. 131–2) had also named Eisenman as an example of a 'post-structuralist' post-modernist, while Robert Stern's essay 'The Doubles of Post-Modern', in *The Harvard Architectural Review*, vol. 1 (Spring 1980), p. 83, had classified Eisenman as a 'schismatic' post-humanist post-modernist rather than as a 'traditional' post-modernist, and classed him together with writers such as Norman O. Brown, Marshall McLuhan and William S. Burroughs, who, as seen earlier, had been chosen by Leslie Fiedler as examples of a 'post-Modernist' move towards the 'post-humanism' of the 1960s. (See chapter 6 for further details of Stern's 1980 essay as well as the previous notes on both Fiedler and Bell.) Eisenman himself, however, has argued with Jencks over the latter's designation of him as a 'post-structuralist' or 'Hassanian' post-modernist and insisted on being called simply a post-modernist, while also being critical of the type of post-modernism defended by Jencks (See Jencks's 'Peter Eisenman: an *Architectural Design* Interview', pp. 53f.)

118 Jencks, 'Peter Eisenman: an *Architectural Design* Interview', pp. 53f. Eisenman's usage of terms in this interview may also be said to demonstrate the need for a clear understanding of the differences between current uses of the term 'post-modernism'. To reduce these differences largely to differences of ideology as Eisenman does in at least two instances in the interview (Jencks, 'Peter Eisenman: an *Architectural Design* Interview', pp. 54 and 56) is also to

miss the many more specific differences in attitude to style or design, as described, for instance by Jencks in his 1980 list of the thirty definers of the 'Modern', the 'Late-Modern' and the 'Post-Modern'. (See Jencks, *Late-Modern Architecture*, p. 32.) Jencks also speaks specifically in his 'Peter Eisenman: an *Architectural Design* Interview', p. 55, of 'thematics, representation, signification, communication, memory' as the 'rhetorical tropes' which 'Post-Modernists' like himself – 'rather than the Hassanian kind' – have been making. When Jencks appeared to be calling Eisenman a postmodernist in Jencks's sense because of Eisenman's talk of enriching architectural language (Jencks, ibid., p. 59), Eisenman had, however, again distinguished his post-modernism from Jencks's according to what may be described as the philosophy of deconstruction by saying that 'to enrich' was for him 'not to give something new value, but to uncover what has been repressed by old values'.

119 See Bernard Tschumi, 'Parc de la Villette, Paris', in *Architectural Design*, vol. 58, nos. 3/4 (1988), Profile 72, 'Deconstruction in Architecture' (London, 1988), p. 33. Ironically (given the appropriation of Baudrillard to the ranks of 'postmodernism'), the then unbuilt Parc de la Villette project had also been condemned together with the Pompidou Centre by Baudrillard in his 'The Ecstasy of Communication', pp. 130f., as one of the public spaces invaded by advertising and its 'gigantic spaces of circulation'. (And see also the note on Baudrillard's criticism of the Pompidou Centre in chapter 3.)

120 See the previous discussion of Wigley. The account given of the Tate Gallery and Academy Group Symposium on Deconstruction at the Tate Gallery in 1988, on p. 7 of the same *Architectural Design* Profile 72 in which Tschumi's 'Parc de Villette' project is described, also comments on how Tschumi and Eisenman were in agreement with Wigley's concept of Deconstruction in architecture as challenging architectural conventions, but adds that they 'disagreed with Wigley's idea of Deconstruction as non-Derridean'.

121 See Andrew Benjamin's comments on this in his 'Derrida, Architecture and Philosophy', in *Architectural Design*, vol. 58, nos. 3/4 (1988), Profile 72, 'Deconstruction in Architecture' (London, 1988), pp. 8–11; and Bernard Tschumi's 'Parc de Villette, Paris', pp. 33–9.

122 See Bernard Tschumi's 'Parc de Villette, Paris', p. 38.

123 See ibid., pp. 38–9. Tschumi's statement would appear to cover much of the architecture which Jencks has categorised as postmodernist on the basis of his emphasis on the importance of the

expression of a complexity of codes and meanings in post-modernist architecture.

124 See the previous description of these definers in the preceding text. In addition to listing double-coding as one of the definers of post-modernism, Jencks also writes in his 'Essay on the Battle of the Labels', p. 227, that: 'Post-Modernists doubly-code their buildings in all sorts of ways – with historical, commercial or vernacular layers of meaning – because they try to communicate with various groups through a partial use of their codes.'

125 Ibid.; and see also the previous note 112.

126 See Jencks, *What is Post-Modernism?*, p. 48. Lyotard's suggestion that Jencks's post-modernism is based in the belief that 'anything goes' is also contradicted by Jencks's affirmation here, as elsewhere, of the necessity for the post-modernist critic to make value judgements rather than embrace the relativism of Lyotard and others.

127 Jencks had begun the passage just quoted from the end of his 1986 text by referring to Peter Fuller's *Images of God: the Consolation of Lost Illusions* of 1985, and to his call for the 'equivalent of a new spirituality based on an imaginative, yet secular response to nature herself'. Jencks had then continued: 'His Post-Modernism, like my own, seeks a shared symbolic order of the kind that a religion provides, but without the religion.' Although Jencks aligns himself with Fuller's views here, Fuller was later to develop an ideal post-modernism which (as will be seen in chapter 5) explicitly excluded any 'double-coding' or preservation of the modern.

128 See Charles Jencks, *Post-Modernism: the New Classicism in Art and Architecture*, p. 7.

129 Later Jencks also writes (ibid., p. 329) that 'with Post-Modern Classicism the meanings, values and forms of Modernism and classicism are simultaneously transformed into a hybrid combination'.

130 See Jencks, ibid., p. 176.

131 Ibid., pp. 40ff.

132 See the Conclusion of chapter 3 on Foster's classification of Schnabel as a 'neo-conservative' post-modernist.

133 Jencks, *Post-Modernism: the New Classicism in Art and Architecture*, p. 8.

134 See the previous discussion of Foster in the Conclusion of chapter 3.

135 Levin's review of Schnabel was published in *The Village Voice* of 18 November 1986 and reprinted in Kim Levin, *Beyond Modernism: Essays on Art from the 70s and 80s* (New York, 1988), pp. 223–5.

Although Suzi Gablik takes Schnabel as an example of a post-modernist in her *Has Modernism Failed?* (New York and London, 1984), pp. 88ff., her view of post-modernism as meaning 'anything goes' has also been seen previously to have suited the relativism of deconstructionist post-modernism better than Jencks's concept of post-modernism.

136 See also Carolyn Christov-Bakargiev's 'Interview with Carlo Maria Mariani', in *Flash Art*, no. 133 (April 1987), p. 60, for an illustration of Mariani's 1986/7 portrait of Schnabel which sets him in classical garb against a background of broken classical columns. As the interview between Mariani and Carolyn Christov-Bakargiev in this same issue makes clear, Mariani has not been averse to using irony in his works, and his neo-classical depiction of Schnabel against a background of broken columns might well be seen by those who see Schnabel's broken cups as characteristic of a 'deconstructionist' post-modernism to have added an extra ironic level to his portrait.

137 See note 135 above.

138 See the section on Foster in the Conclusion of chapter 3.

139 See also the discussion of this point in both the Preface and in chapter 6. The use of adjectival distinctions between two or more theories or examples of post-modernism does not necessarily mean that a proponent of one particular variety of post-modernism may not continue to question another's claim to use the term post-modernism. Once the term post-modernism has been appropriated by a certain theoretician or practitioner it would however seem to be necessary to understand what the person in question means by the use of that term, and how its usage differs from that of others, before arguing further about the appropriateness or not of its use.

140 See Robert Rosenblum's *The Dog in Art from Rococo to Post-Modernism* (New York, 1988), pp. 110–13.

141 Ibid., p. 113.

142 Ibid., p. 111.

143 See Baudrillard, *Simulations*, p. 136.

144 In Baudrillard, ibid., pp. 138ff.

145 See Jacques Derrida's, *The Truth in Painting*, translated by Geoff Bennington and Ian McLeod (Chicago and London, 1987), p. 150. Derrida's text (pp. 175–81) had also dealt with Adami's depictions of the suicide of the author of 'The Work of Art in the Age of Mechanical Reproduction', Walter Benjamin. And see also Andrew Benjamin's comments on Derrida's text on Adami, in Christopher

Norris and Andrew Benjamin, *What is Deconstruction?* (London and New York, 1988), pp. 44ff.

146 In fact Taaffe has been associated with the theories of Baudrillard by several commentators. See, for instance, Douglas Kellner's *Jean Baudrillard: from Marxism to Postmodernism and Beyond* (Oxford and Cambridge, 1989), p. 113, and associated notes.

147 Jencks, *Post-Modernism: the New Classicism in Art and Architecture*, p. 11.

148 Ibid.

149 Ibid., p. 22.

150 Ibid., pp. 24ff.

151 Jencks, *What is Post-Modernism?*, p. 48.

152 Jencks, *Post-Modernism: the New Classicism in Art and Architecture*, p. 36.

153 Ibid., p. 271.

154 See the previous notes on Jencks's agreement with Lyotard on this point, and also Jencks's article 'Post-Modernism and Discontinuity', in *Architectural Design*, vol. 57, nos. 1/2 (1987), Profile 65, p. 6, for a more critical discussion of Lyotard's pushing of his pluralism to an extremist 'war on totality'.

155 Jencks, *Post-Modernism: the New Classicism in Art and Architecture*, p. 271.

156 Ibid., pp. 271–2.

157 Ibid., p. 272.

158 The Greek for dialectic (*dialektike*) can also be interpreted to refer to the art of conversation, and Socrates be seen as having understood the dialectic to be the art of conversation aimed at the clarification of concepts. And see also Jencks's *The Language of Post-Modern Architecture*, pp. 131–3, for an example of his use of the word dialectic to refer to discourse as conversation. In contrast to earlier forms of dialectic, Hegel's nineteenth-century version had also been used by him to suggest that history itself was a part of the dialectic whereby Reason or Spirit was developing towards greater self-consciousness. While the Socratic dialectic is not normally related to a dialogue between historical forms as the Hegelian has been, when it is – as in Jencks's reading of Stirling's Stuttgart project – we do not see history presented as part of a development towards a higher form of abstract and universal consciousness as in Hegel's works, but an individual, or group of individuals, placing two historical styles together in a contrast to illustrate the differences as well as the compatibility of those styles.

159 See the first of Jencks's rules for the post-modern in his *Post-Modernism: the New Classicism in Art and Architecture*, pp. 329f., and the following summary of them in this text.

160 Ibid., p. 315. Earlier (on p. 32), Jencks had also referred to the new collaboration between post-modernist architects, sculptors and artists which can be seen in many post-modern buildings.

161 Ibid., pp. 329ff.; and see also Jencks's article, 'The New Classicism and its Emergent Rules', in *Architectural Design*, vol. 58, nos. 1/2 (1988), Profile 70, pp. 26ff.

162 Jencks, *Post-Modernism: the New Classicism in Art and Architecture*, p. 338. As we have seen previously, Fredric Jameson and those following him have reinterpreted the pastiche used in post-modernist architecture as a form of 'blind parody'. In contrast to Jameson's 'Baudrillardian' redefinition of post-modernist pastiche (see the previous discussion of Jameson's concept of pastiche in chapter 3), it may, however, be said to have functioned as parody often has, as a 'double-coding' of a variety of codes with another (as described, for instance, in Rose, *Parody/Meta-Fiction*) in at least some works of post-modernist art and architecture. Despite his description of parody here as one of the 'lesser genres', Jencks has also explicitly praised it, as in, for instance, his *The Language of Post-Modern Architecture*, p. 93, where he writes: 'One of the virtues of parody, besides its wit, is its mastery of cliché and convention, aspects of communication which are essential to Post-Modernism.'

163 Again (see the note above), it may also be said that parody can use a multiplicity of codes as does irony (see Rose, *Parody/Meta-Fiction*, pp. 51–5, and 'general parody' *passim*), just as pastiche may serve to bring a multiplicity of codes together by pasting the one onto another, as indicated by Jencks himself in his earlier works. (And see also Jencks's tenth rule in which irony, double-coding and eclectic quotation are listed together.)

164 Jencks's awareness of the way in which double-coding may go together with the creation of ambiguity or contradiction in post-modernism can remind us that it is also possible to make several distinctions between the types of parody used in post-modern literature and the arts, including distinctions between specific and general parody, and satiric and ironic parody. In all cases parody may be said to have 'double-coded' one text with another, although in the case of satiric parody one text (or code) will generally be the target of the other, while in ironic parody the different codes embedded in the parody may reflect on each other to modify or

change the meaning of both, or simply to add a variety or complexity of codes to the parody text.

165 See Jencks, *What is Post-Modernism?*, p. 9.

166 See also Rose, 'Parody/Post-Modernism', in *Poetics*, vol. 17 (1988), pp. 49–56.

167 Jencks, *Post-Modernism: the New Classicism in Art and Architecture*, p. 342.

168 The full list of 'new rhetorical figures' given by Jencks (ibid., p. 345) reads: 'paradox, oxymoron, ambiguity, double-coding, disharmonious harmony, amplification, complexity and contradiction, irony, eclectic quotation, anamnesis, anastrophe, chiasmus, ellipsis, elision and erosion'.

169 Ibid., p. 346. Jencks then goes on to suggest that the above may also reflect 'the sense of loss which underlies so many departures which can be characterised with the prefix "post" ', and that Toynbee's use of the term in the 1940s and 1950s had expressed a similar melancholy. (But see also chapter 1 for a slightly different point of view on Toynbee's use of the term in this period.)

170 Jencks, ibid., p. 272, contains the reproduction of the conversation he has had with James Stirling about the symbolism of the centre of the Rotunda. In it Stirling also points out that the three circles of which the grate of the drain is composed are not representative of any sacred symbol like the Trinity but of the 'cross-section of an electric cable'.

171 See Jencks, ibid., p. 294 as well as p. 346.

172 See Jencks, ibid., p. 302, where he criticises the relation of the idea of the 'death of the author' to post-modernist architecture.

173 Ibid., p. 350. Jencks writes here: 'Again it is the viewer who supplies the possible interpretations which lead back to himself, or herself: the presence at the absent centre.'

174 Ibid. Some years earlier Malcolm Bradbury and James McFarlane had written in their 'The Name and Nature of Modernism', in Malcolm Bradbury and James McFarlane (eds.), *Modernism 1890–1930* (Harmondsworth, 1976), p. 26: 'If Modernism is the imaginative power in the chamber of consciousness that, as James puts it, "converts the very pulses of the air into revelations", it is also often an awareness of contingency as a disaster in the world of time: Yeats's "Things fall apart; the centre cannot hold".'

175 Jencks also writes in his *Post-Modernism: the New Classicism in Art and Architecture*, p. 349, that 'Post-Modernism is . . . schizophrenic about the past; equally as determined to retain and preserve aspects

of the past as it is to go forward; excited about revival, yet wanting to escape the dead formulae of the past. Fundamentally it mixes the optimism of Renaissance revival with that of the Futurists, but is pessimistic about finding any certain salvation point, be it technology, a classless society, a meritocracy or rational organisation of a world economy (i.e. any of the answers which have momentarily been offered in the last hundred years).'

176 Jencks also concludes his *Post-Modernism: the New Classicism in Art and Architecture*, p. 350, with the suggestion that it is in the nature of our age to 'simultaneously promote rules and break them'. The basis on which his own rules may be broken in the future will no doubt also be of interest to Jencks, although the specific breakages may not necessarily be accepted by him without further discussion and argument. While his 1987 text might also be seen to have 'interwoven' some ideas from 'deconstructionist' theory into his ideas of post-modernism, in, for example, his concluding point that some post-modernist works refer to an 'absent centre', his further point, that the ideas behind such works cannot be confused with the 'late-modernist' belief in the 'death of the subject' also show that he was still not prepared to understand post-modernism as a movement in which 'anything goes'. (And see also chapter 6 note 22 for information on new work being completed by Jencks at the time that this book was going to press.)

5 Alternative theories

1 See, for example, the discussion of Lucien Kroll in chapter 3.

2 See also the Bibliography to this text for the titles of some of these works by, for example, Lucien Kroll and Rob Krier.

3 See chapter 4, note 64.

4 Heinrich Klotz, *The History of Postmodern Architecture*, translated by Radka Donnell (Cambridge, Mass., and London, 1988), Preface.

5 See chapter 4, note 64.

6 See chapter 4 note 63, and Kenneth J. Frampton, 'Towards a Critical Regionalism', in Hal Foster (ed.), *Postmodern Culture* (London, 1985), pp. 16–30.

7 See Kenneth J. Frampton, 'Some Reflections on Postmodernism and Architecture', *ICA Documents* 4/5 (1986), pp. 26–9. Some of the ideas in this paper are also to be found in Frampton's essays, in Kenneth Frampton (ed.), *Modern Architecture and the Critical Present* (London, 1982).

8 Frampton, 'Some Reflections on Postmodernism and Architecture',

p. 26. Frampton has also written in his 'Towards a Critical Regionalism', p. 19, that the post-modern architecture classified by Jencks has gravitated 'towards pure technique or pure scenography'.

9 Frampton, 'Some Reflections on Postmodernism and Architecture', p. 27.

10 Ibid. Frampton also refers on this same page to a distinction made by Peter Wollen between 'positive and negative avant-garde', in which 'we may think of the positive avant-garde as conceiving of themselves and their work as being totally compatible with the modern project of the Enlightenment and with modernisation; and of the negative avant-garde as being passionately involved with the dissolution of all bourgeois culture, including the positive project of the Enlightenment', and then goes on to describe the 'critical culture' as a 'transmutation of the avant-garde'. As in any such mutation, the degree to which all the elements are affected may need, however, to be spelt out even more clearly than Frampton has on his following page 28, while the adequacy of the original distinction as both a description of past avant-garde and a blue-print for the possibilities for the future might also be investigated more thoroughly. To relate such categories of the avant-garde to Jencks, it may be said that although his theories cannot be seen as agreeing with the negative concept of avant-garde, neither, however, can they be seen to have been used to condone all aspects of modernisation, as suggested in the above concept of 'positive avant-garde'.

11 See Frampton, ibid., p. 26.

12 See Jencks's criticisms of the high-tech architecture which Fredric Jameson and others have termed 'postmodern'. Jencks also describes Frampton's own critical regionalism as late-modernist in the Introduction to the 1984 edition of his *The Language of Post-Modern Architecture* (London), p. 6, and criticises what he describes as Frampton's defence of modernism and criticism of ornament on page 152 of the same text.

13 See Jencks, 'The Post-Avant-Garde', *Art & Design*, vol. 37, no. 8 (1987), p. 17.

14 See Frampton's 'Some Reflections on Postmodernism and Architecture', pp. 26ff., and also note 10 above.

15 See chapter 4 note 99 and its related text. Ironically, both Frampton and Jencks have stressed the importance of the architect's contribution to the establishment of the public realm. (See the discussion of the public sphere or realm in chapter 4 and its note 69, and also Frampton 'Some Reflections on Postmodernism and Architecture', p. 28.)

16 See Portoghesi's opening to the volume edited by Gabriella Borsano, *Architecture 1980. The Presence of the Past. Venice Biennale*
(New York, 1980), pp. 9–13, 'The End of Prohibitionism', p. 9, for
his account of both his belief in the importance of appreciating
historical tradition and of Frampton's disagreement with him over
the Biennale and withdrawal from the committee for the selection of
planners for the *Strada Novissima*, over 'among other things'
Frampton's proposal 'to include Rem Koolhaas'. (As seen
previously, Koolhaas is an architect also included in exhibitions of
'Deconstructivist' architecture.) Jencks's contribution to this 1980
volume was his 'Towards Radical Eclecticism', pp. 30–7.

17 See Paolo Portoghesi, *Postmodern: the Architecture of the Post-
industrial Society* (New York, 1983), p. 7.

18 Ibid., p. 12. Prior to this, on page 10, Portoghesi had written of
Jencks that he was 'the most able of the announcers of this new
show' (the postmodern in architecture), but that while Jencks's
definition of post-modernism as a double-coding 'certainly covers
the unifying aspect of many of the most significant works realized in
the last decade which have overcome the ideological crisis of the
Modern Movement', 'It fails, however, to satisfy the historical need
of relating the shift carried out by architectural culture to the profound changes in society and risks confining the phenomenon to an
area completely within the private realm of the architect, therefore
remaining more a psychological than an historico-critical definition.'

19 Ibid., p. 28.

20 Ibid., p. 7.

21 Ibid., p. 11.

22 Ibid. Portoghesi also writes on page 68, that the new post-industrial
society will no longer need the 'villes tentaculaires', or skyscraper
cities, of late-industrial society, and adds that the new information
technology – able to be worked from the home as much as from the
office – will mean that 'small cities will once again play a role not
only in the consumption and passive reception of the culture of the
metropolis, but also in autonomous creation and valid interlocu-
tion'. Not only might Jencks's emphasis on the need for greater
communication between the builders and users of cities be recalled
here, but it is also interesting to note that he had not only referred in
his *The Language of Post-Modern Architecture*, p. 108, to the way
in which the post-modern interest in the restoration of the public
sphere might be contrasted with the modernist obsession with the
free-standing monument, but had, in the later edition of that work
of 1987 (p. 5), also gone on to speak of the post-industrial society as

one in which work will be carried out in the home and the office rather than the factory.

23 Portoghesi, *Postmodern*, p. 8.
24 Ibid.
25 Ibid.
26 Ibid., p. 11.
27 Ibid., p. 39.
28 Ibid., p. 42.
29 Ibid.
30 Ibid., pp. 42–6.
31 Ibid., p. 72.
32 Ibid.
33 Ibid., p. 73.
34 Ibid., p. 8, and see also its p. 12 for another reference by Portoghesi to Touraine.
35 Ibid., p. 73; and see also chapter 2 note 54 on Touraine's comments on the forces controlling the development of the city, and chapter 4 note 119 on Baudrillard's criticisms of new buildings such as the Pompidou Centre.
36 Portoghesi, ibid., p. 75.
37 As noted previously, Portoghesi's text was published as such in 1982.
38 Fuller's rejection of the theories of both deconstructionist and 'double-coded' post-modernism is treated here not just as a criticism of those schools, as offered, for example, by Habermas, but as part of an alternative theory of post-modernism because of Fuller's related suggestion of a more ideal form of post-modernism than those already in existence. (See also the following section of text.)
39 See Peter Fuller, 'The Search for a Postmodern Aesthetic', in John Thackara (ed.), *Design after Modernism* (London, 1988), pp. 117ff.
40 Ibid., p. 117.
41 Ibid., p. 133.
42 See Peter Fuller, *Theoria: Art and the Absence of Grace* (London, 1988), p. 6.
43 Ibid., p. 45.
44 See also Fuller's 'Towards a New Nature for the Gothic', *Art & Design*, vol. 3, nos. 3/4 (1987), Profile 2, The Post-Modern Object (London, 1987), pp. 8–9.
45 Fuller, *Theoria*, p. 213. Fuller's *Theoria* also refers on p. 183 to the 'aesthetic wastelands of late and post-modernism' and repeats an earlier criticism made by him of the 1987 television series *State of the Art* and of its presentation of post-modernism on *Theoria*, pp. 212ff.

46 Fuller, *Theoria*, p. 213.
47 See Fuller, 'Towards a New Nature for the Gothic', p. 7.
48 Fuller, *Theoria*, pp. 233–4, also speaks of the 'post-modern age' as one in which science is 'rediscovering the aesthetic and spiritual meanings of nature'.
49 See Peter Fuller, 'Art and Post-Industrialism', in his Fuller, *The Australian Scapegoat* (Perth, 1986), p. 37.
50 See 'Towards a Fuller Meaning of Art. Peter Fuller interviewed by Colin Symes', in Fuller, *The Australian Scapegoat*, p. 54. An earlier essay by Fuller entitled 'Conserving "Joy in Labour" ', in *William Morris Today* (London, 1984), pp. 90–3, had also referred on page 93 to the relevance of Morris's ideas to 'post-industrial society' but without developing the connection further.
51 See chapter 4 note 73.
52 See chapter 4 note 73.
53 Fuller, 'The Search for a Postmodern Aesthetic', pp. 130ff. Fuller also writes here that a more sophisticated mathematics and technology might be more sensitive to the variations and detail of nature, and, hence, also more able to describe and reproduce them.
54 See the discussion of Penty in chapter 2 for further information on his theories. Although described as a follower of William Morris, Arthur Penty had also been somewhat more sceptical than Morris about the use of machines to take over the labour which could free men and women for the arts. While Penty has also been seen to have preferred the Norman to the Gothic style in architecture, his criticisms of modern architectural methods and materials, and of the sensibility which accompanies them, are, however, not dissimilar to Fuller's.
55 See, for example, the second volume of Habermas's *Theory of Communicative Action* (Boston, 1987).
56 Both Fuller and Habermas may, however, be said to have extended (like Lyotard) the early Frankfurt School critique of the instrumental rationality increased by modernisation. See, for example, Habermas's *Theory of Communicative Action*, and Fuller's *Theoria*, where he takes up Marcuse's critique of 'technological rationality'.
57 See the discussion of this issue in the section on Habermas in chapter 3.
58 The denial of the agency of the subject in deconstructionist theory (and in Jameson's theory of the 'death of the old bourgeois subject' as well as in those of the 'death of the subject' as such) also suggests both that the subject is incapable of individual 'value-rationality' and in participating in any true consensus about values of the type spoken of by Habermas and others, given that in both cases the

existence of subjects able to make their own value decisions is necessary. As suggested previously, the theory of the 'death of the subject' has also never adequately explained how its own theoreticians have been able to make their choice of agreeing with such a theory, or how this can be done and the theory still remain meaningful, or, even, as Malcolm Bradbury's *Mensonge* has also suggested, how they can write their articles or books in the first place.

59 See also Fuller, *Theoria*, pp. 212ff.

60 See Victor Burgin, *The End of Art Theory: Criticism and Postmodernity* (London, 1986), p. 204.

61 Ibid., p. 2; and see also the previous discussions of Hassan, Fiedler, Jameson and Huyssen.

62 John Fekete (ed.), *Life After Postmodernism* (London, 1988), p. ii.

63 Ibid., p. iii.

64 Ibid., p. xiv.

65 Criticism may also be made of the implication found in some relativist works that the effective critique of the value judgements revealed behind a specific defence of a value also serves to question the existence or validity of that value itself. One problem here is that we may be being offered not only a generalisation from one or more criticisable value judgements to all, but also a covert and even unconscious positing of an unproven identity between the judgement or defence of a value by an individual or group and the value in question. One other common criticism of relativist critiques of the subjectivity of value-judgements is, of course, that these critiques may themselves be condemned as subjective on the basis of their own premisses. Further to the above, Len Doyal and Roger Harris's, *Empiricism, Explanation and Rationality: an Introduction to the Philosophy of the Social Sciences* (London, 1986), pp. 118ff., may also be mentioned here as providing some other philosophical arguments against relativism.

66 See also Charles Jencks, *Post-Modernism: the New Classicism in Art and Architecture* (London, 1987), p. 12, for a description of 'post-logical-positivism' as modern rather than post-modern.

67 See, for example, the Introduction to *The Positivist Dispute in German Sociology* of 1969, English translation by Glyn Adey and David Frisby (London, 1976), which even takes the dispute back to the nineteenth century.

68 See Fekete, *Life After Postmodernism*, p. xii. Fekete refers to both Habermas and Giddens here but not to their specific positions *vis-à-vis* post-modernism.

69 Fekete himself refers (ibid., p. xii) to Giddens's contribution to the

analysis of the 'fact–value' distinction, but avoids discussing both Giddens's views on post-structuralism and the distinctions made by Giddens between the natural and the social sciences. On the latter see, for instance, Giddens's 1984 paper on 'The Social Sciences and Philosophy – Trends in Recent Social Theory', in his *Social Theory and Modern Sociology* (Stanford, 1987), p. 70 where he writes: 'Social science is concerned with concept-bearing and concept-inventing agents, who theorize about what they do as well as the conditions of doing it. Now natural science, as has been made clear in the "newer philosophy of science", involves a hermeneutic. Science is an interpretative endeavour, in which the theories comprise meaning-frames. Unlike natural science, however, the social sciences involve a double hermeneutic, since the concepts and theories developed therein apply to a world constituted of the activities of conceptualizing and theorizing agents.'

70 See Giddens's, 'Structuralism, Post-structuralism and the Production of Culture', in his *Social Theory and Modern Sociology*, p. 89.

71 Ibid., p. 99.

72 The answer to the question of to what extent post-modernists such as Jencks might agree with the description of the dissolution of the 'fact–value' distinction as central to the post-modern may also depend on to what extent that dissolution will be used as a part of any deconstructionist reduction of value to the interpretative viewpoint of its defender, and on the concept of the subject which will be used to describe that defender as, for example, an agent with some degree or other of freedom to make his or her own choices or selections, or as a being who has been 'overdetermined' by the structures of constraint which so often dominate the deconstructionist post-modernist's view of contemporary society.

73 Andreas Huyssen, 'Mapping the Postmodern', in his *After the Great Divide: Modernism, Mass Culture and Postmodernism* (Indiana, 1986; London, 1988), p. 198.

74 Although Huyssen makes a brief reference to Jencks, in Huyssen, *After the Great Divide*, pp. 186–7, it is largely to Jencks as both a critic of modernism and as an advocate for the post-modernist mixing of styles, while he also concludes his discussion of post-modernist architecture on pp. 187–8 by relating it to Robert Venturi, Denise Scott Brown and Steven Izenour's *Learning from Las Vegas* (Cambridge, Mass., and London, 1988), and to what he sees to be the essentially popular nature of the post-modern. Not only has Jencks raised many other issues about post-modernism, including its return to both the subject and to intersubjective communication,

which may be of relevance to those dissatisfied with the reduction of the agency of the subject in deconstructionist or post-structuralist varieties of post-modernism, but he has, in contrast to deconstructionist post-modernists and critics of post-modernist architecture who have tended to speak largely of the male theorists and practitioners of post-modern architecture, also acknowledged the work of several different women artists, architects and theorists in his various works on post-modernism.

75 Here it should also be noted that the suppression of the concept of the subject as agent in structuralist and post-structuralist theory might also be said to have been responsible to at least some degree for the suppression of the idea of the individual woman as an agent capable of making her own value decisions and value-actions in some modern and late-modern feminist theory based on post-structuralist ideas.

76 See E. Ann Kaplan's article 'Feminism/Oedipus/Postmodernism: the Case of MTV', in her *Postmodernism and its Discontents* (London and New York, 1988), p. 42.

77 Kaplan's article goes on to suggest (ibid.) that 'we must continue to articulate oppositional discourses ... if we are to construct new subjects capable of working toward the utopian post-modernism we all hope will be possible', and adds that this 'means not validating or celebrating the erosion of all categories and differences and boundaries – as Baudrillard and his followers sometimes appear to do'. What is missing here is, however, not only the recognition that the type of post-modernism to which she is referring is only one variation on what may be called deconstructionist post-modernism (Kaplan also relies to a large extent on Arthur Kroker's and David Cook's Baudrillardian *The Postmodern Scene: Excremental Culture and Hyper-Aesthetics* (Montreal, 1986) for her account of contemporary post-modernism) but also the discussion of other non-Baudrillardian and non-deconstructionist accounts of post-modernism which already exist.

78 See Jencks on 'Radical Eclecticism' as well as his 1987 rules for the 'Post-Modern' for an indication of his belief in the subject as agent.

79 Problems clearly arise with the statement 'anything goes' if we try to apply it to its own interpretation, where it becomes clear that in order to retain the dictum 'anything goes' we must desist from applying it to itself. (Put in other words, it could be said that if anything goes then even the statement 'anything goes' may be taken to mean anything at all – and, hence, even its opposite 'anything does not go'!) Although some contemporary critics have also

claimed that no stable meaning may be attributed to a text because of the hermeneutic involved in the process of interpreting the words of another, whereby, for instance, a reader may be forced to impose some meanings on a text to obtain a clear message from it, the critical reader should further still be able to give some account of both the overt arguments presented by a text and of the bases of his or her interpretation of them. To most pre-twentieth-century hermeneuticists, the aim of the hermeneutical reading of a text was, moreover, not to increase its 'indeterminacy' in any 'Hassanian post-modernist' sense, but to approximate more closely its covert as well as overt meanings. While some post-modernisms have been developed on more recent and relativistic deconstructionist bases than those of pre-post-modernist hermeneutics, even they have been seen to have needed readers who were able to distinguish their arguments from those of others, and to understand at least something of what they were saying. What the varieties of post-modernisms discussed in this text have shown is, moreover, that, given the recent increase in theories of the post-modern and its related concepts, readers must now be enabled to make even finer distinctions and even more accurate accounts of the arguments of such theories than before.

6 Conclusion and summary

1 See chapter 2 for details.
2 As noted previously in chapter 2, Bell adds that he had also been using the term post-industrial there in contrast to Ralf Dahrendorf's 'post-capitalist' because Bell was dealing with 'sector changes in the economy' while Dahrendorf was discussing 'authority relations in the factory'.
3 See the pages on Touraine in chapter 2 for further details of his concept of the post-industrial society as 'technocratic' and 'programmed'.
4 See also chapter 2, note 32. Toffler does not use the term post-industrial here, but his description of society has been echoed in several other works which have used the term post-industrial to describe future society as one in which new technologies will revolutionise present society and its culture. (And see also his *The Third Wave* of 1980 in which he speaks of a new post-industrial age in terms of a third wave of changes which will include the return of work to the home as 'electronic cottage'.) As discussed in chapter 2,

one other theorist of influence on recent concepts of the post-industrial has been Marshall McLuhan, whose work on new developments in the communication media and their effects may be dated from at least 1960.

5 See Bell, *The Coming of Post-Industrial Society* (Harmondsworth, 1976), pp. 14ff. and the discussion of these and other points relating to Bell's characterisation of the post-industrial society in chapter 2 of this book. As noted in that chapter, some of the ideas developed by Bell in his 1973 work had also been expressed in articles published prior to 1973.

6 Michael Collins has also recently stated in Michael Collins and Andreas Papadakis's *Post-Modern Design* (London, 1989), p. 18, that Pevsner had used the term post-modern as early as his 1961 essay 'The Return to Historicism', republished in his *Studies in Art, Architecture and Design*, vol. II (London, 1968), p. 258, to describe a new 'post-modern anti-rationalism'.

7 Jencks ('Why Post-Modernism?', in 'Post-Modern History', *Architectural Design* Profile 10, in *Architectural Design*, vol. 48, no. 1 (London, 1978), p. 14) has also referred to a use of the term 'post-Modern Movement style' by Joseph Rykwert in the latter's article 'Ornament is no Crime', published in the September 1975 edition of *Studio International*, p. 95. Later, when Rykwert republished this article in his *The Necessity of Artifice* (London, 1982), pp. 92–101, he introduced it (p. 92) by saying that 'If I have a regret about something I published it is for the unfortunate and precocious use of the term "post-Modern Movement style" which I applied here to the work of Paul Rudolph. However, let it stand.' One of the problems with this usage in view of other recent architectural uses of the term post-modern was also that Rykwert (see *The Necessity of Artifice*, p. 97) had described Rudolph as a 'favourite target' for the Venturis.

8 See the discussion of Bell's views in chapter 2 as well as the various notes to Bell.

9 See Stern's 'At the Edge of Modernism', in *Architectural Design*, vol. 47, no. 4 (April 1977), pp. 274–86. Later, in his 'The Doubles of Post-Modern', in *The Harvard Architectural Review*, vol. 1 (spring 1980), pp. 75–87, Stern wrote that he had first used the term post-modern in a paper of 1976 entitled 'Possibly, the Beaux-Arts Exhibit means something after all' (later published in *Oppositions*, vol. 8 (spring 1977), pp. 169–71) to describe 'a shift in mood' in some of the architecture of the time. (See Stern, 'The Doubles of Post-Modern', p. 76, note 4, for further details.)

10 See the discussion of Koehler's views in chapter 1.

11 See the section on Lyotard in chapter 3 for further details.

12 See Stern's 'The Doubles of Post-Modern', pp. 75–87. Stern writes on p. 76: 'Thus the doubles of the Post-Modern: two distinct but interrelated Post-Modern sensibilities: a schismatic condition that argues for a *clean break* with the 400 year old tradition of Western Humanism and a "traditional" condition that argues for a return to, or a recognition of, the *continuity* of the cultural tradition of Western Humanism of which it holds modernism to be a part.' Prior to this Stern had also described the schismatic 'Post-Modern' condition as positing a break with both modernism and the modern period, while the traditional 'Post-Modern' condition is said to 'propose to free new production from the rigid constraints of modernism, especially from its most radical and nihilistic aspects (as exemplified by Dada and Surrealism) while simultaneously reintegrating itself with other strains of Western Humanism, especially those which characterize its last pre-modernist phase, that of the Romanticism which flourished between 1750 and 1850'. Although Stern's 'traditional post-modernism' is not incompatible with Jencks's view of post-modernism as a double-coding of modernism with other more humanistic codes, Jencks's post-1980 choice of the classical code as the most suitable of the latter contrasts with Stern's description of Romanticism as being especially typical of the humanism with which traditional post-modernism is aligning itself, while the schismatic post-modernism which Stern describes as both a 'double' of post-modernism and as something which breaks from modernism is characterised by Jencks, *What is Post-Modernism?* (London, 1986), p. 32, as 'Late-Modern' rather than as 'Post-Modern' or as one of its 'doubles'.

13 See Portoghesi's 'The End of Prohibitionism', in Gabriella Borsano (ed.), *Architecture 1980: the Presence of the Past* (New York, 1980), p. 9 where, for example, he speaks of the 'Post-Modern' as 'The return of architecture to the womb of history' and as the 'recycling in new syntactic contexts of the traditional forms'.

14 See the section on Habermas in chapter 3.

15 See the section on Fuller in chapter 5.

16 See the previous discussion of Fuller's theories in chapter 5 as well as the discussion of Jencks in chapter 4.

17 One recent book entitled *An Introductory Guide to Post-Structuralism and Postmodernism*, by Madan Sarup (New York and London, 1988), not only provides only one brief chapter on the latter subject, but also states on its page 118 that the term 'postmodernism' will be used synonymously with that of 'post-structuralism'.

18 Frank Kermode, *History and Value* (Oxford, 1988), pp. 145–6. This present text has also been critical of deconstructionist post-modernism because of its author's belief in the need for writers on this subject to be critical of theories which not only deny the possibility of establishing any definitions or values for themselves, but at the same time use covertly assumed definitions and values for both the canonisation of their own ideas (including their attacks on the possibility of establishing value or certainty) and the condemnation of those of others. As stated elsewhere in this text, we shall only be able to evaluate the arguments for the values proposed by post-modernist theorists if we are able to understand the often unstated presuppositions and premises on which the defence of them is based, so that one may also hope that clarity of argumentation will be more readily accepted as a precondition of any post-modernist discussion of value in the future than it has been in the past for some.

19 One other recent book on the subject of post-modernity published after the completion of this text, David Harvey's *The Condition of Postmodernity* (Oxford, 1989), also follows Jameson's 1984 article in which he mistakenly describes the Bonaventure Hotel as 'post-modern' (see, for example, Harvey, ibid., p. 88), and uses on his own admission (ibid., p. 338) a mixture of definers from Hassan and others for a contrast of what he terms 'Fordist modernity' and 'Flexible postmodernity'. Like Hassan's, many of Harvey's definers are however as suitable for that which has previously been termed 'modern' as for any new 'post-modern' phenomena, and his claim that the post-modern appears like the modern (following Marshall Berman's 1982 characterisations of modernity) to be characterised by flux because it is, like modernity (as Jameson also claims), a capitalist process (see, for example, Harvey, ibid., p. 342) may be said to be circular in that it is, for one thing, largely his choice of Hassanian late-modernist examples of flux that has set the post-modern up as such in the first place.

20 One other interesting aspect to the growth of post-modern theory which has to be mentioned here, if only, unfortunately, in a final note, is the growth of interest in the topic of the post-modern in Soviet countries with a tradition of criticising Western modernism. What is interesting here is that the 'post-modern' can be used as a term to describe a final farewelling of that modernism, and the development of something independent of it and its traditions, and/or it can be used as a term to mark the farewelling of the Soviet 'modernity' born of Zhdanov's canonisation of Socialist Realism. As elsewhere, the definition of what one's post-modernism or post-

modernity will entail will be dependent to at least some extent on the concept, or practice, of the modern to which it is to be 'post', as also on how that prefix is to be understood and defined with reference to the concept of the modern.

21 I am thinking here especially of Charles Jencks and of his early descriptions of the way in which post-modern architecture may make good some of the errors of modern architecture, as well as of his later statements on the importance of establishing a new pluralism of values. Further to this, and recalling Jencks's own reference to him towards the end of his *What is Post-Modernism?* of 1986, I should also like to make reference here to Sir Ernst Gombrich's discussion of the subject of value in the conclusion of the new fifteenth edition of his *The Story of Art* (Oxford, 1989), p. 498, as well as to its new section on post-modernism, and to also take this opportunity to thank him for other comments, insights and words of wisdom which have assisted both directly and indirectly in the analysis of issues raised in this work.

22 See also note 21 above on the discussions of value by Charles Jencks. At the time at which this manuscript was going to press Jencks was preparing a new work on the 'Post-Modern World', which promised to deal with issues concerning the contemporary world and its future not treated in detail in his previous works, and had also just completed a new, third edition to his *What is Post-Modernism?* of 1986 in which some of those issues were also to be raised. With regard to the latter it is also interesting to note in this conclusion to our study of the major factors characterising the different theories of the post-modern and the post-industrial that when the second, revised, enlarged edition of 1987 of that work had begun the task of looking at some of those issues it had concluded in a way which again affirmed Jencks's view of the post-modern as 'double-coding' the modern with other more plural values and developments (*What is Post-Modernism?*, p. 56): 'Perhaps the ultimate paradox of the Post-Modern situation, the condition built on paradox and irony, is that it can willingly include the Modern and pre-Modern conditions as essential parts of its existence. It has not taken an aggressive stance with respect to an agricultural civilisation, it has not sought to destroy industrialisation, nor put forward a single totalising ideology.'

23 Amongst the values suggested by Jencks in works discussed in chapter 4 we may not only find the value of increased communication, but also that of the production of buildings and works of art which will enrich rather than devalue the life of our cities.

24 According to J.M. and M.J. Cohen's *The Penguin Dictionary of Modern Quotations*, 2nd edn, Harmondsworth, 1980, p. 16, 'The future is not what it was' is a statement attributed to an anonymous professor of economics by Bernard Levin in the *Sunday Times* of 22 May 1977.

Bibliography

Adey, Glyn and David Frisby (trans.), *The Positivist Dispute in German Sociology* (1969). London, 1976.

Adorno, Theodor W. and Max Horkheimer, *Dialectic of Enlightenment*, trans. John Cumming. London, 1986.

Arac, Jonathon, (ed.), *Postmodernism and Politics*. Minnesota and Manchester, 1986.

Babbage, Charles, *On the Economy of Machinery and Manufactures*. London, 1832; 4th enlarged edn, London, 1835; repr. Fairfield, N.J., 1986.

The Exposition of 1851. London, 1851; new impression of 2nd edn of 1851, London, 1968.

Passages from the Life of a Philosopher. London, 1864.

Bann, Stephen, 'A Revolutionary Garden in Versailles', *Art & Design*, vol. 4, nos. 5/6, 1988, Profile 9, 'The Classical Sensibility in Contemporary Painting and Sculpture', pp. 38–9.

Baudrillard, Jean, *The Mirror of Production*, trans. Mark Poster. St Louis, 1975.

'The Implosion of Meaning in the Media and the Implosion of the Social in the Masses', in Kathleen Woodward (ed.), *The Myths of Information: Technology and Postindustrial Culture*. London, 1980, pp. 137–48.

For a Critique of the Political Economy of the Sign, trans. Charles Levin. St Louis, 1981.

'The Beaubourg-Effect: Implosion and Deterrence' (1977), *October*, spring 1982, pp. 3–13.

Simulations, trans. Philip Beitchmann. New York, 1983.

'On Nihilism', *On the Beach*, vol. 6, spring 1984, pp. 38–9.

'The Ecstasy of Communication', in Hal Foster (ed.), *Postmodern Culture*, London, 1985, pp. 126–34.

America, trans. Chris Turner. London and New York, 1988.

Bauman, Zygmunt, *Legislators and Interpreters: on Modernity, Post-*

modernity and Intellectuals. Oxford and Cambridge, 1987.
'Sociological Responses to Postmodernity', *Thesis Eleven*, no. 23, 1989, pp. 35–63.

Bell, Daniel, 'Technocracy and Politics', *Survey*, vol. 16, no. 1(78), winter 1971, pp. 1–24.
'The Post-Industrial Society: the Evolution of an Idea', *Survey*, vol. 17, no. 2(79), spring 1971, pp. 102–68.
The Coming of Post-Industrial Society, (1973). Harmondsworth, 1976.
The Cultural Contradictions of Capitalism. New York, 1976.
The Winding Passage: Essays and Sociological Journeys 1960–1980. Cambridge, Mass., 1980.

Benjamin, Andrew, 'Derrida, Architecture and Philosophy', *Architectural Design*, vol. 58, nos. 3/4, 1988, Profile 72, 'Deconstruction in Architecture', pp. 8–11.

Benjamin, Walter, *Illuminations*, ed. Hannah Arendt; English trans. of 1968 by Harry Zohn. New York, 1969.

Berman, Marshall, *All that is Solid Melts into Air: the Experience of Modernity* (1982). London, 1985.
'The Experience of Modernity' in John Thackara (ed.), *Design After Modernism*, London, 1988, pp. 35–48.

Bernstein, Richard J. (ed.), *Habermas and Modernity*. Oxford and Cambridge, 1985.

Bertens, Hans, 'The Postmodern *Weltanschauung* and its Relation to Modernism: an Introductory Survey', in Douwe Fokkema and Hans Bertens (eds.), *Approaching Postmodernism*, Amsterdam and Philadelphia, 1986, pp. 9–51.

Bonito Oliva, Achille, *Transavantgarde International*. Milan, 1982.

Borsano, Gabriella (ed.), *Architecture 1980: the Presence of the Past. Venice Biennale*. New York, 1980.

Bradbury, Malcolm, *Mensonge*. London, 1987.

Bradbury, Malcolm and James McFarlane (eds.), *Modernism 1890–1930*. Harmondsworth, 1976.

Brzezinski, Zbigniew, *Between Two Ages. America's Role in the Technetronic Era* (1970). Harmondsworth, 1979.

Buerger, Peter, *The Theory of the Avant-Garde*, trans. Michael Shaw, Manchester and Minneapolis, 1984.

Burgin, Victor, *The End of Art Theory: Criticism and Postmodernity*. London, 1986.

Calinescu, Matei, *Five Faces of Modernity*. Durham, N.C., 1987.

Christov-Bakargiev, Carolyn, 'Interview with Carlo Maria Mariani', *Flash Art*, no. 133, April 1987, pp. 60–3.

Clifford, James and George E. Marcus (eds.), *Writing Culture: the Poetics and Politics of Ethnography*. Berkeley, Los Angeles and London, 1986.

Cohen, J.M. and M.J. Cohen, *The Penguin Dictionary of Modern Quotations*, 2nd edn. Harmondsworth, 1980.

Collins, Michael and Andreas Papadakis, *Post-Modern Design*. London, 1989.

Connor, Steven, *Postmodernist Culture: an Introduction to Theories of the Contemporary*. Oxford, 1989.

Coomaraswamy, Ananda K., *The Arts and Crafts of India and Ceylon*. London and Edinburgh, 1913.

Coomaraswamy, Ananda K. and Arthur J. Penty (eds.), *Essays in Post-Industrialism: a Symposium of Prophecy concerning the Future of Society*. London, 1914.

Crook, J. Mordaunt, *The Dilemma of Style: Architectural Ideas from the Picturesque to the Post-Modern*. London, 1987.

Cumming, Hugh, 'Carlo Maria Mariani. An *Art & Design* interview by Hugh Cumming', *Art & Design*, vol. 4, nos. 5/6, 1988, 'The New Modernism: Deconstructionist Tendencies in Art, pp. 17–25.

Current Anthropology, vol. 29, no. 3, June 1988, pp. 405–35.

Dear, M.J. 'Postmodernism and Planning', *Environment and Planning D: Society and Space*, vol. 4, 1986, pp. 367–84.

Debord, Guy, *Society of the Spectacle*. Detroit, 1983.

Derrida, Jacques, *The Truth in Painting*, trans. Geoff Bennington and Ian McLeod. Chicago and London, 1987.

Dictionary of Scientific Biography, ed. Charles Coulston Gillispie. New York, 1970.

Doyal, Len and Roger Harris, *Empiricism, Explanation and Rationality: an Introduction to the Philosophy of the Social Sciences*. London, 1986.

Eagleton, Terry, *Against the Grain: Essays 1975–1985*. London, 1986.

Encyclopaedia Britannica, 30 vols., 15th edn. Chicago, 1982.

Etzioni, Amitai, *The Active Society: a Theory of Societal and Political Processes*. London and New York, 1968.

Featherstone, Mike, 'In Pursuit of the Postmodern: an Introduction', *Theory, Culture & Society*, 'Special Issue on Postmodernism', ed. Mike Featherstone, vol. 5, nos. 2–3, pp. 195–215.

Fekete, John (ed.), *Life After Postmodernism*. London, 1988.

Fiedler, L.A., *The Collected Essays of Leslie Fiedler*, vol. II. New York, 1971.

Fitts, Dudley, *Anthology of Contemporary Latin-American Poetry* (1942). London and Norfolk, Conn., 1947.

Fokkema, Douwe and Hans Bertens (eds.), *Approaching Postmodernism*. Amsterdam and Philadelphia, 1986.

Foster, Hal (ed.), *The Anti-Aesthetic: Essays on Postmodern Culture*.

Port Townsend, Washington, 1983; republished as *Postmodern Culture*. London, 1985.

Recodings: Art, Spectacle, Cultural Politics. Washington, 1985.

Frampton, Kenneth J., 'America 1960–1970', *Casabella*, nos. 359–60, May/June 1971, pp. 24–38.

Modern Architecture: a Critical History. London, 1980.

'Towards a Critical Regionalism', in Hal Foster (ed.), *Postmodern Culture*. London, 1985, pp. 16–30.

'Some Reflections on Postmodernism and Architecture', *ICA Documents*, nos. 4/5, 1986, pp. 26–9.

Frampton, Kenneth J. (ed.), *Modern Architecture and the Critical Present*. London, 1982.

Frankel, Boris, *The Post-Industrial Utopians*. Oxford and Cambridge, 1987.

Fuller, Peter, 'Conserving "Joy in Labour" ', in *William Morris Today*, ICA, London, 1984, pp. 90–3.

The Australian Scapegoat. Perth, 1986.

'Towards a New Nature for the Gothic', *Art & Design*, vol. 3, nos. 3/4, 1987, Profile 2, 'The Post-Modern Object', pp. 5–10.

'The Search for a Postmodern Aesthetic', in John Thackara (ed.), *Design after Modernism*. London, 1988, pp. 117–33.

Theoria: Art, and the Absence of Grace. London, 1988.

Gablik, Suzi, *Has Modernism Failed?* New York and London, 1984.

Garvin, Harry R. (ed.), *Romanticism, Modernism, Postmodernism* (*Bucknell Review*, vol. 25, no. 2). London and Toronto, 1980.

Giddens, Anthony, *The Constitution of Society*. Oxford and Cambridge, 1984.

Social Theory and Modern Sociology. Stanford, 1987.

The Consequences of Modernity. Oxford and Cambridge, 1990.

Gombrich, E. H., *The Story of Art*, 15th edn. Oxford, 1989.

Gorz, André, *Farewell to the Working Class: an Essay on Post-Industrial Socialism* (1980), trans. Mike Sonenscher. London, 1982.

Griffiths, John, 'Deconstructionist Tendencies in Art', *Art & Design*, vol. 43, no. 3, 1988, Profile 8, 'The New Modernism: Deconstructionist Tendencies in Art', pp. 53–60.

Habermas, Juergen, *Strukturwandel der Oeffentlichkeit*. Darmstadt, 1962.

'The Public Sphere', *New German Critique*, autumn 1974, pp. 49–55.

Legitimation Crisis (1973), trans. Thomas McCarthy. London, 1976.

Theory of Communicative Action (1981), trans. Thomas McCarthy. Vol. I, Boston, 1984; vol. II, Boston, 1987.

'Modernity – an Incomplete Project', in Hal Foster (ed.), *Postmodern Culture*, London, 1985. pp. 3–15.

Die neue Unuebersichtlichkeit. Frankfurt am Main, 1985.

Philosophical–Political Profiles, trans. by Frederick G. Lawrence. Cambridge, Mass., and London, 1985.

'A Philosophico-Political Profile', *New Left Review*, no. 151, May/June 1985, pp. 75–105.

The Philosophical Discourse of Modernity, trans. Frederick Lawrence. Oxford and Cambridge, 1987.

Harvey, David, *The Condition of Postmodernity*. Oxford, 1989.

Hassan, Ihab, *The Dismemberment of Orpheus: Toward a Postmodern Literature*. New York, 1971.

'The Question of Postmodernism', in Harry R. Garvin (ed.), *Romanticism, Modernism, Postmodernism* (*Bucknell Review*, vol. 25, no. 2), London and Toronto, 1980, pp. 117–26.

The Postmodern Turn. Essays in Postmodern Theory and Culture. Columbus, Ohio, 1987.

Hebdige, Dick, *Hiding in the Light: on Images and Things*. London and New York, 1988.

Hoffmann, Gerhard, Alfred Hornung and Ruediger Kunow, ' "Modern", "Postmodern" and "Contemporary" as Criteria for the Analysis of 20th Century Literature', *Amerikastudien*, vol. 22, no. 1, 1977, pp. 19–46.

Howe, Irving, 'Mass Society and Postmodern Fiction', in Howe, *The Decline of the New*, London, 1971, pp. 190–207.

Hudnut, Joseph, 'the post-modern house', *Architectural Record*, vol. 97, May 1945, pp. 70–5; and *Royal Architectural Institute of Canada Journal*, vol. 22, July 1945, pp. 135–40.

Architecture and the Spirit of Man. Harvard, 1949.

Hughes, Robert, 'The Decline and Fall of the Avant-Garde', in Gregory Battcock (ed.), *Idea Art*. New York, 1973, pp. 184–94.

Hutcheon, Linda, *A Theory of Parody: the Teachings of Twentieth-Century Art Forms*. New York and London, 1985.

A Poetics of Postmodernism. History, Theory, Fiction. New York and London, 1988.

Huyssen, Andreas, *After the Great Divide. Modernism, Mass Culture and Postmodernism*. Bloomington, Ind., 1986, and London, 1988.

Hyman, Anthony, *Charles Babbage: Pioneer of the Computer*. Oxford, 1982.

International Encyclopedia of the Social Sciences, 17 vols. ed. David L. Sills. London and New York, 1968.

Ionescu, Ghita (ed.), *The Political Thought of Saint-Simon*. Oxford, 1976.

Jacobs, Jane, *The Death and Life of Great American Cities* (1961). Harmondsworth, 1962.

Jameson, Conrad, 'Modern Architecture as an Ideology', *Architectural Association Quarterly*, vol. 7, no. 4, October/December 1975, pp. 15–21.

Jameson, Fredric, 'Postmodernism, or the Cultural Logic of Late Capitalism', *New Left Review*, no. 146, July–August 1984, pp. 53–92.

'Postmodernism and Consumer Society', in Hal Foster (ed.), *Postmodern Culture*, London, 1985, pp. 111–25.

The Ideologies of Theory: Essays 1971–1986. Vol. II: *The Syntax of History*. London, 1988.

'Postmodernism and Consumer Society', in E. Ann Kaplan (ed.), *Postmodernism and its Discontents*. London and New York, 1988, pp. 13–29.

Jay, Martin, *Marxism and Totality: the Adventures of a Concept from Lukacs to Habermas*. Oxford, Cambridge and California, 1984.

Fin de Siècle Socialism and Other Essays. New York and London, 1988.

Jencks, Charles, *Modern Movements in Architecture* (1973). 2nd edn, Harmondsworth, 1985.

'The Rise of Post Modern Architecture', *Architectural Association Quarterly*, vol. 7, no. 4, October/December 1975, pp. 3–14.

'A Genealogy of Post-Modern Architecture', *Architectural Design*, Profile 4, 1977, pp. 269–71.

The Language of Post-Modern Architecture. London, 1977; 2nd revised enlarged edn 1978; 3rd revised enlarged edn 1981; 4th revised enlarged edn 1984; 5th revised enlarged edn 1987.

'Why Post-Modernism?' in 'Post-Modern History', *Architectural Design*, vol. 48, no. 1, 1978, Profile 10, pp. 11–26; 43–58.

Late-Modern Architecture. London and New York, 1980.

'Towards Radical Eclecticism', in Gabriella Borsano (ed.), *Architecture 1980: the Presence of the Past. Venice Biennale*, New York, 1980, pp. 30–7.

Post-Modern Classicism – the New Synthesis, ed. Charles Jencks, published as an *Architectural Design* Profile. London, 1980.

Current Architecture. London, 1982.

Towards a Symbolic Architecture: the Thematic House. London, 1985.

'Translating Past into Present: Post Modern Art and Architecture', *Country Life*, 21 November 1985, pp. 1620–3.

'Essay on the Battle of the Labels Late-Modernism vs Post-Modernism', *Architecture and Urbanism*, January extra edn, entitled 'Charles Jencks', pp. 209–36. Tokyo, 1986.

What is Post-Modernism? London, 1986; 2nd revised enlarged edn 1987.

Post-Modernism: the New Classicism in Art and Architecture. London, 1987.

'Post-Modernism and Discontinuity', *Architectural Design*, vol. 57, nos. 1/2, 1987, Profile 65, 'Post-Modernism and Discontinuity', pp. 5–8.

'The Post-Avant-Garde', *Art & Design*, vol. 37, no. 8, 1987, Profile 4, 'The Post-Avant-Garde: Painting in the Eighties', pp. 5–20.

Architecture Today. London, 1988.

'The New Classicism and its Emergent Rules', *Architectural Design*, vol. 58, nos. 1/2, 1988, Profile 70, 'The New Classicism in Architecture and Urbanism', pp. 22–31.

'Deconstruction: the Pleasure of Absence', *Architectural Design*, vol. 58, nos. 3/4, 1988, Profile 72, 'Deconstruction in Architecture', pp. 17–31.

'Peter Eisenman: an *Architectural Design* Interview by Charles Jencks', *Architectural Design*, vol. 58, nos. 3/4, 1988, Profile 72, 'Deconstruction in Architecture', pp. 49–61.

'The Battle of High-Tech: Great Buildings with Great Faults', *Architectural Design*, vol. 58, nos. 11/12, 1988, Profile 76, 'New Directions in Current Architecture', pp. 19–39.

'The Bank as Cathedral and Village', *Architectural Design*, vol. 58, nos. 11/12, 1988, Profile 76, 'New Directions in Current Architecture', pp. 77–9.

Johnson, Philip and Mark Wigley, *Deconstructive Architecture.* New York, 1988.

Jones, Barry, *Sleepers Wake! Technology and the Future of Work.* Melbourne, 1982.

Kahn, Herman, and A.J. Wiener, *The Year 2000: a Framework for Speculation on the Next Thirty-three Years.* New York, 1967.

Kaplan, E. Ann (ed.), *Postmodernism and its Discontents.* London and New York, 1988.

Kearney, Richard, *The Wake of Imagination.* London, 1988.

Kellner, Douglas, 'Postmodernism as Social Theory', *Theory, Culture & Society*, vol. 5, nos. 2–3, June 1988, pp. 247ff.

Jean Baudrillard: from Marxism to Postmodernism and Beyond. Oxford and Cambridge, 1989.

Kermode, Frank, *History and Value.* Oxford, 1988.

Klotz, Heinrich, *The History of Postmodern Architecture*, trans. Radka Donnell (from *Moderne und Postmoderne: Architektur der Gegenwart*, Braunschweig and Wiesbaden, 1984). Cambridge, Mass., and London, 1988.

Koehler, Michael, ' "Postmodernismus": ein begriffsgeschichtlicher Ueberblick', *Amerikastudien*, vol. 22, no. 1, 1977, pp. 8–18.

Krauss, Rosalind, *The Originality of the Avant-Garde and Other Modernist Myths*. Cambridge, Mass., and London, 1986.

Krier, Rob, *Rob Krier on Architecture*, trans. Eileen Martin. London and New York, 1982.

Kroker, Arthur and David Cook, *The Postmodern Scene: Excremental Culture and Hyper-Aesthetics*. Montreal, 1986.

Kroll, Lucien, *The Architecture of Complexity* (1983), trans. Peter Blundell Jones. London, 1986.

Kumar, Krishan, *Prophecy and Progress: the Sociology of Industrial and Post-Industrial Society*. Harmondsworth, 1978.

Lancaster, Osbert, *A Cartoon History of Architecture*. London, 1975.

Levin, Harry, 'What was Modernism?', in Levin *Refractions: Essays in Comparative Literature*, New York, 1966, pp. 271–95.

Levin, Kim, *Beyond Modernism: Essays on Art from the 70s and 80s*. New York, 1988.

Lipsey, Roger, *Coomaraswamy: his Life and Work*. Princeton, 1977.

Lyotard, Jean-François, *Driftworks*, ed. Roger McKeon. New York, 1984.

The Postmodern Condition: a Report on Knowledge, trans. Geoff Bennington and Brian Massumi. Manchester, 1984.

Les Immatériaux. Paris, 1985.

Immaterialitaet und Postmoderne, trans. Marianne Karbe. Berlin, 1985.

'Defining the Postmodern', trans. Geoffrey Bennington, *ICA Documents*, vols. 4/5, 1986, pp. 6–7.

Le Postmoderne expliqué aux enfants. Paris, 1986.

Que Peindre? Adami, Arakawa, Buren. Paris, 1988.

'Jean-François Lyotard: die Erhabenheit ist das Unkonsumierbare. Ein Gespraech mit Christine Pries am 6.5.1988', *Kunstforum*, vol. 100, April/May 1989, pp. 354–63.

MacFarlane, James, 'Jean-François Lyotard on Adami, Buren and Arakawa', *Art & Design*, vol. 4, nos. 3/4, 1988, Profile 8, 'The New Modernism: Deconstructionist Tendencies in Art', pp. 76–80.

McLuhan, Marshall, *The Mechanical Bride; Folklore of Industrial Man*. New York, 1951.

Explorations in Communication, with E. S. Carpenter. Boston, 1960.

The Gutenberg Galaxy: the Making of Typographic Man. Toronto, 1962.

Understanding Media: the Extensions of Man. New York, 1964.

The Medium is the Massage: an Inventory of Effects, with Quentin Fiore. New York, 1967.

War and Peace in the Global Village, with Quentin Fiore. New York, 1968.

Martin, Wallace, 'Postmodernism: Ultima Thule or Seim Anew?', in Harry R. Garvin (ed.), *Romanticism, Modernism, Postmodernism* (*Bucknell Review,* vol. 25, no. 2), pp. 142–54. London and Toronto, 1980.

Mills, C. Wright, *The Sociological Imagination* (1959). Harmondsworth, 1983.

Modern Painters, ed. Peter Fuller, vol. 1, no. 1, spring 1988.

Morrison, Philip, and Emily Morrison (eds.), *Charles Babbage and his Calculating Engines: Selected Writings by Charles Babbage and Others.* New York, 1961.

Newman, Michael, 'Revising Modernism, Representing Postmodernism', *ICA Documents,* nos. 4/5, 1986, pp. 32–51.

Norris, Christopher, *The Deconstructive Turn.* London and New York, 1983.

'Jacques Derrida: in Discussion with Christopher Norris', *Architectural Design,* vol. 58, nos. 1/2, 1989, Profile 77, 'Deconstruction II', pp. 6–11.

Norris, Christopher and Andrew Benjamin, *What is Deconstruction?* London and New York, 1988.

Onis, Federico de, *Antologia de la poesia española e hispanoamericana (1882–1932).* Madrid, 1934.

Oxford English Dictionary. 1st edn, Oxford, 1933; 2nd edn, Oxford, 1989.

Oxford English Dictionary Supplement. Oxford, 1982.

Pannwitz, Rudolf, *Die Krisis der europaeischen Kultur,* 2 vols. Nuremberg, 1917.

Penty, Arthur J., *Old Worlds for New: a Study of the Post-Industrial State.* London, 1917.

Post-Industrialism. London, 1922.

The Elements of Domestic Design. Westminster, 1930.

Pevsner, Nikolaus, 'Architecture in our Time: the Anti-pioneers', *The Listener,* 29 December 1966, pp. 953–5, and 5 January 1967, pp. 7–9.

Studies in Art, Architecture and Design, 2 vols. London, 1968.

Portoghesi, Paolo, 'The End of Prohibitionism', in Gabriella Borsano (ed.), *Architecture 1980: the Presence of the Past. Venice Biennale*, New York, 1980, pp. 9–13.

Postmodern: the Architecture of the Postindustrial Society. New York, 1983.

Read, Herbert, *Art and Industry: the Principles of Industrial Design* (1934), 3rd revised edn. London, 1953.

Riesman, David, 'Leisure and Work in Post-Industrial Society', in E. Larrabee and R. Meyersohn (eds.), *Mass Leisure*, Glencoe, Ill., 1958, pp. 363–85.

Rose, Gillian, 'Architecture to Philosophy – the Postmodern Complicity', *Theory, Culture & Society*, 'Special Issue on Postmodernism', ed. Mike Featherstone, vol. 5, nos. 2–3, June 1988, pp. 357–71.

Rose, Margaret, *Parody/Meta-Fiction*. London, 1979.

Marx's Lost Aesthetic. Cambridge, 1984.

'Habermas and Post-Modern Architecture', *Australian Journal of Art*, vol. 5, 1986, pp. 113–19.

'Post-Modernism Today: some Thoughts on Charles Jencks's "What is Post-Modernism?" ', in *Reasons to be Cheerful*, George Paton Gallery, Melbourne, 1987, pp. 1–6.

'Parody/Post-Modernism', *Poetics*, vol. 17, 1988, pp. 49–56.

'The Concept of Avant-Garde: from the Modern to the Post-Modern', *Agenda*, vol. 1, no. 2, August 1988, special supplement pp. 23–4.

'Myth in Modern and Post-Modern Theory: from Marx's Theory of Commodity Fetishism to Theories of Reification in Critical and Post-Modernist Theory', in F.J. West (ed.), *Myth and Mythology*, pp. 35–49. Canberra, 1989.

'Theories of the Subject in Post-Modernism from the "Disappearing" to the "Intersubjective" Subject', in Ales Erjavec (ed.), *The Subject in Post-Modernism*, vol. II, Lubljana, 1990, pp. 186–99.

'Innovation and Tradition in Post-Modernism', in *Papers of the XIth International Congress of Aesthetics*. Nottingham 1990, pp. 161–4.

'Post-Modern Pastiche', *The British Journal of Aesthetics*, vol. 31, no. 1, January 1991, pp. 26–38.

Rosenblum, Robert, *The Dog in Art from Rococo to Post-Modernism*. New York, 1988.

Rykwert, Joseph, *The Necessity of Artifice*. London, 1982.

Sangren, P. Steven, 'Rhetoric and the Authority of Ethnography: "Post-modernism" and the Social Reproduction of Texts', *Current Anthropology*, vol. 29, no. 3, June 1988, pp. 405–24.

Sarup, Madan, *An Introductory Guide to Post-Structuralism and Post-modernism*. New York and London, 1988.

Scott Brown, Denise, 'Learning from Pop', *Casabella*, vols. 359–60, May/June 1971, pp. 14–23.
    'Reply to Frampton', *Casabella*, vols. 359–60, May/June 1971, pp. 39–46.
Smith, Bernard, *Place, Taste and Tradition* (1945). Oxford, 1979.
    Australian Painting 1788–1970 (1962). Oxford, 1971.
    'Peter Fuller's Impulse to Destroy', *Australian Society*, March 1989, pp. 41–4.
Somervell, D.C. (ed.), *A Study of History by Arnold J. Toynbee.* Oxford, 1946.
Sontag, Susan, *Against Interpretation and Other Essays.* New York, 1978.
Spengler, Oswald, *The Decline of the West*, trans. Charles Francis Atkinson. London, 1971.
Stearn, Gerald Emanuel (ed.), *McLuhan: Hot and Cool.* Harmondsworth, 1968.
Steinberg, Saul, *The New World.* New York, 1965.
Steiner, George, *Language and Silence: Essays 1958–1966.* London and New York, 1967.
Stern, Robert, 'At the Edge of Modernism' *Architectural Design*, vol. 47, no. 4, April 1977, pp. 274–86.
    'The Doubles of Post-Modern', *The Harvard Architectural Review*, vol. 1, spring 1980, pp. 75–87.
Survey, vol. 16, no. 1(78), winter 1971, pp. 1–77.
Survey, vol. 17, no. 2(79), spring 1971, pp. 102–68.
Swenarton, Mark, *Artisans and Architects: the Ruskinian Tradition in Architectural Thought.* London, 1989.
Taylor, Keith (trans. and ed.), *Henri Saint-Simon (1760–1825).* London, 1975.
Thackara, John (ed.), *Design after Modernism.* London, 1988.
Theory, Culture & Society, 'Special Issue on Postmodernism', ed. Mike Featherstone, vol. 5, nos. 2–3, June 1988.
Toffler, Alvin, *Future Shock.* London, 1970.
    The Third Wave. New York, 1980.
Tominaga, Ken'ichi, 'Post-Industrial Society and Cultural Diversity', *Survey*, vol. 16, no. 1, winter 1971, pp. 68–77.
Touraine, Alain, *The Post-Industrial Society, Tomorrow's Social History: Classes, Conflicts and Culture in the Programmed Society* (1969), trans. Leonard F. X. Mayhew. London, 1974.
Toynbee, Arnold J., *A Study of History.* Vols. 1–6, London, 1939; vols. 7–10, London, 1954.
    An Historian's Approach to Religion (1956). 2nd edn, Oxford, 1979.

'Art: Communicative or Esoteric?', in the collection *On the Future of Art*, introduced by Edward F. Fry, New York, 1970, pp. 3–19.

Tschumi, Bernard, 'Parc de la Villette, Paris', *Architectural Design*, vol. 58, nos. 3/4, 1988, Profile 72, 'Deconstruction in Architecture', pp. 33–9.

Venturi, Robert, *Complexity and Contradiction in Architecture*. New York, 1966.

Venturi, Robert, Denise Scott Brown and Steven Izenour, *Learning from Las Vegas* (1972), revised edn, Cambridge, Mass., and London, 1988.

HRH The Prince of Wales, *A Vision of Britain*. London, 1989.

Weber, Max, *Economy and Society*, ed. Guenther Roth and Claus Wittich. Berkeley, Los Angeles and London, 1978.

Wellmer, Albrecht, *Zur Dialektik von Moderne und Postmoderne*. Frankfurt am Main, 1985.

Welsch, Wolfgang, *Unsere postmoderne Moderne*. Weinheim, 1988.

Wigley, Mark, 'Deconstructivist Architecture', in Philip Johnson and Mark Wigley, *Deconstructive Architecture*, New York, 1988, pp. 10–20.

Wolfe, Tom, *From Bauhaus to Our House*. London, 1981.

Index

Aalto, Alvar, 106, 256 n. 57
absent author, 63f., 84, 148,
    271 n. 172, 277 n. 58; *see also*
    subject, death of and
    decentred
abstraction, 2, 15, 18ff., 45, 46,
    103, 123, 130f., 171, 188 n. 35,
    198 n. 100, 219 n. 33, 231
    n. 133
Adami, Valerio, 143, 216 n. 6, 227
    n. 97, 228 n. 98, 101, 268
    n. 145
Adorno, Theodor W., 61, 86, 89,
    92f., 226 n. 73, 227 n. 91, 241
    n. 207, 242 n. 215, 244 n. 232;
    see also Frankfurt School
agency, *see* subject as agent
agora, 116, 125, 148; *see also*
    public spheres
Aijmer, Goeran, 96f.
Albertsen, L., 232 n. 144
alienation, 45, 56ff., 71, 111, 136,
    137, 152, 225 nn. 70, 73, 230
    n. 122, 139 n. 196
Aliterature, 43
allegory, 4
Althusserian theory, 232 n. 142,
    239 n. 196
anarchism, 44, 47, 48, 49, 50, 52,
    58f., 92, 125, 214 n. 128, 218

nn. 17, 18, 222 nn. 41, 44; *see
    also* nihilism
ancients versus moderns, 15, 194
    n. 72
antinomianism, 38f., 44, 45, 214
    n. 128, 219 n. 25
anti-object art, 20
'anything goes', 3, 60, 137, 150,
    168, 183 n. 3, 267 n. 126, 268
    n. 135, 272 n. 176, 279 n. 79
Arac, Jonathan, 212 n. 114
Arakawa, 227 n. 97, 228 n. 98
archaism, 16, 18f., 189 n. 43, 195
    n. 76
architecture, *see* deconstructionist
    architecture, High Tech
    architecture, late-modernism,
    modern architecture,
    post-modern architecture,
Arendt, Hannah, 259 n. 69
'art for art's sake', 18
Arts & Crafts, 23, 199 n. 10, 200
    nn. 11, 12, 242 n. 217; *see
    also* craft
AT&T Headquarters New York,
    135
avant-gardes, and concepts of, 16,
    32ff., 48, 52, 61, 64, 65, 71,
    83, 91, 93, 94, 101, 123f., 130,
    131, 152, 193 n. 61, 196 n. 84,

208 nn. 80, 86, 223 n. 51, 228
n. 100, 229, n. 112, 236 n.
165, 239 n. 196, 250 n. 2, 256
n. 57, 257 n. 59, 261 nn. 82,
83, 264 n. 104, 265 n. 112, 273
n. 10; *see also* neo-
avantgardism, post-avant-
gardes, transavantgarde

Babbage, Charles, 35f., 210 n. 98,
101, 103, 211 nn. 105, 107,
108, 260 n. 73
Bahro, Rudolf, 201 n. 22
Bakhtin, Michael, 53
Bann, Stephen, 219 n. 31
Baroque style, 73, 113, 116
Barth, John, 44, 191 n. 53, 218
n. 21, 219 n. 26, 222 n. 49
Barthelme, Donald, 44
Bataille, Georges, 224 n. 64, 241
n. 210
Baudrillard, Jean, xii, 4, 26ff., 42,
45, 65, 67, 69f., 72, 78, 79, 80,
125, 137, 141ff., 157, 181 n. 9,
184 n. 11, 185 nn. 15, 16, 189
n. 48, 190 n. 51, 204 nn. 34,
39, 205 n. 42, 44, 48, 217 n.
13, 219 n. 26, 220 n. 36, 224
n. 62, 229 nn. 107, 108, 231
nn. 133, 135, 236 nn. 171,
172, 238 n. 186, 245 n. 238,
266 n. 119, 269 n. 146, 270 n.
162, 275 n. 35, 279 n. 77
Bauhaus, 60, 66, 205 n. 42, 256 n.
56, 265 n. 112
Bauman, Zygmunt, 247 n. 250
Beaubourg, *see* Pompidou
Centre,
Becker, Juergen, 44
Beckett, Samuel, 43, 44, 48, 52,
219 n. 26, 222 n. 49, 225 n. 70
Beer, Max, 201 n. 19

Bell, Clive, 18
Bell, Daniel, 21, 24f., 29–39, 53,
56f., 61, 66f., 161, 170, 173,
187 n. 31, 191 n. 53, 199 nn.
1, 2, 201 n. 22, 202 n. 24, 203
nn. 31, 32, 205 n. 47, 206 nn.
59, 61, 62, 207 nn. 64, 65, 77,
208 n. 87, 209 nn. 90, 92, 210
nn. 96, 97, 211 nn. 108, 109,
212 nn. 110, 114–16, 213 nn.
117, 119, 122, 214 nn. 125,
128, 218 n. 25, 222 n. 41, 224
nn. 61, 64, 227 n. 88, 229 n.
104, 230 n. 118, 241 nn. 208,
210, 246 nn. 239, 240, 259 n.
73, 265 n. 117, 280 n. 2, 281
nn. 5,8
Benjamin, Andrew, 266 n. 121,
268 n. 145
Benjamin, Walter, 33, 208 n. 85,
268 n. 145
Bense, Max, 44
Bergner, Josl, 18, 20, 198 n. 98
Berman, Marshall, 97–100, 123,
181 n. 5, 248 n. 257, 249 n.
266, 283 n. 19
Berryman, John, 197 n. 88
Bertens, Hans, 197 n. 88
Blake, Peter, 135, 137, 138, 140,
262 n. 86
Blanchot, Maurice, 44
Blatteau, John, 152
Bloch, Felix, 36, 211 n. 107
Bofill, Ricardo, 145, 148
Bonaventure Hotel, Los Angeles,
xii, 69, 76ff., 175, 184 n. 4,
196 n. 83, 234 n. 150, 236 n.
172, 237 n. 174, 238 n. 178,
239 n. 190, 245 n. 237, 283 n.
19
Bonito Oliva, Achille, 19f., 46, 123,
198 nn. 101, 104, 261 n. 82

Booth, Wayne, 68, 69
Borges, Jorge Luis, 44, 48, 219 n.
    26
Borromini, Francesco, 113
Bradbury, Malcolm, 271 n. 174,
    277 n. 58
Braverman, Harry, 211 n., 108
Brecht, Bertolt, 44
bricolage, 4
Brown, Norman O., 38, 191 n. 53,
    265 n. 117
Brutalism, 113
Brzezinski, Zbigniew, 21, 25, 170
Buerger, Peter, 93, 196 n. 84, 236
    n. 165, 262 n. 83
bureaucracy, 29, 68, 86, 99, 155,
    157, 206 n. 49, 240 n. 202
Buren, Daniel, 227 n. 97, 228 n. 98
Burgess, Anthony, 191. 53
Burgin, Victor, 163, 176
Burroughs, William S., 38, 44, 191
    n. 53, 218 n. 21, 265 n. 117
Butor, Michel, 44
'Byzantinism', 18f.; *see also*
    Post-Byzantine

Calinescu, Matei, 194 n. 72, 220 n.
    37
capitalism, 4, 23, 28, 37ff., 55,
    56ff., 66ff., 86ff., 130, 152,
    174, 175, 176, 183 n. 2, 184 n.
    11, 200 nn. 13, 17, 201 n. 22,
    207 n. 62, 212 nn. 110, 113,
    114, 229 n. 104, 230 nn. 117,
    118, 239 n. 195, 248 n. 257,
    257 n. 59, 283 n. 19; *see also*
    late capitalism
carnivalisation, 53
Chapman, John Watkins, 180 n.
    1, 193 n. 62, 197 n. 89
Churchill College, Cambridge,
    191 n. 55

classical styles, 156, 159, 160, 235
    n. 161, 255 n. 52, 256 n. 57,
    262 n. 86, 263 nn. 89, 90, 268
    n. 136, 282 n. 12; *see also*
    neo-classicism, post-modern
    classicism
Clifford, James, 247 n. 247
Cohen, Ralph, 12, 193 n. 61
Collins, Michael, 281 n. 6
communication, theories of and
    systems, 25ff., 46, 55ff., 67ff.,
    83, 86ff., 101ff., 154ff., 160ff.,
    170f., 175, 176ff., 195 n. 76,
    203 n. 31, 205 n. 47, 221 n.
    37, 240 n. 202, 255 n. 48, 257
    n. 62, 259 nn. 69, 73, 260 n.
    74, 267 n. 124, 270 n. 162, 274
    n. 22, 281 n. 4, 284 n. 23
computers, 35f., 44, 57, 83, 129,
    161, 171, 210 n. 100, 101, 211
    nn. 105, 107, 252 n. 22, 259 n.
    73
computer society, *see* post-
    industrial society
Comte, Auguste, 36, 209 n. 88
Concept Art, 45, 46
concreteness, 45, 46, 219 n. 33
Connor, Steven, 246 n. 245
consensus, concepts of, 55f., 61f.,
    84, 86ff., 162, 203 n. 31, 213
    n. 116, 240 n. 204, 242 n. 215,
    255 n. 51, 276 n. 58
Constructionism, 52
Constructivism, 131, 196 n. 84,
    223 n. 50, 244 n. 230, 249 n.
    266, 264 n. 108, 265 n.
    112
Coomaraswamy, Ananda K., 22f.,
    169, 199 n. 6, 200 nn. 13, 14,
    201 n. 20, 204 n. 33
Counihan, Noel, 18, 20, 198 n. 98
counter-cultures, *see* post-

modern cults and
counter-cultures

Courbet, Gustave, 137, 139

craft, 23, 90, 123, 183 n. 2, 200 nn.
11–13, 201 nn. 20, 22, 242 n.
217; *see also* Arts & Crafts

Crimp, Douglas, 245 n. 238

critical regionalism, 151 f., 273 n.
12; *see also* Frampton

Crook, J. Mordaunt, 233 n. 146,
238 n. 187

Cubism, 52

Culler, Jonathan, 248 n. 256

cults, *see* post-modern cults and
counter-cultures

Dada, 16, 17, 38, 49, 51, 52, 196 n.
84, 218 n. 18, 223 n. 51, 282
n. 12; *see also* neo-Dada

Dahrendorf, Ralf, 30, 280 n. 2

Dario, Ruben, 13f., 171

Dear, M. J., 239 n. 188, 245 n. 237

Debord, Guy, 4, 184 n. 11

decadence, 11, 14, 47, 78, 189 n.
43, 190 n. 51

decentring, 4, 78, 133, 148f., 185
n. 13, 271 nn. 170, 174, 272 n.
176; *see also* subject,
decentred

deconstruction, concepts of, 40ff.,
131, 167, 215 n. 5, 216 nn. 6,
10, 11, 217 n. 13, 223 n. 50,
226 n. 80; *see also* 'new
modernist
deconstructionists', post-
modernism,
deconstructionist theories of

deconstructionist architecture,
130–4, 181 n. 6, 216 nn. 6, 10,
11, 223 n. 50, 232 n. 143, 264
n. 108, 265 nn. 109, 112, 117,
118, 266 nn. 119–23, 274 n. 16

'Deconstructivist' architecture,
see deconstructionist
architecture

decoration
in modernism, 6ff., 13ff., 19,
22ff., 111, 116, 153, 159, 171,
194 nn. 69, 70, 200 n. 12, 231
n. 133, 242 n. 217
in post-modernism, 95, 96, 107,
113, 115, 123, 125, 134, 144,
146, 147, 159, 173, 187 n. 23,
194 n. 69, 238 n. 185, 242 n.
217, 256 n. 56, 257 n. 63, 258
n. 64, 263 n. 90, 273 n. 12,
281 n. 7

De Porzemparc, Christian, 73

Derrida, Jacques, 41, 42, 49, 87,
92f., 133, 143, 215 n. 5, 216 n.
6, 224 n. 64, 228 n. 101, 241
nn. 207, 210, 244 n. 232, 248
n. 256, 266 n. 120, 268 n. 145

dialectics, 2, 49, 55, 62, 90, 145f.,
149, 183 n. 3, 222 n. 44, 269
n. 158

difference, 50, 167, 279 n. 77

discontinuity, 45, 48, 130–4, 145,
222 n. 49, 263 n. 92

divisions of labour
manual, 23ff., 28, 35, 36, 169,
199 n. 7, 202 nn. 23, 25, 27,
204 n. 33, 210 nn. 98, 103
mental, 29ff., 210 nn. 98, 103,
211 n. 108

Don Quixote, 50

double-coding, dual-coding;
concepts of, 186 n. 20, 194 n.
72, 220 n. 37, 223 n. 49, 233
n. 144, 250 nn. 3, 8, 254 n. 32,
256 n. 55, 257 n. 62, 261 n.
81, 264 n. 93, 267 n. 127, 270
nn. 162–4, 271 n. 168, 274 n.
18, 284 n. 22; *see also* post-

double-coding (*Cont.*)
    modernism, double-coded
    theories of
Duchamp, Marcel, 46, 123, 141

Eagleton, Terry, 245 n. 236
eclecticism, 8, 49, 60, 73, 83, 96,
    115, 118, 123, 135, 143, 145,
    148, 172, 188 n. 33, 233 n.
    144, 146, 234 n. 152, 247 n.
    250, 249 n. 1, 253 n. 25, 259
    n. 73, 270 n. 163, 271 n. 168;
    see also radical eclecticism
Egyptian architecture, 145
Einstein, Albert, 143
Eisenman, Peter, 130, 131ff., 234
    n. 152, 238 n. 187, 265 nn..
    109, 117, 118, 266 n. 120
electronic cottage, 280 n. 4
electronic media, 25ff., 46, 66ff.,
    154, 175, 204 n. 33, 260 n. 73,
    280 n. 4
electronic village, *see* global
    village and world village
Eliot, Thomas S., 43
Engels, Friedrich, 98
Enlightenment, 61, 62, 85, 92,
    151, 153, 172, 190 n. 52, 213
    n. 116, 273 n. 10
ennoblement of work, 24f., 213 n.
    117
environmental art, 45, 46
Equitable Building, St Louis, 79
Etzioni, Amitai, 12, 53, 170, 172f.,
    192 n. 59, 202 n. 30, 203 nn.
    31, 32, 214 n. 125, 223 n. 57,
    224 n. 61
Existentialism, 43
experimentalism, 44, 60, 64, 65,
    66, 94, 130, 172, 174, 192 n.
    58, 228 n. 100, 229 n. 112, 257
    n. 59, 261 n. 82, 265 n. 112;

    see also avant-gardes
Expressionism, 15, 18, 105, 106,
    198 n. 98, 253 n. 25; *see also*
    neo-Expressionism

facadism, 258 n. 64
Fascism, 89, 90, 198 n. 100, 201 n.
    22
Featherstone, Mike, 185 n. 17, 239
    n. 188
Fekete, John, xiii, 164f., 176, 277
    nn. 68, 69
feminism and post-modernism,
    xiii, 166f., 245 n. 238, 279 nn.
    74, 75, 76
Fiedler, Leslie, 11f., 16, 38, 45, 47,
    49, 75, 76, 172, 173, 175, 186
    n. 20, 191 nn. 53, 54, 192 n.
    58, 203 nn. 32 33, 213 n. 122,
    214 nn. 125, 128, 218 nn. 21,
    25, 221 nn. 40, 41, 235 nn.
    161, 162, 165, 265 n. 117, 277
    n. 61
film theory, xiii, 66, 181 n. 9
Finlay, Ian Hamilton, 46, 219 n. 31
Fischer, Michael M. J., 96f., 247 n.
    247
Fitts, Dudley, 12, 13ff., 19, 51,
    171, 193 n. 62, 194 nn. 64–9,
    196 n. 86
Ford, Henry, 143
Fordism, 283 n. 19
formalisms, 16, 235 n. 161
Foster, Hal, xii, xiii, 80, 94–6, 125,
    135, 136, 175, 215 n. 5, 245 n.
    238, 246 nn. 239, 240 242,
    245, 265 n. 117, 267 nn. 132,
    134
Foster, Norman, 80ff., 129, 130
Foucault, Michel, 38, 87, 92f., 224
    n. 64, 241 nn. 207, 210, 224 n.
    232

'Fourth Epoch' concept, 11, 172, 190 n. 52

Frampton, Kenneth, xiii, 149, 151–2, 235 n. 162, 236 n. 165, 245 n. 238, 272 nn. 7, 8, 273 nn. 10, 12, 15, 274 n. 16

Frankel, Boris, 201 n. 22

Frankfurt School, 86, 165, 225 n. 73, 240 n. 204, 241 n. 205, 276 n. 56; *see also* Adorno and Horkheimer

Freud, Sigmund, 49, 143; *see also* neo-Freudians

Fuller, Buckminster, 191 n. 53

Fuller, Peter, xiii, 134, 149, 158–62, 163, 171, 175, 198 n. 99, 201 n. 22, 256 n. 58, 267 n. 127, 275 nn. 38, 45, 276 nn. 48, 50, 53, 54, 56

functionalism in architecture, 2, 8, 60, 80, 88, 91, 104, 107, 115, 125, 153, 188 n. 36, 194 n. 69, 198 n. 100, 244 nn. 226, 230, 252 n. 18, 253 n. 25, 255 n. 48, 258 n. 64, 263 n. 90; *see also* post-functionalism

Futurism, 16, 19, 52, 79, 189 n. 43, 195 n. 76, 272 n. 175

Gablik, Suzi, 137, 248 n. 257, 268 n. 135

Garaudy, Roger, 21

Gardner, John, 48

Geertz, Clifford, 247 n. 250

Gehlen, Arnold, 243 n. 225

Gehry, Frank O., 130, 131

Genet, Jean, 38, 43

Getty Museum, 135

Gibbon, Edward, 190 n. 49

Giddens, Anthony, 165, 207 n. 78, 248 n. 256, 277 n. 68, 69

Gill, Eric, 201 n. 20

global village, 26ff., 44, 45, 203 n. 33, 204 n. 34; *see also* world village

Golding, William, 191 n. 53

Gombrich, Sir Ernst, 134, 284 n. 21

Gombrowicz, Witold, 48

Goodman, Paul, 21, 202 n. 24

Gorz, André, 21, 157, 170f., 205 n. 48

Gothic art and architecture, 22, 159, 160, 276 n. 54; *see also* neo-Gothic

Graves Michael 73, 113, 148, 256 n. 56

Greenberg, Clement, 163, 176

Gropius, Walter, 8, 79, 188 n. 36, 198 n. 100, 256 n. 57

Guild Socialism, 21ff., 169, 200 n. 14, 201 n. 22, 202 n. 24

Gurvitch, Georges, 206 n. 49

Habermas, Juergen, xii, 37, 55, 57, 60ff., 66, 84, 85–94, 95f., 107, 112, 113, 155, 162, 165, 174, 180 n. 2, 181 n. 5, 183 n. 2, 185 n. 16, 196 n. 84, 212 nn. 114–16, 216 n. 11, 223 n. 59, 224 n. 64, 227 nn. 87, 88, 89, 91, 229 nn. 104, 115, 230 n. 124, 234 n. 153, 240 nn. 202, 204, 205, 241 nn. 207, 208, 210, 213, 242 nn. 214, 215, 243 nn. 223–6, 244 nn. 229, 230, 232, 233, 245 n. 238, 246 nn. 239, 240, 245, 249 n. 263, 255 n. 51, 256 n. 57, 259 n. 69, 275 n. 38, 276 nn. 56–8, 277 n. 68

Hadid, Zaha M., 130, 131

Happenings, 45, 49, 51, 63, 64

Harvey, David, 245 n. 237, 248 n. 257, 283 n.19

Hassan, Ihab, xii, xiii, 4, 12, 16, 42–53, 55, 58, 68, 72f., 75, 92f., 94, 101, 125, 130, 131, 173, 175, 176, 183 n. 2, 184 nn. 4, 10, 186 n. 20, 195 n. 79, 196 n. 86, 204 n. 34, 214 nn. 125, 128, 215 n. 4, 216 n. 12, 217 nn. 13, 15, 16, 218 nn. 17, 18, 21, 24, 219 nn. 26, 30, 33, 220 n. 35, 221 nn. 39–41, 222 nn. 44, 45, 47, 49, 223 nn. 50, 51, 56, 224 nn. 59, 62, 226 n. 77, 231 nn. 133, 233 nn. 148, 149, 235 nn. 162, 165, 240 n. 204, 245 n. 236, 252 n.23, 256 n. 55, 265 n. 117, 266 n. 118, 277 n. 61, 280 n. 79, 283 n. 19

Hays, H. R., 12, 13ff., 19, 51, 171, 194 n. 65, 196 n. 86

Hebdige, Dick, 3ff., 27f., 185 nn. 15, 16, 208 n. 85, 245 n. 236

hedonism, 31, 37, 38, 214 n. 125

Hegel, Georg Wilhelm Friedrich, 55, 62, 146, 153, 222 n. 44, 269 n. 158

Heisenberg, Werner Karl, 54, 215 n. 128

Hemingway, Ernest, 43

Heraclitus, 147

hermeneutics, 55, 217 n. 12, 222 n. 45, 278 n. 69, 280 n. 79

high modernism, 65, 75, 84, 130, 163, 176, 229 n. 115, 234 n. 150, 238 n. 185, 239 n. 189, 240 n. 197, 257 n. 59

'high modernist postmodernism', 73, 74f., 234 nn. 150, 157

High Tech architecture, 68ff., 129, 130, 146, 152, 205 n. 44, 238 n. 182, 239 n. 194, 273 n. 12

Himmelblau, Coop, 131

Himmelstrand, Ulf, 207 n. 78

historicism, 71, 85f., 91, 113, 125, 147, 150, 152, 155, 174, 195 n. 76, 198 n. 99, 231 n. 128, 246 n. 245, 257 n. 62, 274 n. 16, 281 n. 6, 282 nn. 12, 13

Hockney, David, 135, 137, 138, 140, 262 n. 86

Hodgkin, Howard, 138, 262 n. 86

Hollein, Hans, 113, 119

Hongkong Shanghai Bank, Hong Kong, 80ff., 129, 130

Horkheimer, Max, 86 89, 226 n. 73; *see also* Frankfurt School

Howe, Irving, 12, 16, 172, 192 n. 58

Hudnut, Joseph, 5ff., 14, 15, 19, 171, 186 n. 22, 187 nn. 24–30, 188 nn. 33, 36, 37, 194 n. 69, 196 n. 87, 250 n. 5

Hughes, Robert, 64

humanism, 49, 78, 124, 133, 135, 137, 148, 174, 175, 235 n. 161, 265 n. 117, 282 n. 12

Hutcheon, Linda, 194 n. 72, 220 n. 37, 261 n. 81

Huyssen, Andreas, 111, 166, 175, 212 n. 114, 221 n. 41, 235 nn. 161, 165, 241 n. 208, 255 n. 44, 277 n. 61, 278 n. 74

hybrid codes, 105ff., 250 n. 8, 252 n. 23, 264 n. 93, 267 n. 129; *see also* double-coding

hybridisation, 53

Hyperrealism, 262 n. 86

hyperreality, 69, 78, 181 n. 9, 184 n. 4, 204 n. 39, 236 n. 171

hyperspace, 4, 69, 78, 237 n. 172, 245 n. 237

ideal post-modernisms, *see* post-modernism, ideal versions of

indeterminacy, 4, 42, 44, 45, 47,

48, 50, 51, 52, 58, 173, 184 nn.
4, 10, 215 n. 128, 217 n. 13,
218 n. 21, 226 n. 77, 247 n.
250, 279 n. 79
India, 23, 183 n. 2, 200 nn. 13, 14
industrial building products, *see*
modern building materials
industrial society, xi, 2, 4, 6ff.,
9ff., 22ff., 29ff., 56ff., 86, 98,
104, 199 n. 7, 201 nn. 20, 22,
202 n. 23, 204 n. 33, 207 n.
64, 208 n. 80, 209 n. 88, 210
n. 96, 230 n. 118, 260 n. 74,
284 n. 22
industrial working class, 6, 9ff.,
16, 98, 172, 207 n. 78
information society, *see* post-
industrial society
instrumental reason, *see*
rationality, instrumental
International Style, 12, 15, 90, 91,
99, 107, 115, 118, 194 n. 69;
see also modern architecture
and Modern Movement.
intersubjectivity, *see* subject, and
intersubjectivity
intertextuality, 50, 222 n. 49
irony, 44, 47, 51, 53, 68, 69, 100,
123, 125, 141, 147, 148, 150,
220 n. 37, 221 n. 38, 224 n.
62, 258 n. 64, 261 n. 81, 263
n. 89, 268 n. 136, 270 nn. 163,
164, 271 n. 168
Isozaki, Arata, 146, 148
Izenour, Steven, *see* Venturi,
with Scott Brown and
Izenour, *Learning from Las
Vegas*

Jacobs, Jane, 103, 110, 251 n. 12
Jameson, Conrad, 104
Jameson, Fredric, xii, xiii, 4, 65–

85, 89, 94ff., 107, 112, 113,
125, 130, 163, 175, 176, 181 n.
9, 184 nn. 4, 11, 185 n. 15,
186 n. 20, 196 n. 83, 200 n.
17, 216 n. 11, 219 n. 26, 223
n. 56, 224 n. 62, 229 n. 115,
230 n. 124, 231 nn. 128, 130,
132, 133, 232 nn. 142, 144,
233 nn. 145, 147, 148, 234 n.
150, 235 n. 162, 237 n. 172,
238 n. 178, 239 nn. 188–90,
195, 196, 240 n. 197, 245 nn.
237, 238, 246 nn. 239 , 242,
245, 255 n. 50, 256 n. 55, 257
n. 59, 264 n. 97, 270 n. 162,
273 n. 12, 276 n. 58, 277 n.
61, 283 n. 19
Jarrell, Randell, 197 n. 88
Jarry, Alfred, 43
Jay, Martin, 240 n. 205, 242 n.
214, 244 n. 229
Jencks, Charles, xii f., 4, 5, 7, 8,
10, 17, 43 46, 50, 59f., 65, 66,
68, 72, 73ff., 87, 90, 91, 96,
99, 100, 101–49, 150f., 152,
153, 154, 155, 156, 158, 159f.,
162, 163, 167, 173ff., 176, 179,
180 n. 1, 181 n. 6, 184 n. 4,
185 nn. 16, 18, 186 n. 20, 187
nn. 23, 32, 188 nn. 34, 35, 191
n. 55, 194 n. 72, 195 n. 76,
196 nn. 83, 87, 204 n. 34, 217
nn. 16, 17, 218 n, 18, 219 n.
31, 220 nn. 35, 37, 221 nn. 38,
40, 41, 223 nn. 49, 59, 226 nn.
81, 83, 84, 228 n. 101, 229 n.
112, 231 n. 127, 232 n. 143,
233 nn. 144–7, 234 nn. 150,
152, 157, 160, 235 n. 161, 236
n. 166, 237 n. 174, 238 nn.
178, 185, 187, 239 nn. 189,
194, 240 n. 197, 243 nn. 223,

Jencks, Charles (*Cont.*)
225, 245 n. 237, 249 n. 266,
250 nn. 3, 4, 5, 8, 251 nn. 10,
12, 15, 17, 252 nn. 18, 22–4,
254 nn. 32, 33, 36, 38, 255 nn.
42, 47, 51, 52, 256 nn. 55, 56,
58, 257 nn. 59–63, 258 nn. 64–
9, 259 nn. 72, 73, 260 nn. 74,
79, 80, 261 nn. 81–3, 262 nn.
86, 87, 263 nn. 88–90, 92, 264
nn. 93, 94, 104, 265 nn. 117,
118, 266 n. 123, 267 nn. 124,
126, 127, 129, 268 n. 135, 269
nn. 154, 158, 270 nn. 159–64,
271 nn. 168–70, 172, 173, 175,
272 n. 176, 273 nn. 8, 10, 12,
15, 274 nn. 16, 18, 22, 278 nn.
72, 74, 279 n. 78, 281 n. 7, 282
nn. 12, 16, 284 nn. 21, 22, 23
Johnson, Philip, 12, 131, 223 n.
50, 250 n. 5
Jones, Barry, 209 n. 88, 211 n. 108
Joyce, James, 43, 66, 222 n. 49

Kafka, Franz, 43
Kahn, Herman, 21
Kant, Immanuel, 62
Kaplan, E. Ann, 167, 279 n. 77
Kearney, Richard, 205 n. 47, 223
n. 56
Kellner, Douglas, 189 n. 48, 205
n. 44, 269 n. 146
Keniston, Kenneth, 21, 202 n. 24
Kenner, Hugh, 218 n. 21
Kermode, Frank, 12, 177, 187 n.
24, 191 n. 54, 240 n. 204
Kitaj, Ron, 135
kitsch, 60, 66, 95, 246 n. 245
Klotz, Heinrich, 79f., 150f., 175,
238 nn. 178, 182, 243 n. 223,
244 n. 226, 255 n. 48, 258 n.
64

knowledge society, *see* post-
industrial society
Koehler, Michael, 12ff., 42, 173,
192 nn. 57, 58, 193 nn. 61, 62,
195 n. 74, 195 n. 74, 80, 196
nn. 83–7, 197 nn. 88, 89, 198
n. 97, 221 n. 39, 224 n. 61,
254 n. 35
Koolhaas, Rem, 130, 131, 274 n. 16
Krauss, Rosalind E., 125, 245 n.
238, 262 n. 83, 264 n. 94
Krier, Leon, 135, 258 n. 69
Krier, Robert, 253 n. 25, 258 n. 69,
272 n. 2
Kristeva, Julia, 217 n. 12
Kroker, Arthur, and David Cook,
279 n. 77
Kroll, Lucien, 88 ff., 112, 187 n.
23, 242 n. 219, 243 n. 223, 272
nn. 1, 2
Kumar, Krishan, 199 n. 1

Lacan, Jacques, 239 n. 196
Lancaster, Osbert, 109, 110f.
language games, 41, 57ff., 61, 263
n. 92
l'art pour l'art, *see* art for art's
sake
late capitalism, 67ff., 115, 175, 184
n. 11, 200 n. 17, 229 n. 108
late-modernism, xii f., 4, 17, 27,
46, 50, 51f., 59, 64, 66ff., 95f.,
100, 107, 115f., 125ff., 136ff.,
152, 173, 174, 175, 179, 181 n.
6, 184 n. 4, 187 n. 23, 191 n.
55, 193 n. 59, 196 n. 83, 214
n. 128, 217 n. 16, 219 n. 33,
229 n. 108, 233 n. 147, 234 n.
150, 237 nn. 172, 174, 238 n.
185, 245 n. 237, 253 n. 28, 257
nn. 61, 62, 258 n. 65, 264 n.
104, 266 n. 118, 272 n. 176,

273 n. 12, 275 n. 45, 279 n. 75, 282 n. 12, 283 n. 19; *see also* High Tech architecture, modernism, post-modernism, deconstructionist theories of, ultra-modernism

Latin American literature, 13f., 171, 193 n. 62

Le Corbusier (Charles Edouard Jeanneret), 113, 256 n. 57

leisure society, 24f., 170, 202 n. 28

'less is more', 15, 105f, 194 n. 70

Levin, Harry, 1, 16, 172, 192 n. 58

Levin, Kim, 137, 267 n. 135

Libeskind, Daniel, 131

life-world, 86, 88, 240 n. 202, 242 n. 214, 244 n. 230; *see also* Habermas

Loos, Adolf, 153, 159, 256 n. 57

Lowell, Robert, 197 n. 88

Luhmann, Niklas, 226 n. 76

Lukacs, George, 86

Lyotard, Jean-François, xii, xiii, 3f., 5, 31, 41, 42, 53–65, 66, 70, 71, 83, 84, 91, 92, 94, 107, 113, 118f., 125, 129f., 134, 144f., 146, 153f., 155, 158, 159f., 164, 173, 174, 175, 176, 181 n. 5, 183 n. 3, 184 nn. 4, 6, 185 n. 16, 208 n. 86, 213 n. 116, 215 n. 4, 216 nn. 6, 11, 217 nn. 12, 13, 221 n. 40, 223 nn. 56, 59, 224 nn. 62, 64, 225 nn. 66, 67, 70–73, 226 nn. 76, 81, 83, 84, 227 nn. 87, 88, 91, 97, 228 nn. 98, 100, 101, 104, 229 nn, 106, 112, 230 nn. 117, 124, 236 n. 171, 239 nn. 190, 196, 255 n. 51, 257 n. 59, 260 n. 74, 261 n. 82, 263 n. 92, 264 nn. 104, 105, 267 n. 126, 269 n. 154, 276 n. 56

McCarthy, Thomas, 86f.

McDonald, Maryon, 248 n. 256

machines and machinisms, 6, 8, 12, 18, 22ff., 102, 116, 188 n. 35, 199 nn. 7, 9, 201 n. 20, 202 nn. 23, 24, 27, 212 n. 113, 236 n. 169, 237 n. 172, 252 n. 22, 276 n. 54

McLuhan, Marshall, 25–8, 45, 67, 191 n. 53, 203 n. 33, 204 n. 34, 265 n. 117, 281 n. 4

Magritte, René, 147

Mallet, Serge, 21

Mandel, Ernest, 67, 200 n. 17

Mannerist, 73, 116

Marcus, George E., 97, 247 n. 247

Marcuse, Herbert, 205 n. 48, 226 nn. 73, 76, 276 n. 56

Mariani, Carlo Maria, 63, 119ff., 135, 137, 227 n. 96, 260 n. 79, 261 n. 80, 262 n. 86, 87, 268 n. 136

Martin, Wallace, 183 n. 2

Martinez, Enrique Gonzalez 13f.,

Marx, Karl, 23f., 34f., 56ff., 98, 100, 206 n. 49, 207 n. 62, 225 nn. 70, 71, 73, 230 n. 117, 239 n. 196, 249 n. 266

Marxisms, 21, 23f., 49, 55, 56ff., 130, 153, 158, 167, 225 nn. 70, 71, 73, 230 n. 118, 122, 239 n. 196, 240 n. 204

Matthews, Harry, 191 n. 53

mediaevalism, 23; *see also* Middle Ages

Merton, Robert K., 31

meta-fiction, 219 n. 26, 222 n. 49

meta-narratives, 3f., 41, 55ff., 83, 84, 119, 130, 144, 153, 155, 160, 167, 173f., 184 n. 3, 208 n. 86, 215 n. 4, 225 nn. 67, 73

Middle Ages, 23, 98, 183 n. 1

middle-classes, 9f., 98, 172
Mies van der Rohe, Ludwig,
    105f., 194 n. 70, 256 n. 57
Mills, C. Wright, 11, 172, 190 n.
    52, 212 n. 110
modern age, 1, 4, 9ff., 15ff.; *see
    also* modernity
modern architecture, xii f., 1, 6ff.,
    14, 15, 22ff., 60, 66, 79f.,
    86ff., 99f.,101ff., 151ff., 169,
    189 n. 43, 194 nn. 69, 70, 72,
    195 n. 76, 199 n. 7, 201 n. 20,
    202 n. 23, 212 n. 115, 229 n.
    115, 237 n. 174, 238 nn. 178,
    185, 187, 242 n. 217, 244 nn.
    226, 230, 251 n. 10, 255 n. 42,
    256 nn. 56, 57, 58, 257 n. 61,
    258 n. 65, 263 nn. 89, 90, 266
    n. 118, 276 n. 54, 284 n. 21;
    see also International Style,
    Modern Movement, and
    modernism
modern art, xii, 1, 16, 18ff., 46,
    62ff., 70ff., 119ff., 141, 147,
    181 n. 1, 189 n. 43, 195 n. 76,
    196 n. 84, 198 nn. 98, 100, 199
    n. 7, 217 n. 13, 227 n. 96, 231
    n. 135, 235 n. 161, 262 nn. 86,
    87, 282 n. 12, 283 n. 20; *see
    also* late modernism,
    modernism
modern building materials, 6ff.,
    22ff., 169, 199 n. 7, 201 n. 20,
    257 n. 63, 276 n. 54
modern culture, *see* high
    modernism, modernism and
    popular culture
modern, definition of, xi, 1f., 5ff.,
    55, 85f., 182 n. 1, 183 n. 2,
    186 n. 19, 249 n. 266
modern epoch, *see* modern age
modern literature, 13ff., 43f., 48,

50, 191 n. 53, 54, 197 n. 88,
    225 n. 70, 251 n. 10
Modern Movement, xii, 8, 106,
    111, 118, 154, 173, 187 n.
    24, 188 n. 36, 238 n. 187, 253
    n. 25, 263 n. 88, 274 n. 18,
    281 n. 7; *see also*
    International Style and
    modernism
modernisation, xi, 1, 2, 7, 21ff.,
    65, 68, 86ff., 111, 129f.,
    151ff., 160ff., 183 n. 2, 227 n.
    91, 244 n. 230, 273 n. 10, 276
    n. 56
modernism, xi, xii, 1, 2, 5ff., 12ff.,
    37ff., 43ff., 59f., 62ff., 65ff.,
    85ff., 101ff., 151, 153ff.,
    158ff., 163, 176, 181 n. 1, 188
    n. 36, 189 n. 43, 192 n. 58,
    194 nn. 69, 72, 195 nn. 75, 76,
    196 n. 84, 198 nn. 98, 100, 212
    n. 114, 214 n. 128, 220 n. 37,
    225 n. 70, 228 nn. 98, 100,
    229nn. 106, 115, 231 n. 133,
    232 n. 144, 234 nn. 150, 157,
    235 n. 161, 238 nn. 178, 185,
    240 n. 204, 241 n. 210, 243 n.
    225, 244 n. 226, 246 nn. 240,
    245, 248 n. 257, 249 n. 266,
    250 n. 8, 254 nn. 35, 36, 255
    nn. 42, 47, 256 nn. 56, 57, 257
    n. 59–62, 260 nn. 70, 74, 79,
    262 nn. 83, 86 87, 263 n. 89,
    264 n. 104, 265 n. 112, 266 n.
    118, 267 n. 129, 271 n. 174,
    273 n. 12, 274 n. 22, 282 n.
    12, 283 nn. 19, 20; *see also*
    high modernism, late-
    modernism, modern art and
    architecture, new modernist
    deconstructionists,
    ultra-modernism

modernity, xi, 1, 2, 41, 55ff., 84,
85ff., 101ff., 152ff, 162, 200 n.
13, 227 n. 88, 228 n. 100, 229
nn. 104, 106, 236 n. 172, 240
n. 204, 241 nn. 208, 210, 249
n. 266, 283 n. 19, 284 n. 22;
see also project of modernity
Moore, Charles, 73, 113, 135, 146
Morris, William, 21, 25, 161, 171,
198 n. 100, 201 n. 22, 276 nn.
50, 54
Mumford, Lewis, 198 n. 100

Nabokov, Vladimir, 48
neo-avantgardism, 17
neo-capitalism, 4, 78; *see also* late
capitalism
neo-classicism, 73, 90, 145, 238 n.
182, 243 n. 222; *see also*
classical styles, post-modern
classicism
neo-conservatism, 55, 61, 87f., 91,
92, 95f., 135, 136, 155, 174,
175, 224 n. 64, 241 n. 210, 246
nn. 239, 240, 245, 267 n. 132
neo-Dada, 12
neo-Expressionism, 172, 250 n. 2,
253 nn. 25, 28, 262 n. 86
neo-Freudian, 37f., 49
neo-gnosticism, 49, 52, 222 n. 44
neo-Gothic, 18f., 189 n. 43
neo-Rationalism, 112
neo-Renaissance, 199 n. 10
Newman, Michael, 231 n. 133
'new modernist
deconstructionists', 63, 228 n.
98
Nicholas of Cusa, 147
Nietzsche, Friedrich, 87, 249 n.
266
nihilism, 31, 37f., 44, 47, 101, 123,
125, 174, 189 n. 48, 204 n. 34,

205 n. 44, 229 n. 107, 231 n.
133, 282 n. 12
Norman architecture, 22, 199 n.
10, 276 n. 54
normless pastiche, 69ff., 95f., 124,
181 n. 9, 184 n. 4, 246 n. 242
normlessness, 69ff., 95f., 124,
157, 181 n. 9, 184 n. 4, 231 n.
130, 246 n. 242
Norris, Christopher, 40ff., 56, 216
nn. 6, 10, 223 n. 50, 248 n.
256
nostalgia, 62f., 70, 73, 147, 228 n.
101, 234 n. 152
'Nothing Post-Modernism', 80

O'Connor, Victor, 18, 20, 198 n.
98
O'Doherty, Brian, 197 n. 89
Olson, Charles, 12, 15, 192 n. 58
Onis, Federico de, 12, 13ff., 16,
19, 47, 51, 171, 193 n. 62, 194
nn. 66, 69, 72
Orage, Alfred R., 21, 199 n. 4
ornament, *see* decoration
Owens, Craig, 245 n. 238
Oxford English Dictionary, 5–12,
18, 21, 182 n. 1, 183 n. 2, 185
n. 18, 186 nn. 19, 20, 187 n.
24, 188 n. 37, 191 n. 53, 193
n. 62, 198 n. 97, 232 n. 144,
233 n. 146, 236 n. 169

Palladio, Andrea, 236 n. 169
Palmer, Richard E., 222 n. 45
Pannwitz, Rudolf, 180 n. 1, 190 n.
51
Papadakis, Andreas, 281 n. 6
Parc de la Villette project, 133, 266
n. 119; *see also* Tschumi
parody, 44, 45, 47, 50, 68, 69, 70,
72, 78, 84, 97, 123, 124, 147,

parody (*Cont.*)
    175, 191 n. 53, 194 n. 72, 218
    n. 22, 219 n. 26, 220 nn. 36,
    37, 222 nn. 47, 49, 231 n. 133,
    232 n. 144, 248 n. 255, 261 n.
    81, 270 nn. 162–4
participation, 44, 46, 49, 115, 218
    n. 18, 220 n. 35
pastiche, 4, 68ff., 75, 84, 95, 112,
    124, 147, 148, 175, 181 n. 9,
    184 n. 4, 219 n. 26, 231 n.
    128, 232 n. 144, 233 n. 146,
    234 n. 152, 239 n. 189, 240 n.
    196, 245 n. 237, 246 nn. 239,
    242, 245, 247 n. 250, 270 nn.
    162, 163
Pataphysics, 43, 49, 218 n. 18
Penty, Arthur, 21–5, 29, 104, 161,
    169, 195 n. 76, 199 nn. 2, 6, 7,
    9, 10, 200 nn, 11, 12, 14, 17,
    201 nn. 19, 20, 22, 202 nn.
    23–8, 204 n. 33, 206 nn. 57,
    58, 210 n. 103, 211 n. 108, 212
    n. 113, 213 n. 117, 227 n. 88,
    230 n. 118, 236 n. 169, 242 n.
    217, 252 n. 22, 257 n. 63, 276
    n. 54
Performance art, 49, 51, 64; *see
    also* Happenings
performativity, 57ff., 205 n. 48,
    226 nn. 73, 76
Perreault, John, 12, 20, 192 n. 58,
    197 n. 89, 254 n. 35
Pevsner, Nikolaus, 12, 118, 172,
    191 n. 55, 196 n. 87, 250 nn.
    2, 5, 253 nn. 25, 28, 281 n. 6
Photo-Realism, 75, 262 n. 86
Picasso, Pablo, 217 n. 13
pluralism, 49, 53, 90, 92, 103, 104,
    112, 115, 118, 125, 144ff., 150,
    160, 221 n. 38, 223 n. 53, 238
    n. 185, 249 n. 1, 250 n. 8, 254

n. 32, 258 n. 64, 263 n. 92,
    269 n. 154, 284 nn. 21, 22
Poirier, Richard, 218 n. 21
Pompidou Centre, Paris, 80f., 236
    n. 172, 238 nn. 185, 186, 255
    n. 52, 266 n. 119, 275 n. 35
Pop Art, 45, 46, 66, 75, 141, 234 n.
    160, 235 n. 161, 246 n. 245,
    252 n. 24, 262 n. 86
Pop Fiction, 12, 47, 191 n. 53
Popper, Sir Karl, 61
popular culture, 38, 47, 66, 70, 75,
    76, 78, 84, 89, 93, 94, 143,
    163, 173, 175, 191 n. 53, 234
    n. 160, 235 nn. 161, 162, 236
    n. 165, 239 n. 189, 240 n. 197,
    242 n. 215, 278 n. 74
Portman, John, *see* Bonaventure
    Hotel
Portoghesi, Paolo, xiii, 113, 114,
    149, 151, 152–8, 174f., 256 n.
    56, 274 nn. 16, 18, 22, 282 n.
    13
positivism, 164f., *see also* post-
    logical positivism
post-avant-gardes, 91, 93f., 123,
    152, 228 n. 101, 261 n. 83; *see
    also* avant-gardes, neo-
    avantgardism,
    transavantgarde
Post-Byzantine, 18f.
post-capitalism, 30, 230 n. 118,
    280 n. 2
post-Christian, 10, 38, 145, 172,
    212 n. 113, 214 nn. 125, 128
post-ethical capitalism, 37–9, 67,
    212 n. 110, 229 n. 104
post-functionalism, 238 n. 187
post-history, 11, 243 n. 225
Post-Impressionism, 198 n. 97
post-industrial society: definitions
    and theories, xi, xii, xiii, xiv,

1f., 7, 20, 21–39, 56ff., 66ff.,
83, 118, 129, 152, 154, 156,
157f., 160ff., 166, 167, 168,
169–71, 172ff., 176, 177, 178,
179, 180 nn. 1, 3, 181 nn. 9,
187 n. 31, 193 nn. 59, 62, 199
nn. 1, 2, 7, 200 n. 17, 201 n.
22, 202 nn. 24, 28, 203 nn. 31,
32, 204 n. 34, 205 nn. 47, 48,
206 nn. 48, 59, 62, 207 nn. 65,
77, 78, 209 nn. 90, 91, 92, 210
nn. 96, 97, 211 nn. 108, 109,
212 n. 115, 214 n. 128, 224 n.
61, 225 n. 71, 226 n. 76, 230
nn. 117, 118, 239 n. 190, 252
n. 22, 259 n. 73, 260 n. 74,
264 n. 99, 274 n. 22, 276 n.
50, 280 nn. 2–4, 281 n. 5, 284
n. 22
post-logical positivism, 164f., 176,
277 n. 66, 278 nn. 69, 72
post-middle-class age, 9ff., 16,
172, 197 n. 90, 206 n. 59; *see
also* Toynbee
Post-Modern Age, 9ff., 15ff.,
56ff., 171, 172, 187 n. 31, 206
n. 57; *see also* Toynbee
post-modern anthropology; *see*
post-modern ethnography
post-modern architecture, xii, xiii,
1, 2, 3, 4, 5, 6ff., 12, 17, 18,
46, 47, 59f., 66, 68ff., 85ff.,
95f., 99f., 101–49, 150ff.,
171ff., 181 n. 6, 183 n. 3, 184
n. 4, 185 nn. 16, 18, 186 nn.
19, 20, 22, 187 nn. 23–32, 188
nn. 33–6, 191 n. 55, 194 n. 69,
195 nn. 72, 76, 196 nn. 83, 87,
212 n. 115, 216 n. 11, 218 nn.
17, 18, 220 n. 37, 223 n. 49,
224 n. 59, 230 n. 124, 231 nn.
128, 132, 232 nn. 143, 144,
233 n. 146, 234 nn. 150, 152,
157, 160, 235 nn. 161, 162,
236 n. 169, 237 n. 174, 238
nn. 182, 185, 187, 239 nn.
189, 190, 240 nn. 196, 197,
242 n. 215, 243 n. 223, 244
nn. 226, 230, 245 n. 237, 246
nn. 239, 240, 245, 249 n. 1,
250 nn. 5, 8, 251 nn. 15, 17,
252 n. 23, 253 nn. 25, 28, 254
nn. 31, 36, 255 nn. 48, 52, 256
nn. 55, 56, 57, 257 nn. 59–62,
258 nn. 64–9, 259 n. 72, 260
n. 74, 261 n. 81, 263 nn. 89,
90, 92, 264 nn. 93, 99, 266 nn.
118, 123, 267 nn. 124, 129,
270 nn. 160, 162, 271 nn. 168,
170, 274 n. 18, 278 n. 74, 281
nn. 6, 7, 9, 282 nn. 12, 13, 283
n. 19, 284 nn. 21, 23; *see also*
post-modernism, double-
coded theories of
post-modern art, xii, xiii, 1, 2, 5,
16, 17, 18ff., 46f., 62f., 95f.,
119ff., 135ff., 186 n. 19, 219
n. 31, 227 n. 96, 260 n. 79,
261 n. 80, 262 n. 86, 268 n.
136, 270 nn. 160, 162
post-modern classicism, xii, 107,
112, 116ff., 135ff., 156, 159,
174, 175, 186 n. 20, 238 n.
182, 249 n. 1, 255 n. 52, 258
n. 68, 260 n. 80, 267 n. 129
post-modern criticism, 173, 191 n.
53, 214 n. 128, 218 n. 21
post-modern cults and counter-
cultures, 37ff., 45, 172, 191 n.
53, 203 n. 32, 214 nn. 125,
128, 222 n. 41
post-modern, definition of, xi ff.,
1–2, 3–20, 40ff., 101ff., 150ff.,
169ff., 180 nn. 1, 2, 3, 181 n.

post-modern, definition (*Cont.*)
  9, 193 n. 62, 194 n. 69, 250
  nn. 5, 8, 268 n. 136, 279 n. 79;
  see also prefix 'post'
post-modern ethnography, 94,
  96–7, 181 n. 5, 215 n. 1, 247
  nn. 246, 247, 250, 248 nn.
  255, 256
post-modern geography, 239 n.
  188, 245 n. 237, 283 n. 19
post-modern literature, 11f., 43ff.,
  172, 173, 191 nn. 53, 54, 192
  n. 58, 197 n. 88, 214 n. 123,
  218 nn. 18, 21, 270 n. 164
post-Modern Movement style,
  281 n. 7
post-modern science, *see* science,
  modern and post-modern
post-modern sociology, 55, 205 n.
  48, 214 n. 128, 224 n. 59, 247
  n. 250
post-modern sublime, *see*
  sublime, modern and
  post-modern
post-modernisation, xii, 1, 27f.;
  see also modernisation and
  post-modernity
post-modernism
  deconstructionist theories of,
  xii, xiii, 3f., 17, 33, 37ff., 40–
  100, 125ff., 130ff., 136ff., 158,
  160, 163, 164f., 167, 173ff.,
  181 n. 4, 184 n. 4, 196 n. 83,
  204 nn. 34, 39, 208 nn. 85, 86,
  213 n. 122, 215 n. 4, 5, 216
  nn. 6, 11, 217 nn. 12, 13, 16,
  222 n. 41, 223 n. 56, 224 n.
  62, 229 n. 107, 231 n. 132, 244
  n. 229, 245 n. 237, 247 n. 250,
  248 nn. 255, 256, 252 n. 23,
  263 n. 92, 264 n. 104, 265 nn.
  117, 118, 266 nn. 119–23, 267

n. 126, 268 nn. 135, 136, 272
  n. 176, 275 n. 38, 276 n. 58,
  278 nn. 72, 74, 279 nn. 77, 79,
  283 nn. 18, 19; *see also*
  deconstructionist architecture
double-coded theories of, xii,
  xiii, 5, 17, 43, 46, 47, 48, 73ff.,
  87f., 90, 100, 101–49, 150f.,
  158, 160, 167, 173ff., 186 n.
  20, 188 nn. 34, 35, 194 n. 72,
  196 n. 23, 201 n. 20, 220 n.
  37, 223 n. 49, 226 nn. 83, 84,
  231 n. 127, 233 nn. 144, 146,
  234 nn. 150, 152, 157, 160,
  235 n. 161, 237 n. 174, 238
  nn. 182, 185, 187, 243 n. 225,
  245 n. 237, 249 n. 1, 250 nn.
  3, 8, 251 n. 17, 252 n.23, 254
  n. 32, 255 n. 52, 256 nn. 55,
  56, 257 n. 62, 258 nn. 64–9,
  259 n. 72, 261 n. 81, 263 n.
  90, 266 n. 123, 267 nn. 124,
  127, 129, 270 nn. 160–4, 271
  n. 168, 272 n. 176, 274 nn. 18,
  22, 275 n. 38, 278 n. 74, 282
  n. 12, 284 nn. 22, 23
ideal versions of 158ff., 175f.,
  267 n. 127, 275 n. 38
optimism in, 10f., 190 n. 49
pessimism in 10f., 64f., 189 n.
  48, 190 nn. 49, 51
spelling of, 5, 184 nn. 4, 10, 186
  n. 20, 193 n. 62
tracers of theories of, 181 n. 9,
  184 nn. 4, 10
see also 'Nothing Post-
  Modernism' and Soviet
  post-modernism
post-modernity, xii, 1, 2, 4, 16,
  53ff., 65ff., 94ff., 166ff., 222
  n. 45, 228 n. 100, 240 n. 204,
  284 n. 22; *see also* modernity,

post-modernisation, post-modernism
post-Protestant work ethic, 37ff., 172, 191 n. 53
post-relativism, 166
post-scarcity, 25
post-structuralisms, 63, 71, 93, 95, 97, 130, 131, 136f., 165, 175, 215 n. 5, 222 n. 49, 228 n. 101, 230 n. 122, 232 n. 142, 239 n. 196, 244 n. 232, 248 n. 256, 265 n. 117, 278 n. 69, 279 nn. 74, 75, 282 n. 17
post-war, 9ff., 198 n. 97
post-Western, 9ff., 172
prefabricated building, 6ff., 22, 172, 187 nn. 23, 27, 188 n. 36
prefix 'post', xi, 1, 2, 15, 24, 28, 45, 46, 85, 102, 180 n. 1, 186 n. 20, 198 n. 97, 222 n. 41, 230 n. 118, 235 n. 161 , 271 n. 169, 284 n. 20
pre-industrial, 23, 151, 160ff., 169, 200 n. 13, 210 n. 96, 252 n. 22
Pre-Raphaelites, 18f, 195 n. 76
programmed society, 28f., 170, 280 n. 3; *see also* technocratic society and Touraine
project of modernity, 55, 60ff., 85ff., 155, 162, 174, 181 n. 5, 213 n. 116, 227 n. 87, 229 n. 104, 240 n. 204, 242 n. 214, 243 n. 225, 244 n. 232; *see also* Habermas
proletariats, *see* industrial working class
Protestant work ethic, 37f., 191 n. 53; *see also* post-Protestant work ethic
Proust, Marcel, 43
Pruitt-Igoe housing estate, 108, 110ff., 113, 118, 256 n. 56

public spheres, 88ff., 112, 116ff., 148, 154ff., 160, 255 n. 51, 258 n. 69, 259 n. 72, 260 n. 80, 266 n. 119, 273 n. 15, 274 n. 22

Queen Anne style, 116, 199 n. 10, 257 n. 63

Rabelais, François, 53
Rabinow, Paul, 97, 247 n. 247
Rader, Melvin, 198 n. 100
radical eclecticism, 73f., 83, 104, 113, 234 n. 152, 252 n. 18, 279 n. 78; *see also* eclecticism
Raphael, 124, 127, 262 n. 86
Rationalism (in architecture), 104, 112, 113, 255 nn. 47, 48, 256 n. 57, 281 n. 6
rationality
    instrumental, 86ff., 226 n. 73, 227 n. 91, 241 n. 205, 242 n. 215, 276 n. 56
    purposive, 86, 183 n. 2
    value, 86, 241 n. 205, 276 n. 58
    see also value, discussions and theories of
Read, Sir Herbert, 201 n. 20
Realism, 16, 18ff., 60, 93, 123, 198 n. 98; *see also* Social Realism, and Socialist Realism
Reich, Wilhelm, 191 n. 53
reification, 56ff., 71, 86, 225 n. 71, 230 n. 122
relativism, 40ff., 53ff., 134, 144f., 159, 160, 162ff., 183 n. 3, 241 n. 207, 267 n. 126, 268 n. 135, 277 n. 65, 279 n. 79
Renaissance, 1, 4, 15, 22f., 95, 148, 182 n. 1, 199 n. 10, 272 n. 175
res publica, see public spheres

Richta, Radovan, 21
Riesman, David, 21, 25, 170, 199
n. 2, 202 nn. 26, 28
Roberts, Stone, 137
Rococo, 73, 141
Romanesque, 145
Romanticism, 49, 73, 282 n. 12
Ronan Point tower block, 255 n.
42
Rorty, Richard, 185 n. 16
Rose, Gillian, 223 n. 59
Rosenblum, Robert, 141
Rossi, Aldo, 73, 112, 135, 157, 255
n. 48
Rothko, Mark, 62f.
Rudolph, Paul, 281 n. 7
Ruskin, John, 21, 25, 159, 160,
161, 162, 175, 198 n. 100, 201
n. 22, 202 n. 25
Rykwert, Joseph, 281 n. 7

Saarinen, Eero, 106, 191 n. 55, 253
n. 28
Sade, Marquis de, 43
Said, Edward W., 245 n. 238
Saint-Simon, Claude-Henri, 29,
32–4, 36, 206 n. 49, 208 nn.
80, 86, 209 nn. 88, 90, 91, 210
n. 103, 211 n. 108, 249 n. 266,
262 n. 83
Salle, David, 147
Sangren, P. Steven, 96f., 226 n.
80, 248 n. 256
Sartre, Jean-Paul, 44, 225 n. 70
Sarup, Madan, 282 n. 17
satire, 68, 69, 124, 233 n. 144, 262
n. 86, 270 n. 164
Scheutz, George, 35
Schinkel, Karl Friedrich, 145, 255
n. 52
'schizophrenic' culture, 50, 75,
113, 125, 239 n. 189, 256 n.

55, 264 n. 93, 271 n. 175
'schlock', 66, 234 n. 160
Schnabel, Julian, 95f., 135ff., 267
nn. 132, 135, 268 n. 136
Schwarzkogler, Rudolf, 64
science
modern, 6, 7, 29, 31, 32ff., 41,
55ff., 65, 85, 144, 174, 208 n.
80, 210 nn. 103, 104, 211 nn.
105, 107, 108, 212 n. 110, 225
nn. 71, 73, 229 n. 104
post-modern, 10, 29ff., 56ff.,
170, 172, 203 n. 31, 205 n. 47,
206 n. 57, 214 n. 128, 226 n.
77, 230 n. 118, 276 nn. 48, 53
science fiction, 12, 66, 191 n. 53
Scott Brown, Denise, 235 n. 162;
see also Venturi, with Scott
Brown and Izenour, *Learning
from Las Vegas*
Scruton, Roger, 134
self-reflexivity, 45, 122, 160, 219
n. 26, 222 n. 49, 241 n. 207
semiotics, 49, 103, 105, 115, 251 n.
15, 17, 252 n. 18
service economy, 30ff., 129, 170,
207 nn. 77, 78, 212 n. 115, 230
n. 118, 260 n. 74; *see also*
post-industrial society
skyscrapers, 189 n. 43, 274 n. 22;
see also High Tech
architecture
Smith, Adam, 35, 36, 210 n. 103,
211 n. 108
Smith, Bernard, 18ff., 103, 171,
186 n. 20, 195 n. 75, 197 n.
90, 198 nn. 95, 98–100
Smithson, Peter, 102
socialism, 21, 24f., 28f., 56f., 197
n. 90, 201 nn. 19, 22
Social Realism, 18ff., 103, 171, 198
n. 98

Socialist Realism, 283 n. 20
'society of the spectacle', 4, 67, 68, 184 n. 11
Somervell, D. C., 9ff., 172, 189 nn. 40, 42, 221 n. 39
Sontag, Susan, 45, 49, 218 nn. 21, 24, 231 n. 133
Soroki, Pitirim, 18
Soviet post-modernism, 283 n. 20
Sanish literature, 13f., 171
Spengler, Oswald, 10f., 190 n. 51
Stein, Gertrude, 43
Steinberg, Saul, 121, 122
Steinerg, George, 218 n. 21
Stern, Robert, 173, 174, 250 n. 2, 265 n. 117, 281 n. 9, 282 n. 12
Stirling, James, and Wilford and Associates, 76, 116, 117, 124f., 128, 135, 145f., 147, 148, 186 n. 20, 238 n. 182, 269 n. 158, 271 n. 170
structuralism, 12, 37, 165, 215 n. 5, 222 n. 49, 248 n. 256
Stuttgart, State Gallery, 76, 116, 117, 124f., 128, 135, 145f., 148, 186 n. 20, 238 n. 182, 255 n. 52, 263 n. 89, 264 n. 92, 269 n. 158, 271 n. 170
Styron, William, 48
subject
    as agent, 10f., 58f., 74, 84, 148f., 154ff., 165, 167, 190 n. 51, 207 n. 62, 211 n. 108, 213 n. 116, 228 n. 101, 239 n. 196, 271 n. 173, 276 n. 58, 278 n. 69, 72, 279 nn. 74, 75, 77, 78
    death of, 39, 64f., 70ff., 74, 83f., 95, 137, 141ff., 148f., 175, 225 n. 70, 228 n. 100, 232 n. 142, 240 n. 196, 241 n. 207, 246 n. 242, 271 n. 172, 272 n. 176, 276 n. 58
    decentred, 44, 58f., 71ff., 78f., 84, 95, 165, 167, 175, 190 n. 51, 228 n. 101, 232 n. 142, 245 n. 236, 271 n. 174
    and intersubjectivity, 61, 65, 74, 86ff., 148f., 154ff., 240 nn. 202, 204, 241 n. 205, 274 n. 22, 278 n. 74
    overdetermination of, 230 n. 122, 232 n. 142, 239 n. 196, 278 n. 72
sublime
    modern, 62f.
    post-modern, 62f., 174, 224 n. 59
super-industrialism, 203 n. 32; *see also* Toffler
Surrealism, 15, 16, 17, 38, 43, 52, 91, 93, 196 n. 84, 236 n. 165 282 n. 12
Symbolisms, 13f., 19, 43, 49, 103, 107, 116, 123, 129, 144, 146, 163, 171, 242 n. 214, 252 n. 17, 256 n. 56
system-world, 86, 88, 240 n. 202, 242 n. 215, 244 n. 230; *see also* Habermas

Taaffe, Philip, 141ff., 269 n. 146
Taylor, Frederick Winslow, 211 n. 108
technetronic society, 25, 170; *see also* post-industrial society
technocratic society, 28f., 170, 206 n. 49, 280 n. 3; *see also* post-industrial society
terror, concepts and uses of, 52, 58f., 66, 68
Toffler, Alvin, 25, 170, 203 n. 32, 214 n. 125, 280 n. 4
Tominaga, Ken'ichi, 33f., 208 n. 87, 209 nn. 88, 91

Touraine, Alain, 21, 28–9, 157,
    158, 170, 205 n. 48, 206 n. 49,
    275 nn. 34, 35, 280 n. 3
Toynbee, Arnold J., 9ff., 12, 15f.,
    18f., 42, 47, 49, 73, 171, 172,
    186 n. 20, 187 n. 31, 188 nn.
    37, 40, 189 nn. 42, 43, 48, 190
    nn. 49, 51, 192 n. 58, 193 n.
    62, 195 nn. 73–6, 196 n. 86,
    197 n. 90, 206 nn. 57, 59, 214
    nn. 125, 128, 219 n. 25, 221 n.
    39, 233 n. 149, 271 n. 169
transavantgarde, 19f., 60, 123, 198
    nn. 101, 104, 229 n. 112, 261
    n. 82, 262 n. 86
Tristram Shandy, 50
Tschumi, Bernard, 130, 133, 265
    n. 116, 266 nn. 119–23
Tyler, Stephen A., 97, 247 n. 247

Ulmer, Gregory L., 245 n. 238
ultra-modernism, 6ff., 13, 16, 51,
    101, 172, 187 n. 23
Ungers, Matthias, 135
Updike, John, 48
Utzon, Jorn, 191 n. 55

Valéry, Paul, 43, 190 n. 49
value, discussions and theories
    of, 37ff., 74f., 86ff., 112, 134,
    135ff., 143ff., 156ff., 158ff.,
    163ff., 176ff., 203 n. 31, 227
    nn. 88, 91, 267 n. 126, 277 n.
    65, 283 n. 18, 284 nn. 21,
    23
Venice Biennale 1980, 85f., 151,
    152, 157, 174, 274 n. 16
Venturi, Robert, 48, 73, 75, 79, 99,
    103, 105ff., 113, 119, 133, 135,
    146, 240 n. 197, 249 n. 264,

    251 n. 15, 252 n. 24, 253 nn.
    25, 30, 254 n. 31, 281 n. 7
*Complexity and Contradiction
    in Architecture*, 48, 75, 79,
    103, 105ff., 133, 251 n. 15, 253
    nn. 24, 25
with Denise Scott Brown and
    Steven Izenour, *Learning
    from Las Vegas*, 75, 105, 221
    n. 38, 234 n. 160, 235 n. 162,
    236 n. 165, 251 n. 12, 252 n.
    24, 278 n. 74
vernacular architecture, 89, 113,
    199 n. 10, 257 nn. 62, 63
Vico, Giovanni Battista, 49
'villagism', 23, 200 n. 13, 203 n.
    33
Vitruvius, 236 n. 169
Vonnegut, Kurt, Jr, 191 n. 53

Waiting for Godot, 52
Wales, HRH The Prince of, 232 n.
    144
Warhol, Andy, 46, 75, 141, 235 n.
    161
Weber, Max, 86, 88, 183 n. 2, 200
    n. 13, 207 n. 62, 227 n. 88
Wellmer, Albrecht, 242 n. 214
Welsch, Wolfgang, 180 n. 1, 190
    n. 51, 197 n. 89
Wiener, Anthony J., 21
Wigley, Mark, 131, 223 n. 50, 264
    n. 108, 265 n. 112, 266 n.
    120
Wilson, Edmund, 43, 44,
Wolfe, Tom, 103, 235 n. 161, 251
    n. 10
Wollen, Peter, 273 n. 10
Woolgar, Steve, 215 n. 1
working class, *see* industrial
    working class
world village, 46, 119, 204 n. 34,

259 n. 73; *see also* global
village
Wright, Frank Lloyd, 195 n. 76,
198 n. 100, 256 n. 57

Yeats, William, 43, 271 n. 174

Zevi, Bruno, 156